The Creation of
the Cowboy Hero

ALSO BY JEREMY AGNEW
AND FROM MCFARLAND

*Alcohol and Opium in the Old West:
Use, Abuse and Influence* (2014)

*The Old West in Fact and Film:
History Versus Hollywood* (2012)

*Entertainment in the Old West:
Theater, Music, Circuses, Medicine Shows,
Prizefighting and Other Popular Amusements* (2011)

*Medicine in the Old West:
A History, 1850–1900* (2010)

The Creation of the Cowboy Hero

Fiction, Film and Fact

JEREMY AGNEW

McFarland & Company, Inc., Publishers
Jefferson, North Carolina

LIBRARY OF CONGRESS CATALOGUING-IN-PUBLICATION DATA

Agnew, Jeremy.
The creation of the cowboy hero : fiction, film and fact / Jeremy Agnew.
      p.   cm.
Includes bibliographical references and index.

ISBN 978-0-7864-7839-2 (softcover : acid free paper) ∞
ISBN 978-1-4766-1814-2 (ebook)

1. Western films—United States—History and criticism. 2. Cowboys in popular culture. 3. Western stories—History and criticism. 4. West (U.S.)—In motion pictures. 5. West (U.S.)—In literature. I. Title.
PN1995.9.W4A519 2015   791.43'65878—dc23
                2014040982

BRITISH LIBRARY CATALOGUING DATA ARE AVAILABLE

© 2015 Jeremy Agnew. All rights reserved

No part of this book may be reproduced or transmitted in any form or by any means, electronic or mechanical, including photocopying or recording, or by any information storage and retrieval system, without permission in writing from the publisher.

Cover images: iStock/Thinkstock

Printed in the United States of America

McFarland & Company, Inc., Publishers
Box 611, Jefferson, North Carolina 28640
www.mcfarlandpub.com

For Greg, the cowboy,
and Liz, his cowgirl.

Table of Contents

Timeline of Notable Influences on the Perception of the Western Hero ... ix
Preface ... 1

1. There Have to Be Heroes ... 5
2. The Legend Begins ... 17
3. The Lure of the Dime Novels ... 28
4. The Great Showman ... 44
5. Buffalo Bill's *Wild West* ... 56
6. More and More Wild West Shows ... 74
7. Our Cowboy Heroes ... 83
8. Flickering Images ... 95
9. Tom Mix and the Flashy Showmen ... 109
10. Pulp Magazines and Mass-Market Paperbacks ... 120
11. Warbling Cowboys and the Silver Screen ... 134
12. Brooding Heroes ... 152
13. And a Suitable Heroine ... 166
14. Violence Returns ... 183
15. The Image Persists ... 199

Postscript ... 215
Chapter Notes ... 219
Bibliography ... 227
Index ... 231

Timeline of Notable Influences on the Perception of the Western Hero

1682	Publication of the first Indian captivity narrative by Mary Rowlandson.
1803	President Thomas Jefferson purchases the Louisiana Territory, which opens up land for settlement of the West.
1823	James Fenimore Cooper publishes *The Pioneers,* which features Natty Bumppo, the first Western hero of fiction.
1826	Cooper publishes *The Last of the Mohicans.*
1840s	Development of the steam-powered rotary printing press leads to the widespread availability of novels at cheap prices.
1860	Beadle & Adams publish their first dime novel.
1861–1865	The American Civil War pits the Union against the Confederacy.
1864	Start of the transcontinental railroad as the Union Pacific pushes towards the West Coast to meet the Central Pacific building eastwards from California.
1866–1880	Height of the cowboy era, with cattle drives from Texas to Kansas to supply eastern markets with beef; height of the gunfighting era in the Old West.
1869	Completion of the transcontinental railroad; Ned Buntline publishes *Buffalo Bill, the King of Border Men,* the first dime novel about William F. "Buffalo Bill" Cody.
1870s	Cody appears onstage in a series of melodramatic plays with Western themes.
1876	Lt. Col. George Armstrong Custer and his troops of the Seventh Cavalry are annihilated in the Battle of the Little Bighorn in Montana.
1880s	Peak popularity of dime novels; first dude ranches cater to Easterners who want to live the life of the cowboy.
1881	The bloody gunfight at the O.K. Corral takes place in Tombstone, Arizona.
1884–1910	Buffalo Bill's *Wild West* presents a limited image of the West created around spectacle and drama.
1887	The cowboy as a hero makes his first literary appearance in Prentiss Ingraham's *Buck Taylor, King of the Cowboys.*
1890s	Generally accepted period for the closing of the Western frontier, which creates a nostalgia for the "good old days," leaving the public enthusiastic for Western stories and motion pictures.
1895–1910	The first motion pictures record Western life but are mostly documentation of events, such as cattle round-ups.

1902	Owen Wister publishes *The Virginian* and creates the first identifiable cowboy hero, a character who will influence western literature and motion pictures for many years to come.
1903	*The Great Train Robbery* sparks an increased interest in Western films.
1910s	Broncho Billy becomes the first identifiable Western movie hero.
1912	Zane Grey publishes *Riders of the Purple Sage,* a novel that will strongly influence the form of subsequent Western novels.
1910–1915	William S. Hart popularizes the good badman hero in his movies.
1920s	Western movies become longer and contain more plotting; the dour hero of W.S. Hart gives way to the flashy image of Tom Mix; first appearance of pulp Westerns; rodeo gradually replaces Wild West shows as live cowboy entertainment.
1929	The stock market crash in New York leads to the Great Depression, which also depresses movie attendance.
1930s	Silent movies give way to sound; Ken Maynard adds songs to his films; decline of the A Westerns and rise of the B Westerns; the Production Code is introduced to clean up movies; the rise of the singing cowboy.
1939	*Stagecoach* revitalizes interest in A Westerns; first cheap paperbacks appear.
1946	*Duel in the Sun* brings sex back to the Westerns.
1950s	B Westerns disappear from movie houses; heroes of A Western movies become driven by inner psychological defects; rise of television Westerns.
1960s	Peak years for the television Westerns; Italian-made "spaghetti" Westerns present a new type of hero, who is more of an antihero.
1969	*The Wild Bunch* is a milestone in movie violence.
1980	*Urban Cowboy* and the TV series *Dallas* spark a craze for big hats, boots, western clothing, and cowboy music among city folk.
1980s	Very few Westerns are being produced, but the occasional offerings are violent and gritty.
1990	*Dances with Wolves* wins the Academy Award for Best Picture.
1992	*Unforgiven* wins the Academy Award for Best Picture.

Preface

Genres must regularly transform themselves ... imaginatively manipulating classic givens ... if they are to maintain a compelling hold over their audiences—Lee Mitchell[1]

A buckskin-clad frontiersman wearing a fringed coat and a coonskin hat, a good badman covered in dust, a laconic lone gunfighter, a singing cowboy outfitted in sequins, a morose roving gunman racked by internal doubt and turmoil, and an antihero, squinting and unshaven wearing a poncho. Which one of these is the hero of countless Western movies and books? The answer, of course, is all of them. Each has represented the Western "hero" at different times during the last 200 years.

Which of these heroes is the true representation of the West? From a historical perspective, none of them. The Western "cowboy" hero is a mythic persona created and propagated by dime novels, pulp fiction, television, and Hollywood movies. Much has been written about this imaginary cowboy as the Western hero, but in reality the cowboy did not settle the western United States and had only a minor impact on its history. In spite of this, the cowboy has become the major cultural icon for the West.

The image of cowboys as Western heroes is certainly still with us today. During a recent stroll around some tourist-oriented shops in my hometown in the West, I noted a candy bar labeled "Cowboy Chocolate Bar." The label said it was "inspired by the West." I also found two recently-published cowboy cookbooks, a book of cowboy poetry, a variety of cowboy hats, boots and moccasins, and a joke roll of John Wayne cowboy toilet paper (in the interests of good taste I will not repeat the rest of what the label said, but many readers will have probably seen the same item in novelty gift stores).

While most of us tend to think of the hero of Westerns as unchanging, the portrayal of the hero figure has changed significantly over time. While preparing the manuscript for one of my previous books, *The Old West in Fact and Film* (McFarland, 2012), research emphasized to me how much the image of the cowboy hero has changed with the evolution of books and motion pictures and the changing tastes of audiences. This present book discusses various depictions of the hero and the factors that created and influenced his changing image from his introduction in roughly 1800 to the present. It will not be a specific history of Western literature, music, art, film, or individual cowboy movie heroes, but it blends relevant parts of these elements into the overall theme of the Western hero.

I approached this subject with some trepidation. While conducting my research, I ran across the statement that "scholars have examined the phenomenon of the cowboy ad nauseam."[2] In my study of the available literature, however, it would appear that the mass appeal of the Western myth has not generally made it popular for scholarly research. In reality, it can be a mine of cultural information because the image of the cowboy hero is so important and popular that it has had a major impact on the American memory of the history of the West.

The two most successful creations of American filmmakers have been the Western and the gangster movie. Hallmarks of both genres are violence, chase scenes, criminal activity, and simplistic morals. Both involve male bravado, along with guns as desirable objects and rituals for their use. Such popularity may reflect the importance of these icons in the fantasy life of Americans or may be related to a wishful yearning for the days of the frontier when a man was self-reliant and had to protect himself. Perhaps this is also linked to nostalgia and a way of recapturing a past that people are reluctant to lose. Or perhaps violent plots help to serve as an escape from the confinement of an industrial society. Many critics feel that Western plots of the 1960s and 1970s reflected American politics and fears, such as the Kennedy era of the early 1960s, Russia, American involvement in Vietnam, the Watergate scandal, and the Cold War. *The Wild Bunch* (1969), for example, has been interpreted by some critics as an allegory about the war in Vietnam. Others critics, such as Jon Tuska, disagree and point out that this was not what director Sam Peckinpah had intended.[3] None of this is my area of expertise, so I shall leave further analysis to critics and psychologists.

As in my prior book, the present volume not going to be a history of Western filmmakers or stars, other than material that relates directly to the hero image. These individuals have been discussed in detail elsewhere. As I stated in the preface to my previous book, I do not write movie criticism, and I do not analyze movies. This is not my area of expertise, desire, or intent. I intend to follow these same guidelines in this book. Similarly, I have tried not to inject my own opinions or criticism of particular books or movies into my writing, but have attempted to stick to facts. Nor will I analyze the intent of filmmakers other than the perception I gained from what is seen on the screen. Other excellent books may be consulted for movie analysis and criticism.

The reader of this book should keep in mind that, in many instances, the portrayal of a particular version of the Western hero is a result of outside factors. The motivation for making a Western isn't always based solely on historic, artistic, or technical achievement. Commercial reality often plays a large part in the final result. The media of mass culture of any era are in business to make a profit. A movie has to appeal to an audience who will pay hard-earned money to see it. If there is no profit, there is no business. The Western has always been a safer bet than many other types of film, and Hollywood cranked out cowboy movies in the 1950s knowing that any Western would get extensive bookings across the country. *Broken Arrow* (1950), for example, grossed $3.5 million and *Shane* (1953) grossed more than $9 million (on an estimated budget of $3.1 million).[4] As Will Wright wrote in *Six Guns and Society*, "Westerns are not myths but are commercial products made by professionals for the sake of profit. This argument ... goes on to contend that American tastes and preferences are not reflected but molded in successful films by the powerful studio heads, directors, and movie stars."[5] From publishers of dime novels to contemporary filmmakers, all try to appeal to the widest audience and want to make as much money as possible.

As will become apparent in the text, the expectations and demands of readers, viewers, and moviemakers have all influenced the public's perception of the Western hero. When popular sentiment changes, so must a filmmaker in order to survive. As a result, business interests have commercialized the Western past as publishers and studios tried to make their particular image of the West be the most compelling to ensure the largest audience. Movies are intended to make money and are judged by their success at the box office.

One significant influence on the genre has been that readers and movie audiences are notoriously fickle. Fiction writers and movie producers often do not know what the next significant trend will be until it happens. As a result, when a book or movie type becomes unexpectedly popular, a host of imitators will leap forward to copy and over-exploit it until audiences get tired and move on to the next trend. Two examples spring to mind. During the late 1910s film star William S. Hart created the dusty, disheveled good badman on the screen as an extremely popular depiction of the Western hero. By 1920, however, audiences had tired of this repeated formula and turned to the newer, flashy showmanship of movie star Tom Mix. As a consequence, Hart faded away as a major Western performer and Mix's vision became the new "authentic" Western hero. Similarly, after the success of Sergio Leone's popular trilogy of so-called Dollars spaghetti Westerns in the 1960s, cowboy heroes all started to look like a scruffy, unshaven Clint Eastwood.

The visual image of the West in popular culture is the Hollywood image. Millions of people have conceived their perception of the American West from watching movies and reading pulp novels and magazines written by authors who threw in large dashes of their imaginations. Hollywood filmmakers have always taken liberties with the facts and have expressed their interpretation of the West as the "authentic" one. The heroes of these Western fictions were, therefore, for the most part invented, glorified, sensationalized, romanticized, distorted, and made into legends. Of relevance here is the "cone effect," proposed Edward Whetmore. The result is what is called "constructed mediated reality" (CMR).[6] This says that all entertaining programs exaggerate and magnify real life in order to make it more interesting and entertaining. Therefore novels or films make stories set in the West more intense and violent, exaggerate sexual themes, and make cowboy life appear more colorful than real life. Audiences then perceive this media reality to be the norm and modify their thinking to conform to it, eventually incorporating it into their own lives. Because many of our contemporary perceptions of the Western hero have come to us from Hollywood, much of this book will discuss his changing image in the movies. For examples I have tried to mostly refer to films that are well known, so that the reader may be familiar with them, but I have also included other examples as appropriate.

Before beginning, I should explain three conventions that I have used in this book. In some places I have chosen to generically refer to the land west of the Mississippi that features in Western novels and movies as the "West," with a capital W. This terminology is not meant to represent a specific geographical area of the American West, but rather the mythic West of imagination and legend. I have also used this convention with "Western," which refers to books and movies that depict the cowboy and the West, as well as other descriptors. In a similar sense I have chosen in some places to use the generic term "White Man" or "the Whites" to describe the nameless, faceless pioneer, cowboy, gunman, and other non–Indian immigrant to the West in pulp novels and motion pictures.

In some parts of the text, I have similarly used names that may not represent the politically-correct terminology of today, like "Native American," "First People," "First Nation," and similar names for American Indians.[7] I have done this on purpose, both because "Indian" was the name that was in use at the time in describing the Old West and because "Indian" in this context does not represent a particular Native American culture or tribe.

Rather, the name describes the nameless, faceless fictional foe of the White Man used as the villain in dime novels and films. Furthermore, most of the "Indians" in motion pictures were not played by American Indians but by actors of white and other races and did not represent the true cultures they were supposed to. For these reasons, therefore, it seemed appropriate to retain the original language of literary and script writers. It should be understood, however, that the real American West contained many different cultural, ethnic and immigrant groups who were equally important to the development of the real West. No disrespect is intended by the use of any of these names.

Another convention is that, in the context of this book, I will use the word *persona* to mean a little more than its usual dictionary meaning of a character in a novel or a movie. I will use it to also describe the semi-fictional character that many show business people and movie stars (or their publicists or movie studios) created as their show business or screen image apart from their real life. The word *persona* is derived from a Latin word that means "theatrical mask." This description is appropriate in this context, as many of the real-life Western heroes and movie heroes projected an appearance to the world that masked their real selves.

The first chapter of this book will present an overview of the Western hero. The rest of the chapters will trace the image of the hero and his place in the fictional West, from early novels and movies to the present, and discuss how that image has evolved due to changing audience expectations and economic pressures on various media to create a profitable product.

In closing, I would like to point out that the quotes at the beginning of each chapter are worth reading and thinking about. Though most of them are laced with irony, they concisely sum up what this book—and the mythic Western hero—is all about.

1

There Have to Be Heroes

Myth is the language of historical memory—Richard Slotkin[1]

Escapist fare about the Old West, set against its historically rich and exciting background, has appeared in every narrative form of entertainment from books, radio, movies, pulp fiction, television, and photographs to paintings, ballet, and sculpture. Many of the stories have centered around heroes who are cowboys, Indians, gunslingers, and sheriffs involved in gunfights, cattle drives, and wagon trains. The single connecting feature is that these stories are set in the West. Marketing tie-ins have included hats, clothes, guns, comics, books, beer, food, automobiles, and cigarettes.

Stories of the classic West and the settlement of the frontier beyond the Mississippi provide action, romance, and conflict between good and evil that is resolved by the handsome cowboy hero. Over the years, the "Western Frontier" has become the most visible symbol of the American spirit, and the grandeur of the West serves as a scenic backdrop for many stories of conflict between lawlessness and social order. At the end of the conflict, the hero wins the thanks of the community, often the heroine, and perhaps some tangible reward in return. Watching the hero ride off into the sunset provides the audience a satisfactory resolution and escape from reality.

As this type of story proliferated, the historical American West became two places. One was a real place and time that had its own sequence of events and history. The other was a mythic place associated with the fantasies of movies and books. For people raised in the 1950s, for example, the most memorable vision and images of the West are those associated with Western films, rather than the open spaces of trans–Mississippi America.

The Myth of the Frontier West

The story of the Western Frontier is the oldest, most characteristic, and longest-lived of all American myths. The American Old West of myth is set at a point in history where savagery and lawlessness are in decline, as the frontier is being settled by an advancing wave of law and order, but challenges to its civilization remain.

Myths are stories drawn from history, which is itself preserved as a set of narratives that eventually become a series of vivid images. For hundreds of years many hero myths have been incorporated into romantic literature about knights in exotic lands and men who fight for wealth and glory. Their characteristics are usually bravery, gallantry, courage, and a long-suffering nature. These are valiant warriors who overcome tremendous odds to win the fair

Pint-sized movie fans of the 1950s often dressed up to emulate their favorite cowboy heroes. This youngster is complete with white hat, gaudy Western shirt with pearl buttons and white piping, candy cigarette dangling from his lips, twin cap pistols in his gunbelt, and a BB gun rifle (albeit apparently with a bent barrel). It appears that this young buckaroo couldn't afford a real pair of cowboy boots (Author's collection).

maiden. Knight images in the Old West include Davy Crockett defending the Alamo, the bravery of the lawmen in the shoot-out at the O.K. Corral, and the heroic but doomed nature of Custer's Last Stand.

As history is transformed into myth, it is interpreted in different ways by the teller of the story, whether through oral tradition or the written word. This has occurred from the time of early cavemen sitting around a campfire relating oral history and gradually embellishing it into myth. Today we have newspapers, movies, books, and television to serve the same purpose. Interpretation and selective retelling, even by professional historians, may gradually alter the original facts. In entertainment, these changes are often related to what the author or screenplay writer and the reader or movie viewer see as a dramatic narrative. As a result, historical elements that tend to maximize conflict, suspense, and the moral qualities of a story may be emphasized at the expense of other factual but less dramatic events that do not make as good a tale. In this way, popular stories of the West tended to focus on brief dramatic moments of conflict, and other, more mundane, details were often downplayed. Eventually this became a blend of fact and fiction, reality and fantasy, in which the real West was inaccurately remembered and portrayed.

A boost to the myth of the West came from dime novels and mass-circulation national newspapers of the late 1800s, as well as stage melodramas and Wild West shows. By the end of the nineteenth century the popular Western story had achieved a form where the historic West served as a springboard for extravagant and fantastical tales of adventure far removed from historical reality. Historical events were changed to suit the story. Dime novels full of wild improbable stories by authors such as Ned Buntline sold in the hundreds of thousands. Buffalo Bill's *Wild West* and the *Miller Brothers' 101 Ranch Wild West Show* reenacted exciting slices of Western history and life, creating the urge in children and even adult city dwellers to live on the open range. Later, Western movies and television did the same for a different generation. In this way, the cowboy became the romantic figure representing the entire West.

The dream of boys and girls in the 1940s and 1950s was to be like Ralphie (Peter Billingsley) in *A Christmas Story* (1983), who dressed in a sequined cowboy outfit as he vanquished villains and protected the family and home with his trusty Red Ryder BB gun. Kids of that era dressed like movie-cowboys, walked in stilted John Wayne fashion, rode make-believe horses, and carried toy revolvers. Young fans ran around in checkered shirts, bandanas, hats and boots emulating their heroes and playing cowboys and Indians as they acted out Western characters and roles. Their fast guns were cap pistols and their bicycles stood in for their faithful steeds as they shot it out with dastardly villains.

Fanciful Publicity

The rapid westward expansion that lasted from about 1865 to the closing of the Western frontier around the turn of the twentieth century is the basis for the myth. Though pioneers started to settle Oregon and California in the late 1840s, the major settlement of the West took place after 1865 and the end of the American Civil War. The rallying cry was "Manifest Destiny," the concept that White Americans had the moral obligation to displace existing Native American cultures and settle the vast empty areas between the Mississippi and the Pacific Coast.[2] Between 1855 and 1875 various gold and silver rushes, along with the completion of the transcontinental railroad, spurred settlement of the Great Plains and the Far West. Tens of thousands of gold seekers, cattlemen, settlers, and farmers flocked to populate the wide-open spaces.

Much of the expansion was accompanied by books, magazines, and travel guides that eulogized the benefits of living in the West and the riches to be found there. Typical books that had a significant influence on the American public were the reports of Lewis and Clark (who traveled the West from 1804 to 1806), the expedition of explorer Lt. Zebulon Pike in 1806, and Francis Parkman's 1849 *The Oregon Trail*, which described his travels in the West. Some books were accurate, but many were fiction that came from the minds of writers hoping to cash in on the migration trend and make a quick dollar. The earliest travel guides were obviously mostly inaccurate because exploration of the West was still in its infancy.

In a self-perpetuating circle, the myth was then used to boost further westward expansion and rapid growth that conquered the wilderness and displaced and subjugated the Native American tribes that inhabited it. Part of the myth involved the conflicts of the pioneers struggling with an unfamiliar environment and hostile natives. The border between the Indians and the Whites continually moved westwards until the wilderness ended at the Pacific Ocean.

The West became a symbol of all that America stood for: freedom, justice, self-reliance, and the pioneer spirit. But it also became characterized by events that in reality were only brief dramatic moments. The great cattle drives that molded the role of cowboys into a legend lasted for only about fifteen years, from 1865 to 1880. Cattle round-ups, wagon trains, and gold rushes were only short phases of the history of the West. The period that Native American Indians posed a real threat to settlers lasted for only about thirty years, yet that period has been extended in movies to show a permanent state of the defenders of civilization standing up to lawlessness and savagery.[3] Most of the West's communities were peaceful and life in them was routine. In the movies this has been transformed into formula towns with rustlers, desperadoes, and outlaws roaming the streets and being involved in constant shoot-outs with marshals and sheriffs. Shootings and killings in the real West were rare and were treated seriously by the law, not in the casual manner of the movies.

Where Was "the West?"

The first question in considering Western heroes is in defining the geographical location of "the West." Was it the eastern forests where James Fenimore Cooper's heroes fought Indians on foot? Was it beyond the Cumberland Gap made famous by Daniel Boone? Was it Kentucky and the land of the backwoodsman fighting Indians? Or was it the red sandstone buttes of Monument Valley and the deserts of Arizona where sheriffs and badmen shot it out on the main street and the cavalry constantly campaigned against the Indians? It was all of these. This is not the country of the United States west of the Mississippi, rather it is "the West," a timeless never-never land of great expectations and grand illusions that was part of the expanding frontier.

In the beginning, all of America was some vague frontier to the west of the East Coast. The land of the West was perceived as a vast uncharted territory of lawlessness that Easterners were not familiar with, but envied. "The Frontier" then moved across the West at the forefront of a wave of civilizing influences. Early tales placed the Western frontier at the Allegheny Mountains, and only later in the American West and Southwest. When President Jefferson purchased the unknown, uncharted, and unexplored Louisiana Territory from France in 1803, the West became the land beyond the Mississippi. The term "Wild West" for this land did not come into common use until after the Civil War.

A Heroic Background for Heroes

In the first half of the nineteenth century, Americans did not travel as widely as they do today, and many people spent their entire lives within a few miles of where they were born. Early interest in the West was stimulated by painters who helped to solidify the heroic image with a background of an idealized version of the Western landscape. Before black-and-white photography developed around the mid–1800s, the best way many easterners could "see" the West was through the eyes of artists. Their paintings soon turned the West into a mythological place, even before filmmakers added to it with their own images. As early as 1841 the Texas $2 bill contained a romantic image of a cowboy wearing a tall hat who was mounted on a pony with a rope in his hand.[4]

George Catlin was a painter who studied Native Americans, trappers, buffalo, and Western landscapes in the 1830s. In the 1860s and 1870s artists Albert Bierstadt and Thomas Moran created a mythic Western landscape with a series of huge inspirational romanticized paintings in the style of Thomas Cole and Frederick Church, and the earlier Hudson River School of painting in the East. These artists created sublime views of the Rocky Mountains and Sierra Nevada scenery on giant canvases showing the full majesty of these mighty mountains.

Idealized, almost sentimental, images of the West were sketched and painted in enhanced dramatic ways by artists Charles Russell and Frederic Remington. Both Remington and Russell painted the elements of dime novels and popular melodramas by featuring galloping horses, blazing six-guns, and dramatic Indian ambushes. They were among the premier myth-makers of the West, creating images of what they felt the West should have been instead of what it really was. Remington in particular was fascinated by the conflict between the Whites and the Indians. In 1886 he traveled the Southwest with General Nelson Miles on a campaign against the Apaches in Arizona. The artist sketched and painted fierce men in equally fierce conditions that ran the gamut of the Western cavalryman's experiences. Out of this came such paintings as *Cavalry Charge on the Southern Plains*, *Forsythe's Fight on the Republican River*, *Through the Smoke Sprang the Daring Young Soldier*, *A Dash for the Timber*, and *Last Cavalier*. Cavalry scenes were one of Remington's favorite subjects and many of his paintings appeared in *Harper's Weekly*.

Remington did not wish to be a reporter of the real West but considered himself to be an image-maker by presenting more drama than authenticity. He did not record facts but painted a carefully constructed image of the West with scenes of cowboys in Indian fights, cavalry in action, and cattle stampeding. His was an imaginary frontier of action, tragedy, and violence, with typical Westerners for subjects, such as old mountain men, Indians, trappers, and old-style cowboys. After 1899 Remington turned more frequently to cowboy subjects in paintings such as *The Fall of the Cowboy* and *The Stampede*. He once said, "Cowboys are cash."[5] His cowboys were often portrayed in clothing that real cowboys didn't wear, as can be seen by comparing his paintings with photographs of contemporary cowboys. But his success told him what people wanted to see, so he continued to paint his heroes in action, frozen into moments of drama. Though Remington visited the West, he painted most of his pictures in his studio in New Rochelle, New York.[6] His world of melodrama, death, violence, and tragedy was portrayed by 2,750 paintings and drawings, 25 bronzes, 8 books, and many magazine articles.[7]

Film director John Ford said that he studied Remington's paintings and tried to reproduce the artist's images and use of color in his films. To echo the feel of these pictures Ford asked cinematographer Winton Hoch to study Remington's paintings when he was filming *She Wore a Yellow Ribbon* (1949). Henry Fonda posing in *My Darling Clementine* (1946) is similar to the pose struck by the soldier in Remington's *The Alert* (1888).[8]

Another important painter of Western legend was Charles Schreyvogel. After he visited Buffalo Bill's *Wild West* and was captivated by what he saw, he decided to make the West and Indian fighting his specialty. He traveled the West taking notes and making sketches, then created paintings at his house in Hoboken, New Jersey. Examples are *My Bunkie* and *Rescue at Summit Springs*. His favorite models were said to be a local handyman and the son of a champagne salesman. Not all the details of his paintings were authentic or accurate, but they presented stirring scenes of battle.

In 1904 artist N.C. Wyeth from Delaware visited the West, actually working for three months on a cattle round-up. Afterwards he created a series of stirring images of cowboys, cattle, and his Western adventures. He became one of the most sought-after illustrators, and his paintings appeared in almost every important periodical of his time.

The Mythic West of Hollywood

A lone rider, a small isolated figure moving slowly against an awesome natural background of vast open plains and towering mountains. A dust-laden town where tight-lipped gunfighters, dance-hall girls, trail-weary cowboys, and demure bonneted housewives mingle under the scorching sun. A swarm of Indians on the warpath, circling a wagon train. These are images straight from the Hollywood version of the West. The West of this myth was a land of moral certainty set against vistas of awesome splendor and beauty. The good guys who triumphed over the bad guys were brave, dependable, honest, and true. Movies have become the vision of Western history for many Americans, in spite of the fact that few of these films are historically accurate.

The Western movie is an idealized vision of the experience of settling the West. In reality, settling the land was hard, grueling work, with the constant threat of accidents, marauding Indians, and fatal illnesses hanging over the emigrants. Skills required on the frontier were courage, independence, an understanding of the land, and a willingness to act forcefully. The real West was conquered by settlers and exploiters who came for farming, cattle, timber, trapping, and prospecting. The Native Americans were beaten into submission and removed through a series of wars. This real West was not as attractive as the adventures, fantasies, and swift action depicted by Zane Grey and other Western authors.

A topic that fascinated nineteenth-century readers and audiences who attended Western movies was the cowboy's saloon antics and feuds. Photographs like this staged one from 1907, titled "A Dispute with the Bartender," fueled the myth that cowboys were always drunk, armed, and "on the prod," looking for a fight. The two men leaning on the bar are pointing their guns at the bartender and wearing wooly chaps to portray rough, tough cowhands (Library of Congress).

The classic West of Hollywood was set between about 1865 and 1890, or from the end of the Civil War until the end of the Western frontier years. This period included gunfights, cowboys, cattle drives, Indian Wars, discovery of gold, wild mining camps such as Deadwood and Cripple Creek, and the building of the railroad. Through these Western films, audiences created their own mental image of the West. The Western movie had to seem real and authentic while still conforming to audience fantasies, such as setting, costume, and the heroic behavior of the genre. Some liked the eastern wooded landscapes of early silent Westerns. Some preferred the stark, treeless landscapes of William S. Hart, with its choking dust. Others objected to the musical numbers and fancy clothes of Roy Rogers and Gene Autry as being unrealistic and historical mockery. None of these images, however, were true visions of the real West.

The Hollywood Western is a national myth, a global icon, and cornerstone of American identity. Hundreds of Hollywood Westerns have claimed to be the "true story" by presenting authentic history and being factual.[9] But movies are not obligated to depict exact history. Many filmmakers have taken the facts and "interpreted" them for their own purposes. The concern was not to depict the West as it was, but to interpret it as an enduring myth. Critic

Jon Tuska was discussing producer Darryl Zanuck, director John Ford, and their film *My Darling Clementine* (1946) when he said, "Historical reality simply meant nothing to them. Their commitment was to a fantasy world that, even if populated by characters with the names of real persons who once had lived, was nonetheless to serve as an embodiment of certain accepted moral and political values, constructed according to definite cinema story conventions, a prescription favoring certain social attitudes."[10]

Some movies were quite open about it. *The Plainsman* (1936), directed by Cecil B. DeMille, included a disclaimer that "the story that follows compresses many years, many lives, and widely separated events into one narrative."[11] *Sutter's Gold* (1936) was honest when it said that the story is "not taken from the pages of history. Rather, it is legend and fiction, inspired by fact." Historian Alvin Josephy, Jr., writing about *They Died With Their Boots On* (1941), was more blunt when he said, "The screenwriters and director Raoul Walsh based much of the production on known historical facts, though they embellished, refashioned, twisted, and distorted most of these facts into their own hodgepodge of truth and melodramatic fairy tale."[12] As author Frank Dobie said, "What happened doesn't matter. What people like to believe does."[13]

The Mythic Western Hero

There were no cowboy heroes until they were invented. The traditional myth of the frontier idealized the White male adventurer as the hero. The movie cowboy is a man on a horse with six-shooter and no home who travels around the West solving problems. This concept came from a conglomeration of ideas in the 1890s, fed by writers and artists but, interestingly, supported and encouraged by westerners themselves. The Hollywood cowboy is a tough, self-reliant character who spends his money on gambling, liquor, and women. He wears a Colt .45 revolver and carries a Winchester '73 rifle on his saddle, can look after himself, and takes good care of his horse. He may have an unhappy past, or a wife killed by Indians or the villain, or maybe he has been unjustly blamed for a killing.

The Western hero arrived in print in the 1820s with James Fenimore Cooper's Hawkeye, was reborn in the dime novels and pulp magazines in the last half of the nineteenth century, was promoted in film starting at the turn of the twentieth century, and continued into television in the 1950s. This lonely and rugged hero captured the imagination of millions exposed to American culture. He is central to the myth of America's last frontier. He is a man of intense action, but he retaliates only after he is provoked. His triumph is good over evil, a preservation of the way of life, the defense of the weak and innocent. In the Western comedy *The Paleface* (1948), however, dentist "Painless" Peter Potter (Bob Hope) displays all the characteristics that are the exact opposite of the traditional Western hero. He exhibits lechery, cowardice, false pride, and incompetence at gunfighting.

The Western movie modernized the myth of the knight-errant in a form of morality play in which good conquered evil. The knight figure was changed into the cowboy who went around rescuing damsels in distress and righting wrongs. The hero and the villain were reduced to a simple pair of antagonists. The good versus the bad. Other heroes were the mountain man, the cavalryman, the gunfighter, the lawman, and the scout. Just as the West was a vague place set somewhere among the mountains of the Rockies or the deserts of Utah and Arizona, the heroes (almost always White Anglo-Saxon males) who populated this mythic landscape were a vague combination of integrity, morality, chivalry, honor, courage, and self-reliance. This was the ideal hero.

Hollywood Westerns tended to focus on the lone gunman. Like the hero of legend, the traditional hero of the Westerns is skilled in battle, knows his opponent, and shows no fear in the face of danger. The hero is the embodiment of good. He is an upright, clean-living, sharp-shooting WASP who respects the law, the flag, women, and children. He is self-reliant and solves problems his own way. He is always the best fighter and wins fistfights and gunfights.

Audience expectations are that the hero will also be romantic. Similar to the gunfighter hero of *Shane* (1953), he is gentle and courteous, with a hint of nobility. No wonder many of these cowboys were called "Knights of the Range." Writer Zane Grey even used this description as the title of a novel. The hero dresses smartly, rides a white horse that is his closest companion, holds up justice, and doesn't seek personal gain.

The hero may sacrifice women, family, friendship, and a settled life, and envy those who have these things. He often faces loneliness, again like Shane, who is a drifter. However, he is often redeemed by a woman, friendship, a home, owning land, or after he protects a town. All he really wants to do is to settle down, but that is often denied him. When Shane (Alan Ladd) leaves after the final shoot-out, he says, "I gotta be goin' on." When Joey (Brandon de Wilde) asks why, Shane says, "Man has to be what he is, Joey. Can't break the mold. I tried it and it didn't work for me." In *The Magnificent Seven* (1960), the gunfighters Chris

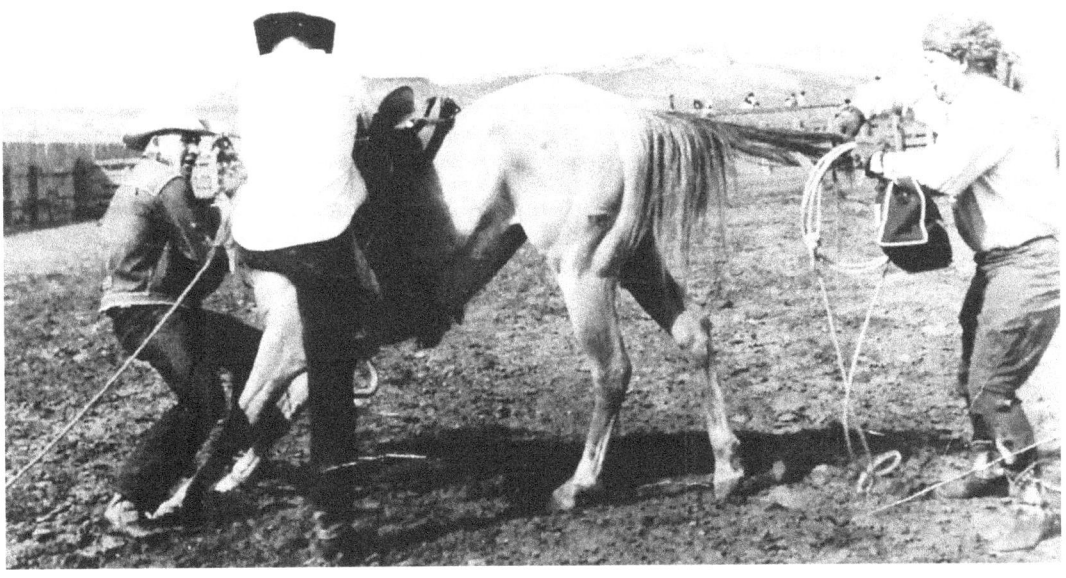

The image of the Western cowboy hero lives on with rodeo performers, seen here in small-town New Mexico in the mid–1950s. A rider gingerly tries to mount a wild horse while a wrangler holds the head and the rodeo clown holds the tail. The clown plays a vital part in rodeo as he distracts enraged stock if the rider is thrown off. This one is plaiting the horse's tail to bewilder the horse and amuse the audience (Author's collection).

and Vin have to move on or change from gunfighters into something else, as does Chico (Horst Buchholz) who hangs up his guns and becomes a farmer. He willingly abandons the freedom and individuality of a gunfighter for a woman and a farmer's life.

Over the years, changes have been made in the hero to reflect shifting values in society and in the audience. If the audience does not accept and sustain a particular type of hero, he has to change or he will fade away to be replaced by another embodiment of the hero. The entertainment industry has to maintain a profit or it too will die away, so Hollywood has to respond to changing audience tastes. The audience identifies with heroes who reflect its own morality, taste in lifestyle, and attitudes towards the situations the cowboy becomes involved in. The Western must supply escapist entertainment without too much challenge to the intellect or imagination.

Villains

The classic Western villain is the embodiment of the bad man. He is a banker, land-grabber, rustler, or big rancher who tries to take land away from little ranchers. He is concerned only with advancing his own skullduggery and is often a smooth talker with designs on helpless women. Villains are never nice or friendly to anyone. They are always complaining, bragging, threatening, or insulting. Sometimes the villain is reduced to almost a caricature. For example, in the 1930s Westerns he dressed in black, rode a black horse, and was doomed to lose.

The hero's conflict often involved Indians as villains. In the classic Hollywood period generic Indians existed as hordes of faceless, nameless enemies to be mown down by the hero and his companions. Their specific identity was blotted out. In later plots, the expendable Indians were replaced by expendable Mexicans, as in *The Professionals* (1966) and *The Wild Bunch* (1969). In *Butch Cassidy and the Sundance Kid* (1969) the expendables were Bolivians. In *Two Mules for Sister Sara* (1970) they were replaced by expendable French soldiers. By the time of *No Country for Old Men* (2007) and *The Last Stand* (2013) and changing social issues, the villains were transformed into expendable drug dealers.

Real-life Heroes

As well as the fictional Western heroes created by movies and television, prominent real-life Western figures underwent the scrutiny of novelists and moviemakers. The exploits of real-life Westerners such as Kit Carson, Buffalo Bill Cody, Wild Bill Hickok, and Wyatt Earp were seized by dime novelists, and later by Hollywood, and turned into colorful symbols of American legend. Many of these heroes became fictional characters while they were still alive. Real-life outlaws such as Jesse James and Billy the Kid were psychopathic killers but were elevated by dime novels and the legend of the West into heroes with Robin Hood status. Sometimes there were attempts to follow historical facts; however, more often these people were portrayed as fictitious heroes in stories based on common myths. The real people disappeared under the weight of dime novels and screenplays.

Books and screenplays made some of these frontier legends famous. Wyatt Earp and Doc Holliday, for example, were relatively minor characters in the West until they were propelled into prominence by the book *Wyatt Earp* by Stuart Lake. The real gunbattle at the O.K. Corral was a relatively minor incident in a lawless territory until it was featured in movies such as *My Darling Clementine* (1946) and *Gunfight at the O.K. Corral* (1957). Equally violent was a gory real gunfight in Perry Tuttle's dance hall and saloon in Newton, Kansas, on August 19, 1873, during which five men were killed and four wounded.[14] Today this fight is all but forgotten except by historians, but the O.K. Corral lives on. Similarly, Wyatt Earp lives on in legend, but other notable lawmen, such as Bill Tilghman, Billy Brooks, Charlie Bassett, and Dallas Stoudenmire, have vanished into obscurity.

Standardized Hollywood Plots

Hollywood Westerns integrated the literary and historical traditions of the myth into a blend of fiction and history. As a result, Westerns became the primary vehicle for transmission of the myth. The Western comes from a long tradition of Wild West literature that dominated the mass media and audience tastes of nineteenth-century America. The genre started with a hunter rescuing the heroine from the Indians. The tradition of these early sentimental novels gave way to pulp literature. As readers' appetites for violence and spectacle grew, writers who had previously churned out adventures, sea stories, and romances turned to the Western to cash in on the growing market. To add spice to plots, some heroes evolved into morally ambiguous figures, such as bandit Deadwood Dick, who was finally redeemed by the love of a good woman. A particularly popular plot was a lone stranger riding into a troubled town, cleaning it up, and gaining the respect of the local townspeople and the admiration of the local schoolmarm.

The classic hero, whether in Westerns or in another genre, is a man from whom something has been taken. He becomes involved in extraordinary adventures to resolve the situation through his superior skills, then reverts to his original status at the end. One popular plot involved the hero pretending to be one of the bad guys and his true heroic nature remaining hidden until the end. He may play the part of an outlaw who is really a lawman as he works undercover or in disguise as one of the crooks to expose the villain's dastardly plot. Sidebar 1–1 summarizes some common Hollywood plots.

Sidebar 1–1
Common Hollywood Western Plot Lines

1. **Pioneer Achievements.** The building of the railroads, the coming of the transcontinental telegraph and stagecoach lines, large cattle drives. *The Iron Horse* (1924), *Dodge City* (1939), *Pony Express* (1953).

2. **Wanderers and Searchers.** A roving cowboy, gunfighter, or mountain man becomes involved in searching for someone or something. *The Searchers* (1956), *MacKenna's Gold* (1969).

3. **Ranch or Towns.** Conflicts between groups, such as cattlemen against rustlers or sheepmen, farmers against cattlemen. *To the Last Man* (1933), *The Sheepman* (1958).

4. **Justice and Revenge.** Revenge for a crime committed against the hero. *The Bravados* (1958), *Last Train from Gun Hill* (1959).

5. **Indian Romance.** A White man marries an Indian and either becomes an outcast because of racial intolerance or the wife dies to prevent miscegenation. *The Vanishing American* (1925), *Broken Arrow* (1950).

6. **Outlaws.** The hero is either an outlaw or a reformed outlaw. *Jesse James* (1939), *The Law and Jake Wade* (1958).

7. The Lawman. One man stands as a lone enforcer of justice, with or without his own townspeople. *High Noon* (1953), *The Last Stand* (2013).
   8. The Army. The cavalry versus Indians in countless plots. *Fort Apache* (1948), *Escape from Fort Bravo* (1953).

Western novels, and particularly Western movies, developed with very definite guidelines about moral and dramatic conventions. The action tended to be stereotyped into barroom fights and brawls, poker games in smoky saloons, gunfights in empty streets, ambushes from behind rocks, cavalry chases, Indian attacks, and mysterious strangers riding into town. Cattle drive themes were popular, because rip-roaring cattle towns provided a location where lawless behavior could be acted out, often without retribution. The supporting cast, of course, was the marshal and the saloon girl, with the cattle baron and some homesteaders thrown in to provide conflict. Any plot must contain conflict, so villains, cheating cowards, overbearing bullies, and similar characters are part of the story.

Hollywood Western plots were sometime adapted from previous movies and relocated in the West. *Mutiny on the Bounty* (1935) became *Red River* (1948). *Gunga Din* (1939) was adapted into *Sergeants 3* (1962).[15] *The Adventures of Robin Hood* (1938) became *The Mark of Zorro* (1940). *The Charge of the Light Brigade* (1936) became *They Died with Their Boots On* (1941).

The narrative plot of Westerns always leads to resolution of the plot in a final spectacular gunfight. But this has to contain the concept of a fair fight, with the antagonists walking down the street in the bright sun towards each other, equally armed, weapons plainly in sight. This type of final gunfight became a requirement and Hollywood movies had to conform to this audience expectation created by the myth. If there was no final gunfight audiences were disappointed. For that reason some films, such as *The Big Country* (1958), did not do well at the box office. This particular movie deviated from standard plotting by changing and distorting the conventional image of the Western myth with a hero who is an easterner who hasn't shot a gun in ten years.

Some critics have charged that "all Westerns are alike." To some extent this is accurate. Westerns do have a limited set of situations, landscapes, and actors. Western towns are full of stock characters, such as the mild-mannered storekeeper, the genial doctor who drinks, the newspaper editor who tries to right wrongs, the upright blacksmith, the decent woman, and the legendary prostitute with the heart of gold. Though these characters are seen now as stereotypes, when they were first introduced they were considered to be part of a new fresh approach to plotting.

2

The Legend Begins

The true point of view in the history of this nation ... is the Great West—Frederick Jackson Turner[1]

The most powerful part of the early myth the public believed about the West was created by the written word. Fictional stories published in various cheap formats increased in national circulation, as in well as size and complexity, after the 1840s. The Western novel, like other works of popular fiction, was a commercial product intended to provide entertainment for the reader and provide a decent income for the writer.[2]

In the nineteenth century, readers were fascinated by men such as Daniel Boone and Davy Crockett, who were part of Manifest Destiny. The nation wanted to read tales of adventurous and courageous white men advancing into the threatening wilderness. Because audiences wanted to read about heroes, writers supplied them with heroes who were skilled hunters and Indian fighters. Part of the myth of the frontier was that the White hero could think and fight better than anyone, so these individuals were depicted as strong-willed, self-motivated, and relying on their own skills for survival.[3]

Captured by Indians

One of the first published heroic tales was not fiction. In 1682 Mary Rowlandson published an account of her captivity during King Philip's war between Indians and New England settlers. In 1676 a band of Indians raided the village of Lancaster, Massachusetts, killed thirty-five colonists and took twenty-four captives, including Mary Rowlandson and several other women.[4] Mrs. Rowlandson, the wife of a minister, was made a slave of Indian warrior Metacom (King Philip), chief of the Wampanoag.[5]

In Rowlandson's popular book, titled *The Sovereignty and Goodness of God* and first published in 1682, she wrote a sensational account of being taken deep into the woods and of witnessing Indian ceremonies. The book was a best seller and went through at least fifteen editions. In a classic piece of self-promotion, the title page of the 1773 edition intones, "A Narrative of the Captivity, Sufferings and Removes of Mrs. Mary Rowlandson, who was taken prisoner by the Indians with several others, and treated in the most barbarous and cruel manner by those vile savages."[6] Rowlandson spent eleven weeks with the Indians, until she was freed after a ransom was paid.

A fundamental part of this frontier narrative was the struggle between men of White and Indian races for the body of a woman. Rowlandson's tale of captivity symbolized the capture of Christianity and civilization. This made sensational reading, due to the prevailing simplistic ideology that races should not mix. However, Mrs. Rowlandson's story of her trials and tribulations was a strongly moral one. She described how she resisted physical and spiritual temptations while with the Indians, thus vindicating her moral character and the strength of her values. In this story, the final triumph of civilization was her rescue as a White woman after being held captive. Mrs. Rowlandson's book stimulated the publication of a host of similar stories, most of them emphasizing the more lurid details. The plot of a white woman captured and mistreated by Indians was popularly known as a "captivity narrative."

The popular theme of these captivity stories was that of a woman kidnapped by Indians and her rescue by a hero or hunter or woodsman—or a combination of all three—who tracks her through the forests. This rescue-in-the-nick-of-time concept was used commonly in later Western films. Typically the cavalry rides to the rescue just before the wagon train or settlers are overwhelmed by the Indians. This takes place in the movie *Stagecoach* (1939), where the cavalry arrives just in time to fend off the pursuers. Another example occurs in *Escape from Fort Bravo* (1953), where the last few of the motley group escaping from the besieged fort are rescued just as they are about to be overrun. The fear of kidnap by Indians promoted by books such as Mary Rowlandson's provided villains in the form of Indians abducting white women. Thus one way that the hero could prove his bravery was by rescuing the heroine. The Indians, on the other hand, were portrayed as generic villains who were barbaric, ruthless, and evil.

In the early decades of the 1700s, the real-life captivity narrative was expanded into fictional form. These tales recounted the stirring deeds of daring Indian fighters and similar heroes battling Indians and the elements in the wilderness. The typical story started with a hunter (always male) who was completely at ease as he traveled through the deep woods. Then the plot thickened when a White woman or girl was captured from her familiar civilized surroundings by Indians. She was dragged kicking and screaming into the dark sinister woods where there was danger at every turn and Indians lurked behind every tree. Rescue by the gallant hero came, of course, by the end of the book.

All the land to the west of civilization was seen as a dark, forbidding place. Part of the allure for readers was a plot fueled by a fear of the unknown West and capture by Indians. Women readers, in particular, had a morbid fascination that this might happen to them.

The Importance of Leatherstocking

In the literary world of the first half of the nineteenth century, the frontier hero stood as a barrier between civilization and the savagery that was presumed to exist just beyond the Western frontier. Civilization was equated with progress, which was promoted as the American ideal. The hero was a man who tamed the wilderness and made it safe for civilization.

The hero of these novels was often dressed in a buckskin outfit to authenticate the image of the experienced woodsman. In spite of his seemingly humble appearance, the man underneath was often an aristocratic or upper-class character. His background might be that of a British nobleman as in *The Pioneers* or a Virginia planter as in *The Last of the Mohicans*. Even in *The Virginian* the main character was given the background of a Southern gentleman with eastern respectability underneath his rough cowboy exterior.

The creator of the original Western hero in American popular literature was James Fenimore Cooper. Cooper wrote historical romances with plots formed around variations of the core characters of a hunter, a captive, and a savage. Cooper's first novel, published in 1820 and titled *Precaution*, was not particularly well received. He persisted and the next year wrote *The Spy*, which launched his career as a novelist. His later books were highly successful and were translated into dozens of languages.

Cooper's major literary achievement was a series of five historical romances known as the Leatherstocking Tales. The books were centered around the adventures of fictional woodsman Natty Bumppo and his interaction with the lives of settlers on the Western frontier. Bumppo was also known variously as Hawkeye, Leatherstocking, Pathfinder, and Deerslayer. During the nineteenth century this character as a hero was borrowed, imitated, plagiarized, and parodied. His heroic persona served as the protagonist for serious novels and was the prototype for the hero of countless stage melodramas and dime novels. Later pulp writers and novelists further developed and expanded the basic formula initiated by Cooper.

The Leatherstocking stories were not written in a chronological sequence of Natty Bumppo's life. The first of the tales was *The Pioneers* (published in 1823), set in 1793, with Bumppo aged between seventy-one and seventy-three. The next was *The Last of the Mohicans* (1826), set in 1757, with him aged around thirty-six or thirty-seven. The third was *The Prairie* (1827), set in 1805, when Bumppo was somewhere between eighty and eighty-seven. This was followed by *The Pathfinder* (1840), set in 1759, with Bumppo around thirty-eight or thirty-nine. The final book of the series was *The Deerslayer* (1841), set in 1740, with Natty Bumppo aged twenty-three or twenty-four.

The most enduring of the books has been *The Last of the Mohicans* (1826), which was possibly based on the real-life kidnapping by Indians and rescue of Daniel Boone's daughter, Jemima, and two of her companions in 1776.[7] The book was written in the style of the time, which is a little difficult to read today. Bumppo tends to be long-winded and the Indians in the stories are very talkative, in contrast to the cowboys of later pulp novels, who could be downright taciturn. The writing is sentimental and romanticizes the Indians. Nevertheless, the book has remained extremely popular and has sold millions of copies. It has been claimed that this was the most widely read American novel of the nineteenth century.

The essential plot revolves around the British Fort William Henry, which is under siege by the French in 1757. The primary characters besides Hawkeye are Major Duncan Heywood, Colonel Munro and his two daughters, Cora and Alice, and the evil Magua the Huron. Echoing the sentiment of the time, Cooper gave this description in the introduction about the native warrior of North America: "In war, he is daring, boastful, cunning, ruthless, self-denying, and self-devoted; in peace, just, generous, hospitable, revengeful, superstitious, modest, and commonly chaste."[8]

Cooper's books furthered the nineteenth-century concept of not mixing White and non–White races, in a literary theme that emphasized the popular perception that "bad" Indians always wanted to kidnap and sexually possess White women. This was seen as the equivalent of polluting the women, both morally and racially. Any "mixing" that did occur had to be solved by the author killing off one or more of the participants. In *The Last of the Mohicans* this concept is thinly veiled in the following excerpt: "'Die!' repeated Cora.... '[T]hat were easy! Perhaps the alternative may not be less so. He would have me,' she con-

James Fenimore Cooper broke literary ground when he developed the character of Natty Bumppo, also known as Leatherstocking, Pathfinder, and Deerslayer. In Cooper's time the forests of the East were considered to be dangerous, unknown places populated by fierce Indians who were always ready to ambush men and kidnap women. This illustration from a 1910 version of *The Last of the Mohicans* shows Leatherstocking, friendly Indians, and one of Munro's daughters traveling silently through the deep forest (Library of Congress).

tinued, her accents sinking under a deep consciousness of the degradation of the proposal, 'follow him to the wilderness ... to remain there: in short to become his wife!'"[9]

To avoid the concept of forced White miscegenation, which was distasteful to nineteenth-century sensibilities, Cora's heritage is described as "mixed": "Her complexion was not brown, but it rather appeared charged with the color of the rich blood, that seemed ready to burst its bounds."[10] To make her background even clearer, Cooper delicately described Cora's mother thusly: "She was the daughter of a gentleman of those isles, by a lady whose misfortune it was ... to be descended, remotely, from that unfortunate class who are so basely enslaved to administer to the wants of a luxurious people."[11]

Though violence will be discussed in detail in a later chapter, it is worth noting that graphic violence was often a part of these early Indian-versus-Whites novels. In the fierce fight between the protagonists and the Huron Indians in *The Last of the Mohicans*, Uncas is described "leaping on an enemy, with a single, well-directed blow of his tomahawk, cleft him to the brain."[12] Even grimmer is an incident that occurs during Magua's attack on the retreating inhabitants of the fort. One of the Indians grabs a baby from its mother's arms and "his bantering but sullen smile changing to a gleam of ferocity, he dashed the head of the infant against a rock, and cast its quivering remains to her very feet."[13] Just for good measure the Indian also kills the mother, with a savage blow to the head with his tomahawk. This was pretty grim reading for 1826. In other instances, Cooper tones down the action. When Hawkeye shoots Magua at the end of the book, it is described as his rifle "pour[ing] out its contents."[14]

Although Cooper created frontier romances and the first Western hero, he was also responsible for much of the generic hero myth. His version of the myth included a wide variety of White and Indian social and racial stereotypes showing extreme good and evil and a mix of characteristics between. Contrasting concepts included a White man raised as an Indian and Indians who exhibited White ideas.

Cooper also promoted the American idea that it is acceptable for the hero to take action outside the law in the pursuit of justice. The notion was that good always triumphed over evil if the good had high civilized moral values.[15] Leatherstocking, as the hero, is a man who stands outside civilization and retaliates against the agents of savagery with death and violence because of his own superior morality. His violence is used to end their violence. He has little compunction about the morality of his actions and takes no responsibility for them. This foreshadowed the later antiheroes of the spaghetti Western films of the 1960s. Then as now, European and American audiences responded enthusiastically to Cooper's new type of hero.

Real-life Heroes

Looking for new twists on plotting and in search of more frontier heroes for their books, novelists seized on real-life westerners. Two of these real-life heroes were Daniel Boone and Davy Crockett. Though both Boone and Crockett were important historical figures in their own right on the frontier, they were elevated to almost legendary status after being discovered by dime novelists. Later real-life Westerners who received similar treatment were mountain man Christopher "Kit" Carson and showman William F. "Buffalo Bill" Cody.

Men like Kit Carson, Jim Bridger, and "Wild Bill" Hickok became better known as dime-novel heroes than for their historical deeds in real life.

Daniel Boone (1734–1820)

The American hero as an Indian fighter was exemplified by the career of backwoodsman Daniel Boone, who achieved near mythic status. Over his lifetime, Boone built a legitimate reputation as a strongly individualistic woodsman, expert trailblazer, and daring scout. He was adept at Indian warfare and had a vast store of knowledge of his opponents. He may have even been a model for the hunter-heroes of James Fenimore Cooper's romantic adventure novels. Boone had a small farm in the backwoods of the Appalachian Mountains of North Carolina and Virginia in the 1760s. In 1769 he traveled to Kentucky in search of free land and a life away from the confines of civilization. He led a group of settlers through the Cumberland Gap to found a town named Boonesborough and later became an important figure in politics who was transformed into a local folk legend.

Boone started on the path to become a mythic hero as a result of a pamphlet called *Kentucke* (1784) written by John Filson.[16] Filson was a friend of Boone and accompanied him on several expeditions. Though the pamphlet portrayed Boone as a mythic hero, it was also a thinly disguised sales brochure to promote to immigrants and investors the development of land along the Ohio River. The text linked Boone's adventures to the wilderness West that Filson was trying to sell as a new Garden of Eden. He described a wild and exotic landscape with weird rock formations, strange animals, lush meadows of flowers, vast herds of buffalo, springs with curative powers, and air that was good for the health.[17] Local Indians were presented as the Noble Savage.

Boone went on to be the subject of countless stories, novels, and films, which culminated in a television series that ran from 1964–1970.

Davy Crockett (1786–1836)

Davy Crockett was also a real outdoorsman and woodsman who became an important literary property. As such, he was the most successful frontier legend since Daniel Boone.

In 1831, a play titled *The Lion of the West* by James Kirke Paulding, based on the real-life Davy Crockett, became very popular. Two years later an unknown author wrote *Life and Adventures of Colonel David Crockett of West Tennessee*. Noting the popularity of the play and the book, Crockett quickly brought out his own biography. The book, written primarily by himself and published in 1833, was titled *Narrative of the Life of David Crockett of the State of Tennessee*. By doing this, Crockett, already an adept storyteller, became the author of his own legend and was one of the first to create his own literary persona. The book became very popular and sold between 5,000 and 10,000 copies, which was a large number at the time.[18] The demand for more of his stories led to another book in 1834 titled *Sketches and Eccentricities of Col. David Crockett of West Tennessee*, ghost-written by James S. French. Books and plays like this made readers in the East believe that the West was a place of romantic adventure, financial independence, and potential fame. This image helped to create and propagate the legendary West and the people who lived there.

Kit Carson (1809–1868)

By the mid–1800s, interest in the frontiersman fighting Indians in the forests of the East started to fade. Tomahawks and muskets, along with heroes dressed in coonskin caps and moccasins, were seen as being out of date. The reading public wanted a new, fresh, more contemporary hero. In response, writers of sensationalist stories looked for someone different to promote. The new fictional model became Kit Carson, plainsman, trapper, Indian fighter, and frontiersman.

The real Christopher "Kit" Carson was an authentic frontiersman, born in 1809 in Kentucky. Carson was not a tall man. He had a slight frame and was only about five feet four inches tall. He appeared shorter, as he was bow-legged from years in the saddle. He had stringy brown hair that hung down to his shoulders and a scar on his left ear, and his body was covered with old knife and bullet wounds. To be able to communicate with the varied cultures of the Southwest, he could speak Spanish, French, and several Indian languages. He smoked a pipe but rarely drank.

A capsule look at his career shows a life of an authentic Westerner and mountain man. He ran away to the West at age sixteen, arriving in New Mexico in 1826. During the late 1820s, Carson and his family lived in the tiny village of Taos in northern New Mexico, which became the most important market and supply center for trappers west of St. Louis.[19] From

The real mountain man Kit Carson made his home in Taos, New Mexico, an important trading town for fur trappers in the early 1800s. Carson and his family lived in this modest one-story, four-room adobe house in Taos from 1843 until 1867, when they moved to Boggsville, Colorado. Carson died at the hospital at nearby Fort Lyon in 1868 and is buried in Taos (author's collection).

1829 to 1831 Carson was an apprentice trapper in California. From 1831 to 1841 he was a trapper and mountain man. Between 1842 and 1849 he served as a guide for exploratory expeditions into the West led by John Charles Frémont ("The Pathfinder"). From 1861 to 1867 he had a Civil War military career that carried into the postwar Indian campaigns in the West. In 1868 Carson was appointed superintendent of Indian Affairs in Colorado. It was Carson and a military force that finally broke the resistance of the Navajo Indians in Northern Arizona and relocated them to a reservation at Bosque Redondo (Fort Sumner) in New Mexico. In 1867 Carson left the army and moved to Boggsville in southeast Colorado.[20] He died in May of 1868 at age fifty-nine at nearby Fort Lyon, Colorado.

Even before Carson's death, the legend makers were hard at work. Under their torrents of verbal hyperbole, the new fictional Carson became a national hero. The man and his exploits were magnified by early biographers, then embellished and exploited by later writers of dime novels who made him into a fearless champion and defender of virtue. He was perceived as the new hero of the wilderness of the Rockies and the West.

The real Carson first came to the public's attention when he was a scout for General Stephen Watts Kearny during the Mexican war, and after that for Frémont in the 1840s. Carson was the one who traveled across the country as a dispatch rider to bring the news of Frémont's capture of California to Washington. Newspapers reported Carson as a modern version of Daniel Boone and Davy Crockett all rolled into one.

The fictional version of Carson, invented by Charles Averill, first came to the attention of the reading public in *Kit Carson: The Prince of the Gold Hunters*, published in 1849. In this improbable yarn, the literary Carson killed scores of Indians and rescued a young girl captured by savages. He was a self-confident man of action and a supreme outdoorsman who never lost a battle. In spite of Carson's small build in real life, Averill gave his fictional hero a "mighty frame," "massive arms," and "prodigious strength." The hero was at least six inches taller than Carson's real five-foot-four and was a big man with rippling muscles. The plot moved along at a brisk pace and was full of cliff-hangers. The fictional story contained a prairie fire, a treasure cave, and a perilous escape from the Indians. Averill claimed that the yarn was based on facts, but apparently he did not take the trouble to learn much about Carson or even obtain permission to use Carson's name as his fictional hero.[21] One of the false "facts" in the book was that Carson was the discoverer of the original California gold strike in 1848.

Carson's literary persona was loosely based on minimal facts and expanded by myth. His image eventually diverged into two forms. One appeared in dime novels that were intended for mass circulation among the lower and middle classes. The other was found in the better class of fiction, which was published in hard cover and was intended for a more "respectable" reading public. This latter version tended to overlook Carson's two Indian wives in real life and made his manners and ways more gentlemanly. The literary Carson of the paperback novels became the hero of dashing but violent exploits, a wild hunter battling Indians and evil renegades with a heavy dose of the standard rescue plot. The Carson that appeared in the higher class of novels was a more genteel character, though still a man of violence, and a hunter, avenger, and rescuer of women.

Eventually more than seventy books were written with Carson as a hero, an avenger of Indian depredations, rescuer of women captured by Indians, and all-around superb outdoorsman. Typical of the Carson pulps were *Rocky Mountain Kit's Last Scalp Hunt, The*

The imaginary exploits of authentic plainsmen, trappers, Indian fighters, and frontiersmen were turned into dime novel fodder by writers of sensationalist fiction looking for a new type of hero at a time when frontiersmen dressed in coonskin caps and moccasins were seen as being out of date. In this illustration from *Puck* magazine in 1912, a young Boy Scout meets some of the heroes of the dime novels in the form of Daniel Boone, California Joe, Kit Carson, Texas Jack Omohundro, Buffalo Bill Cody, and Davy Crockett (Library of Congress).

Fighting Trapper: Kit Carson to the Rescue, and *Kit Carson's Last Bride: The Flower of the Apaches*.[22] These stories made his persona famous. The adventures that Carson supposedly engaged in became so outlandish that even Carson was surprised. The cover of one dime novel showed Carson holding a beautiful woman he has just rescued, with both of them surrounded by dead Indians. After examining the picture, Carson is said to have commented, "Gentlemen, that thar may be true, but I hain't got no recollection of it."[23]

A biography published by De Witt Peters in 1859, titled *The Life and Adventures of Kit Carson, the Nestor of the Rocky Mountains, from Facts Narrated by Himself*, fueled the legend. But even Carson commented that "Peters laid it on a little thick."[24] Unfortunately there was also a downside to having to live up to the reputation of a hero. One time on the Oregon Trail, Carson met a man from Arkansas who had heard about the famous scout. "I say, stranger, are you Kit Carson?" the man said. Carson replied that he was. The man supposedly looked at him in disappointment and said, "Look here, you ain't the kind of Kit Carson I'm looking for."[25] When General William Sherman first met the man who was credited with so many daring deeds, he said that to his surprise that Carson was a small, stoop-shouldered man with reddish hair and a freckled face and did not look like the hero he was.

In 1849 the real Carson accompanied an army expedition searching through New Mexico to find and rescue a white woman named Ann White, who had been captured by Jicarilla

Apaches. Unfortunately, only a few minutes before the troops found the camp to rescue her, one of the Indians killed her with an arrow. Searching the camp afterwards, Carson found a copy of a pulp novel by Charles Averill that had probably belonged to Mrs. White. Part of the plot described the rescue of a girl kidnapped by the Indians. Carson was always disturbed by this find and wondered if the book had given her false hope that he would come to rescue her.[26] By 1900 some of Carson's popularity as a subject for pulp novels had faded, though his fictional self would be revived in the 1940s and 1950s for comic books and television. He is remembered today chiefly by the many places named after him, such as the towns of Kit Carson and Fort Carson in Colorado, Carson City in Nevada, Carson National Forest in New Mexico, and 14,165-foot Kit Carson Mountain in Colorado.

Other mountain men were also turned into heroes. An example is the legend of John "Liver Eating" Johnson, which became the basis for the novel *Mountain Man: A Novel of Male and Female in the Early American West*. The book was later made into the movie *Jeremiah Johnson* (1972).

George Armstrong Custer (1839–1876)

Another popular all–American hero was Lt. Col. George Armstrong Custer. Custer rose to become the youngest brevet general in the Union army, was a Civil War hero, and afterwards became a legendary Indian fighter.[27] Because of his youth, he was popularly known as the "Boy General." He was a charismatic and flamboyant leader. His final Indian fight and death at the Little Bighorn in Montana elevated his exploits to the level of national myth.

On July 19, 1876, less than two weeks after the Bighorn battle, the *New York Daily Graphic* published a full-page illustration by William de la Montagne Cary titled *The Battle on the Little Bighorn River—The Death Struggle of General Custer*. The image showed Custer standing high and tall with Indians swirling all around him. This interpretation was the first to establish the concept of the "Last Stand" and make it part of the Custer legend.[28]

The core of the Custer myth is found in his own book, *My Life on the Plains; or, Personal Experiences with Indians*. In addition, much of the publicity that elevated Custer to the rank of a folk hero came from the pen of his wife, Elizabeth Bacon Custer, popularly known as "Libbie," who continued to promote her husband's memory long after his death. The daughter of a Michigan lawyer, Libbie was a respected society lady. She perpetuated and magnified the memory of her husband as a hero and the martyr of the Little Bighorn in a series of books that glorified Custer's life in the West. She started in 1885 with *Boots and Saddles; or, Life in Dakota with General Custer*, which was a glowing account of her marriage to Custer and their life on the frontier. The book sold 15,000 copies in the first nine months after publication. She followed it with *Tenting on the Plains; or, General Custer in Kansas and Texas* and *Following the Guidon*.

Another of the heroic Custer images that impressed the public was a series of paintings of the final battle at the Little Bighorn. One of the most popular was an eleven-foot by twenty-foot canvas titled *Custer's Last Rally* by John Mulvaney. Mulvaney spent two years researching the historical details in an attempt to portray the battle correctly. Other popular images of the battle were *General Custer's Death Struggle* by Henry Steinhegger, *Custer's Last Stand* by Frederick Paxon, and *Custer's Last Fight* by Cassily Adams, all painted in the late 1900s. All of them show Custer fighting valiantly with saber and revolver at the climax of the battle as he is about to be overcome by Indians. The latter version was converted into a lithograph by Otto Becker (who modified the painting as he created the lithograph) and at least 200,000 were distributed by Anheuser-Busch Brewing Company.[29] A study of the many illustrations of Custer's Last Stand by historian Don Russell led him to conclude that the Battle of the Little Bighorn has been the most frequently depicted moment in all of American history. He found a thousand different representations of the scene on paintings, lithographs, calendars, books, dime novels, and comic books.[30]

Custer was subject to a wide variety of opinions. The heroic version of Custer was a favorite subject of movies in a direct retelling of the battle, such as *They Died with Their Boots On* (1941). In *Santa Fe Trail* (1940), Ronald Reagan played Custer as handsome, jovial, and sensitive to the problems of slavery. In *Little Big Man* (1970), however, Richard Mulligan portrayed him as a megalomaniac racist. The Custer legend was also used as the basis for Custer-like film plots, such as *Fort Apache* (1948), where the entire command is wiped out in an Indian attack.[31] In these plots the Indians were depicted as war-like savages and unchangeable in nature as they resisted the coming of the White man.

Henry Wadsworth Longfellow wrote a poem about the Custer battle titled "The Revenge of Rain-in-the-Face." The tone of the piece contains references to how the savage Indians attacked Custer, though in reality it was the other way around.

Debunking the Heroes

In the 1970s some revisionist historians attacked the legends of Boone, Crockett, Carson, and Custer as frontiersman heroes. Carson, for example, instead of being the valiant hero of the times, became the killer of defenseless Indians and a racist who tried to exterminate the Navajo. Though in one sense this was partially true, the reality of the situation was somewhere in the middle. In real life, Carson was a friend of the Indians and fought to protect and preserve their way of life; however, he was also an army officer and had to follow the orders of his superior officers. With controversy over government Indian policy surrounding him, Carson once said, "I don't know if I did right or wrong, but I always did my best."

All four of these men fought Indians, either in defense of their homes or as soldiers at war in the military. In fighting Indians, all were carrying out the accepted practices of the time. Boone and Crockett were protecting their homes and the settlers. Carson was well liked in the West, but he was indeed an Indian fighter who resisted fighting them until directly ordered to by the army. Custer sought military glory, which brought him to an unexpected fate.

3

The Lure of the Dime Novels

If history does not support the moral message, then history must be altered."—John Ford[1]

During the mid–1800s, coinciding with the early settling of the West, a fundamental change took place in the technology of book production. This publishing revolution started with the development of the steam-powered, high-speed rotary press that allowed the widespread sale of cheap publications. In 1846 one rotary press was developed that could produce 290,000 copies of a newspaper each hour.[2] By 1865 a further important printing development was that the paper feeding these high-speed presses was supplied from huge rolls, instead of in single sheets, thus improving efficiency. This improved technology widened the expansion of newspapers and created the weekly story magazine. Wide distribution of publications was further encouraged when the post office lowered mailing rates for magazines to two cents per issue in 1857.

The advances in printing also led to the publication of cheap editions of romances, melodramas, and lurid adventure fiction that became known as "dime novels." This was sometimes also called "steam literature" after the steam presses. A sequence was thus set in motion that led to the creation of the sensationalist dime novels, then to pulp fiction, and eventually to mass-market paperbacks.

Industrialization, mechanization, and urbanization in the United States brought about major social and cultural changes that were reflected in the book industry. By the 1840s the industrial revolution had brought compulsory public education to the masses and by 1861 America had the highest literacy rate in the world at 58 percent of the total population.[3] Books became part of the popular culture and many of the major publishing houses that are still in business today were founded. Another change was that books began to use the everyday language of the masses.

The popular magazine industry started to flourish around the same time. *Harper's Weekly* was founded in 1850, *Atlantic Monthly* in 1857. The magazine industry grew from 700 individual publications in 1865 to over 5,000 by 1900.[4] These magazines published short stories, poems, serialized novels, essays, and commentaries. There were several intellectual levels of magazines. At the bottom of the scale were cheaply printed sensationalistic lower-class journals like the *Spirit of the Times* and the *Police Gazette*. To appeal to the middle-class there was a series of more literate magazines, such as *Harper's Weekly* and *Frank Leslie's Illustrated Weekly*. Literary and cultural journals for intellectuals were the likes of *Atlantic Monthly* and *North American Review*, which was the first literary magazine in the United States.

Periodicals typically contained stories of thrilling action, courtly love, and melodramatic

The publication of a veritable torrent of dime novels, pulp magazines, comic books, and cheap novels about gun-slinging Western heroes fueled an interest in the West among young and old alike. Young boys wanted to run away to become a cowboy and adult males dreamed of marrying a pretty cowgirl and living on a ranch in the West (Author's collection).

adventure, all illustrated by garish woodcuts. In the 1880s *Harper's Weekly*, *Scribner's Magazine*, *Knickerbocker*, and *Atlantic Monthly* started to publish more Western fiction and print correspondence from travelers to the West. Along with this were articles, letters to the editor, and the same type of miscellaneous material that makes up today's general circulation magazines. One of the most successful magazines that published Western fiction was Street and Smith's *New York Weekly*. Longer stories were often serialized and ran over several issues, frequently ending each installment with a cliff-hanger to entice readers to buy the next issue. The long-winded story titles that were in style at the time ended up being a synopsis of the action of the plot. For example, *The Banner Weekly* serialized a story between July 6 and September 28, 1889, with a title that was a mouthful: *The Wild Steer Riders; or, The Red Revolver Rangers: A Story of Lawless Lives, Love, and Adventure in the Lone Star State*.[5]

A very popular journal was *National Police Gazette*, more commonly known as the *Police Gazette*, founded in 1845. The owner after 1876 was Richard Kyle Fox, a man who showed intuitive judgment for what the public wanted. Fox's formula was the sensational reporting of crime and human interest stories, accompanied by dramatic illustrations. Fox made the *Police Gazette* into an illustrated tabloid style of publication that specialized in lurid coverage of events in the Wild West, murders, and scandalous events that involved women. Typical were stories that concentrated on the violence and killing in Texas caused by marauding bands of outlaws and raids by Comanche and Kiowa after the Civil War. Fox turned the *Police Gazette* into an immensely popular weekly magazine in the East in the late

1800s with nationwide circulation through subscription. Between 1865 and 1900 news journals like this that specialized in scandalous and sensational reporting included sensationalistic headlines and stories about crime, sex, and violence. These journalistic excesses became known as "yellow journalism."[6] The popularity of the *Police Gazette* was given a nod of recognition in the film *Cat Ballou* (1965), which used vintage period woodcuts similar to the magazine as illustrations for the titles.

Other changes in publishing occurred after the completion of the transcontinental railroad, at a time when the eyes of the country were focused on the West as a land of opportunity. Settlers went west by the thousands to seek gold and free land. To match this trend, new stories were needed in American frontier adventure fiction. The land of Leatherstocking had long since been settled and the time of Boone and Crockett was past. These plots had become stale and the public was ready for something else. The demand for new heroes was met by the dime novel, which offered adventure and romance for the lowest price then known.

The Dime Novels

"Dime novel" was a generic name for the inexpensively produced mass-market fiction paperbacks that appeared from about 1860 to 1910 from multiple publishing houses. The format of the dime novel was a small paperback book of about 100 pages in length, containing a short novel (novelette) of about 30,000 words. Many had plots set in the West. Early Western dime novels described hunters and scouts outfitted with flintlock rifles and coonskin caps and featured men who had outrageous manners of speech and dress. The newer type of hero fought Indians and bandits and rescued heroines. Very few of these books, however, had a plot where the hero was involved with being a cowboy or dealing with cattle, and any cowboys who appeared in these novels did nothing that a real cowboy would do. The open range and herding cows was not part of the fictional Western vision. The closest to a cowboy was an occasional hero like fictional Texas lawman "Moccasin Mat," who had a horse that came when Mat whistled.[7]

Dime novels were cheap sensationalist fiction produced primarily for audiences of working-class men and women, with heroes who were a continuation of the frontier fighter invented by Cooper. The typical cover showed the hero engaged in a fierce fight using a knife or firing a gun. The books were cheaply printed on poor paper with a high acid content and were subject to rapid yellowing and decomposition. Because of this and their lurid content, they were often called "yellowbacks." Few examples have survived until now because the paper became fragile with time and disintegrated when handled.

The stories in dime novels were a continuation of earlier costume dramas, with the protagonist as a form of knight-errant. Plots were sensational and melodramatic, featuring outlaws, bandits, villains, lost loves, and damsels in distress. As Ted Hayden (John Wayne) says in *West of the Divide* (1934), "Oh, I see, like a dime novel. We eliminate the old gent, you marry the gal and get the ranch." The heroes of this overblown style of fiction, whether real like Kit Carson or fictional like Deadwood Dick, took on whatever characteristics the writer wanted the hero to have, and the plots covered whatever the writer thought the public wanted to hear and whatever met their preconceived notions of the West. Sensationalism was the key to commercial success and the pressure was on authors and publishers to supply what readers wanted and to repeat it to retain their audience.

The key to success was action. Some series of dime novels specialized in thrillers about spies, pirates or soldiers. Many were written with cliff-hanging elements that fed popular fantasies and romantic mythology about Western outlaws and Indians. To persuade buyers, the cover usually depicted some dramatic element of the tale, such as the heroine in distress, Indian attacks, or the villain lurking around to shoot the hero. Schoolboys and youths read these stories in the barn and late at night in bed by candlelight. Adults scorned them but read them in secret. In *Cat Ballou* (1965), Catherine Ballou (Jane Fonda), a young schoolteacher traveling out West in 1894, is pretending to be reading a book of Tennyson poems, but inside it she is hiding and reading a dime novel titled *Kid Shelleen and the Massacre at Whiskey Slide*.

Beadle & Adams

In the mid–1800s, most quality novels and romance books sold for about $1.50, which at the time was more than a day's wages for a workingman. Hoping to create a business opportunity, printer and publisher Erastus Flavel Beadle had the idea of publishing novels of 25,000 to 35,000 words in length and selling them for only 10 cents.

In 1858 Erastus joined forces with his brother, Irwin P. Beadle, who was a publisher in New York. The two founded a company originally called I.P. Beadle & Company. In 1860 they started to publish children's books, joke books, and various handbooks, all priced at ten cents. These were the original dime novels. The firm also published as Beadle & Company, and Beadle & Adams with business associate Robert Adams. The Beadles and Adams groups published various series of books under the banners of Pocket Novels, Beadle's Boys Library, Pocket Library, Story and Adventure, The New Dime Novels, Dime Library, and Beadle's Boy's Library. Beadle also came out with a half-dime library for boys aged eight to sixteen who might not have ten cents. Examples were the Nickel Library and Beadle's Half-Dime Library. Beadle's Dime Novels issued a new title every two weeks or so and published 321 titles between 1860 and 1874.[8] Between 1860 and 1865 Beadle sold more than 4 million copies of dime novels.[9]

Most dime novels were written very rapidly. They were not intended to be serious literature but were written as escapist reading for youths and the everyday man, such as loggers, soldiers, sailors, and others. The books were small and could be easily carried in a pocket. The publisher paid authors anywhere from $75 to $200 per book.[10] Most of the writers were from the East and had never been to the West, but they responded valiantly to the new trend and started churning out highly imaginary Wild West tales by the score. They used stock plots and characters, often repeating themselves frequently. Typical of the lurid Western titles was *Jack Long; or, Shot in the Eye: A True Story of Texas Border Life*. Another was *Pacific Pete, Prince of the Revolver* by Joseph Badger.

To fuel their prolific publishing output, Beadle used an estimated 250 authors. Many of them had various aliases and often wrote under several pen names at the same time. A thousand words an hour (about three double-spaced typewritten pages) was not unusual for some prolific authors. A 70,000-word novel could be completed by a fast writer in only a week. Author Albert W. Aiken, for example, whose specialty was Western stories, cranked out novels at a furious rate. Beadles could count on him for a new manuscript every Saturday night.

Some critics claimed that the low cost and low literary worth of many of these stories aimed them at people from the lower classes; however, dime novels were popular with readers of all stations of life. Publishers were smart businessmen who wanted to reach the widest possible audience. Stories were intentionally written in "popular" style to appeal to a wide range of readers and the low cost made them available to even the reader with little money. Increasing urbanization brought about by the industrial revolution boosted the sales of these books to fill the need for escapist literature as a form of entertainment. Similarly, during the Civil War, dime novels were read by soldiers who needed an escape from boredom between battles. This boosted sales for Beadle & Adams, as books were sent to army camps in bales like firewood and the cheap novels were read by the troops until they fell apart. Similar markets for this inexpensive escapist reading material were ships, railroads, and logging and mining camps.

Books from Beadle & Adams generally sold for ten cents, but despite their name, not all dime novels sold for a dime. The name was only generic. Some sold for as much as twenty-five cents, others for as little as five cents. Dime novels typically sold from 35,000 to 80,000 per title, which was a successful number for that time.

The cutthroat dime novel business was dominated by the Beadles until 1889, when Erastus retired with a fortune. He died 1894, and Beadle & Adams went out of business in 1898.

Improbable Plots

Dime novels included stories about circuses, sports, schools, pirates, smuggling, and every imaginable hero that young boys admired. Most of the novels were Westerns and frontier tales, with heroes who were frontiersmen, cowboys, and bandits. Many heroes came back in novel after novel. Popular also were historical stories with settings on the high seas, during major wars, or in exotic locations. Many were about the "Indian War," but exactly which war was not specified. In spite of this, plots killed off faceless and nameless Indians in droves.

The fiction of the dime novels was overblown and full of melodramatic style, as each dime novel tried to outdo the others. The stories focused on action and fast-paced conversation. The West was mostly considered to be all one place, either the high plains and prairies of eastern Colorado, Nebraska, and eastern Montana, or the Mountain West with dense forests, cascading streams, and fast-running rivers. One popular theme was the rise to fame of a poor but honest lad. Plots often included the brave hero, who for one reason or another appeared in the guise of a simpleton, or a girl who puts on boys clothing to be near her lover and follow him to war or danger. These types of plots appealed to the working class and sold thousands of copies.

Female characters were young, innocent, and beautiful. Some were determined and resilient, though they knew their places as daughter, mother, or wife. Others had the tendency to faint or be weak in the face of danger. In line with the moral thinking of the times, even though maidens were captured by Indians and some were tortured or scalped, their "honor"

Erastus and Irwin Beadle churned out hundreds of cheap dime novels between 1865 and 1898, featuring the exploits, real or imagined, of frontier heroes who were also real or imagined. This one, attributed to Buffalo Bill himself, is titled *Death Trailer, the Chief of Scouts* (Author's collection).

(virginity) was kept intact. These women might be captured and suffer torment or death, but all of them remained virgins to the end.[11]

Though Beadle & Adams dominated the industry, other publishers were quick to come out with their own dime novels. Elliott, Thomes and Talbot of Boston followed in the early 1860s. George P. Munro, a former employee of Beadle & Adams, started up a series called Munro's Ten Cent Novels in 1863. Another competitor was Frank Tousey, who started publishing in 1878. Robert M. DeWitt of New York started DeWitt's Ten Cent Romances. Richmond and Company of Boston published Richmond's Novels. Other publishers of dime novels were M.M. Ballou of Boston, Carey & Hart of Philadelphia, and Fredrick A. Brady of New York. Beadle & Adams produced 3,688 issues, Munro 1,362, and Tousey 2,154.[12]

One of the most important competitors of Beadle & Adams was the publishing firm of Smith & Street, who started publishing dime novels in 1889 and produced 2,802 issues.[13] They were one of the five major dime novel publishers in New York. Founders Francis Scott Street and Francis Shubael Smith published Smith & Street's *New York Weekly* (subtitled *A Journal of Romance, Amusement & Useful Knowledge*) until 1887, when Street died and Smith retired. The firm continued to be a major publisher of pulp novels into the 1930s. Among others, they published *Mammoth Monthly Reader* and the *Sea and Shore* series. Street & Smith later published a series of pulp novels about the James brothers and other outlaw bandits.

Dime novels were of two general types, romances for the women and adventure dominated by Western settings for the men. Also popular were boys' and girls' series books, which were aimed at the younger reader. Fiction set on the frontier or in the West was the most popular. Of the 1,500 novels published by Beadle & Adams after 1860, three-quarters of them dealt with the West.[14] Typical heroes were lawman and gambler Wild Bill Hickok, sharpshooter Annie Oakley, frontiersman Texas Jack Omohundro, and cowboy Buck Taylor.

Dime novel publishers produced not only Westerns but also crime and adventure stories. If a plot line became popular in the dime novel world, then it was instantly copied by competing publishers. For example, sea stories based on the success of the Yankee traders were very popular in the 1870s and 1880s.

Cowboys in the dime novels had a flourishing but relatively short life. Then Western plots disappeared and were replaced by detective stories. In an effort to maintain the Western story, some of these detective stories were set in the West. Author Albert Aiken, for example, sent his police spy hero Joe Phoenix out West for several adventures. Edward Wheeler had his Western bandit Deadwood Dick act as a detective in over half his stories. Wheeler also created "Denver Dol, the Detective Queen." Though detectives appeared in dime novels in the 1870s, their popularity grew with the introduction of the Old Sleuth series, which first appeared in 1885. In 1886 St. George Rathbone created "Sombrero Sam, the Cowboy Detective." Street & Smith retaliated in 1891 with the Nick Carter series.

Most of the American dime novels made their way across the Atlantic and were reprinted in England. There they received the nickname of the "penny dreadful" and the "shilling shocker." The terminology came from the name of the English coins, the penny and the shilling, which were used to purchase them.[15]

Rough Language

Even though dime novels contained descriptions of violence and mayhem, the publishers were careful about the language they allowed. Editors scrutinized manuscripts and particularly removed anything to do with alcohol or profanity. Though dime novels were intended for soldiers, sailors, railroad men, loggers, and hunters, part of the intended audience was also youngsters, so no impolite language could be included and nothing salacious was allowed. Street and Smith were particularly careful not to offend their readers.

Though dime novel publishers were sensitive to any offensive material in their stories, this was also true throughout Victorian culture. The rape of white women by Indians, for example, was replaced by the euphemistic "outraged" in military reports. Also, no swear words or spoken vulgarity were allowed. Considered very strong was the publication of "d----d." Later, even in *The Virginian*, the epithet that Trampas throws out to the Virginian during their contentious card game was published as "you son-of-a-..."[16] Indians were never allowed to be called "red devils," because that was considered to border on profanity.[17]

In *Giant George, the Ang'l of the Range: A Tale of Sardine-Box City, Arizona* author James M. Cain wrote, "Hoop-La! Set 'em up! Sling out yer p'ison before I stampede through yer hull business! I'm ther 'Bald-headed Eagle o' ther Rockies,' an' are a-huntin' sum galoot what's got ther sand ter stomp on my tailfeathers. Shove out a bar'l o' bug-juice afore I bu'st up yer sherbang; fer my feed-trough are chuck full o' cobwebs, an' as dusty as Chalk Canyon. Hoop-La!"[18] This was considered to be rather rough language for the times. Reportedly even Beadle & Adams were shocked, but they published the story anyway.

Another example of the peculiar language that dime novelists thought was used by mountain men was this one from *The Luckless Trapper; or, The Haunted Hunter* by William Reynolds Eyster (aka Captain Lew James). At one point the trapper Bill Blaze exclaims, "Minks and mushrats! Blam'd if she ain't Dick Martin's gal! A trump, by mitey! She's cleaned out the hull b'iling; stampeded ther corral, an's bringin' the pick o' the lot into camp! Bill Blaze an' her'll move inter Black Load camp rejoicin'. Waugh!"[19]

Many contemporary critics considered that this lurid type of literature—with its dreadful language, violence, and questionable values—to be a bad influence on youth. Religious leaders worried about a decline in morals, an increased rate of crime, and even deviant behavior in the young, and attacked dime novels from the pulpit. They felt that sensationalist prose and violent characters and plots, along with convoluted moral messages in the plots, changing identities of some of the characters, and confusion of right and wrong would send an improper message to impressionable youths. Many intellectuals viewed dime novels as immoral and dangerous to the minds of others, especially the young and the working class. They viewed dime novels as a sinister threat to American youth, and certainly as bad as smoking.

Significant Dime Novels

Maleska

The first fictional Beadle & Adams dime novel was *Maleska: The Indian Wife of the White Hunter* published in 1860 by Ann Sophia Stephens, the previous author of a number of romances. The book was very popular and sold more than 300,000 copies. Considering that the population of the country at the time was about 30 million and the literacy rate was about 20 percent this was an impressive number.[20] The book started a trend in cheap novels that one scholarly observer called "a literary pestilence."[21]

SETH JONES

In 1860 Beadle & Adams also brought out *Seth Jones; or, The Captives of the Frontier* by Edward Sylvester Ellis.[22] Ellis was a nineteen-year-old schoolteacher who continued to write 159 dime novels until 1916. *Seth Jones* was a Leatherstocking type of hero who behaved in a manner similar to James Fenimore Cooper's heroes. *Seth Jones* rivaled *Maleska* for sales and went on to become one of the bestsellers of its time. The book sold 60,000 copies almost immediately and eventually sold an estimated 500,000 or so copies.

Maleska presented a picture of a gray and tragic frontier. *Seth Jones*, on the other hand, was White, masculine, and triumphant. It became the blueprint for the dime novel Western and heroic White men rescuing White women from the clutches of the dreaded Indians.

DEADWOOD DICK

By the 1870s, suspense and action added further sensationalism to the tales in dime novels. In 1877 Edward Lytton Wheeler created a heroic, intelligent, handsome, and chivalrous character that he named Deadwood Dick. Dick eventually went on to feature in thirty-three novels produced by Beadle & Adams. He was a plainsman who "sorted out wickedness in mining camps," but also foiled stage robberies and kidnappers. He was virile, violent, and invincible in combat, though not totally pure in thought and deed, and he spent a lot of time with Calamity Jane. He was able to defeat all his enemies and prevail in every situation. One of his distinguishing characteristics was that he liked to utter "a wild sardonic laugh." He and others like him were so well-portrayed in the dime novels that many readers believed that they were real people. The character of Deadwood Dick may have been loosely based on a Deadwood stagecoach driver named Richard Cole, though four other men also claimed to be the authentic Deadwood Dick.[23] Wheeler was reported to be a bit of a character himself. He called most people "pard" and adopted the life of a Westerner.[24] In reality, he spent most of his life in Pennsylvania.

The Deadwood Dick series introduced a new variation and fresh approach to the traditional frontier hero, as Dick was the first dime novel hero who was an outlaw in disguise. However, even though Dick was a bandit hero, the publisher was careful not to promote any bad behavior in the character that might influence youth the wrong way and bring criticism to the series. The theme of reformed outlaws such as Deadwood Dick, which explored the possibility of being both good and bad at the same time, became popular among audiences. The good bad-man hero that was later portrayed with immense success by film actor William S. Hart in the 1910s had its origin in this type of dime novel.

Wheeler's first novel in the series was *Deadwood Dick, the Prince of the Road; or, The Black Rider of the Black Hills*. Dick sought to avenge the wrongs done to him by rich White men by robbing stagecoaches. To maintain the popular White woman rescue theme, this first story also included a character named Fearless Frank, who rescues seventeen-year-old

Alice Terry from captivity by Sioux Indian chief Sitting Bull. To add lurid detail to the story, Sitting Bull strips Alice to the waist to have her flogged. Frank quickly persuades the chief to release her and she is once again properly clothed as dictated by Victorian propriety.

Unlike the earlier backwoodsman tales, Indians were rarely portrayed as the villains in these stories. The villains rather were the wealthy classes, such as eastern industrial capitalists, stockbrokers, and business managers. All of these were considered by working-class readers to be the privileged class and the elite rich and represented wealth gained by corrupt means. Rapid urbanization, industrialization, and the rise of big business had created distrust of the managing classes by the common working man and created the feeling of being exploited. These novels provided a way that the working man could temporarily escape from the drudgery of his job into a fantasy world and become a Western hero who could right all wrongs.

Deadwood Dick became so popular that the other dime novel publishers had to have their own lawbreaker heroes. Street & Smith's Log Cabin Library, for example, contained a large percentage of outlaw stories. When desperate novelists ran out of characters to invent, they turned to real historical people and sensationalized the outlaw careers of Jesse James, the Younger brothers, Billy the Kid, and the Daltons. These bandits and dangerous outlaws in real life were turned by writers into the nineteenth-century American equivalents of European highwayman or gallant Robin Hoods. In the 1880s Jesse James and others rose to the level of folk hero status.

Given the prevailing Victorian morality, it was unethical to make a bandit the hero of popular books. Therefore, in order to make the outlaw's actions acceptable to readers, writers gave him a veneer of respectability. He was described as a courtly and chivalrous man, especially when interacting with women. Writers also created a means to justify his actions. In the fictional stories about Jesse James, Jesse and his brother Frank were supposedly unjustly persecuted and driven outside the law, so they sought revenge against those who had wronged them. In Deadwood Dick's case, the justification for his bandit career is the death of his foster parents and the looting of their estate by the dastardly Filmore brothers. Dick pursues them legally, but without success. He finally resorts to taking the law into his own hands and eventually strings them up by the end of the book. The essence of the plot was that Dick had been wronged by powerful villains who were supported by the law, so his actions were justified. It was the familiar theme of the little guy fighting back against the establishment. As Deadwood Dick sought revenge and justice, he became popular with working-class readers who felt that nineteenth-century industrialists and bosses oppressed them and ruled their lives. But not everybody was in favor of the idea of righting wrongs forced on innocent men. Protests were made to the postmaster general, who threatened to take away cheap second-class mailing privileges to try to control what was seen as a decadent trend.[25] But by then it was too late and the heroic outlaw had become a staple of Western dime-novel literature.

Wheeler added romance in the form of Calamity Jane, who first appeared in Wheeler's *Deadwood Dick, the Prince of the Road; or, The Black Rider of the Black Hills*. Calamity Jane was described as having a "trim boyish figure" (unlike the real Martha Jane Canary) and "a wonderful wealth of long glossy hair." *Deadwood Dick on Deck; or, Calamity Jane, the Heroine of Whoop-Up* is about miners escaping from the clutches of absentee mine owners, a compelling contemporary topic in the West.[26] In the early novels, Dick was unable to persuade Calamity Jane to marry him. She and Deadwood Dick did, however, eventually marry in

Dime novels and illustrated newspapers of the late nineteenth century created and immortalized many of the mythical ideas about the Old West. Though a few instances of cowboys forcing someone to dance while they shot at his feet did occur, dime novels enhanced and perpetuated rough-and-tough images of the West like this staged scene. These images carried over into early movies and reinforced the myths of the Wild West. A scene of a bowler-hatter Eastern dude dancing while saloon patrons shoot at his feet was used in the early film *The Great Train Robbery* (1903), a movie that stirred great interest in Westerns (Library of Congress).

1881, four years after the first story appeared. Apparently unsatisfied with the way that the plots were going, Wheeler killed off both characters in Deadwood Dick's final book, *Deadwood Dick's Dust; or, The Chained Hand.*

Now able to start again with a fresh approach, in 1883 Wheeler created Deadwood Dick, Jr. Curiously he was not the son of the original Deadwood Dick, but simply another character who appropriated the name. Junior appeared in more than ninety-seven Beadle & Adams novels, performing so many of the same deeds as to be indistinguishable from his predecessor. He addressed himself to contemporary problems that were of concern to the workingman of the time. In one story, for example, Deadwood Dick, Jr. leads the miner's union in Leadville to win a "fair wage" for the members. Wheeler also wrote dime novels that featured characters such as Rosebud Rob, Sierra Sam, High Hat Harry, and the curiously named Nobby Nick.

In response to the popularity of Deadwood Dick, competitive publishers Street & Smith produced a series of novels about Diamond Dick. The creation of William W. Cook (the pen name of W.B. Lawson), Diamond Dick may have been based on the real-life Richard

Tanner, who was a scout for George Armstong Custer and later a trick shot in a Wild West show.[27] Many imitations followed, such as Hurricane Bill, Mustang Sam, Pacific Pete, and Panther Paul from the pen of author Joseph Badger, and Daredeath Smith from Leon Lewis.

Two of the Authors

Several thousand authors wrote dime novels, some of them full time and others only part time to earn extra income.

One prolific author was Edward Ellis. He also used the pseudonyms James Fenimore Cooper Adams, Boynton Belknap, Capt. Latham C. Carleton, Frank Faulkner, Capt. R. Hawthorne, Lt. R. H. Jayne, Billex Muller, Emerson Rodman, Seelin Robins, among others.

One of Beadle's most prolific authors was Colonel Prentiss Ingraham, a veteran of the Civil War. He started writing in 1870 and wrote until his death in 1904. Depending on the source, his estimated total novel output was between 500 and 1,000 titles, with a likely number of over 600. Precise numbers become uncertain, as most dime novelists wrote under multiple pen names, making it hard to attribute stories to the correct author. Of the more than 500 novels based on Buffalo Bill Cody, Ingraham may have been the author of over 200. A typical one that he is known to have written was *Buffalo Bill's Big Contract*. Ingraham supposedly wrote one entire 35,000-word dime novel in a twenty-four hour period. Afterwards, he is reported to have modestly remarked, "I was both tired and hungry when I finished, for I had had only a sandwich or two, eaten as I worked."[28]

As well as writing extensively about Buffalo Bill, Ingraham penned several novels very loosely based on the life of William Levi "Buck" Taylor, a real-life shooting and trick-riding show star. Taylor, a real cowboy who had excellent skills with horses and cattle, was an original member of Buffalo Bill's *Wild West* troupe and worked on Cody's ranch in Nebraska. In 1887, Ingraham wrote Taylor into a novel that was ostensibly a biography. The full, long-winded title was a mouthful: *Buck Taylor, King of the Cowboys; or, The Raiders and the Rangers: A Story of the Wild and Thrilling Life of William L. Taylor*. This book, which appeared in *Beadle's Half-Dime Library* on February 1, 1887, featured Taylor as the first of the real cowboy heroes. Ingraham also wrote *Buck Taylor, the Saddle King; or, The Lasso Rangers' League*; *The Cowboy Clan; or, The Tigress of Texas*; *Buck Taylor, the Comanche Captive*; and *Buck Taylor's Boys; or, The Red Riders of the Rio Grande*. Then Taylor stories faded from the dime novels.[29] To promote the books, Ingraham gave Taylor the title "King of the Cowboys" long before movie star Roy Rogers was given the same name by Republic Studios.

Seeking another real-life hero, Ingraham wrote *Texas Jack, the Mustang King* about scout, hunter, and sometime stage actor John Burwell "Texas Jack" Omohundro.

Glorifying the Outlaws

Looking for ever more sensational material and noting the popularity among readers who liked and identified with Deadwood Dick, many of the dime novel writers turned to outlaw tales. These new protagonists were not only violent, but they also offered a different set of moral values than the earlier heroes. Characters such as the fictional Deadwood Dick and the real-life outlaw Jesse James were bandits supposedly responding to injustice done to them by corrupt officials who represented the powerful rich classes. Examples of these novels were *The Bandit King*; *The James Boys in Missouri*; *The Younger Brothers*; and *The Road Agents*. In a similar vein, Richard K. Fox wrote *Bella Starr, the Bandit Queen; or, The Female Jesse James*.

Jesse and Frank James

The first to try to persuade public opinion towards the side of the James brothers was newspaperman Major John Newman Edwards. Edwards was a major influence in transforming the image of Jesse James from the reality of a ruthless robber and murderer to a fictional modern prince of bandits who led a Robin Hood–like band. Edwards started his campaign with an inflammatory editorial titled "The Chivalry of Crime" in the *Kansas City Times* on September 27, 1872, after a robbery by the James gang at the Kansas State Fair, during which a child was shot and injured. In spite of this, Edwards denied their guilt, justified their crimes, and praised their bravery and valor. He continued to glorify and defend the James gang in a similar manner until his death in 1889. To a large extent, Edwards invented Jesse James' public persona.

Edwards continued to champion the cause of the James boys in a book titled *Noted Guerillas; or, The Warfare of the Border*.[30] Edwards called Jesse James a Southern version of the frontier hero and made him out to be a hero of folk legends. He was attributed with characteristics such as superb horsemanship, a favorite horse, skill with a pistol, and a love of revolvers, characteristics that were later given to movie heroes. James was promoted as a misunderstood knight-errant. This, however, was not the reality. History suggests instead that the James brothers were cold-blooded, murderous thieves and there never was any evidence that they robbed from the rich to give to the poor.[31]

Frank James, Jesse's brother, went to Kansas as a "Border Ruffian" in 1855. He and Jesse, who was only sixteen, enlisted in Quantrill's Raiders at the start of the Civil War and spent it as guerrillas. Jesse soon became one of the deadliest and most skilled of the guerrillas. The band used terrorism and reprisals against public officials, prisoners, and the general civilian population. Their mission was to terrify as well as to kill. Unlike army soldiers, captured guerrillas were subject to summary trial and execution.

After the war the James gang continued looting and stealing, using the tactics they had learned as guerrillas. By 1869 the James boys and their gang had turned to robbery. They were different from most common criminals because they were supported by the press and by local civic leaders who had been displaced by the war. Newspaper editors and local landowners mythologized Jesse's exploits. Supporters even tried for amnesty from the state legislature. Part of the myth made Jesse a "guerrilla" rather than a common criminal (even though the Civil War guerrillas were far worse) and his postwar deeds were seen as championing their lost cause. By the end of the 1870s publishers were cranking out a series of lurid dime novels that celebrated the "heroic" deeds of the James gang.

Similar to justification of the exploits of bandit Deadwood Dick, journalists and dime novel writers portrayed the activities of Jesse James and his gang as morally justifiable opposition to oppressive banks and scheming railroads. They characterized Jesse as having the moral values of the White hero. They made him out to be a man of the wilderness, a natural leader, and a noble character, but with a tendency towards savage violence and merciless revenge when he was wronged.[32]

The public myth that Edwards created about the James boys being persecuted was given a boost when Pinkerton detectives hot on their trail threw some type of device that exploded through the window of the home of Jesse's mother and stepfather on January 26, 1875. Jesse's mother, Zerelda Samuel, was injured so badly in the explosion that her right hand had to be amputated. More tragic, the blast mortally wounded nine-year-old Archie Peyton Samuel, half-brother of Jesse and Frank.[33]

The James gang received national attention when they switched from robbing local banks to robbing trains, which was a federal offense. Jesse was again characterized as being persecuted and driven into outlawry by the railroads and holding up trains was considered to be his way of avenging himself. This was considered to be acceptable because Jesse was supposedly motivated by courage and manhood to right wrongs. Thus the James legend was essentially rewritten in 1880 to become a conflict with oppressive railroads.[34] Another author who championed the cause of the James boys was Frank Triplett, who penned a book titled *The Life, Times and Treacherous Death of Jesse James*, in which Jesse was portrayed as an aristocratic hero.[35] This book became part of the foundation of the outlaw's literary mythology as an avenger of the wrongs unjustly forced on his family. The rich capitalists that forced him into outlawry were characterized as "white trash."

In the end, the real Jesse was shot in the back of the head by his cousin Bob Ford while Jesse was hanging a picture on a wall of his house on April 3, 1882.[36] The motivation was reward money posted by the governor. After Jesse's death, John Edwards helped to negotiate Frank's surrender on October 4, 1882. After a series of trials and legal manipulations, Frank was released from prison in February 1885. Mrs. Samuel, Jesse's crippled mother, continued to promote the legend of Jesse James by selling souvenirs in the form of pebbles from Jesse's grave at twenty-five cents each. Her supply was reputedly replenished from a nearby creek.[37] She also sold horseshoes that supposedly came from the two brothers' horses. All one can presume is that the brothers had a great many horses.

By 1901 both Street & Smith and Tousey were publishing James novels. Street & Smith published a dime-novel series under the banner of The Jesse James Stories: Original Narratives of the James Boys. Issue No 1. was titled *Jesse James the Outlaw*. Over the next two years 277 stories appeared in Tousey's *James Boys Weekly* and New York Detective Library, and in Street & Smith's Jesse James Stories. Tousey's James was driven to become a guerrilla and a life of crime by the whipping of his father.[38] Street & Smith started publishing James Boys stories as part of their Log Cabin Library, with stories featuring the James gang alternating with detective stories. Publishers presented these stories as authentic by crediting them to detectives who worked on the cases. Street & Smith claimed that their authority was Captain Jake Shackleform, credited as a Western detective who had actually hunted Jesse James. Tousey's source was supposedly an unnamed "New York detective." James stories blended with detective fiction as eastern detective heroes went West to hunt James, and the dime-novel James gang went East and appeared in New York adventures.[39] The postmaster general threatened Frank Tousey, one of the most active publishers of these lurid and sensational books, with canceling second-class mailing privileges if his company did not tone down some of the inflammatory titles. Public clamor against these stories became so great by 1903 that the government brought pressure to bear on both firms and they discontinued these publications.[40]

The James family continued to promote the Jesse James legend with several motion pictures, such as *Jesse James Under the Black Flag* (1921) and *Jesse James as the Outlaw* (1921), produced by Mesco Pictures, in which the James family had a financial interest. The general theme was that Jesse was forced into outlawry and how others' crimes were blamed on him. Jesse James, Jr. starred as his father. Mainstream moviemakers took up the cause with *Jesse James* (1927) with Fred Thompson, a popular movie cowboy.

Billy the Kid

Billy the Kid was a small-time local outlaw involved in the bloody Lincoln County cattle war in New Mexico before authors of dime novels grabbed his story with both hands. Legend says that he shot twenty-one men by the time he was twenty-one, but the reality is probably more like six to ten over a four-year career. One dime novel was written before the Kid's death, *Billy the Kid, the New Mexico Outlaw; or, The Bold Bandit of the West* by Edmund Fable. In real life, Billy was tracked down and killed by sheriff Pat Garrett in 1881 at Pete Maxwell's ranch near Fort Sumner, New Mexico. It was not until after Billy's death that he was elevated to the status of folk hero. Dime novelists, of course, amplified the myth over a very short period of time.

Contributing to Billy's wronged-outlaw legend were fictional books such as Francis W. Doughty's *Old King Brady and "Billy the Kid"; or, The Great Detective's Chase*. Brady was a fictional detective, thus the author was attempting to authenticate the story by blending the real and the fictional. More accurate was Barton W. Currie, who wrote about Billy the Kid in *Harper's Weekly* in September 1908. Currie said, "With the band of desperadoes he led, he raided ranches, 'shot up' towns, killed, burned houses and committed outrage after outrage with the blind recklessness of a maniac." Currie called him a "bandit chief." These stories do not agree with the historical facts.

The Authentic Life of Billy the Kid, written in 1882, was credited to Pat Garrett but was really the product of Marshall Ashmun Upson, a former reporter for the *New York Herald* who was a friend of Garrett's and lived in nearby Roswell, New Mexico. The original long and windy title was *The Authentic Life of Billy, the Kid, the Noted Desperado of the Southwest, Whose Deeds of Daring and Blood Made His Name a Terror in New Mexico, Arizona and Northern Mexico*, a mouthful that set the tone for the rather overblown account inside. The book publicized Billy the Kid and made Pat Garrett out to be a hero and in the process helped to manufacture the legend. Upson claimed that he ghost wrote the book to make it sell.[41] Another boost to the legend came when Walter Noble Burns wrote *The Saga of Billy the Kid* (1926), which made Billy out to be a hero. Also contributing to the legend was a play titled *Billy the Kid* (1903) by Walter Woods and a series of later questionable movies about Billy's life.

After the exploits of Billy the Kid were fictionalized, the image of the cowboy grew as a romantic figure. But even in 1887 a visiting Englishman noted that the persona of the cowboy was already turning into a myth as an idealistic figure with many virtues.[42]

James Butler "Wild Bill" Hickok

Not all real-life dime-novel heroes were outlaws. Writers seized on any Western characters that they felt they could embellish and use for the image of heroes. One who fitted the heroic mold was James Butler "Wild Bill" Hickok, gambler and part-time lawman. Hickok was an imposing figure, over six feet tall, with broad shoulders. He was an authentic frontiersman, but he later adopted a style of clothing and accessories that were described in the dime novels. This included dual pistols, long hair, and buckskin clothing like the frontier scouts. This appearance was considered to be symbolic of the frontier of the dime novels and in the eyes of readers made him into a "real" Westerner. This image supposedly connected him closer to untamed nature, fierce animals, and the wilderness. This style of clothing was, however, outdated by the time he appeared in Kansas after the Civil War.

Wild Bill Hickok became a celebrity after an 1865 interview with Colonel George Ward Nichols, a journalist looking for colorful Western characters. Nichols published an account of Hickok's fight with Dave McCanles on July 12, 1861, in *Harper's New Monthly Magazine*. Nichols' version was a vivid, but mostly exaggerated and inaccurate, account of the real fight.[43]

Hickok's persona was soon adopted by the dime novelists. The first dime novel story about Wild Bill, titled *Wild Bill, the Indian Slayer* appeared as issue no. 3 of *DeWitt's Ten Cent Romances*, a monthly magazine of action stories. The cover showed Hickok surrounded by opponents with knives, with the bodies of the vanquished spread around him on the ground. Issue no. 10, which featured *Wild Bill's First Trail*, showed him in fierce hand-to-hand combat with an Indian wielding a tomahawk as Hickok prepares to knife him.

The Mythmakers

The concept of the mythmaker in the form of a journalist who glorifies these men and turns them into dime-novel heroes is acknowledged in several movies, among them *The Man Who Shot Liberty Valance* (1962), *Buffalo Bill and the Indians* (1976), and *Unforgiven* (1992). *The Man Who Shot Liberty Valance* (1962) contains the classic line uttered by the editor of the *Shinbone Star*, Maxwell Scott (Carleton Young), who declares, "This is the West, sir. When the legend becomes fact, print the legend."

In *Unforgiven* (1992), W.W. Beauchamp (Saul Rubinek) is writing a biography of English Bob (Richard Harris), who shows up in the town of Big Whiskey, Wyoming, in 1880. Beauchamp is writing a dime novel about Bob titled *The Duke of Death*, which portrays English Bob as a gallant defender of women and lightning-fast on the draw. In Beauchamp's version, English Bob shot Corky Corcoran during a fair fight in the Blue Bottle Saloon in Wichita. Beauchamp does reluctantly admit that in the publishing business certain liberties are taken with the pictures on the cover. Sheriff Little Bill (Gene Hackman), however, who was there for the fight, says that in reality Bob was drunk and shot Corcoran in cold blood after Corcoran shot himself in the toe and his revolver exploded. Little Bill satirizes the title of the dime novel by pronouncing it as "The Duck of Death."

4

The Great Showman

The Western hero is a subject whose roots are in history, whose image has been transformed into myth, and whose chief function for the contemporary audience is to provide popular entertainment—Rita Parks[1]

William F. "Buffalo Bill" Cody was arguably the most famous American of his time. His stature grew from a minor character on the frontier to become a show business personality and entertainment industry. Along the way his background and image became myth and lore. His flamboyant persona was boosted by dime novels, newspaper stories, stage melodramas, and his Western extravaganza, the *Wild West*. He and his show created a heightened interest in the American West during the last two decades of the nineteenth century. The continued success of his show business enterprise was maintained by publicity men, boosters, barkers, and skilled handlers. Under the adroit direction of Ned Buntline, John Burke, Nate Salsbury, and others, the image of Buffalo Bill grew to be a larger-than-life myth. In one program for the *Wild West* from 1886 he was presented as "the representative man of the frontiersmen of the past."

Buffalo Bill became one of the prime creators of the image of the heroes of the frontier by focusing on a handful of events and people that became symbols for the Old West. Fierce, painted Indians in war-bonnets and their attacks on the Deadwood stagecoach, the settler's cabin, and the circled wagon train represented the West to millions of attendees in the audience. Cody spent his life selling a romantic vision of the West and believed that he was presenting history.[2] In his early years, Buffalo Bill had been a buffalo hunter, a guide, a scout, and a teamster, among other activities, though he was never a cowboy. His show cowboys, though, represented the West as they rode bucking horses, roped steers, and rescued the Deadwood Stage from Indians.

Cody was a real person, but most of the legends and persona that surrounded him were created by his press agent and Cody himself. The early Buffalo Bill legend was developed over a series of dime novels, then after 1882 around himself as the star of the *Wild West*. He eventually even came to believe the myth.

Ned Buntline

The story of the fictional Buffalo Bill started with one of the kings of the pulp writers, Edward Zane Carroll Judson, better known under his primary pen name as Ned Buntline. Buntline wrote adventure stories about the sea, sports, and the Mexican war, covering an estimated span of over 400 dime novels. He also penned temperance tracts. Though best known for his role in promoting Buffalo Bill as a Western hero, Buntline wrote only twenty-five "Western" novels.[3]

Judson had a varied career before becoming a full-time professional writer. His own account of his background blended reality with myth, as did his later writings, and many of the details of his real life are obscure. As a boy, Judson ran away from home to serve on a ship in the navy. After he returned to civilian life he started a sensationalist magazine called *Ned Buntline's Own*. Possibly as a link to his days at sea, Judson wrote under a variety of pseudonyms with a definite nautical flavor, such as Charlie Bowline, Frank Clewline, and Jack Brace, as well as his most famous, Ned Buntline. On a ship, a buntline is one of the ropes attached to the bottom of a square sail.

Judson took part in the Seminole Wars in Florida during the 1830s. He later served in the Union army for a short while during the Civil War but eventually deserted.[4] During the later rewriting of his biography, he credited himself as the Union army's chief of Indian scouts and gave himself the title of colonel. He has also been characterized as a bigamist, teller of tall tales, and general scoundrel.[5] He wrote for *Knickerbocker* magazine as early as 1838. His later career focused on newspaperman, publisher, editor, writer, temperance lecturer, and social reformer.

Judson was also a bit of a philanderer. He shot and killed a man in Nashville who accused Judson of having an affair with his wife. As a result, an angry mob grabbed him from jail in order to lynch him. The unruly mob started to hang him, but luckily a bystander cut the rope just in time (other accounts say that the rope broke) before he choked to death.[6] Among his other activities, Judson led an Irish immigrant mob in the Astor Place Riot against British actor William Macready on May 10, 1849, in New York. Twenty-two were left dead and 144 injured after the militia fired on the rioters. Judson served a year in prison for helping to incite a riot.[7]

Cody's Early Days

Until 1869 and his leap to fame in dime novels, Cody was a minor Western character. He had been a farmer, teamster, drover, trapper, Civil War soldier, stagecoach driver, buffalo hunter, and army scout. He also claimed in his autobiography to have been a Pony Express rider. His autobiography is the only source for this and the story may have evolved out of his later reinvented persona.[8] Most of Buffalo Bill's Indian fighting involved small-scale skirmishes that took place in the 1860s and 1870s.

Cody received his nickname of "Buffalo Bill" after he hunted buffalo to feed construction workers on the railroad from the fall of 1867 through most of 1868.[9] He reportedly killed more than 4,000 animals in eighteen months. His was a common nickname on the frontier and there were many "Buffalo Bills" who were scouts and hunters in Texas, Kansas, and the Dakotas in the 1860s and 1870s.[10]

In August of 1868, Cody acted as a civilian scout for the Tenth Cavalry. The duties of a scout included tracking Indians, acting as a courier to carry dispatches between military posts, hunting game for food as required, and acting as a guide for visiting dignitaries and army officers. Curiously, it wasn't a requirement for scouts to know much about

Indians. Cody did, however, have genuine skills as a tracker, Indian fighter, and buffalo hunter.

Buffalo Bill in the Dime Novels

The completion of the transcontinental railroad in 1869 brought tourists, journalists, and dime novelists to the West looking for material to sensationalize for their stories. That same year, Judson, as the writer Ned Buntline, was one of those who traveled to the West. His goal may have been to meet Wild Bill Hickok. Reportedly he did meet Hickok, but the two men did not get on well and Buntline apparently did not find the literary inspiration he was looking for.[11]

In July of 1869 Buntline stopped at Fort McPherson, Nebraska, to interview Maj. Frank North about an Indian skirmish that had become known as the Battle of Summit Springs. The fight had taken place in May of 1869 when a battalion of the Fifth Cavalry had marched north from Fort Lyon, Colorado, to rescue two German immigrant women, Mrs. Maria Weichell and Mrs. Susanna Alderdice, and an infant who were being held captive by a band of Cheyenne.[12] The troops caught up with the Indians at Summit Springs, in the northeast part of Colorado. During the fight, a chief named Tall Bull was killed. After the skirmish, Cody claimed that he had shot Tall Bull. Several others, however, claimed that they were the one who killed him. In all the confusion of the fight, there has never been a clear picture of who did what, though there is no evidence to dispute Cody's claim.[13]

Buntline wanted to use this sensational true story as the basis for a dime novel. He also needed a figure he could turn into a dime novel hero. For some reason North did not want to be interviewed and supposedly said that a man asleep under a nearby wagon, who turned out to be Cody, would fill Buntline's need for adventure stories. But it may have also happened that Buntline was passing the fort on his way back East from California and ended up chatting with Cody.[14] However the meeting happened, Buntline changed his stories to feature Buffalo Bill. Cody was perfect for the part of a Western hero. He was a scout for General Eugene Carr, and army scouts projected Buntline's desired heroic image of the frontier. Cody was an impressive six-foot-two, was tall and muscular, had long curly hair, and looked the part in buckskin clothing.

Buntline's first novel about Cody was titled *Buffalo Bill, the King of the Border Men*. This tall tale appeared in serial form in Smith & Street's *New York Weekly* between December 23, 1869, and March 10, 1870. The novel later became the basis for Buntline's play *Buffalo Bill, the King of the Border Men*. To put it mildly, Buntline's prose stretched the truth, such as including Wild Bill Hickok (whom Bill had not yet met) and having Bill's mother (who was already dead) give him sterling character endorsements. Though Cody received his nickname of "Buffalo Bill" earlier from buffalo hunting, the name does not seem to have been popularly applied to him before Buntline called him that in this dime novel.[15]

The account was not what would now be considered a Western, but was a lurid tale from the Civil War in Kansas. It was a fictional story of adventure and revenge, with Buffalo Bill and Wild Bill Hickok teaming up to defeat a gang of "border ruffians." The story starts with the murder of Buffalo Bill's father by the villainous Jake M'Kandlas in Missouri when Bill was a boy. In the best melodramatic fashion, Bill, of course, swears revenge. After Cody

Battles between the U.S. Army and the Plains Indians between 1865 and 1890 were commonly fought on windswept rolling hills such as these. Stirring Indian battles were the basis for Cody's later recreation of his fight with Tall Bull at Summit Springs, his fight with Yellow Hair at War Bonnet Creek, and Custer's Last Stand in Montana that appeared in stage plays, dime novels, and Cody's later Wild West. These lonely marble markers show where a group of soldiers fell during the Battle of the Little Bighorn (author's collection).

grows to manhood, he joins Hickok to rescue Buffalo Bill's (fictional) sister Lottie, who had been captured by Dave Tutt, one of the M'Kandlas gang. This story did have some vague basis in fact, as the real Hickok had killed a gambler named Dave Tutt in a gunfight in Missouri in 1865. The real Hickok was also in a fight with a man named Dave McCanles at the Rock Creek stage station in Nebraska in 1861. Buffalo Bill and Wild Bill, however, did not meet until 1864. In the novel, Hickok is called "Hitchcock."[16]

Buntline's plotting used the extravagant phrasing and blood-and-thunder prose popular at the time. When Buntline described Bill's family, he said, "A noble-looking, white-haired man sits by a rough table, reading the Bible aloud. On stools by his feet sit two beautiful little girls—his twin daughters—not more than ten years of age, while a noble boy, twelve or thirteen, stands by the back of the chair where sits the handsome, yet matronly-looking mother." The villain is introduced with the following rhetoric: "Hark! The sound of horse galloping with mad speed towards his house falls upon his ear."[17] This melodramatic sample comes from chapter 18: "'Mercy—we surrender!' shouted a huge villain, already down with a bullet in his brawny breast. 'Take the mercy your gang gave my father!' shouted Buffalo Bill, and his knife clove through the villain's skull."[18]

Starting with Buntline's first effort in 1869, Buffalo Bill eventually starred in 557 dime novels by twenty different authors. His fictional persona appeared in Beadle's Dime Library, Frank Tousey's Wide Awake Library, and Street & Smith's *New York Weekly*. Buntline also wrote *Buffalo Bill's Best Shot; or, The Heart of Spotted Tail*, which appeared as a serial in *New York Weekly* in 1872. *Buffalo Bill's Last Victory; or, Dove Eye, the Lodge Queen*, was a serial publication starting on July 8, 1871, followed by *Hazel Eye, the Girl Trapper: A Tale of Strange Young Life*. The latter story is a little unusual in that it features a female heroine. Hazel Eye may, however, have been modeled on poetess Anna Fuller, whom Buntline had married in October of 1871.[19] Buntline's last dime novel about Buffalo Bill was titled *Buffalo Bill's First Trail; or, Will Cody, the Pony Express Rider*, published in 1885. Buntline wrote only a few novels about Cody, but Colonel Prentiss Ingraham, who started ghostwriting for Buffalo Bill around 1880, may have produced over 200 more under various pseudonyms.

Buffalo Bill appeared as the hero of more dime novels than any other real or fictional character than perhaps Jesse James. These dime novels helped to establish his mythic persona and expanded both his personal legend and that of the Wild West.

Buffalo Bill on Stage

After the success of his dime novel about Cody, Buntline saw an opportunity for further profit by bringing the real hero to the public by way of the stage. Buntline persuaded Buffalo Bill and Bill's old friend "Texas Jack" Omohundro to appear with him in a play. As a result, Buffalo Bill made his stage debut on December 18, 1872, at Nixon's Amphitheater in Chicago in *The Scouts of the Prairie*. The play went on to St. Louis, Cincinnati, Philadelphia, and New York. *The Scouts of the Prairie* was not factual, but it was based on Buntline's imagination and the frontier myth of brave heroes fighting against overwhelming odds, using their skills with guns and ropes to subdue savage Indians and save the beautiful maiden. The Indian maiden in this case was played by actress and dancer Giuseppina Morlacchi, who had performed in Italy, London, and Spain.

Buntline supposedly wrote the drama in four hours. The plot was based on the dime novel *Buffalo Bill's Last Victory; or, Dove Eye, the Lodge Queen*, which had already been published, so it is possible that it could indeed have been written in such a short time.[20] *The Scouts of the Prairie* was a stage drama that included a dozen or so Indian "supers," which was short for "supernumeraries," a theatrical term for stage actors in nonspeaking parts. The film industry now calls them "extras."

Buntline featured himself in the play as Cale Durg, an old trapper. Durg was an alter ego for Buntline, just as Buntline was the alter ego of the real Judson, who loved disguises, costumes, and role-playing.[21] Buntline often posed for photographs in his buckskin costume from the play and dressed up in it for giving public lectures. He made Durg a wise and experienced frontiersman and mountain man who followed the principles of justice and morality. Durg was described in *Hazel Eye, the Girl Trapper* as "a giant in stature, dressed from head to foot in the skins of panthers, with the hair outside, his face covered with a rough shaggy beard, his hair long, and like his beard fiery red."[22] By contrast Buntline was stocky and slightly shorter than average, but he did have red hair, a booming voice, and a glib tongue. Buntline killed off Durg in the second act after a long temperance lecture that reflected Buntline's own leanings.

Again echoing his own personal background and sentiments as a temperance crusader, Buntline depicted Buffalo Bill's character as a similar crusader by putting words into his mouth such as "there is more fight, more headache—aye, more *heart* ache in one rum bottle than there is in all the water that ever sparkled in God's bright sunlight. And I, for the sake of my dear brothers and sisters, and for the sweet trusting heart that throbs for me alone intend to let the rum go where it belongs and that it not down my throat." When Cody (in reality a hearty drinker) read this, he is reported to have responded with somewhat profane surprise.[23]

The plot was standard melodrama. Durg's ward was a virtuous white woman called Hazel Eye, who is rescued by the good Indian, Dove Eye, played by Morlacci. Then Buffalo Bill and Texas Jack enter and shoot all the Indians. Buntline included plenty of gunfire in each act to add to the action-packed spectacle. In the final scene Hazel Eye is in Bill's arms and the curtain comes down.

The play was not a slick production. Cody was tongue-tied, the actors forgot their lines and sometimes said the wrong lines, but the audience didn't care and the drama played to packed houses. The audience came to observe the real-life heroes of the West and the opportunity to see the principals as themselves was more interesting to many than the play itself. Reviewers and critics were not so kind and ridiculed both the actors and the plot, but the play was still a smash hit with the public. Critics felt that the acting skills of the principals were less than polished and objected to some parts of the production, for example when red flannel cloth was substituted for scalps.

The dialog was somewhat stilted, using flowery Victorian melodramatic stage prose such as "Hark! Is not that the distant howl of a wolf?"[24] This should not have been unexpected, as Buntline was a dime novelist. Indeed, the original dime novel *Buffalo Bill's Last Victory; or, Dove Eye, the Lodge Queen* includes the following typical extracts of dialog when Dove Eye is reflecting on her rescue by Buffalo Bill: "'Dove-Eye has no words to thank the brave pale-face with,' said she. 'Her life has been saved by him and she will be his slave forever.' 'He is brave as the bravest and beautiful as a lone pine upon a hill-top,' she said. 'Dove-Eye will be *his* slave or she will cook meat for no man.' 'There is no warrior like him in all the tribes,' she murmured, as she rode on. 'Dove-Eye must win his love or die.'"[25]

The Scouts of the Prairie was not informative, educational, or factual. It was simply a fanciful, imaginative interpretation of the heroic mythology of the West that used the same elements as pulp novels and, later, Western films and television series. Brave heroes fighting overwhelming odds, skill with guns, fights with Indians, and the rescue of a beautiful maiden were what the public wanted.

The Scouts of the Prairie played its final performance on June 16, 1873. Buntline and Buffalo Bill parted ways, as Bill felt he did not get a fair share of the profits. Buntline tried to repeat his show with other performers, but they were not a success without the presence of Cody, the authentic frontiersman and scout.

Buffalo Bill started the next season with Omohundro, Wild Bill Hickok, and Morlacci in *The Scouts of the Plains*, which was almost a repeat of *The Scouts of the Prairie*. Buffalo Bill, Texas Jack, and Wild Bill played themselves. Morlacchi played a part named Pale Dove. Again, most of the dialog was right out of the dime novels, such as "fear not, fair maid; by heaven you are safe at last with Wild Bill, who is ever ready to risk his life and die if need be in defense of weak and defenseless womanhood."[26]

Hickok did not take the part of a showman seriously. He had the unpleasant habit of shooting blank cartridges at the legs of the extras who played the Indians, which caused nasty powder burns. Cody kept asking him to stop, but Hickok persisted.[27] Hickok didn't seem happy with show business and left the show at Rochester, New York.

In 1873 Omohundro and Morlacci married and left in 1874 to form their own combination.[28] Cody persevered without them and the Buffalo Bill combination toured for the next ten years. His plays were typical frontier melodramas of rescuing a white woman from Indian captivity and restoring her to her family and home.

Stage Melodramas

In his early stage career Cody was a real frontiersman and scout who, as an actor, portrayed a frontiersman. This started the confusion between Buffalo Bill's real life and his stage persona. The basic plot of his first plays were that the Indians capture the girl, the scouts fight their way through the wilderness to rescue the maiden, and she falls in love with one of them. The early plays were animated dime novels in a simple melodramatic format. This appealed to the audience, so, in turn, these plays stimulated more dime novels and plays, and the cycle was repeated.

A typical Western melodrama from the turn of the century was *Girl of the Golden West*. The play was originally written in 1905 and was later novelized by the author before undergoing four film adaptations. The Girl (as she is referred to in the play) falls in love with Dick Johnson before she finds out that he is also the bandit Ramirez. He vows to himself to reform. While he is visiting The Girl at her cabin he is wounded by the jealous sheriff, who wants to marry her himself. The sheriff wants to take Johnson back to town to hang him for a robbery at the local saloon, but The Girl challenges the sheriff to a game of poker for the best of two hands out of three that she can keep him. She wins and nurses Johnson back to health. After Johnson recovers, he comes back to town to see her. The sheriff again wants to arrest him, but The Girl and the sheriff toss a coin for who will get Johnson. It turns out that the coin the sheriff uses is a rare Spanish coin that was stolen from the saloon, so he is unmasked as the real robber, and Johnson and The Girl go off together. This is an example of the good bad-man being reformed. Many of these plays were mediocre, but enthusiasm for the West made them extremely popular.

Cody's Stage Days

Between 1872 and 1876 Cody alternated between scouting for the army in the summer and theatrical work in a series of Western melodramas in the East in the winter. He had considerable legitimate skills as a scout, but his presence was also used to bring favorable publicity to the army. Cody understood the interest among the public in entertaining images of the American West. As a consequence, his theatrical career and his abilities as a civilian scout and hunter started to become intertwined. Cody encouraged and developed the myth as part of his stage persona. One of the areas where fact and fiction blurred together was the origin of the "first scalp for Custer" that became part of the Buffalo Bill legend. This incident

Stage melodramas reflected stories from the dime novels with the same tales of dashing heroes, brave heroines, evil villains, and plenty of action. This poster from 1898 shows a scene from a play called *A Fortune Hunter*. Pictured here is "The Rescue at Eagle Rock Ranch." The valiant Nellie bars the door with her left arm as she holds the villainous Mexicans at bay (Mexicans were commonly used as generic villains, similar to generic Indians). She holds a gun in her left hand while other action swirls around her in the background. Western stage productions such as these were immensely popular and were partly what led Buffalo Bill into pursuing a career as a showman (Library of Congress).

was the basis for Cody's stage melodrama written for the 1876–1877 season by Colonel Prentiss Ingraham, *The Red Right Hand; or, The First Scalp for Custer*, which used Cody's real duel with Indian chief Yellow Hair as the climax of a fictional hostage rescue situation.

The real incident started when Cody was scouting for the Fifth Cavalry in the summer of 1867. Army troops including Lt. Col. George Armstrong Custer and the Seventh Cavalry had moved towards the Black Hills of South Dakota and tried to encircle a large gathering of hostile Indians. The tactic failed and Custer's last battle at the Little Bighorn took place on June 25, 1867.

Meanwhile, to the southeast, Cody and other scouts were tracking a band of Cheyenne. They caught up with them on July 17 at War Bonnet Creek (also called Hat Creek in War Department records) near Montrose, Nebraska, and entered into a minor skirmish. The fight erupted very rapidly, and afterwards reports of what had happened became confused. Apparently Cody and one of the warriors, named Yellow Hair, surprised each other and opened fire.[29] Cody's horse stepped in a prairie dog hole and fell, then Cody shot at the charging Indian. Afterwards Cody rushed over and scalped him and supposedly shouted, "The first scalp for Custer!"

Several parts of the reported story sound suspiciously like fiction. For example, these particular Indians had not been at the battle at the Little Bighorn, Yellow Hair was not a war chief, his was not the first scalp taken, revenge had nothing to do with the crude, almost-accidental killing, and the skirmish was historically unimportant. Cody had nothing to do with Custer's fight on the battlefield and had not even found out about Custer's death until July 7. Custer and Cody had been only briefly and distantly associated with each other during the Indian wars on the Plains that lasted from 1867 to 1870. Nonetheless, Cody appeared as Custer's trusty scout in a series of dime novels.

Cody was not wearing his usual scout's outfit of buckskins that day, but was wearing one of his Mexican stage costumes made of black velvet with scarlet trim and silver buttons and lace. This was the type of costume dime novelists had made the public believe was a proper costume for a Westerner. Cody planned to later stand in front of an audience on the stage in this supposedly authentic plainsman's garb and say he took the first scalp for Custer. In this way the fact and the story would blend together to reinforce the legend. The event was certainly real, but it was heavily laced with elements of fiction. One of the first articles about the battle was written by Lt. Charles King for the *New York Herald* six days after the fight. He wrote it at Cody's request and phrased it as a somewhat overblown recounting of the fight.

The story and legend became even more dramatic in Cody's 1879 autobiography, in which the almost-accidental killing of Yellow Hair now started with a shouted challenge that resulted in a sensational hand-to-hand fight to the death with knives, Cody eventually stabbing the Indian. Soldiers who were present afterwards described the fight as less glamorous and over quickly. These witnesses confirmed that Yellow Hair was shot and not killed in a knife duel. The story of the "duel" was emphasized by Cody and in a later biography by his sister. In this way the image of Cody waving the dead Indian's scalp became part of the Cody legend. Cody used the real scalp as part of his theatrical advertising until he received complaints about exhibiting the gruesome relic. His autobiography contains a sketch of him waving Yellow Hair's scalp in the air as he stands over the dead Indian. This also helped to authenticate the showmanship and image of the later stage play. The fight was reproduced as a woodcut, the cover of a dime novel, a poster, and several heroic paintings.

Buffalo Bill came from a long line of storytellers such as Davy Crockett and Jim Bridger.[30] All loved to tell tall tales embellished by their imaginations. Buffalo Bill's legend was expanded by his mythmaking machinery and commercial capitalism, and he remained at the forefront of marketing for the rest of his life.

The Hero Reinvented

Much of what we know about Buffalo Bill Cody comes from his autobiography, *The Life of Hon. William F. Cody, Known as Buffalo Bill*, first published by Frank E. Bliss in 1879 in Hartford, Connecticut. Experts feel that most of it was probably written by Cody rather than by a ghostwriter. However, much of what is contained in it must be regarded as suspect. For example, Cody claimed that he rode for the Pony Express out of Julesburg, Colorado, in 1859. He soon started saying that he had been the first rider for the route. The Pony Express did not start until 1860 and so obviously had no riders in 1859. In addition, none of the stations he listed as stops were correct. Three eyewitness accounts that supposedly corroborate him being a rider become suspect under investigation. Three other, more reliable, accounts by his sister, his former teacher, and Cody himself, place him in school in Leavenworth, Kansas, at the time.[31] Interestingly, he did not say anything about the Pony Express to newspapermen during interviews until 1874.[32] In his autobiography Cody also claimed that he had the scars of 137 wounds from Indians, though his wife told reporters that she had noticed only one. In spite of legend, he left the Union army as a private, the same rank he held when he entered. The autobiography also contains fanciful connections to Wild Bill Hickok, the Mormon War, and other exploits, including being a spy during the Civil War. Cody was helped in the later reinvention of his persona by John Burke, press agent for Cody's *Wild West*. Together the two of them wove together elements of dime novels, Cody's stage persona, and his real life adventures to produce a conglomerate character.

In 1872, Cody ran as a candidate for a seat in the Nebraska legislature. He lost by forty-two votes. He later claimed that he had won the race but had resigned the seat to go on the stage due to popular demand.[33] After this supposed win, he called himself "The Honorable William F. Cody." Just like the earlier Western hero Davy Crockett, this title helped to boost his image by creating the impression of a frontiersman who had risen to an important role of state leadership.

By 1887 Cody was calling himself "Colonel Cody" and was listed as such in the *Wild West* show program. Although he was an army scout, Buffalo Bill was never in the regular army. Scouts were civilian employees. His elevation to the rank of colonel was an honorary appointment as an aide-de-camp to the Nebraska State Militia by John Thayer, the governor of Nebraska, in 1887. By then the Indian Wars were almost over (they ended in 1890). The appointment was engineered by Cody's publicity agent, John Burke, to improve Cody's status on the European tours.[34] Cody later backdated this rank to 1867 in order to add status to his earlier scouting adventures.

The civilian status of scouts led to a different problem. Cody received the Congressional Medal of Honor in 1872 for guiding a detachment of troops to recapture horses that had been stolen by Sioux Indians. For their roles in the skirmish, Cody and three of the soldiers were recommended for the medal by Colonel J.J. Reynolds, commandant of the Third Cavalry. Until 1918 the Congressional Medal of Honor was the only medal that was awarded to military personnel. The medal had a wide range of uses and could be awarded for as little as being a good soldier. Cody's medal was revoked in 1916 because as a scout he was a technically a civilian and the medal could be awarded only to active duty soldiers. Cody's medal was finally reinstated on January 12, 1989, with the opinion that Cody, though a contract army scout, had performed with the necessary bravery to have been awarded the medal.

Buffalo Bill became what we would call today a show-business celebrity. During his stage appearances and later when he performed in the *Wild West,* his publicity staff created and shaped a public perception of the person and his accomplishments, as movie studios did for later Western film stars. His staff made him the most recognized character of his time. Dime novels, stage plays, and his *Wild West* performances reflect his constructed identity. Though he was an accomplished buffalo hunter, scout, and Indian expert, his personal memories tended to blend with the stories he dramatized and with his public persona. In turn, his persona turned into a national memory.

Buffalo Bill Cody received his nickname from hunting buffalo to feed railroad workers on the Kansas Pacific Railroad in 1867 and 1868. As a result of widespread hunting, the buffalo (more correctly American bison, *Bison bison*) declined almost to extinction by the 1890s, when only about 1,000 animals remained. Only determined efforts by individuals such as Teddy Roosevelt as well as intensive breeding programs allowed the numbers to return again. The birds perched on the back of the animal shown here will pick off parasites such as ticks (author's collection).

It was essential for Cody to look the part of a Western frontiersman. Even early in his career, when he worked as a guide for hunting trips, Cody created an image of the frontiersman for himself. As part of his personal publicity, he distributed photos of himself with long hair and a goatee, dressed in fringed buckskin clothes and a broad-brimmed hat. This was the type of appearance that experienced trappers, scouts, and frontiersmen were supposed to present and what his supporters and public expected. He liked boots that were thigh-high (over twenty-six inches tall), a fashion statement that set the trend for later Wild West showmen and performers. Expansion of Cody's frontier persona came with his autobiography, which contained his version of his battles, perilous situations, and daring exploits.[35] The purpose of the book was to establish Cody's authenticity and "genuine frontier credentials" as a scout, hunter, and guide.

Even professional historians have found it difficult to separate fact from fiction. Some historians, for example, feel that Cody's account of his first Indian killing is overly dramatic and that the incident may never even have taken place.[36] As another example, the glorified Yellow Hair incident was a great opportunity for publicity and showmanship. Buffalo Bill helped to write the news report by Charles King in the *New York Herald,* which helped to authenticate his dramatized performance in the later play that supposedly re-created the event.[37] Buffalo Bill's involvement with the real event helped to verify it and create an association with Custer, another famous Western hero. During the performances of the *Wild West,* this linkage was expanded to portray him as the would-be rescuer of Custer.

P.T. Barnum was a great showman who was associated with hoaxes, fakery and, as he put it, "humbug." As a piece of unconscious irony, a photograph of Cody's office at the Irma Hotel in Cody, Wyoming, around 1910 shows a picture of Barnum on the back wall.[38]

5

Buffalo Bill's *Wild West*

The amusements of a people are the best index of their character—John Burke, publicist for Buffalo Bill[1]

More than any other person, Buffalo Bill portrayed the West in mythical terms, expanded the legend of the frontier and Western heroism, and turned the cowboy into a national hero. Dime novelists helped to shape the public vision of the West, but what really popularized it was the series of stage plays featuring Buffalo Bill. However, by around 1880 stage melodramas like *The Scouts of the Prairie* started to lose their audiences. A further limitation was that Cody's combination company was restricted in what it could present on a stage due to obvious size and physical limitations.

Cody searched for something else to continue his show business career and the eventual result was the arena extravaganza named Buffalo Bill's *Wild West*. Cody took a few elements of the West—such as Indians, buffalo, stagecoaches, and cowboy action—and created an illusion that audiences thought was the reality of the West. The show offered a heady aroma of animals, smoke, dust, and gunpowder, with panoramic backdrops of the West, rousing visual action, stirring spectacle, and noble figures on horseback. The show's publicity men shaped Buffalo Bill's *Wild West* around what experience had taught them the public wanted. Audiences were presented with cheap and convenient entertainment, and they loved the sensory stimulation of the fights between cowboys and Indians, the sound and feel of pounding hoofbeats and galloping horses, and the echo of gunshots around the arena. Riders in the show never walked but always galloped, speeding up the tempo and giving the impression that the West was always in a hurry.

The public was eager for heroes and by the time Buffalo Bill created the *Wild West*, his reputation as a genuine Western hero was well established. The show was a sensation and was extremely successful between 1883 and 1916. It made the public believe that life in the West was a series of death-defying adventures. As a result, at the turn of the twentieth century millions of Americans and Europeans thought they remembered the Wild West because they had seen it in Buffalo Bill's spectacle. His *Wild West* show blurred the lines between entertainment and education, fiction and fact. Though most of the performers had personally experienced the Old West and its lifestyle, Cody's interpretation of the West was drawn from dime novels and contemporary sensationalist journalism. These hazy recollections of national memory were supported by a combination of Western literature, art, and the popular culture of dime novels and sensationalist magazines.

The Early Wild West Shows

Wild West shows had made a fitful start forty years before Buffalo Bill created his popular spectacle. One of the earliest took place on August 31, 1843, at a racetrack in Hoboken, New Jersey. In June, innovative showman P.T. Barnum found out that a man named C.D. French (real name Fitzhugh) had brought fifteen buffalo calves to Boston, probably to exhibit them. Barnum purchased them for $700 and hired French as their keeper. Barnum then used the animals to stage a "Grand Buffalo Hunt," which was supposed to be a display of Western roping skills.

On the day of the show, French, dressed up as an Indian, chased the buffalo around the arena. The calves were terrified, broke out of the arena, and promptly vanished into a nearby swamp to hide. Only a few were recaptured. Needless to say, the show was not a great success. To make the disastrous performance worse, one spectator died after he fell out of a tree he had climbed to escape from the thundering rush of the fleeing buffalo.[2] Even though the show was not a success, Barnum, being an astute businessman, made a profit as usual. He had secured the concession for the ferry that customers had to use to reach the racetrack.[3]

Barnum regularly exhibited Indians at his Boston Museum in the 1840s, where they performed war dances and demonstrated battles on the stage for fascinated audiences. In 1860 Barnum went into partnership with James C. "Grizzly" Adams and created another show that featured bears, wolves, lions, and buffalo. Adams eventually died from wounds sustained from repeated mauling by his bears.[4] In the 1870s Barnum used Indians in his traveling exhibitions to demonstrate their style of everyday living, and included a battle scene between the Indians and a band of Mexicans.[5]

Other promoters also put on Western shows. In 1855 *Tyler's Indian Exhibition* tried to simulate a buffalo hunt. Another of what could be considered the forerunners of the Wild West shows was the first rodeo staged at Deer Trail, Colorado, which featured bronco busting. A third was a Fourth of July celebration in Cheyenne, Wyoming, in 1872, which featured steer riding.

One famous Westerner who participated in an early Wild West show was Wild Bill Hickok. In August of 1872, Hickok was part of a show at Niagara Falls that featured buffalo. This so-called Grand Buffalo Hunt was staged by Colonel Sidney Barnett, the son of Thomas Barnett, who owned a museum at Niagara Falls. His hope in doing this was to attract more tourists to the museum. The intent was for a group of Indians to chase the buffalo while shooting blunt arrows at them and then finally capture them with lassos. To headline the show, Barnett hired Texas Jack Omohundro, the well-known hero of dime novels. Omohundro backed out of the show at the last minute and Barnett hired Hickok as his replacement. Unfortunately for Barnett, the expense of putting on such an extravagant show was far greater than the box office receipts. This contributed to the Barnetts eventually losing their museum.[6]

Cody and Doc Carver

Buffalo Bill's entry into Wild West show business began in 1882 when he organized a Fourth of July celebration named the "Old Glory Blowout" for North Platte, Nebraska. The show included rodeo-like displays of cowboy skills in which a thousand cowboys competed for prizes in marksmanship, riding, roping, horse races, and bronco busting. Cody put on a demonstration of hunting buffalo, shooting at the animals with blanks from horseback. Buffalo Bill always characterized this as the original Wild West show, though there had been others before him.

The North Platte celebration was such a success that in 1883 Cody teamed with W.F. "Doc" Carver to put on the *Hon. W.F. Cody and Dr. W.F. Carver's Rocky Mountain and Prairie Exhibition*, which opened on May 19, 1883, in Omaha. The show included Indians, cowboys, Mexicans, and a cowboy band. The stars were Cody, Carver, and Captain Adam H. Bogardus, a trapshooter who billed himself as "America's Champion Shot." Carver and Bogardus were legitimately considered to be two of the best exhibition marksmen in the world at the time. Cody was also a remarkable marksman in an age when shooting skills were prized.

Doc Carver was billed as "The Evil Spirit of the Plains" and "The Championship Marksman of the World." He received the nickname of "Little Doc" from his father because he cared for wounded animals when he was young. Carver claimed that he had mingled with many famous frontier characters, such as Wild Bill Hickok, General Custer, and Texas Jack Omohundro; however, his adventures on the plains were never accurately documented.[7] Carver always boasted that he played a vital role in winning the West, even though there was no evidence for his claims.

Disagreements between Cody and Carver caused a falling-out at the end of 1883. After the two split, Carver joined with Captain Jack Crawford to form the *Carver and Crawford Wild West*. Their show lasted until 1885. Carver went on to appear in several other Wild West shows over the following years.

Buffalo Bill's Wild West

The largest and most popular of the Wild West shows was Cody's *Wild West*. Cody did not like his spectacle to be called a Wild West "show," as he felt that it represented history rather than a show, so it was always called simply the *Wild West*. The *Wild West* continued to be a successful popular entertainment for more than thirty years and was a major influence on the American perception of the frontier West. The show created the same image during equally successful overseas tours in Europe and Australia. The show toured England, Scotland, France, Spain, Germany, Belgium, and Italy, and even Austria, Hungary, Poland, Romania, Serbia, and the Czech Republic. The creator and chief attraction was Cody himself. The show was targeted for the urban middle class, and particularly at women. Like watching a movie or television today, the *Wild West* offered an escape from reality and the daily grind of the working class.

The *Wild West* presented gaudily dressed performers in almost nonstop action. Featured acts were horse races with Indian riders, foot races between Indians and cowboys, a Pony Express demonstration, an Indian attack on the Deadwood stage, an attack on a settler's cabin, shooting exhibitions, and horse riding skills. These different acts and scenes were presented as typical frontier history. Though Buffalo Bill wanted everything in the show to be authentic, he featured only the elements of the West that contained action, adventure, and

One of Buffalo Bill's show acts was to ride around the arena shooting at glass balls thrown into the air by an assistant. This photograph glamorizes his act by showing him riding with an Indian helper in the open air in front of a painted backdrop. Though Cody used small birdshot in his rifle for safety reasons, he was indeed a superb shot and thrilled audiences with his shooting ability (author's collection).

spectacle, thus Cody's entire presentation became part of the powerful myth of the West. Audiences believed that they were being educated as well as entertained, and thought the show was real history.

The *Wild West*, publicized as "America's National Entertainment," was Cody's primary mythmaking enterprise. The presence of real cowboys, horses, buffalo, Indians, stagecoaches, and shooting brought gripping entertainment to audiences in thousands of performances. It blurred the lines between reality and entertainment, history and myth. As the show matured, the acts became larger and more complex, and the costumes and staging became more and more elaborate. Special effects eventually included a prairie fire, a sunset, and a cyclone.

The show was performed in the open air. The promoters claimed that shooting acts would damage an overhead tent, though the small lead shot they used would travel only about eighty to one hundred yards, making this reason improbable. Instead, the outdoor setting was carefully staged to give the show the feeling of being in the Western outdoors under open skies. Performing in the outdoors also gave the impression that the cowboys were hardy Westerners who could shrug off any inconvenience of rain or wind.

Though the *Wild West* was make-believe, all circus-type entertainment featuring animals and action-packed performances were inherently dangerous. Indians, cowboys, horse handlers, and support workers were injured from time to time. Performers suffered broken arms, dislocated shoulders and hips, concussions, sprains, fractures, and cracked ribs, from dealing with horses and livestock and from the dangerous stunts they performed in the arena. Even Cody was injured on more than one occasion. There were very few days when one of the performers or crew didn't suffer some sort of injury.

The show featured buffalo, deer, and elk, which were unusual animals for eastern audiences. Buffalo Bill himself reenacted a buffalo hunt by chasing half-a-dozen buffalo around the arena on horseback while shooting at them with blanks. This was pure showmanship. In reality, commercial buffalo hunters didn't hunt from horseback. Instead, they set up a stationary stand overlooking the herd they intended to shoot. Buffalo were not very bright animals and would not spook at the sound of a shot. They simply continued grazing while animals around them were being killed. After the hunter had shot enough buffalo, teams of butchers, skinners, and freighters moved in to process the carcasses for skins and meat.

For most of the *Wild West* shows, the regular and very popular climax was the "Attack on the Settler's Cabin," which featured a White mother and her children under attack. During the fighting, Buffalo Bill rode to the rescue, which symbolized him as the savior of the West. Cody never actually performed such a rescue during his lifetime, but this was symbolic of the Western myth. The act appears to have been added by show manager Nate Salsbury after he became a managing partner in 1884, and it was part of the program from 1884 to 1907.

Cody promised accuracy and said that the show was "reality itself." He put his name on his show because he felt that he had participated in the real events. Admittedly the show's cowboys had been genuine cowboys and the Indians were always authentic, though both were perhaps portrayed a little freely. Though the show claimed historical authenticity, it used the theatrical conventions of showmanship and melodrama, including stirring music and colorful costumes. The Indians were Sioux in feathered headdresses and fiercely painted faces. They wore ornate costumes and were bare above the waist. The Mexican performers wore satin jackets and pants and large sombreros. One part of the performance was called "Cowboy Fun," which showed cowboys wearing six-guns and wooly angora chaps doing rope tricks and bronco busting.

Buffalo Bill portrayed the Western hero as masculine, courageous, and full of self-confidence. Even though cowboys were the focus of Western novels and movies, they had a relatively small place in the *Wild West*. The gunfighter of the movies had no place at all in the show. The cowboys appeared as a supporting cast, such as the rescuers in the stagecoach attack, and for riding, bronc-busting acts, and "cowboy fun." Indians racing around the arena on horseback and whooping confirmed for viewers the perception of the Indian as a wild savage. After the performance, the audience could visit the show camp and see how the performers lived and chat with real Indians and cowboys.

The acts were introduced by announcer Frank Richmond, and later Henry Clifford, who added commentary during the performances. Both had very powerful voices that carried clearly to the audience without a need for artificial amplification. The show started with a grand entry as various groups rode into the arena while Richmond introduced them. Buffalo Bill entered last. Horses were featured in 25 percent of the acts, careening around the arena in various races, such as an Indian on horse pitted against one on foot, or a cowboy versus a Mexican vaquero. The show included women riders and a Pony Express demonstration with various ways to mount, dismount, and gallop off at high speed.

The "Fight with Yellow Hair" was an act that featured cowboys and Indians riding menacingly towards each other as Yellow Hair threw out a challenge to Buffalo Bill. They shot at each other, then went into face-to-face, hand-to-hand combat, with Cody armed with a knife and Yellow Hand with a spear. In the end, Cody, of course, "knifed" Yellow Hair and took his scalp. Then the remaining cowboys and Indians charged at each other and had a wild skirmish.

Buffalo Bill's success was at its height in 1893. He was a celebrity, a well-known figure who attracted public attention, as much for who he was as for what he had done. He generally acted as himself, with the exception of portraying Custer at times.

Nate Salsbury

Cody met Nathan "Nate" Salsbury in the spring of 1882, though they did not enter into a business partnership until later.[8] Salsbury was an experienced showman in his own right. He formed a variety act in 1875 called "Salsbury's Troubadours" and managed it for the next twelve years. His group presented a musical comedy show that featured songs, dances, and comic routines blended together.

Salsbury was a good entrepreneur and organizer, and Cody eventually hired him to be in charge of business and showmanship for the *Wild West*. Salsbury organized the tours, hired the performers, and helped to shape the show. He was probably instrumental in adding the "Attack on the Settler's Cabin," the climactic scene that was very popular with audiences. Like the earlier captivity narratives, for many people this symbolized an attack on White womanhood, domesticity, and the family. The audience was thrilled at the rescue by the noble White scout and his cowboys.

John Burke

Another key player in the team that made the *Wild West* a success was John M. Burke, the show's longtime publicist. Burke was no stranger to Buffalo Bill, as Cody had previously hired him in 1883 as press agent for Carver's show and hired him earlier to do publicity for some of Cody's stage plays.

Burke, who had been a newspaper editor and manager of a show troupe, was a master at his job, which was inflating stories and turning them into exciting material for the press. He handled all the publicity and gathered the crowds. He was one of the best publicity agents in the business. During his long career with Cody, Burke changed some facts and invented others, over the years developing many of the legends that helped to define the *Wild West*.[9] Burke entered into the part of a showman and began to call himself "Major" Burke. He wore the same style of long hair and broad-brimmed hat that the *Wild West* performers did.[10]

Burke poured out a constant stream of anecdotes, stories, and *Wild West* show history. He and his team produced a booklet that was used to authenticate the *Wild West* by describing every aspect of the show. In 1893 he authored a book titled *"Buffalo Bill" from Prairie to Palace*, a volume that was bursting with publicity and promotion.[11] Not missing a trick, vendors sold copies of this autobiography to show audiences. Copies were also distributed to the press and to Buffalo Bill's interviewers. Booklets such as one titled *A Peep at Buffalo Bill's* Wild West were sold as souvenirs of the performance.

Burke, Salsbury, and Cody understood the value of advertising. Burke's advance men went into towns ahead of the performers and covered buildings with advertising posters that depicted scenes from the show. The advertising was sensational and melodramatic. Some posters showed a single scene; others were montages, pictures of performers, or scenes from the show. Many had Buffalo Bill featured in a prominent position. Posters were extensively pasted on storefronts, the outsides of barns, outhouses, fences, and anywhere else the men could find open space. The property owners were glad to allow this, as they were given free tickets to the show in return. The advance men also bought space in newspapers and flooded the town with handbills and heralds (two-sided announcements for the show, printed on cheap, brightly colored paper called "circus paper"). Heralds were usually distributed by hand to advertise traveling shows. The advance men sometimes also distributed couriers, which were small newspapers that advertised the show. At the same time, Burke's publicity agents supplied a constant stream of prepared stories about the show. When the performers arrived, headliners such as Cody, Annie Oakley, and Buck Taylor gave press interviews.

The desired audience of all entertainers at the time was middle class women, with the expectation that they would bring their husbands, children, and families to the show. Burke's advertising was intended to appeal specifically to them. Though Burke and Cody wanted to attract women, by definition the *Wild West* was a violent show full of gunplay, like the raid on the settler's cabin and the attack on the stagecoach. The boisterous spectacle of all this action, of course, was very appealing to the men in the audience.

The Trick Shooters

In an era that had a national fascination with shooting and firearms, displays of marksmanship played a popular and important role in the *Wild West*. Shooting acts in the *Wild*

West made up about 25 percent of the show, emphasizing White male skill in a way that made it seem acceptable. Superior skill at marksmanship was considered in the 1880s and 1890s to be a manly sport and was a favorite of the males in the audience. Beyond that, proficiency with a firearm was considered to be a practical and necessary form of self-defense in the Wild West.

Cody himself was an excellent shot with shotgun, rifle, and revolver. Part of his performance consisted of riding around the arena shooting at balls thrown into the air by an assistant. Cody's shooting skills were supported (though not financially) by the Winchester Repeating Arms Company, one of the most successful of the rifle manufacturers. In turn, Cody endorsed Winchester rifles and would speak highly of them and his use of them.[12] In this way, both promoted each other. Buffalo Bill also promoted Colt revolvers and endorsed the Colt advertising statement that they were used in his show. He also endorsed Du Pont cartridge powder, Savage automatic pistols, and firearms made by the Remington Arms Company.

Posters for the *Wild West* always featured plenty of firearms, and guns were promoted in the show as being essential to the preservation of life and defense of the home in the West. The show's cowboys were shown wearing guns for all their activities, included riding bucking broncos, which would have been impractical in real life. Such images made guns appear to be an essential element of the Western frontiersman's outfit.

For safety, Cody and the other sharpshooters in the show used cartridges containing small lead shot instead of a solid lead bullet, and the shells were loaded with a light charge of powder so that the shot would not carry far. Shot dispersed quickly and would travel for only about eighty to one hundred yards, whereas a solid lead bullet could travel for a mile or more and be very dangerous. While shooting in Baltimore, Cody had accidentally hit and injured a boy in the audience. After that he made sure to only use shot and to take proper precautions.[13] For added safety, performers typically fired towards the open end of the U-shape that defined the arena.

The use of shot also made the glass balls used in the shooting performances easier to hit. Most of the clay targets, glass balls, and other targets that performers broke were hit at a range of about twenty yards. At that distance the spread of the shot was about three inches across. The shooter's skill, however, should not be underestimated. Even using shot, the targets were nonetheless difficult and skill was required to hit them accurately.

Adam Bogardus

One of original trick-shooters in the *Wild West* was Adam Bogardus—formerly with Cody in *Hon. W.F. Cody and Dr. W.F. Carver's Rocky Mountain and Prairie Exhibition*—accompanied by his four sons. Their act was referred to as the Bogardus "shooting quintette." This suggested a family association that Cody and Burke wanted to promote among the audience, similar to popular contemporary singing groups.[14]

Annie Oakley

The most popular performer next to Buffalo Bill was Annie Oakley, born Phoebe Ann Moses in Darke County, Ohio, in 1860. She took the stage name of Oakley when she started

performing shooting acts in theaters. Unlike some similar shooting acts—such as lighting a match, snuffing out a candle with a single shot, and splitting apples, all of which were performed with fakery on stage—Annie's act was genuine.[15] When she provided meat to restaurants in her youth, she specialized in providing birds that were hit in the head, so that the shot did not spoil the meat.

When Adam Bogardus left the *Wild West*, Salsbury recommended Oakley as a replacement. Cody was dubious at first but decided to give her a chance. He quickly invited her to join in 1885 after he saw her perform. Cody later realized that a woman sharpshooter was a novelty and would help to attract women customers, which was what he wanted. Further promotion and publicity helped to make her one of the headliners of the show. She could shoot a dime held between her husband's (Frank Butler) thumb and forefinger, shoot the ember from a cigarette in his lips, and slice a playing card that he held sideways. She could also shoot accurately while looking in a mirror with the rifle held backwards over her shoulder. The *Wild West* rarely advertised individual performers, but Oakley received star billing.

Annie Oakley turned out to be an important marketing asset for the show. As many women in the audience were unaccustomed to gunfire, ladylike Annie was used in the first shooting act to put them at ease. Both Cody and Annie were seasoned performers who understood the importance of costumes and appearance. Annie made her own costumes and added her own designs. She was well liked by middle-class audiences because she appealed to them as a respectable domestic woman. Only five feet tall, Oakley was an arresting show personality. Theatrical gestures and a sense of drama permeated her act. Instead of walking out into the arena, she tripped out, bowing, waving to the audience, and blowing kisses. She stamped her foot when she made a difficult shot, and pouted when she missed one. Oakley wore boots and wore her hair loose and full, which few women did at the time.

Annie Oakley stayed with the show for sixteen years. Oakley and Butler originally blamed a train wreck they were in on October 29, 1901, as the cause of her retirement. At the time, Butler said she was uninjured, but he later said she suffered terrible injuries to her hip. She appeared in a shooting contest in December 1901 and gave the impression of being in good health.[16] The true cause, as reported in the *Chicago Daily News* in 1901, was that she had been left in a scalding bath at a hot springs for forty minutes instead of one minute. As a result, her hair turned white and her skin became mottled.[17] Oakley's own scrapbook contained a notation that the problem was due to an inattentive attendant at a spa at Hot Springs, Arkansas, who made the bath too hot for too long.[18]

LILLIAN SMITH

In 1885 there were sixteen female sharpshooters touring the United States.[19] Another excellent exhibition shooter who performed in the *Wild West* from 1886 to 1888 was Lillian Frances Smith, also known as "The California Girl." She was an outstanding shot with rifle, shotgun, and revolver. To distinguish her from Annie Oakley, who was billed as the "Cham-

Opposite: **Buffalo Bill and Sitting Bull.** The famous Sioux Indian chief appeared in Cody's *Wild West* during the 1885 season for four months. Custer's death at the Little Bighorn was still vivid in American memory and Sitting Bull was often booed as he rode around the arena, even though he had not participated in the actual battle. He was very fond of Annie Oakley and dubbed her Little Sure Shot as a sign of his respect (Library of Congress).

pion Markswoman," Smith was billed as "The California Huntress and Champion Girl Rifle Shot."[20] She was a big girl and single, and found it hard to compete with the tiny Oakley, the popular married show-woman. Rivalry over their shooting skills and their age difference may have been partially responsible for Smith's leaving the show. She was married for a while to one of Buffalo Bill's show cowboys, James "Jim Kid" Willoughby, but in 1889 she ran off with another man.[21]

After Smith left the *Wild West*, she continued as a markswoman in other shows, billed as a Sioux Indian princess with the stage name of Princess Wenona. She may have had Indian blood but was probably not an Indian princess. Hazy biographical information invented by her publicity team makes it hard to determine the truth.[22] She performed wearing dark makeup in an act with Frank C. Smith (also known as C.F. "California Frank" Hafley) in *California Frank's All Star Wild West Show*. They were billed as "Wenona and Frank—The World's Champion Rifle Shots." She could shoot out a candle flame, trim the ash on Frank's cigar, and break small balls attached to his hat. She could even shoot a dime out of his hand without injuring him.[23] Frank was also an expert pistol shot and rifle shot and a veteran performer formerly with Buffalo Bill.

In 1904, Lillian and Frank tested bulletproof vests that had been specially made for the Czar of Russia and his wife. Lillian shot at Frank point-blank with a pistol while he was wearing one of the vests. When Lillian died, among the effects she left to the Oklahoma Historical Society were a beaded blanket, a buckskin dress, four Winchester rifles, two Smith & Wesson pistols, a pair of silver-plated spurs—and one of the bulletproof vests she had tested for the czar.[24]

Trick Riders

As well as female sharpshooters, Salsbury and Cody hired other female performers, including trick riders such as Georgia Duffy (who was married to cowboy performer Tom Duffy), Della and Bessie Ferrell, and Emma Lake Hickok (the stepdaughter of Wild Bill Hickok).

One of the most popular trick riders and sharpshooters was William Levi "Buck" Taylor, who was known as the "King of the Cowboys." He was the first authentic cowboy hero and appeared in several dime novels. The six-foot-four Taylor had been a real cowboy and herded cattle from Texas to Wyoming. He was a featured performer in the *Wild West* for ten years as a trick rider, roper, expert marksman, and genuine cowboy.

Buffalo Bill's "Indians"

Indians in the *Wild West* were generalized and all dressed the same, with feathered headdress and war paint, and rode an Indian pony. Any differences between tribes were minimized and the result was to create a generalized Plains Indian identity with a lack of individual tribal features. As visitors after the show saw Indians living in teepees, Americans came to believe that all Indians lived and dressed like the Sioux performers and lived in teepees. These stage Indians were passed off as Arapaho, Cheyenne, Pawnee, Crow, Shoshone, or Sioux, depending on the needs of the show. Though some Pawnee and Arapaho were in the show, almost all were Lakota Sioux from the Northern Plains. Though Buffalo Bill had previously used White supers (extras) in his stage melodramas, he did not use them in the *Wild West*. All the Indians had a real tribal heritage to protect the authenticity of his show. This made the rest of the show seem more believable. However, even though the Indians were genuine, they were generic. They were played as war-painted, ferocious aggressors to be defeated and killed. The show glorified the wholesale killing of Indians by White cowboys in pitched battles.

The Cowboy Band

The arena action in the *Wild West* was accompanied by the Buffalo Bill Cowboy Band. Manager Nate Salsbury's background in musical shows may have influenced and expanded the use of music during the performance. Music helped to set the mood of the show, particularly by using a fast-paced tempo to add to the tension of action scenes. The band was led for many years by William Sweeney, who also played the cornet.[25]

To introduce the show, the band played "The Star-Spangled Banner" at the beginning of each performance as an overture.[26] Interestingly, at that time this melody was not the national anthem, and it did not become so until 1931. Another favorite piece of music was Custer's regimental march, "Garry Owen (also spelled Garryowen)," played in honor of Custer's Last Stand.

The Deadwood Stage

One of the most popular acts in the *Wild West* was the "Attack on the Deadwood Stage." As the horse-drawn stagecoach raced around the arena, it was attacked by a band of Indians and road-agents who performed a furious chase involving the use of guns and flaming arrows. To add to the drama, a smoke machine was installed inside the coach to make it look like it had caught on fire.[27] Just in the nick of time, Buffalo Bill would arrive with a group of cowboys and drive the Indians away. Part of the thrill for the audience was that prominent dignitaries rode in the stage during the attack. The announcer asked for volunteers but usually filled it with local officials or members of the press. The stirring chase was billed as a "Startling and Soul-Stirring Attack upon the Deadwood Mail Coach."[28]

Cody's publicists and announcer Frank Richmond claimed that the coach was the real Deadwood stage that traveled the route from Cheyenne, Wyoming, to Deadwood, South Dakota, and was an authentic historic relic saved from abandonment. In reality, the stage had been specially ordered from the Cheyenne and Black Hills Stage Line for the *Wild West*.[29]

The Drama of Civilization

In the winter of 1886, instead of closing, as most traveling shows did, Salsbury rented Madison Square Garden for a season of winter performances. To script the show, he hired dramatist Steele Mackaye, a famous New York actor, playwright, and producer who was known for his theatrical innovations. The show, called *The Drama of Civilization*, was based on the history of American pioneering from the colonies to the mining era. It was a stage spectacle that combined nature, history, and action, at the same time again blurring reality and fiction. All the familiar elements of the *Wild West* were used, including cowboys, Indians, and shooting acts.

The stage scenery included gigantic backdrops, 40 feet high and 150 feet long, that were vivid paintings of forests, prairies, and mountains. The huge paintings were set up at the rear of the stage with small props—such as trees, saddles, or a wagon—cleverly placed in the foreground to create an illusion of depth and allow the action in the foreground to blend back into the painting. Stage entrances were cut into the paintings, so that horses and men could appear to be entering from beyond the immediate foreground.

The program was broken into several separate scenes of American history. Trick riding, roping, and displays of marksmanship were included where appropriate. The first scene was called "The Primeval Forest," which showed the wilderness of the Indian tribes before the arrival of White Americans. The scene ended with a rough-and-tumble fight performed by the Indians. "The Prairie" showed a buffalo hunt, the arrival of pioneers, and life on a cattle ranch, and ended with the inevitable fight between the cowboys and the Indians. "The Mining Camp" demonstrated Pony Express riding, shooting skills, the holdup of the Deadwood stagecoach, and the attack on the settler's cabin. The spectacle was claimed to be an educational history lesson; however, like the *Wild West* it was based on, it showed only the sensational parts of the history of the West.

The Drama of Civilization concluded with a thrilling spectacle that showed the destruction of the frontier mining town of Deadwood City by a cyclone. This special effects triumph was first presented in Madison Square Garden. To simulate the power of a tornado, workmen dug a trench across Twenty-seventh Street to a steam generator that powered four six-foot industrial fans. The artificial hurricane was enhanced by the addition of real leaves thrown into the air by stagehands and blown around the stage. This spectacular staging could be used only in locations where suitable support machinery was available.

Custer's Last Rally

The Drama of Civilization included the staging of an act called "Custer's Last Rally," which was Cody's version of Custer's last fight at the Battle of the Little Bighorn. The performance was a little unusual for Cody's show, as it was a depiction of a real event as opposed to the fictional acts using the generic settler's cabin or the Deadwood stage. Custer's stand appeared only intermittently throughout the years. The Indians were supposed to be Sioux and Cheyenne. Cody's cowboys played immaculately uniformed, all–White soldiers, thus altering the memory of Custer. In reality, the army contained widespread ethnic diversity and included troops who were Irish, English, German, African American, and Italian, often dressed in unmatched and tattered uniforms. Cody's version of all–White troops reinforced the contemporary theories about race and civilization, which included the image that White Anglo-Saxon cowboys, settlers, and troops defeated the Indians and civilized the West.

Cody wore a wig of long flowing hair to impersonate Custer and brandished a sword, even though Custer had cut his hair short the previous year and did not have a sword at the Little Bighorn battle.[30] Later, Cody assigned the role of Custer to cowboy Buck Taylor so that, as Buffalo Bill, Cody could stage a futile dash to rescue Custer. Again, this was a distortion of the facts, as Cody was nowhere near the battle and did not know about it until ten days afterward. The fictional melodrama ended with a banner bearing the motto "Too Late," which implied that Buffalo Bill had almost saved Custer.

The backdrop to "Custer's Last Rally" was 49 feet high and 440 feet long. On a clear, cloudless day outdoors, the painted sky on the canvas blended with the real sky at the top. The cowboys dressed as soldiers, representing Custer's troops, rode in the foreground toward the Indians. In a masterful stroke of clever staging, the Sioux came into the arena out of the entrances cut into the background canvas.

Cody tried for accuracy of detail. He grew a long beard with a moustache and long hair, like Custer. He dressed in fringed buckskins, thigh-high boots, and a broad-brimmed hat. When Libbie Custer wrote her memoirs, *Tenting on the Plains*, in 1887, she praised Cody's performance as Custer and commented that Cody bore a great likeness to the general.[31] She was very pleased with the depiction of "Custer's Last Rally" and felt that it was an accurate representation—even though she had never seen the real battlefield in Montana. Libbie attended the premier, which helped to authenticate the accuracy of the performance in the minds of the audience.

The End of the Wild West

As the *Wild West* entered the early 1900s and the era of Indian fighting had passed into history when the last Native Americans were confined to reservations, Buffalo Bill the scout started to be viewed as an antique type of hero. In an attempt to modernize the frontier hero image, in 1893 Cody added an increased emphasis on military displays of riding drills. These military drill teams were made up of cowboys and cavalrymen to form *Buffalo Bill's Wild West and Congress of Rough Riders of the World*. Cody rode at the head of a grand parade at the opening and closing of each performance as the "King of the Rough Riders." As commander of these "Rough Riders," Buffalo Bill became a modern hero as the country went into World War I. Though the publicity implication was that the performers were linked to Teddy Roosevelt and his charge up San Juan Hill during the Spanish-American War, the name "rough rider" was a generic old-time cowboy name that was applied at the time to any genuine expert horseman and had been applied to Western horsemen in dime novels since before 1880.

When Nate Salsbury became ill in 1894, Cody entered into an arrangement with James Bailey of the Barnum and Bailey Circus to furnish transportation equipment and manage the routes and business aspects of the show. Bailey arranged for the show to do many short stands, which was feasible, as the newly expanded American railroad system made it possible to transport the show easily from town to town. In 1896 the show traveled 10,787 miles in 190 days and gave 332 performances.[32] In this way Cody was able to visit many smaller cities and provide more opportunity for rural audiences to see the show. However, the stress of constantly being on the road contributed to a decline in Cody's health. His hair was graying, he had become heavier, and he now required eyeglasses for his shooting act.[33]

Buffalo Bill defined the national memory of the West through his show *Wild West*, though his vision of the real West was limited to elements that contained action, spectacle, and adventure. Audiences believed they were being educated as well as entertained and thought the show was real history. Colonel Cody is pictured here in his later years, in 1907, as Wild West shows were in decline (Library of Congress).

Cody was not a good money manager. The more he made, the more he spent and the more he invested poorly. In 1909 financial difficulties forced him to merge the *Wild West* with Gordon W. Lillie, who had previously worked for Cody and was now another Wild West proprietor, known in show business as Pawnee Bill. Together they formed *Buffalo Bill's Wild West Combined with Pawnee Bill's Great Far East*, more commonly known as "The Two Bills Show."

At one time Gordon Lillie had worked at the Pawnee Indian Agency. While there, he learned their language and served as an interpreter and teacher at the agency school, which gave him his show name.³⁴ Lillie later went on the road with Buffalo Bill to act as an interpreter for the Pawnees in the *Wild West*. In 1886, he married May Manning, an educated girl from Philadelphia, who became an excellent trick shot and horseback rider. She learned to ride and rope and became so good that she earned the titles of "Princess of the Prairie," the "New Rifle Queen," and the "World's Champion Woman Rifle Shot."³⁵ She was later a headliner in Pawnee Bill's Wild West show. By 1910 another problem for Cody was that other Wild West shows, such as *Miller Brothers' 101 Ranch Wild West Show*, had become serious competition. In 1910 Cody started a series of "Farewell Exhibitions," which lasted until 1912.

The new entertainment form of motion pictures was also providing stiff competition for live shows, so the two Bills decided to enter into film production. In 1910, the Buffalo Bill and Pawnee Bill Film Company produced three reels of film showing acts from the *Wild West*.³⁶ In 1912 they produced *The Life of Buffalo Bill (Col. Cody)*. Though obviously older now, Cody demonstrated his tracking skills, unsaddling his horse and then using a dream sequence of vignettes from his supposed earlier life where he fought Indians, rescued a stagecoach, and captured notorious bandits. In this way he tried to claim authenticity by blending his persona with Western events.

Cody appeared in eleven films between 1894 and 1917. In 1913 he tried to film *Indian War Pictures*, re-creating battles from the Indian Wars, to pay off some of his mountainous debts. The screenplay was written by the same Charles King who wrote cavalry novels and the story of Cody's battle story with Yellow Hair for the *New York Herald*.³⁷ Cody reenacted the battles of Summit Springs and War Bonnet Creek as he had in the show arena. He used real soldiers borrowed from the army through his connections with General Nelson Miles, an authentic Indian fighter. The army was happy to provide the troops, as the publicity it created was a recruiter's dream. Miles insisted that the battle of Wounded Knee be reenacted on the original site. The Indians used in the film, however, were not amused and threatened to use real bullets instead of blank cartridges.

The film was released in different versions with different editing and different running times. In various versions it was also known as *The Last Indian War*; *Last Indian Battles*; *Indian Wars*; *Buffalo Bill's War Pictures*; *Indian War Pictures*; and *Indian Wars Refought by United States Army*.³⁸ The film was heavily advertised, but few movie theaters chose to book it. It did poorly at the box office and the receipts were not enough to pay off Cody's debts. Unfortunately the original film deteriorated and has been lost. Cody later said that making movies was harder than running his *Wild West*.³⁹

Cody had a poor season financially in 1913, so he arranged for a six-month loan from Henry Tammen, the co-owner of the sensationalist newspaper *Denver Post*. When the show performed in Denver, the attendance was still poor, so Tammen foreclosed on the debt and Cody lost the show. In 1914 and 1915, Cody toured with the *Sells-Floto Circus* (also owned by Tammen) at a salary of $100 a day. In 1916 he toured with the *Miller and Arlington Wild West Show*. Cody died on January 10, 1917, in Denver while staying with his sister.

Buffalo Bill's Legacy

Various theories have been proposed for why the *Wild West* was so popular. In Catlin's time, audiences were satisfied with paintings, displays, and lectures about the West. In the era of Cody's *Wild West*, though, the public demanded spectacle, and circuses and similar outdoor amusements were popular. Cody accordingly combined elements from stage plays, circuses, and rodeo to create a historical pageant. Audiences liked bloodshed, violence, conflict, and galloping horsemen. Cody's show personified all this.

Buffalo Bill should be remembered for making the cowboy into a hero of the great myth of the American West. Prior to this, cowboys were considered to be ruffians, desperadoes, and bandits. Cody presented them in romanticized episodes of frontier life, spectacular fights between Indians and cowboys who always won the fight, attacks on cabins and stagecoaches, and demonstrations of superior marksmanship.

Buffalo Bill's legacy was promoting the myth of the use of violence in the conquest of the West. The show glorified violence. Most of the show was a spectacle of White men defeating Indians. There was very little dialogue in the acts, which emphasized the elements of conflict. Cody blurred the lines between fact and myth, history and melodrama. He used cowboys in the show, but they were dressed in white ten-gallon hats, furry chaps, and gleaming guns and were not the reality of sweat-stained ranch hands. Paintings, photographs, and magazine illustrations had made the scenic landscapes of the West familiar to most Americans, so audiences who attended the *Wild West* easily absorbed the image of the West presented in the show. Buffalo Bill himself, dressed in fringed buckskins, and with a moustache, goatee, and shoulder-length hair, looked the part of a legendary hero. The organizers and promoters of the *Wild West* used image, salesmanship, and promotion to make Buffalo Bill into a modern celebrity.

Cody created American historical memory through the medium of popular entertainment and the Western theme of a program that appealed to patriotism by showcasing the uniqueness of frontier life. As Cody toured abroad he was an unofficial ambassador for the United States, presenting the West in a positive light. He represented a nation with an exciting frontier past and showed the different people from the Plains.

Cowboys were represented as rough-and-tough as they had to be on the frontier. Bram Stoker, the author of *Dracula*, met Buffalo Bill in 1887. The character of the American cowboy Quincey Morris, who finally kills the vampire Dracula with a Bowie knife through the heart, was loosely patterned after Buffalo Bill's powerful cowboy image.

The movie *Buffalo Bill and the Indians* (1976) included Ned Buntline (Burt Lancaster), one of the men who originally invented Buffalo Bill's show-business persona. At one point Ned toasts Bill (Paul Newman) and yells out, "Buffalo Bill, the thrill of my life to have invented you." He also says, "No ordinary man could realize what tremendous profits could be made by telling a pack of lies in front of witnesses like it was the truth."

The *Wild West* received endorsements from leading figures on the authenticity of the show. Despite this, the performances were guided by the myth of the West and reduced history and events to "typical scenes" that coincided with popular literary mythology. The Plains segments of the shows were like their descriptions in the dime novels. The eastern forests were from Cooper's novels. The show also made the cowboys into a symbol of Whiteness, which made them easier to market to a middle-class audience. Publicity separated White cowboys from Mexican vaqueros and left out black cowboys completely.

Paul Reddin in his book *Wild West Shows* gave an apt summary when he said, "The Wild West show reduced the western saga to a morality play in which Cody, along with scouts and cowboys, represented the forces of good and civilization and Indians and a few errant white road agents symbolized evil and barbarism."[40]

Later movies continued the myth with offerings such as *Buffalo Bill* (1944) with Joel McCrea. The popularity of Annie Oakley continued in *Annie Oakley* (1935) with Barbara Stanwyck, and on Broadway with Ethel Merman as Oakley and a movie of the same name, *Annie Get Your Gun* (1950), with Betty Hutton.

An unusual tribute to Buffalo Bill's show appeared in *Yodelin' Kid from Pine Ridge* (1937). Smiley Burnette played Colonel Millhouse, who runs a Wild West show complete with bulldogging, steer riding, and an attack by Indians who ride round and round a couple of wagons in the arena.

6

More and More Wild West Shows

History blended with pleasant instruction—Advertisement for the Buffalo Ranch Real Wild West[1]

Wild West shows proliferated after the popularity of Buffalo Bill's *Wild West*. Young men in particular were fascinated by his images of the West and admired Cody's flamboyant performers. To match the arena cowboys, real riders of the range assumed that this was what they were supposed to wear, and they dressed the part. Contemporary studio photographs show many real and would-be cowboys dressed in their Sunday best, holding a gun to match the image.

Cody's competitors put on similar extravagant shows full of buckskin-clad scouts, Indian warriors in war bonnets, and cowboy sharpshooters. Another standard feature of these shows that came from the *Wild West* was an Indian attack on a settler's home with the cavalry riding to the rescue. The shows also featured marksmanship, horsemanship, and heroic frontier deeds promoted by flashy four-color posters that reinforced the myth of a glorious and romantic American frontier that had never really existed. Typical of these shows were *Buckskin Ben's Wild West and Dog and Pony Show*; *Cherokee Ed's Wild West*; *Diamond Bar Ranch Wild West*; *Tiger Bill's Wild West*; *Hulberg's Wild West and Congress of Nations of the World*; and *Texas Bud's Wild West*.

Charles H. Thompkins, who produced *Thompkins' Real Wild West and Frontier Exhibition*, was a Texas cowboy and was part of Buffalo Bill's *Wild West* before striking out on his own in 1910. Advertising trumpeted that his show featured cowboys, cowgirls, Indians, and Mexicans "who know no fear or failure in reckless feats," and offered a "daily dalliance with death."[2] In 1887 showman Joe Shelley produced *Mexican Joe's Wild West*. Doc Carver found a new partner in 1887 and produced *Wild America*. The scope of these shows ranged from large spectacles similar to Buffalo Bill's *Wild West* to small rural shows with only a few broken-down horses and fewer performers.

Some shows did well, some did not. *Tiger Bill's Wild West* toured America from 1909 to 1934. The *Cole Younger–Frank James Wild West*, on the other hand, for some reason was not well received by the public and lasted for only one season in 1903.[3] *Indian Joe Wild West* and *Montana Frank Shows* also lasted only one season. *Col. Tim McCoy's Real Wild West and Rough Riders of the World* did even worse. Formed in 1938, it toured for three weeks, from April 14 to May 4, and was bankrupt within a month.[4]

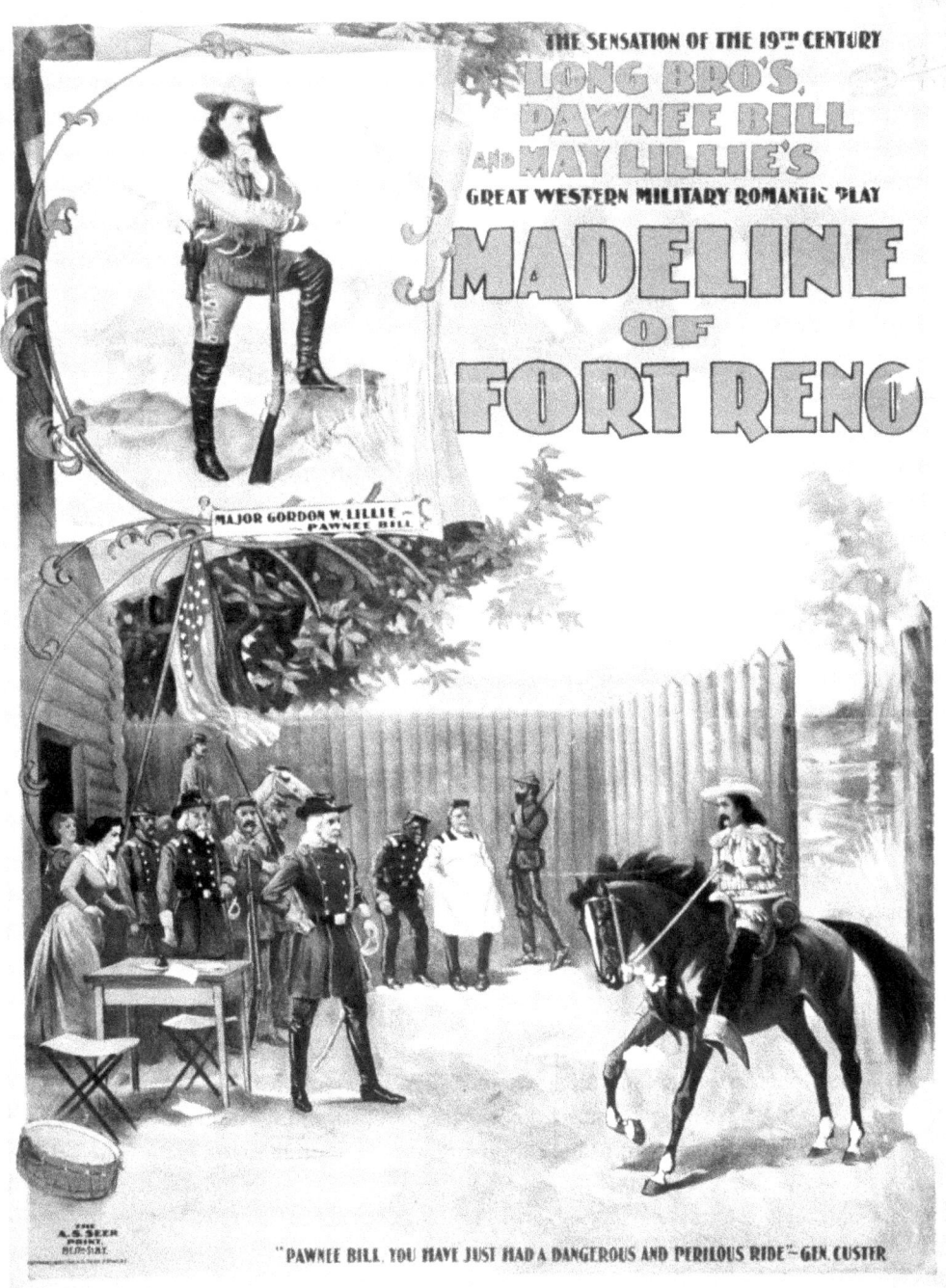

Pawnee Bill (the show business name of Gordon W. Lillie) was another Wild West show proprietor who ventured into show business. He was joined by his wife, May Lillie, an excellent trick shot and horseback rider. Bill's show included elephants, camels, Japanese acrobats, boomerang throwers from Australia, Bedouin Arabs, and dancers from Ceylon. Pawnee Bill and Buffalo Bill joined forces from 1908 to 1912 to form *Buffalo Bill's Wild West Combined with Pawnee Bill's Great Far East*, more commonly known as "The Two Bills Show" (Library of Congress).

The Pawnee Bill Show

Before Pawnee Bill and Buffalo Bill combined their shows, Pawnee Bill had a Wild West show that contained the original *Wild West* plus motley elements from the Far East that included elephants, camels, Japanese acrobats, boomerang throwers from Australia, Bedouin Arabs, and dancers from Ceylon.

The Miller Brothers' 101 Ranch Wild West Show

One of the best known of the Wild West shows was the *Miller Brothers' 101 Ranch Wild West Show*. The Miller Brothers' 101 Ranch was a real ranch, started by Colonel George Washington Miller in the Oklahoma Territory. Before Miller died, he urged his sons, Joseph (Joe), Zack, and George, to buy more land. The ranch and its associated farming operations eventually grew into an immense cattle ranch that covered 110,000 acres near Bliss, Oklahoma. As well as raising livestock, the Millers farmed wheat, corn, and oats.

The ranch became so big that it contained its own schools and churches and a complete road system. Lush orchards grew apples, cherries, and peaches. Dairy cattle provided milk and butter, and meat came from thousands of head of cattle, mules, hogs, and horses. The ranch supported a cider mill, a cannery, packing plants, poultry farms, a dude ranch, a tannery, an electric power plant, an oil refinery, an ice plant, dairy operations, woodworking shops, a laundry, and a cafe. The Millers even operated their own train, with 150 freight cars. A ranch store on the property was a combination of department store and trading post. The entire operation was called by its residents the "Hundred and One" or the "101."

The ranch employed 300 ranch and farm workers who ate one beef cow per day and consumed the eggs from 1,000 chickens. Cowboys roped and branded cattle and tamed horses. Farmhands harvested crops. Blacksmiths, carpenters, and teamsters supported the vast operation. The ranch employed one team of men whose only job was to fix fences. Oil was discovered on the ranch in 1911.

The Millers started to dabble in show business when Colonel Miller staged a "roundup" (really a rodeo) in Winfield, Kansas, in 1882. In 1905, Miller's sons staged their first large-scale Wild West show, which included a roundup and buffalo chase, for several convention groups. The show started with a parade of ranch employees and local Indians and included cowboys displaying rodeo skills such as roping and riding bucking broncos. Other parts of the program showed Indians hunting buffalo and an attack on a wagon train. The Millers followed the contemporary trends in Wild West entertainment and did not try to develop new ideas but included Indian battles, sharpshooters, herds of buffalo, trick riders and ropers, and bucking horses. In September 1905, the Millers joined *Mulhalls' Congress of Rough Riders and Ropers* in a three-day show presented in Coffeeville, Kansas. The show was a great success.

The Millers wanted to keep the image of the Old West alive. The concept of showcasing the ranch and its workers as the idealized image of the West was so successful that the Millers decided to develop a show that would make the ranch a monument to the days of the Old West. The idea was to promote demonstrations of Old West ranch life, including rodeos and a Wild West show. In 1907, the Millers took their show to Norfolk, Virginia, to the

Jamestown Exposition. It was so successful that they decided to become professional showmen and present the show on a regular basis. Their show opened in 1908 in Ponca City, Oklahoma.

Through their show, the Millers helped to promote the cowboy and his way of life as a romantic image, and the pageant became a showcase for the Millers' many skilled riders, ropers, and bulldoggers. Over time, the show matured into sensationalized acts performed by cowboys and cowgirls in gaudy costumes, including trick shooters, wranglers, ropers, and wild horse riders. The Millers hired the best band director they could find, as music was important in all the Wild West shows to set the mood. Stirring marches and up-tempo music helped to create tension in the various acts.

The Millers' publicity campaign said that they used employees from the 101 Ranch in the show; however, many of the performers were actually professionals who were hired specifically as performers. Native Americans from the Ponca tribe, from whom the Millers had acquired much of their land, were in the show but they were not featured performers. The Millers also added sideshows that were typical of the times, including freaks, sword-swallowers, giants, midgets, snake-handlers, and temperance lecturers.

The performance opened with a grand revue, followed by acts of sharpshooting, bronco riding, and bulldogging. The show contained some violence, including a rather gruesome piece of drama where a group of cowboys supposedly captured a horse thief and dragged him to death behind a horse. They also performed re-creations of Indian massacres and scalp dances.[5]

A new direction opened for the Millers in 1911 when they decided to enter the motion

A standard act in many Wild West shows was the "Attack on the Settler's Cabin." In this version the Indians have attacked, with one even on the roof of the cabin and another hiding off to the left, when the show's cowboys arrive to drive them away to the sound of gunfire, war whoops, and up-tempo music from the cowboy band (author's collection).

picture business. The opportunity arose when the Millers decided to winter the show in Los Angeles at the end of the season instead of returning to the ranch in Oklahoma. Most of the performers stayed at the St. Marks Hotel or in cottages in Venice, a small community just south of Santa Monica.[6] Seeing an opportunity, several independent Western filmmakers approached the Millers to see if they could use the Millers' stock and performers in their movies. Finally the Millers struck a deal with the New York Motion Picture Company, which had filmed several earlier Westerns in New Jersey.[7]

As the $2,000-a-week deal included the Miller performers, New York Motion Picture Company gained the use of seventy-five cowboys, twenty-five cowgirls, thirty-five Indians and their squaws, twenty-four oxen, and assorted bison, horses, stagecoaches, and wagons.[8] The film company started to make Westerns under the name of Bison 101, a combination of the names Bison Moving Picture Company and the 101 Ranch. The results included *War on the Plains* (1912), which featured the 101 riders and Indians. Bison later hired Sioux, Cheyenne, Pawnee, Osage, and Comanche Indians, all of whom (like Buffalo Bill's Indians) were costumed and represented as if they were from a single tribe.

Bison 101's filming was based at Inceville, a large movie ranch on the California coast just north of Malibu.[9] To boost ticket sales, crafty publicity agents started a rumor that the Indians at Inceville were so dangerous that security guards had to be employed to keep them from scalping the rest of the cast and crew. Another lively (but false) rumor was that the movie producers had to constantly check to make sure that the Indians had not loaded their guns with live ammunition instead of blanks.[10] Millers' performers continued to work in films into the 1920s. The years between 1908 and 1916 were the best and most lucrative years for the Millers' Wild West show. Their show was so appealing that kids, and even grown men and women, dreamed of running away from home and becoming Wild West performers or working hands at the 101 Ranch.

One of the problems that the Millers had in maintaining an audience was that they tied their show specifically to the ranch, instead of vaguely and generally to the mythic West as Cody had. The Millers tried to stick to ranch-type performances and felt that Cody and the others were moving in a direction that made their shows more like a circus. The Millers finally realized that they had to do the same. They tried to revitalize their show by including camels, elephants, and acts representing the Far East. They renamed the show *The Miller Brothers' 101 Real Wild West and Great Far East*. In an attempt to attract audiences, they added good-looking young women as dancers and horsewomen. Physical attractiveness and youth was a must and, though some dancing experience was helpful, it was not considered essential. The girls' contracts specified that they had to wear appropriate costumes and dance if requested. The Millers' showgirls promoted the simple and wholesome Western way of life. They abandoned corsets and other restrictive Victorian dress, and even rode astride their horses with split skirts. This was a radical change from Cody's *Wild West*, where women performers had to wear skirts and were not allowed to wear trousers even for riding.[11]

Cowgirls became fashionable around 1890. Dressed in colorful costumes and wide-brimmed hats, these women rode bucking broncos, roped steers, and rode in races. They were popular in Wild West shows and easterners fantasized about wild Western women riding horses, packing six-shooters, and doing death-defying tricks on horseback. One poster for *Pawnee Bill's Historic Wild West* offered "beautiful daring Western girls and Mexican Senoritas" riding broncos and performing tricks on horseback. These performances were an outgrowth of women working on ranches. Riding sidesaddle was inconvenient, dangerous, and difficult, so they rode astride the saddle using split skirts in what was called "clothespin style." Riding like this was at first considered unacceptable for proper Victorian women and scandalized local cowboys. It was associated with wild and dangerous women like Calamity Jane (though outlaw Belle Starr rode sidesaddle). The women prevailed, though, and riding sidesaddle went out of style around the turn of the century. Women performers also popularized cowboy hats with very wide brims. Their brims in the early 1900s were often seven inches wide and crowns were seven or eight inches tall.

Women competed in rodeos as early as 1904, riding bucking broncos and wrestling steers. This was dangerous work for women and several cowgirls performing in Wild West and rodeo events were seriously injured. In 1917 Juanita Perry was killed while performing when her horse fell. In 1929 Bonnie McCarroll was killed in the Pendleton Round-up rodeo when her horse fell on her. Faced with bad publicity, rodeo organizers eliminated women's bronc riding and women were gradually phased out of similar events. The prize money was low, the danger high, and women's participation faded away in the 1940s. Women continued to participate in rodeo but in show events, such as barrel racing and calf roping.

In 1916, when the Millers' show was the last Wild West show still on the road, Buffalo Bill Cody appeared briefly with them. For riding around the arena Cody received a fee of $100 a day and a percentage of the receipts. The Millers' show hung on until early in 1918. After this, no Wild West shows toured the country. The Millers' show continued erratically into the 1920s, but attempts to introduce new acts did not reinvigorate audiences. When they reopened in 1925, the Millers had added ballet dancers, a chorus of girls, and trained elephants. The Millers tried to return to the show circuit, but they and their show were too late.

Another unfortunate factor in their decline was the Great Depression. Though the Millers had the ranch to finance their entertainment efforts, falling box office receipts, rising costs at the ranch, and lowered prices for farm products took their toll and the ranch collapsed in the 1930s. The Miller show went into bankruptcy and closed for good in 1931, following the death of two of the brothers, Joe and George. Their beloved Oklahoma family ranch went into receivership and was sold at auction.

The Rising Showman Tom Mix

One of the most successful performers to come out of the Miller Brothers' ranch show was Tom Mix, who subsequently went on to a successful movie career.

Mix was born Thomas Hezikiah Mix in 1880 in Mix Run, Pennsylvania. When he turned eighteen he dropped Hezikiah in favor of Edwin, which was his father's first name. Before becoming a Wild West and movie performer he had a varied career, including physical fitness trainer and boxing instructor.[12] From this point forward his real past became clouded by distortions and half-truths.

When the United States declared war on Spain in 1898, Mix enlisted in the military, hoping to fight in Cuba. Instead, he was assigned to an artillery unit that guarded the Du Pont gunpowder works in Delaware. He was honorably discharged in 1901. When the Boer War started in Africa, Mix reenlisted, hoping to fight at last. However, bored with army life, he took a furlough in 1902 to visit his new wife and never returned. He was officially classified as a deserter, but the army never pursued any action against him.[13]

Mix was a bartender at the Blue Belle Saloon in Guthrie, Oklahoma, when he met Joe and Zack Miller and they offered him a job.[14] During his employment at the 101 Ranch, he learned to ride and rope well enough to compete in rodeos. He also helped to entertain guests at the 101 Ranch's dude ranch operation. He specialized in telling tall cowboy tales (called "windies") to guests, during which he included some of his own magnified exploits.

In April 1905, Mix appeared with many of the Millers' riders in Colonel Mulhall's Wild West show at Madison Square Garden as a twenty-five-year-old cowhand calling himself Tom Mixco from Mexico. The show included bronco busting, a demonstration of a Pony Express ride, an Indian war dance, and trick riding and roping. One of the featured performers was Lucille Mulhall, the daughter of Colonel Zack Mulhall, who started *Mulhall's Congress of Rough Riders and Ropers* in 1899. Called the "Queen of the Range" and "America's First Cowgirl," she specialized in lassoing bulls and tying them up. She also rode bucking broncos.[15] She was a champion roper and in one event roped eight horses at the same time.

After Mix joined the 101 show, he rapidly rose to the level of featured performer. For a while he played the part of the horse thief who was dragged to death behind a horse. After Mix became a movie star, he re-created this stunt for the film *The Law and the Outlaw* (1913) in a scene where his foot catches in a stirrup and he is dragged behind his horse. In 1909 Mix joined the Wilderman Wild West show, then Will A. Dickey's *Circle D Wild West Show and Indian Congress*, where he tended the livestock.

Mix used his marksmanship and riding and rodeo skills in his movies. He was a natural actor and played what was necessary in his films, unlike Cody, who wanted authenticity in his Wild West show. Mix's early Westerns featured tough masculine characters, and he played whatever the script called for, whether it was cowboy, sheriff, Indian, Mexican, horse thief, or outlaw.

Mix's background in ranching and the Millers' show were a useful common combination for early movies. Moviemakers often visited Wild West shows to film action shots. For their part, performers wanted employment during their shows' off-seasons and they were quite willing to do daredevil stunts. In this way, the heroes of Wild West shows, early movies, and rodeo performances were all interconnected. Many of the movie star heroes of the 1920s and 1930s, such as Buck Jones, William Boyd, Hoot Gibson, Ken Maynard, and Tim McCoy, appeared in Wild West shows and developed their cowboy skills there.

From 1929 to 1931 Mix appeared in the Sells-Floto Circus that Buffalo Bill appeared in. In 1934, Mix purchased the Sam B. Dill Circus and converted it to the *Tom Mix Circus and Wild West*, but it was not a success and eventually failed. The stock market crash in 1929 cost him a great deal of money and he ended up in trouble over taxes.

Decline of the Wild West Shows

As America moved into the twentieth century, Wild West shows started to lose their appeal. The Wild West show as an entertainment form began to decline in popularity from about 1905 to the end of the traveling Wild West shows in 1917, which resulted in a marked slump in profitability. One reason was that the up-and-coming entertainment form of the

After Wild West shows faded away in the late 1910s, rodeo started to rise as a popular sport and carried on the skills that early cowboys riding the range had to perform as part of their jobs. Rodeo is still popular today. This cowboy is competing in tie-down roping (formerly called calf roping), where a rider has to rope a calf from a galloping horse, dismount, throw the calf, and tie its legs together. The fastest time among the competitors wins the event (author's collection).

movies could provide excitement for audiences without having to transport a huge show of horses, riders, and scenery all over the country. Movies were a novelty and had the power to surprise, such as when actor Justus Barnes shoots into the audience from the screen at the beginning (or end, as the exhibitor desired) of *The Great Train Robbery* (1903).

The Wild West shows had evolved to meet the demands of American audiences but, like other forms of entertainment, the public eventually started to lose interest and turn to something else. There were no major Wild West shows on the road by 1918, though they were partially replaced by shows that featured cowboys backed by circus and vaudeville acts. The Wild West shows disappeared completely in the 1930s as a result of competition from movies and changes in public tastes in entertainment. While they lasted, the Wild West shows had unparalleled success as part of the Western mythmaking enterprise. However, even as the Wild West shows declined, rodeo, which could be thought of as the offspring of the Wild West shows, underwent a sudden increase in popularity. Today, the biggest and most famous of the rodeos are Frontier Days in Cheyenne, Wyoming; the Calgary Stampede in Alberta, Canada; and the Oregon Round-Up in Pendleton, Oregon.

When the Wild West shows vanished and ranching declined, many out-of-work cowboys headed for Hollywood. Stunt riders were needed in the movies to perform ever more daring pieces of action. Cowboys heard that a man could make more money for falling off a horse than he ever made by staying on it working with cows. Film employment was uncertain for these cowboys, but if they hung around, a director would probably show up and hire them for a day. In this way, real cowboys acting as extras filmed against the rugged backdrop of the West created a further link in the hero myth.

7

Our Cowboy Heroes

Lean and lanky, sitting tall in the saddle and wearing a white hat, riding wild and free across the plains, defeating outlaws and rescuing the defenseless—Holly George-Warren[1]

Towards the end of the 1880s the cowboy entered American popular literature and came to the forefront as a new type of Western hero in Wild West shows. Cowboys began replacing the frontier woodsmen as a cultural icon. The tomahawk of the early Indian sagas in the forests of the East was traded for the six-gun, the cowboy hat, and high-heeled cowboy boots. As the cowboy's popularity grew, his image was expanded by journalists from eastern newspapers, dime novelists, and Wild West shows. Later, pulp novels, radio, movies, and television added their input and interpretation to the myth. Today the name "cowboy" conjures up various images: the hero of dime novels, the Wild West show performer, the Hollywood actor, the singing cowboy of radio and movies, and modern dude ranch wranglers and rodeo performers.

Buffalo Bill created a clean-cut cowboy image in the *Wild West* and made his work and lifestyle seem glamorous. Kathryn Esselman sums this up: "The modern cowboy here became defined through a process of wedding the traditional frontiersman to the knight while visually defining him according to the conventions set by Buffalo Bill's Wild West Show and the Western melodramas."[2] The cowboys' performances consisted of riding bucking broncos and demonstrating horsemanship, roping skills, and steer riding, much of which later became part of the sport of rodeo. This image of "cowboy fun" was enhanced by performers like Buck Taylor, who performed trick shooting and exhibitions of riding skills. One of Taylor's riding tricks was to gallop on horseback across the arena at full speed and pick up a hat or handkerchief as he did so.

When the cowboy figure had appeared earlier in fictional stories of the West, he was usually only a minor figure and not the gallant hero.[3] These tales concentrated mostly on desperadoes against a background of the West's rugged wilderness, and the cowboy was represented as just another violent and lawless inhabitant of the frontier. But by the 1890s, the cowboy started to move into the spotlight as the primary Western fictional hero. In the romantic myth, the cowboy was a strong taciturn loner who rode the range with no apparent purpose and no visible means of support. He became willingly or by circumstance involved in dangerous situations when he encountered a town, a bad-man, or a woman. Plots were basically good versus evil or one of several variations on that theme. The cowboy hero was allowed to kill selectively and unpunished to right wrongs and punish the villain.

The mythic image of the cowboy hero was that of a pistol-packing, whiskey-drinking knight of the plains who symbolized rugged individualism. He was a dashing crusader against evil on the plains. The hero was typically an outsider who was unable to fit into society and, as a result, wandered from place to place. He was silent, kind, noble, generous, patriotic, pious, slow to anger, and quick to avenge his (or the heroine's) honor. The hero was also strong, gentle, handsome, and good to his horse, and though he was often tempted to dally with the saloon girl, he didn't usually do anything about it.

The Real Cowboy

Before Wild West shows became popular, Americans, particularly those in the East, didn't know much or really care about cowboys until the rise of the dime novel entrenched the Western cowboy hero as a cultural icon. In time, with the help of Wild West shows, the cowboy image was transformed into a romanticized vision of rugged individualism. To the readers of dime novels and audiences at Wild West shows, the concept of men wearing guns and high-heeled boots out West as they conducted their daily lives created an image of self-assurance and manliness. The armed cowboy became a symbol of chivalry, courage, honor, and loyalty.

Cody's version of Western history in the *Wild West* proposed that cowboys were a force in expanding and settling the West, which they weren't. In real life, cowboys worked on ranches or were common laborers on horseback hired to drive cattle from Texas to shipping railheads in Kansas. The basic requirement for the job was to be able to stay on a horse for long periods of time. Cowboys on ranches rounded up and branded cattle, gathered hay, mended fences, and performed the other monotonous chores that kept a cattle ranch running. They were generally overworked, underfed, and poorly paid. Cowboys on the cattle drives made about $30 a month, giving them about $90 for an entire summer's work. Cowboys were not colonizers, farmers, town founders, merchants, or railroad builders, though occasionally they were horse thieves, murderers, or stage robbers. The cowboy was not the same as a cattleman. The cowboy was the unskilled laborer who worked for the cattleman and was a hired hand who had to work hard to earn his pay or be fired.

Opinions of cowboys varied. In 1883, *Frank Leslie's Illustrated Weekly* stated that, "morally, as a class, they are foul-mouthed, blasphemous, drunken, lecherous, utterly corrupt. Usually harmless on the Plains when sober, they are dreaded in the towns, for then liquor has the ascendancy over them."[4] But within a few years, as stories about cowboys became popular in dime novels and national magazines, the image underwent a reversal. In 1886, *Harper's Weekly* had a completely different opinion: "Cow-boys as a class are brimful and running over with wit, merriment, good humor.... Altogether cow-boys are a whole-souled, large-hearted, generous class of fellows."[5] Some still see him as the upright hero of the West, while others remember him as a wild, lawless loner always gunning down those who stood in his way.

The original name "cowboy," written as "cow-boy" or "cow boy," was derogatory. The name was originally used for bands of guerrilla outlaws who stole cattle and sold them to the British during the American Revolution, and in the 1870s to Texas bandits who rustled Mexican cattle.[6] Cow-boys in the Arizona Territory were responsible for the bloodshed in the 1880s that culminated in the fight at the O.K. Corral and a threat by President Chester Arthur in 1882 to impose martial law. In the movies the name was first applied to working

7. Our Cowboy Heroes

Real cowboys and their lifestyle were not as glamorous as they were depicted in movies and dime novels. The men worked long hard hours in the saddle, branding, dehorning, castrating, and doctoring cattle, as shown here in 1891. They often even had to break and tame their own horses. They were not the slick gunmen of the movies and their employers typically did not allow them to carry guns while on the job (Library of Congress).

ranch hands, then it was generically applied to anyone who rode a horse and carried a Colt .45 and used his gun to uphold justice. Another name for a cowboy was "waddy," also spelled "waddie." This name was used particularly for a cowboy who drifted from ranch to ranch helping out during busy times.

The alternate name of "cowhand" appeared as early as 1847 but was not generally used until about 1880.[7] Before that the name *vaquero* had been used to describe early Spanish settlers who worked with cattle. The most popular name, and that used in the Kansas cattle towns in the 1870s, was "drover" because that described what a cattle worker did.[8] The names herder, herdsman, and cowboy were occasionally used but not commonly. Then the name caught on with dime novelists who used it to describe a quick-tempered, gun-slinging, no-account character.

As Buck Rainey has pointed out, the real cowboy was mostly drab, hardworking, hard-drinking, illiterate, shabbily dressed, oversexed, and not particularly ambitious.[9] The life of a real cowboy was not particularly pleasant. Life on the cattle trail involved dangerous river crossings, rustlers, hostile Indians, stampedes, drought, torrential rain, hail, snowstorms, sleet, mud, quicksand, tornadoes, poor water supplies, prairie wildfires, snakes, mosquitoes, ticks, and belligerent cattle. The cowboy had to work under a scorching sun in choking clouds of dust, with an ever-present danger of lightning and violent thunderstorms. As old-time cowboy Ramon F. Adams said, there was little romance "in gettin' up at four o'clock in the mornin', eatin' dust behind a trail herd, swimmin' muddy and turbulent rivers, nor in doctorin' screw worms, pullin' stupid cows from bog holes, sweatin' in the heat of summer and freezin' in the cold of winter."[10] Being a real cowboy was hard and boring and involved monotonous work.

Being a roving cowboy on the trail did not lend itself to family ties or romantic relationships. It was difficult for men spending three months or more on a cattle drive to court, marry, and have a family. Besides, most didn't come into contact with decent women. Cowboys were typically in their late teens or early twenties so they could perform the intense physical work required of them and moved on to other jobs by their thirties.

The cowboy's flamboyant clothing was largely based on practicality. A large-brimmed hat protected his face and neck from sunburn and his eyes from the sun's glare. High-heeled boots for riding were designed to slip easily out of the stirrups in case the cowboy was thrown from his horse. His gun was for protection against desperadoes, wild animals, or hostile Indians in the remote reaches of the West.

The mythic cowboy was always a crack shot who could demonstrate fancy gunplay. Movie cowboys could shoot the head off a rattlesnake or the gun out of someone's hand. They were expert at fanning, twirling, and other fancy gun tricks. Real cowboys, though, were typically not good gunmen. They did not have the time or money for ammunition to continually practice their skills in order to become expert shots. A common expression among cowboys was that "he could not hit the side of a barn if he was in one."[11] Their saloon fights were often just threats and bluster instead of gunplay.

In spite of the image of cowboys swaggering around town shooting at everything in sight, many towns and counties in the West banned guns. A Nebraska law of 1867 said that a man should not carry gun, knife or club with the intent to assault another. The 1880 New Mexico statutes said that it was unlawful for a man to carry a weapon (concealed or otherwise) in any settlement in the territory except for his own defense and that of his family. Texas had ordinances against carrying a concealed weapon with the intent of harming another. In the 1870s, cattle towns such as Dodge City and Wichita had ordinances against carrying any weapons in town.

The Virginian

While Buffalo Bill legitimized the cowboy through his *Wild West*, Owen Wister's novel *The Virginian*, published in 1902, took over the image of the mythical cowboy from Cody. In it Wister brought the cowboy into new prominence in what is generally considered to be the first serious Western novel. The Virginian's image echoed Buck Taylor, and action sequences in the novel reflect the Wild West shows, with plenty of riding, shooting, and fighting. Wister blended the new cowboy hero with Wyoming's past and threw in the ingredients of adventure fiction, which were love, action, and good versus evil. Wister's writing was an artistic treatment of the West based on hero themes. He created a West that was a land of freedom, honesty, and integrity, where the wicked received the appropriate punishment.

When the hero (he has no name in the book other than the Virginian) is introduced in the book, Wister describes him in terms of cowboy worship and almost homophilic admiration. His description of the Virginian from the first few pages of the novel reads, "Lounging there at ease against the wall was a slim young giant, more beautiful than pictures. His broad, soft hat was pushed back; a loose-knotted, dull-scarlet handkerchief sagged from his throat; and one casual thumb was hooked in the cartridge-belt that slanted across his hips.... The weather-beaten bloom of his face shone through it duskily, as the ripe peaches look upon their trees in a dry season. But no dinginess of travel or shabbiness of attire could tarnish the splendor that radiated from his youth and strength.... Had I been the bride, I should have taken the giant, dust and all."[12]

The Virginian was a dashing loner in a big hat who charmed the ladies. He had all the characteristics we now associate with movie cowboys of the 1930s, but he was not representative of the cattle frontier or of the real cowboy. He was honest, healthy, virile, strong, shrewd, and gallant, living in Wister's West that was an idealized vision of a West that never was. *The Virginian* was a cowboy novel without cows. Near the end of the novel the Virginian says he does not want to be associ-

Author Owen Wister invented the first cowboy hero when his wrote his 1902 novel, *The Virginian*. This book became the template for cowboy novels even though it is a cowboy novel without cows. Wister is generally credited with inventing the classic concluding showdown between the hero and the villain, and their final gunfight (Library of Congress).

ated with the Wild West cowboy, but he and his story have become the legend. The public was obviously hungry for a new hero and the novel was an instant success. *The Virginian* went through fifteen reprints in its first year.[13] By 1904 it had sold 300,000 copies and by 1920 over a million.

Owen Wister was born in Philadelphia in 1860 and graduated from Harvard. He journeyed to the West looking for a moderate climate for his health and to gather material for a novel. He fell in love with the West and was disappointed that it was disappearing. The result was that he wrote *The Virginian*, in which he presented his own romantic vision of the West, marked by chivalry, honor, and romance, and he championed what he saw as the superiority of Western virtues. He invented the nomadic Western loner as the hero and his Virginia cowboy was what he wanted a Western hero to be. The Virginian is a genteel southerner who uses his wits but adds violence if necessary. He shares Wister's nostalgia for the vanishing West.

Wister is also generally credited with inventing the classic concluding showdown between the hero and the villain, and their final gunfight. Previous novels included shootings and even duels, but not in the way that Wister portrayed the showdown. Wister romanticized the fictional situation of the gunfighter's walk-down and gunfight where the good and the bad face each other on the street with an even break. In the real West these instances were rare. One of the few face-to-face shoot-outs was a duel between Wild Bill Hickok and Davis Tutt that took place in Springfield, Missouri, on July 21, 1865. Most gunfights in the real West tended to be drunken brawls in saloons rather than showdowns on the main street. But Wister's showdown became the norm for fiction and film. After a suitable buildup, the climactic gunfight is over in two sentences: "A wind seemed to blow his sleeve off his arm, and he replied to it, and saw Trampas pitch forward. He saw Trampas raise his arm from the ground and fall again, and lie there this time, still." As he watches the smoke curl up from the two revolvers, the finale is summed up: "'I expect that's all,' he said aloud."[14]

A type of rough-hewn "Code of the West" appears in Wister's novel. The hero gives the villain a warning to "get out of town" (or vice versa) and, if he doesn't, a final conflict and shoot-out are inevitable. In the novel, "Trampas broke suddenly free. 'Your friends have saved your life,' he rang out, with obscene epithets. 'I'll give you till sundown to leave town.'"[15] Trampas is characterized as a villain because he shoots someone in the back. In other words, he didn't adhere to Wister's Code of the West.

For Wister the "cowboy code" was a Western version of the code of honor of the southern gentleman, including courtesy and gallantry. At the same time, it was a grim code of honor and ritualized violence, as it emphasized a final duel to the death to end the feud. In real life in the Old West most gunfights started over insults and escalated immediately into threats that then led to shooting with no further warning. The practical code of the real Western gunman was self-preservation. Shoot first before you get shot.

The Virginian tries to explain his heroic code of honor to Molly when he says, "Can't yu' see how it must be about a man. It's not for their benefit, friends or enemies, that I have got this thing to do." When he tells her that he has to fight, he says, "I could not hold up my head again among friends or enemies."[16] Even though the Virginian says that he's gotta do what he's gotta do, Molly gets down on her knees to plead with him not to fight: "At that word she was at his feet, clutching him. 'For my sake,' she begged him. 'For my sake.'"[17]

The book is famous for two immortal lines. One is when the Virginian and Trampas are in a poker game and Trampas says, "Your bet, you son-of-a-...." In response, the Virginian unholsters his gun and replies, "When you call me that, smile."[18]

Even though Wister tried to portray cowboy language, some of his renditions were not much better than the dime novels, as shown by this song:

> If you go to monkey with my Looloo girl,
> I'll tell you what I'll do:
> I'll cyarve your heart with my razor, AND
> I'll shoot you with my pistol, too—[19]

The real cowboy's language did have its own ring to it, but it was often earthy and occasionally obscene, as noted in songs and limericks that have been collected by researchers.[20] Most of the naughty language used in books and early movies were bowdlerized into the likes of "goldern," "son-of-a-gun," "dern right," "shucks," and "heck."[21]

The Virginian contains some preconceived notions about cowboys and Westerners that had been spread to the East by sensationalistic newspapers. For example, a typically eastern

Though James Fenimore Cooper developed the original hero of the forests, it was Owen Wister who first propelled the cowboy into the spotlight as a literary hero in his Western novel *The Virginian*, first published in 1902. In this poignant scene from the book, Molly is kneeling as she pleads with the Virginian not to go out and face the final showdown with the villain (author's collection).

thought for the time was expressed by Molly's aunt when she says about the Virginian, "I suppose there are days when he does not kill people."[22] In the late 1870s and early 1880s almost every issue of two popular contemporary periodicals, the *Police Gazette* and *Frank Leslie's Illustrated Weekly*, had some lurid article about cowboys. The two delighted in reporting sensational description of wild and lawless behavior. The *Police Gazette* of September 6, 1879, said of cowboys, "While in town his home is in the saloons and the dance houses. He soon gets gloriously drunk and then begins to yell like a wild Indian and shoots off his big revolvers promiscuously into the crowd. He is little else than a crazy demon at such times and woe betide the man who crosses his path." By 1885 the popular periodicals were proclaiming that the real cowboy was just another indication of the crudeness and lack of sophistication of the Old West.

Though *The Virginian* was a groundbreaking story, it showed some unevenness. This is because the novel is composed of two different Virginians in two separate success stories. In the first part, told by a first-person narrator, the Virginian is an individualist who does not stray from his Western code as he lives a free life in the West. In the second part he advances from a working cowboy to the ranch foreman, and then to a full partner of the cattle ranch. Along the way he becomes educated and marries a refined young woman from the East. This second part, which includes the shoot-out with Trampas, is told from the point of view of the author. The cause of this unevenness may be partly explained by the fact that Wister worked into the plot seven previous short stories he had written about the Virginian that had appeared in *Harper's Weekly* and *Saturday Evening Post* between 1893 and 1902. Four of them were published between 1893 and 1897, and three in 1901 and 1902. As in the novel, three were written from a first-person point of view, and the other four from the point of view of an omniscient narrator. Wister did not rewrite the collected novel for consistency. *The Virginian* was originally subtitled *A Horseman of the Plains*.[23]

The Virginian was written after the very real Johnson County War of 1889 in Wyoming. But similar struggles between cattlemen and settlers were still being fought, and these struggles were incorporated into the novel. The overall moral of the story is that a young man born in poverty who inherently has exceptional skills and moral character can rise from the ranks to become a successful businessman. Of course it should be pointed out that the Virginian was not a typical cowboy, even for fictional cowboys. Over the course of the novel, he rises to ranch foreman, marries a cultured woman from the East, and goes on to become a prosperous businessman. Very few real cowboys could achieve that. But the premise provided wish-fulfillment for the reader.

The book was turned into a stage play, and in 1914 it became one of Hollywood's first full-length Westerns. The movie was remade at least four times and eventually became a television series that ran between 1962 and 1971. Though various elements of the plot were changed in each version, the Virginian himself came across as a gentlemanly knight of the Plains who was brave, strong, honest, and compassionate.

The Fictional Cowboy Image

The Virginian was the prototype for a new type of hero and the general plotting and structure of *The Virginian* have been immortalized in countless cowboy novels, movies, and television programs. His persona was grabbed by writers and filmmakers and gradually changed into a cowboy who appears in plots that are almost stereotyped. This mythic cowboy lives in a world where men are men. Even when he is the town marshal or owns a successful ranch, he appears unemployed. He is a man of leisure. He spends much of his time in the saloon playing poker in the evening or camping out in the wide open spaces. He owns one set of clothes, his horse, and his gun. As portrayed on the screen, he is usually a solitary and rugged hero who works alone—or sometimes with a sidekick. This cowboy hero has no past, no particular friends, never starts a fight but always wins it, and does not draw first. He shows limited interest in women. Sometimes he rides into town with only his saddlebags, but he somehow miraculously conjures out of them a clean new suit, a white shirt, and even a new full-sized cowboy hat. He is apparently not a poor man. He always seems to have adequate money in order to eat, gamble and drink in the saloon, and leads a comfortable life at the local hotel or boardinghouse. He can ride a horse faultlessly, draw a gun faster than anyone else, and shoot better than everyone. He loves the wide expanses of land in the West and his horse. The hero always lives in about 1870, though not the real 1870 of history.

Cooper's Leatherstocking was on foot as he moved silently around the eastern forests, but the fictional Western cowboy hero has to have a horse. An unhorsed cowboy is small and uninspiring and loses dignity. A horse has great value as an image of power, authority, and leadership, as symbolized by the Lone Ranger rearing up on Silver at the beginning of each show of the television series. The cowboy's horse is bigger and stronger than a man. The hero's horse is a matter of life and death in the vast open spaces of the West and makes it easier to cover the untracked deserts and mountains, but it is also his companion. The hero becomes one with his horse and will give it his last drop of water. A handsome bridle and saddle are part of the image and the 1930s movie hero had to have a fancy tooled leather saddle. Saddle, bedroll, and rifle all add to the image of tough, reliable, self-sufficient masculinity.

The mythic cowboy also has to have various guns, including revolver, carbine, rifle, or shotgun, to back up his virility and toughness, to resolve physical conflicts, and to bring order to the frontier. A man without a gun would not be able to defend himself in the supposed dangerous frontier world of dime-novel villains and bad-men, so the revolver became an essential accessory. The hero has to have great skill with it and be faster on the draw than the villain. The final gunfight is the classic climax of the Western novel or film that brings resolution of the plot. A gun was considered to be used well and wisely by the hero, but not by the bad-man. As author John Lenihan has pointed out, "the heroes were usually those who displayed an expertise at shooting quickly and accurately as well as the wisdom to shoot discriminately and justly."[24]

Several other Hollywood characteristics were added to the mythical gunman. The sinister-looking gunman's crouch, for example. This serves no practical purpose in a gunfight, but adds to the visual menace during a showdown. Similarly, riding a galloping horse while sitting upright is contrived. Leaning forward in a riding crouch, such as that used by jockeys, lowers the center of gravity, gives less wind resistance, and allows better control of the horse. But the straight-up posture, like that used by William S. Hart, creates a much more heroic image. Another contrived item was the practice of "throwing bullets" seen in many of the B Westerns, where the shooter brings the revolver down sharply in the air while he is pulling the trigger so it looks like the bullets are being thrown out of the barrel. This may look dramatic, but it produces rotten aim.

The dime novels described the hero in sensual terms such as tall, muscular, sinewy, sunburned, prime of manhood, rugged, slim, lean, a giant, and virile. Some critics have gone so far as to suggest that these descriptions, coupled with riding a horse and shooting a gun, suggest blatant overtones of sexual symbolism. However, phallic symbolism of power and sexuality is beyond this book and lies in the realm of Freudian psychologists.

One of the enduring heroic characters of movies is the roving gunfighter who fights violence with violence. Like the chivalrous image of the cowboy, his myth has been exaggerated by Hollywood. In one scene in *The Magnificent Seven* (1960), the men are sitting around philosophizing on their lives as gunfighters. The new recruit to the ranks, Chico (Horst Buchholz), asks, "Your gun has got you everything you have. Isn't that true?" Vin (Steve McQueen), lamenting the life of a gunfighter, replies, "After a while you can call bartenders and faro dealers by their first name. Home, none. Wife, none. Kids, none. Prospects, zero." Chris (Yul Brynner) and the others add, "Places you're tied down to, none. People with a hold on you, none. Men you step aside for, none. Insults swallowed, none. Enemies, none." The sentiment of the movie gunman as a loner is echoed further at the end of the film when Chris and Vin survey the village as they are leaving. Chris echoes the mournful credo of the movie gunfighter: "We lost. We always will." This emphasizes the legend of the lone gunfighter. On the contrary, real gunmen, both good and bad, were usually married and many had children, just like the other settlers and inhabitants of the real West.

In reality, mythic characters have to remain mythic. When the woman gets the hero at the end of the movie, he stops being a cowboy or gunman—or whatever he is—and settles down, like Will Kane (Gary Cooper) in *High Noon* (1952). Or his life becomes that of Will Munny (Clint Eastwood) in *Unforgiven* (1992). He marries, has children, and settles down to farming in a life of drudgery. He becomes someone, or something, other than the wandering gunman. Having a wife and being a family man change everything. As Munny says of his wife, "She cured me of drink and wickedness." That would be the end of the legend.

The Cowboy Code

The days of the Western frontier could be described as vigorous independence. Independence in the worst sense often led to killing, which was part of survival on the frontier and so became part of the legend of the West. The myth was, however, that a man who took up a gun to civilize the West was a good guy, not a killer criminal. It comes as a surprise to the audience if the hero doesn't have a gun, such as in *Destry Rides Again* (1939) or *The Man Who Shot Liberty Valance* (1962). We expect every red-blooded cowboy hero to have a gun. As part of the supposed Code of the West of fiction and film, the hero has to make the fight fair. He keeps his gun in its holster until his opponent draws first, and the code says you don't shoot an unarmed man. Much of the code came from the chivalry of duels in the South. The cowboy hero is perceived as a form of Western knight, so the code became a concept of honor and insult that must be avenged.

Author Jenni Calder puts it this way: "According to the mythic code the badman will crouch behind a rock, rub dirt on the barrel so that the glint won't betray him, and shoot a man in the back. The good man will face his enemy and make sure his enemy is facing him. He will call out to warn him before he draws and fires. These are the rules of the game. It is a clear-cut code which provides a fair-minded, gentlemanly license to kill. In the West killing in self-defense, even if you provoked your enemy to draw on you, was always justifiable homicide."[25]

Contrast this with what really happened in the Old West. In a real gunfight, the man who started to draw first and had his gun in his hand first would always win.[26] This was an inescapable fact based on the reaction time of the human nervous system. Though Charley Waite (Kevin Costner) in *Open Range* (2004) pulled his gun in a most unsportsman-like fashion and shot one of the bad guys in the face without warning, the reality is that he was the one who survived the confrontation. Real lawmen tried to go into a fight with their gun in their hand, usually with the hammer already cocked. Serious gunfighters and lawmen used a cocked shotgun.

In the cowboy-gunfighter myth, it was acceptable for the hero to kill to resolve the conflict in the plot, even if he was not a lawman, and walk away. In the real West it was not so simple. Even lawmen who killed in the line of duty had to answer to coroner's courts, judicial hearings, and formal trials. After the famous shoot-out at the O.K. Corral, the Earp brothers, who represented the law in Tombstone, were summoned to the courtroom to answer charges of murder for the killings of the McLaurys and Billy Clanton. Eventually the charges were dismissed, but only after lengthy legal hearings.

John Wayne

The ultimate Western cowboy hero in many people's minds is John Wayne. Wayne, one of best-known movie actors in the world, played other film roles but has always been identified with the cowboy. His popularity can be measured by the fact that his films grossed $800 million.[27] Wayne is a good example of an actor blending with his screen persona. When he started making movies for Warner Brothers they wanted the audience to think that he was not just another actor in a role but a real cowboy adventurer named John Wayne. In the six Westerns he made for them in 1932 and 1933 he was always named John. This was an extension of the blurring of screen persona and the real actor that was developed by Buffalo Bill Cody fifty years earlier.

Wayne tried to play the Western cowboy with reality. He felt that stars of the 1920s and 1930s were too perfect. He wanted to play a real man who drank and smoked, got mud on his clothes, and fought dirty if he had to. Roy Rogers always fought fair, even if his opponent didn't. Wayne, however, tried to be more realistic in his portrayal of the hero. He believed that the outcome of a fight was survival and if his screen character wanted to win, he had to fight as his opponent did. Wayne's character was not above hitting his opponent unexpectedly if it was necessary for him to win a fight. He did have his limits, however. In the original script for *The Shootist* (1976), when one of Books' (John Wayne) assailants was wounded and trying to get through the barroom door, Books was supposed to shoot him in the back. Wayne, however, said he would not do that as it would be "unthinkable for my image."[28]

Wayne's career started at a time when Western stars differentiated themselves by their costumes. Wayne's Western look became almost a uniform. In his movies, he often wore dusty, frayed jeans or pants, the same battered hat, dusty boots, and the same .45 Colt in the same holster behind his right hip. Wayne's bib-front shirt with two rows of buttons going up the front and widening towards the shoulders emphasized his chest and became a trademark.[29] In his movies, if he liked the girl he kissed her. This was the new Western hero according to Wayne.

Wayne's early film *Tall in the Saddle* (1944) would today be considered a stereotype of the Western movie plot. He plays a well-dressed, laconic, mysterious cowboy who rides into town with no visible means of support but with enough money to spend. One of the women in the plot is a prim, demure blonde from the East, with her hair worn up in the style that women of the late 1800s did wear in real life, and she wears dresses. The other woman is a fiery brunette with long loose hair in a style reminiscent of the 1940s (when the movie was indeed made), who dresses for most of the movie in leather chaps. She plays an independent woman who runs the ranch. When her father sends Wayne up to the line camp, he says, "Don't mind working a lone hand, do you?" Wayne replies, "I like working that way." After a run-in with both women, Wayne says, "No woman is going to get me hog-tied and branded." And they don't—well, at least until the last scene of the picture when one of them does.

Though John Wayne's career as a Western hero has long been a subject of mockery and comedic impressions (such as the way his walk was satirized in *The Birdcage* [1996]), for the most part Wayne did not play a typical cowboy in a typical Western. His screen portrayals show differences, from *Fort Apache* (1948) to *The Searchers* (1956) to *True Grit* (1969) to *The Cowboys* (1972). He generally played a determined man of honesty, loyalty, and integrity. In *True Grit* (1969), however, Wayne went against his previous heroic image by playing an old, fat, crotchety, hard-drinking, profane character.

Wayne was subject to ups and downs in his career. As the depression hit, his starring role in *The Big Trail* (1930) was not greeted with commercial success, which was one factor that led studios to stop production of major Westerns for the rest of the 1930s. This failure had the additional effect of hurting Wayne's emerging movie career and he had to go back to making B Westerns. His career as a star bounced back at the end of the decade with *Stagecoach* (1939), a movie that was responsible for reviving the demand for Westerns in the 1940s. *Stagecoach* (1939), which pioneered the social Western, was received with great acclaim and was a huge commercial success.

Wayne played cowboys for almost fifty years and helped to define the contemporary version of the Western hero, much as Tom Mix did in his day. Wayne was consistently a popular Hollywood actor, but his popularity came at the expense of being limited to certain roles. His link between his screen roles and his real self became so intricately identified with the Western that he was perceived to be an authentic representative of the Old West. His screen persona was so strongly identified with cowboy roles in Westerns that this was what audiences expected and his roles started to blur between the character and the real man. Conversely, like Buffalo Bill, Wayne became so identified with the Western genre that his pictures were perceived as authenticating his movies.

8

Flickering Images

Risking the charge of overstatement, Westerns, especially Western movies, are thus far the single most important American story form of the twentieth century—Jack Nachbar[1]

One of the twentieth century's most influential mediums has been motion pictures. Cinema is driven by its product and marketed in terms of genre, the popularity of the genre, and the star system. The Western film, like any other movie genre, has constantly changed as a result of contemporary social conditions, audience demographics, tastes, and censorship, and associated changes in exhibition, distribution, and technical developments in film production.

The Wild West shows of the last two decades of the nineteenth century created the showman cowboy hero and paved the way for his successor in Western movies. Many of the acts from these live shows were duplicated by the heroes of early Western films, both in documentaries and in fictional plots. The cowboy, then, became the leading male hero of Western movies. Some of these Western stars achieved the status of fantasy figures.

Motion pictures brought a profound change to the nation's culture and permanently impacted the public's leisure and entertainment activities. Western films became popular partly because they could be viewed anywhere, at any time, at a local theater instead of making a special journey to see a Wild West show or rodeo. Movies affected how the nation saw itself and its history. Though early film patrons believed that they were seeing an educational and historical part of the nation's past, in reality filmmakers deliberately manipulated the past and reconstructed historical events to lure crowds of paying patrons. Due to commercial necessity, the motion picture industry has always adapted its product to variations in public desires to appeal to the widest possible audience. As Fenin and Everson complained, "reconstruction of historical events was and still is changed to suit the script."[2]

In 1925, the production of Westerns numbered 227. For most of the years between 1926 and 1967, Westerns made up 25 percent of the movies being made. Over 4,000 Western movies were made in the sound era alone. By the 1950s a large number of Western series appeared on television. Forty-eight series were on the air in 1955 alone.[3] This overexposure started a decline in Western feature film production.

Humble Beginnings

In 1894 the first Kinetoscope, a mechanical device that rapidly flipped a series of still pictures in front of the viewer's eye to create the illusion of motion, was demonstrated in

New York. Though not a movie as we now know it, the concept was popular with viewers, as it created movement in pictures. That same year, the first true motion pictures and movie projector were demonstrated in Paris by the Lumière Brothers. Edison's Vitascope projector debuted in the United States in 1896 and forever changed the face of popular entertainment. Later that year, short films were commonly being shown in vaudeville theaters.

Movies soon broke away from vaudeville to become a separate entertainment form. From 1905 to 1910 was the era of the Nickelodeon, a room with a projector and a screen that showed movies for an admission price of a nickel—hence the name. This became an ideal form of cheap entertainment for adults and families with little money to spare. Estimates are that by 1908 there were between 8,000 and 10,000 Nickelodeons in the United States.[4] Early movies were filmed in black and white and were silent because a method of recording and synchronizing sound and the visual image had not yet been developed. This was not all bad, as silent movies presented no language barrier to the incoming flood of immigrants to the East Coast, who spoke many different languages.

The First "Westerns"

Films with a Western theme have been part of the motion picture industry since its beginning. Part of this was fueled by the popularity of previous Western stage melodramas, dime novels, and Wild West shows. The Edison Company made many short documentary films about the West, including *Cattle Fording Stream* (1898); *Lassoing Steer* (1899); *Herd of Cattle* (1901); *Broncho Busting Scenes, Championship of the World* (1902); *A Bucking Broncho* (1903); *Driving Cattle to Pasture* (1904); *Rounding Up and Branding Cattle* (1904); and *Bucking Bronchos* (1904). Documentary short films showing travel in the West were also popular. Examples are *Canyon of the Rio Grande* (1898); *Coaches Arriving at Mammoth Hot Springs* (1899); *Lower Falls, Grand Canyon, Yellowstone Park* (1899); and *A Trip Through the Yellowstone Park, USA* (1918). Many of these early silent Westerns showed a romantic, nostalgic, and sentimental view of the West.

Edison's Company filmed anything and everything, including parts of Buffalo Bill's Wild West. *Annie Oakley* (1894) documented Oakley shooting at glass balls. *Parade of Buffalo Bill's Wild West Show* (1898) and *Buffalo Bill's Wild West Parade* (1902) showed Buffalo Bill entering New York in a parade.

Though not the first Western with a fictional story, *The Great Train Robbery* (1903), filmed by director Edwin S. Porter for the Edison Company, created an enthusiastic interest in Westerns and the West among the movie-going public. The story was a straightforward one where a gang of bandits holds up a train (which was a contemporary real event), robs the passengers and shoots one, is chased by a posse from town, and then is confronted in a final shoot-out with guns blazing on both sides. The film was longer than most previous ones, running for eleven minutes, or about one reel.[5] The camera technique was more sophisticated and featured changing camera angles instead of the previous typical static camera position, and the editing was used to help tell the story. Though not the first fictional story to use these advanced techniques, this picture used them to great advantage and to the delight of audiences.

After the success of *The Great Train Robbery*, Edison and his competitors churned out

Reading about contemporary real train robberies in the newspapers and fictional ones in dime novels in the late 1890s, along with sensational images like this lithograph created in 1896 depicting a daring railroad holdup, created an awareness and heightened interest in train robberies, which led to later popular motion pictures such as *The Great Train Robbery* (1903) and *The Great K & A Train Robbery* (1926) (Library of Congress).

a series of train robbery films to try to repeat its success. Examples are *The Little Train Robbery* (1905) and *The Hold-Up of the Rocky Mountain Express* (1906). To try to create a newer element than train holdups as the basis for plots, moviemakers turned to bank robberies, cranking out such gems as *The Bold Bank Robbery* (1904) and *The Great Bank Robbery* (1913). The theme of stagecoach robbery, such as the two-minute long *Western Stage Coach Hold Up* (1904), was used for further variety. Many of these early Western movies were direct descendants of dime novels and stage melodramas and consisted of little more than a chase and a fight. They were filled with guns, knives, abductions, robberies, chases, and fights. Cowboys in them might be villains or heroes.

The popularity of *The Great Train Robbery* (1903) helped to shape the image of future Westerns. Audiences were thrilled by the tale of the train robbery, the chase, and the final shoot-out. Other filmmakers naturally rushed to copy these criminal elements. Examples were *A Lynching at Cripple Creek* (1904) and *The Hold-Up of the Leadville Stage* (1904) made by Harry Buckwalter, who was filming promotional movies in Colorado for Selig Polyscope Company. Selig developed the basic format for the Western by combining Colorado scenery with elements of crime, stage melodrama, and the Wild West shows. These films were characterized by holdups, chases, gambling, and shooting played out against scenic landscapes in the West.

Violent crime pictures were popular. In the fictional *Cowboy Justice* (1904), a gambler shoots a cowboy, then is dragged out to a flat prop tree and lynched by the victim's friends. British filmmakers followed the crime trend with *A Daring Daylight Burglary* (1903) and

Trailed by Bloodhounds (1903). Some early filmmakers followed the Cody recipe for authenticity by combining scenes and stories from the dime novels and stage melodrama with authentic details of landscapes and costume. Plots featured sheriffs, outlaws, bad Indians, good Indians, Mexican villains, and heroic outlaws. Edwin Porter's *Life of a Cowboy* (1906) contained a rudimentary plot line of a bandit and a band of Indians robbing a stagecoach, then being thwarted by a heroic cowboy. After 1909 the number of Westerns increased as filmmakers found they could produce them easily and inexpensively. The increase was also driven by a rapid growth in the number of nickelodeons, which created a rising demand for movies.

Part of the attraction of Western movies was their background scenery of the open spaces of the West, represented by vast plains, high mountains, and harsh desert scenery. Sprinkled somewhere in this untamed film version of nature were the beginnings of White civilization represented by ranches, forts, and small towns populated by sheriffs, saloons, banks, schools, and churches. Towns were represented by a few isolated buildings peopled with extras who appear to just wait around for any dramatic confrontation.

Filmmakers went to the West to create sensational films with the unique and authentic scenery of real locations. A second reason, however, was to avoid the Motion Picture Patents Company (also known as the Edison Trust), formed in the East by a group of motion picture studios and distribution companies in 1908 with the goal of trying to monopolize the production of motion pictures. The group even went to the length of persuading Eastman Kodak to sell raw film stock only to member companies. As part of an overall strategy, the group did not give special recognition to individuals as stars, because they did not want actors to become popular and demand higher wages. Independent producers who filmed in the West to escape control of the Motion Picture Patents Company Trust started to feature actors as "stars" as a way of attracting repeat audiences to their films to see favorite performers. In this way, actors such as Douglas Fairbanks and Charlie Chaplin gained more control over their pictures and received higher salaries. The courts eventually declared the trust to be an illegal restraint of trade and it was officially terminated in 1918. Thus was the star system born.

The first generation of fictional Western movies reinforced the popular ideas about the American West that easterners gained from the sensationalist dime novels and newsmagazines such as the *Police Gazette*. As early as the 1910s, critics of Westerns wanted to change this representation of the West. Reviewers complained that too many of the plots and themes were adapted from the sensationalist media, which indeed they were. Some felt that there was a lack of "realistic pictures."[6] The opinion of some was that the criminal activity and lurid violence that had crept into movies should be reduced. Others felt that the association with dime novels, stage melodramas, and cheap sensational journalism was a working-class entertainment and they claimed that there should be loftier ideals. Still others wanted to introduce more romantic elements and more heroic figures who could convey moral lessons. One suggestion was to go back to the theme of the Wild West shows, which had provided a romanticized view of the West and performers who appealed to all age groups as heroic figures. Even other critics complained that there were just too many Westerns to the exclusion of other type of movies.

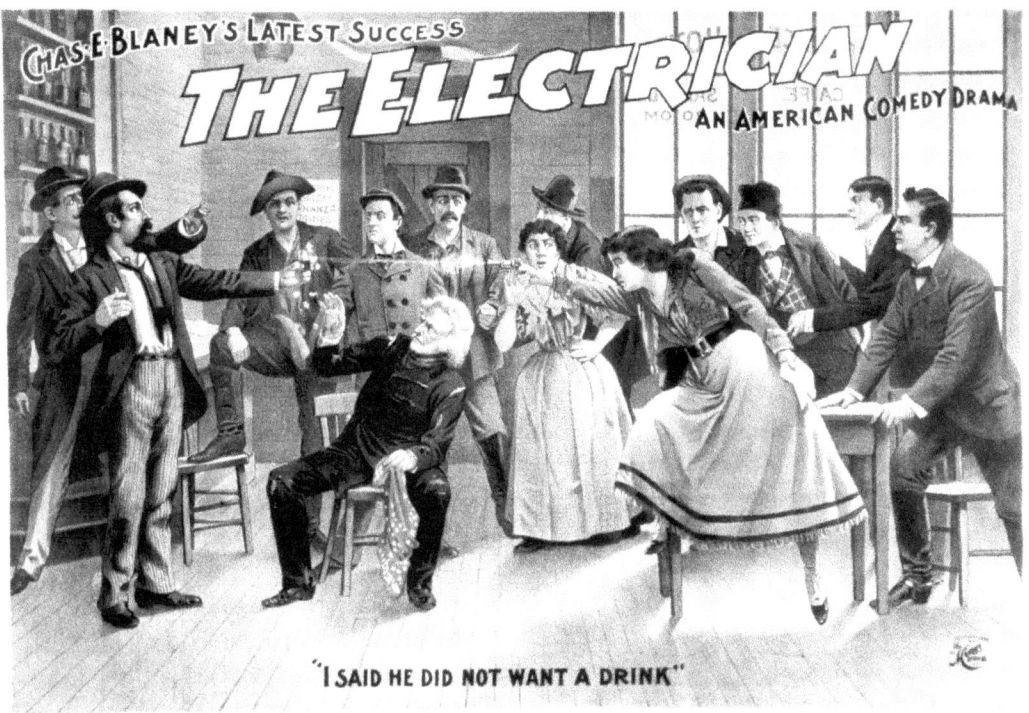

An 1898 advertising poster from *Tom Edson, the Electrician*, a comic satire based on the use of the newfangled electricity. This spunky heroine shows that she is a crack shot as she shoots the glass out of a man's hand to make her point (Library of Congress).

The Indian Era

Filmmakers looking for new plots to set in a Western landscape discovered the Indians and made them the focus of some of the earliest Western motion pictures. At first these were not fictional stories, but reflected a documentary approach that showcased Native American culture. One example was *Sioux Ghost Dance* (1894) filmed by the Edison Company. Similar short movies were *Carrying Out the Snakes* (1901), which featured the snake ceremony of the Hopi tribe in Arizona, and *Wand Dance, Pueblo Indians* (1898). The later *A Pueblo Legend* (1913) featured authentic dancers from the Isleta Pueblo, just south of Albuquerque, New Mexico. Other documentary films included the thirty-second *Serving Rations to the Indians* (1898).

As movie attendance rose in popularity during the early 1900s, fictional plots were added that centered around Native Americans as the noble savage. Indians were presented as being superior to the Whites, interestingly at a time when Indians were not particularly prominent in popular culture. Typical films were *The Red Girl* (1908), *The Aborigines Devotion* (1909), *Her Indian Mother* (1910), *A Redskin's Bravery* (1911), *For the Papoose* (1912), and *Hiawatha* (1913). Filmmaker D.W. Griffith made several motion pictures with Indian themes in 1908, including *The Redman and the Child*; *The Girl and the Outlaw*; *The Red Girl*; and *The Call of the Wild*. This type of Indian film became very popular in Europe.

One obsessive theme in these fictional stories was an Indian hero who became involved with a White woman. In a typical example of this type of plot, a noble Indian leaves the reservation to be an athlete in college. He is marginally accepted in the White world because he is a natural athlete and excels at sports, but he is not accepted socially. Among early silent movies with this theme were *Red Eagle's Love Affair* (1910), *Strongheart* (1914), *Braveheart* (1925), and *Redskin* (1929). In *The Squaw Man* (1914) Dustin Farnum played a disgraced English earl who ends up with a squaw and a half-breed child. At the end he accidentally (but conveniently for the plot) shoots his wife.

In *The Vanishing American* (1925), an adaptation of the Zane Grey novel of the same name, Nophaie (Richard Dix) dreams of peace and prosperity for his people but finds only treachery at the hands of the local Indian agent, Henry Booker (Wallace Beery). Nophaie gains support from a few of the local residents and from the heroine, Marian Warner (Lois Wilson), whom he loves. He joins the army and fights in World War I, but comes back to find that Booker has taken over the land. During the inevitable conflict, Booker is killed and Nophaie is mortally wounded. This romantic view of the Indian was that he was a god-like pagan. He was portrayed as fierce, but lacking knowledge of the ways of the White world. His primitive ways were forgiven because they were accompanied by his child-like simplicity.

The other approach to Indians was to show them as villains to be cut down in vast numbers. Earlier dime novels had described the valiant White man killing Indians by the score. In keeping with this plot device, some early Hollywood movies portrayed the Indian as a savage enemy to be defeated in the inexorable westward movement of the White man. Settlers, prospectors, cattlemen, and soldiers were shown as considering the Indian to be a ferocious adversary who had to be swept aside as he was standing in the way of westward expansion. These Indian plots were not so noble and the Indians were made out to be brute savages. They were shown as swarms of colorfully clad figures on horseback attacking civilized White pioneers in wagon trains or ambushing unsuspecting riders in order to stop pioneer expansion. Representative of this type of plot was *The Battle at Elderbush Gulch* (1913), with Lillian Gish and Mae Marsh appearing as a young mother and child caught up in savage Indian warfare. In reality, by the early 1880s only about 250,000 Native Americans remained, roughly a quarter of their number in the early eighteenth century.

By the end of the silent movie era in the late 1920s, the Indian had essentially vanished as an individualized character, as critics complained of too much crime, too much violence, and too many interracial relationships with Indians. The B Westerns of the 1930s and 1940s did not use Indians as leading characters in plots and many of them did not have Indians in them at all. Though a few later movies used an Indian theme, notably *The Battle at Apache Pass* (*Cochise*) (1952), *Broken Arrow* (1950), and *Geronimo* (1962), the Indian as a hero did not continue.

Broncho Billy Anderson

The huge success of *The Great Train Robbery* (1903) helped to generate public enthusiasm for Western movies. At first there was little competition for moviemakers who used a background in the West. Then the popularity of Westerns brought an inrush of competition. Everyone started filming them and the domestic market became flooded. These early movies were different from later Westerns in that they had no identifiable hero. Film historians generally accept that Broncho Billy, the creation of filmmaker Gilbert Anderson, was the first recognizable Western movie hero.[7] This set the format for Westerns for years to come.

Anderson, born Max Aaronson, was originally an actor who did not have much success on the stage, so he turned to movies. He wangled his way into *The Great Train Robbery* (1903), playing three roles as one of the train robbers, a railroad passenger from the train who is shot during the robbery, and the dude who has his feet shot at in the dance hall scene. Anderson later teamed up with George Spoor to create Essanay Film Company ("Ess" for Spoor and "Ay" for Anderson) to film Westerns. Anderson and Essanay felt they could make a different type of product and thus increase profits. Over the next nine years, Anderson came up with a successful formula for the good bad-man. Following a popular trend in dime novels, Broncho Billy became the bad-man with a heart of gold.

Anderson's first Broncho Billy movie was *Broncho Billy's Redemption* (1910), filmed with himself in the lead role. Between 1905 and 1922 Anderson had 467 credits as director, many of them with Broncho Billy titles such as *Broncho Billy's Redemption* (1910), *Broncho Billy's Last Spree* (1911), *Broncho Billy's Oath* (1913), and *Broncho Billy's Strategy* (1913). When Anderson filmed *Broncho Billy and the Baby* (1915), unfortunately he didn't obtain the screen rights to the story, which was a common practice at the time. The screenplay was adapted from a short story, "Broncho Billy and the Baby," by Peter B. Kyne, that appeared in *Saturday Evening Post* earlier that year. Luckily Kyne liked the movie and didn't sue, though he did demand a royalty. The film was a success and Anderson continued to use the character of Broncho Billy.

Anderson's Broncho Billy movies were not connected narratives. Anderson played a good man in some and a bad-man in others. In some of the plots he was killed off, but he was back to life in the next. In many of these films he played the part of an outlaw who underwent a change into a reformed citizen over the course of the plot. Around 1911 Anderson started to deemphasize crime and pushed non–Whites into the background. The White man became the central protagonist and certainly by 1912 a recognizable Western hero had emerged.

What distinguished Broncho Billy movies was that Billy was a repeating central character that appealed to audiences. Anderson focused on personality rather than on the spectacle that characterized contemporary Westerns. Billy was typically an outlaw who underwent reformation, but one with a sense of responsibility towards women and children. With Broncho Billy, Anderson tried to create better entertainment for families and at the same time be a role model to teach moral lessons to children. He affirmed Victorian values and made the movie theater an attractive place for middle-class families. Anderson often drew on evangelical themes, especially redemption, and used Christian themes in his movies. Examples were *Broncho Billy's Christmas Dinner* (1911), *Broncho Billy's Bible* (1912), and *Broncho Billy's Sermon* (1914). These themes helped to make him popular with middle-class women.

To maintain character recognition, Broncho Billy appeared in a standardized costume that consisted of utilitarian baggy denim pants, a simple dark shirt with a collar, leather gauntlets on his wrists, boots, and a wide belt. In these films, Anderson projected a character who was a combination of a loner, a country hick, a crime fighter, and a detective. Broncho Billy was not a gunfighter, an Indian fighter, or a savior of wagon trains.

By 1914 the character of the good badman had been overused. Broncho Billy's popularity declined around 1915 as both Anderson and the public began to tire of the character and the repeated plots. In 1916 Anderson decided to end the series. He had intended to continue making movies, but he and Spoor dissolved their partnership. This effectively ended Anderson's movie career and he left the motion picture business. His financial success in the movies allowed him to pursue his goal of returning to the theater. Although he had done well in movies, his theatrical judgment was not as good and he became financially drained.[8]

Al Jennings

In the early days of the movies, many of the lawman and outlaws who lived out real events in the West—men such as Al Jennings, Bill Tilghman, Emmett Dalton, Frank James, and Cole Younger—were still alive and the West had not changed much from their heyday. One of those who turned to acting but was not as successful as Broncho Billy in his portrayal of the West was Al Jennings, a reformed Oklahoma bank robber. He found employment in the film industry in Tulsa, which was a major location for making Westerns between 1907 and 1920 before Hollywood became the center of film. Jennings was only recently out of jail for train robbery when he starred in *The Bank Robbery* (1908). Filmed around Cache, Oklahoma, and directed by real-life former frontier lawman Bill Tilghman, the plot vaguely paralleled *The Great Train Robbery* (1903). It created confusion of reality and fiction, as the film and the real events were so close in time.

Jennings later went to Hollywood and became a film star and producer. He strove for authenticity, but the more authentic he tried to be, the less successful his films were. The problem was that his representation of the West was what he knew well, which was Oklahoma around the turn of the century. His outlaws, for example, wore battered Fedora hats and jackets that made them look like city tramps. He showed Indians living in little houses and dressing like farmers. While his depiction was authentic for Oklahoma for that time period, it was localized and did not fit the mythic image of the West desired by audiences and portrayed in dime novels, Wild West posters, magazine articles, and other films.[9] Audiences wanted to see Native Americans in full Plains Indian battle costume riding colorful horses. They wanted films of cowboys versus Indians, and battles between Indians and soldiers.

In 1908 Al Jennings filmed *A Round-Up in Oklahoma*, which told the story of a group of cowboys herding cattle up the trail from Texas to Kansas who are attacked by Indians. Tilghman produced *The Passing of the Oklahoma Outlaws* (1915) about the crimes of several of the real Oklahoma outlaws such as Al Jennings, Henry Starr, Bill Doolin, Cattle Annie, and Little Britches.

Thomas Ince and Inceville

The relationship between Wild West shows and motion pictures goes back to the beginning of movies. In 1894 William K. Dickson made films of performers from Buffalo Bill's *Wild West* in Edison's Black Maria studio in West Orange, New Jersey.[10] In 1909 Selig made pictures with the *Miller Brothers' 101 Ranch Wild West Show* using performers both as actors and to perform stunts. The ranch cowboys used their riding skills, dexterity with a rope, and other show tricks in simple melodramas. Selig also used *Will Dickey's Circle D Ranch and Wild West Show and Indian Congress* to provide cowboys, Indians, and various props in movies such as *Ranch Life in the Great Southwest* (1910).[11]

One of the filmmakers who had a significant influence on early Westerns was Thomas H. Ince. New York Motion Picture Company hired Ince, who had a background in legitimate theater and stage management, to develop a new type of Western. He leased a large tract of land in Santa Ynez Canyon, north of Santa Monica in California, to film Western dramas that included Indian attacks on settlers, wagon trains, and stagecoaches. Ince leased the Millers' 101 Ranch cowboys and wrote film plots to make the best of the troupe's capabilities, including riding stunts and other popular elements of the Millers' Wild West show. Filming on outdoor locations in the canyon gave the pictures a feel of realism. Ince tried to be realistic in costuming and his films showed what authentic cowboys from the 101 Ranch show wore. Many of the plots were thin, but viewers didn't notice that in all the spectacle. *Custer's Last Fight* (1912), for example, was little more than a filmed version of Cody's *Wild West* reenactment of the event.[12]

William S. Hart

By the mid–1910s, as Broncho Billy movies were fading, the popularity of William S. Hart was on the rise and Hart became the new embodiment of the Western hero. Hart was born in Newburgh, New York, in 1865. As his fame as a movie star grew, he revised the story of his early life, exaggerating his connections to the West of cowboys and Indians.

Hart became a professional stage actor and spent thirty years touring the United States in classical and contemporary plays. While he was in California, he contacted former fellow actor and old friend Thomas Ince to discuss producing Westerns. Ince was not enthusiastic and told Hart that the American public was becoming tired of Westerns.[13] But Ince let him try anyway, so Hart started making movies in 1914 at age forty-nine. Eventually the studio staff created a consistent screen persona for Hart that made him a very marketable character. Hart's movies preached values and projected a moral sense and set of values and behavior that he felt American people should conform to.

He was a very popular romantic lead and in his stoic way kissed both the heroine and the bad girl. He was six-foot-two, which made him appear heroic and dominant among the crowds of villains, dance-hall women, and Mexicans who appeared in his movies.[14] His films were intended to appeal to a wide audience, and especially to middle-class white women, who were the prime audience that movie exhibitors wanted to attract. His Westerns emphasized the traditional values of home, family, and church. Many of the middle-class women who made up Hart's audiences liked his Victorian values of godliness, self-control, sentimentality, and honor. As a result, Hart dominated Westerns from 1916 to 1919. Some of his movies had bold themes for the times. In *The Testing Block* (1920), Sierra Bill (William S. Hart) kidnaps Nelly Gray (Eva Novak) and takes her into the mountains, where they build a cabin and she has his son, Buster.

Broncho Billy created the original movie theme of the hero being reformed and redeemed by the love of a good woman. This concept also became a central theme in many of Hart's films. Hart played complex characters tormented by internal struggles with good and evil. In a typical Hart Western the heroine persuades Hart's character as a bad man to convert to Christianity and dedicate himself to social reform. In the end, he emphasizes the moral values of virtue, goodness, and right. Like Broncho Billy, Hart seldom fought Indians.

Hart's craggy and tough screen persona matched the landscape he showed in his Westerns. He depicted the West as he thought it had been and painted a stark, grim, and unyielding version of the West. His movies were characterized by gritty, ramshackle towns and characters in drab, well-worn clothing. The action was often played out against clouds of dust, just as in the real West.

Hart tried to be realistic in his version of cowboy clothing. He realized that authentic Western clothing had to be sturdy enough to provide long wear under rough working conditions and cheap enough to fit a cowboy's budget. He wore frock coats that were dusty and shiny from wear and cheap colorful shirts that the old-time Westerners liked to wear. Hart started the convention that the Western gambler was dressed in a long black coat. His costumes were utilitarian and simple. His towns were scruffy and rundown. The surrounding landscapes were desert-like, with only sparse grass and erratic brush. Critics claimed that his visual look was realistic and authentic, but it is perhaps better described as harsh. He portrayed the West as raw, violent, and somber.

Hart's Western society consists of card-sharps, brothel-keepers, racketeers, and Mexicans. "Mexicans" at the time were treated like "Indians," as nameless, faceless stereotypes that were automatically associated with villains. Hart himself was the prototype of the strong, silent heroes of the Western screen. In *"Blue Blazes" Rawden* (1918), just his screen name hints of a man who is raw, untamed, and uncivilized. Hart's previous work as a Shakespearean actor, playing characters such as the scoundrel Iago in Shakespeare's *Othello*, made him very good at portraying villains in Westerns. He had a subdued but intense style of acting. To show anger, for example, he hunched over and assumed a menacing pose.

Hart brought to his movies a male code of honor that belonged to an older Victorian era. His heroes were deeply moral, self-righteous, and melodramatic. He specialized in playing a bad man, such as an outlaw or gambler, who was redeemed by the love of a good woman—or sometimes by a child, the love of his horse, or his sister. He used this same formula with minor revisions in all his movies. In several films, as a villain he was indeed reformed by his love for his horse.[15]

Hart's good badman character reflected the fictional dime-novel treatments of bandits like Jesse James or Deadwood Dick. The concept was that the hero was basically good but had been driven to commit a crime by extreme circumstances. He fought the nameless, faceless enemies of the common man: the railroad, banks, large oppressive corporations. He took command of the situation with his cleverness and innate judgment, and his superior physical and mental skills. He was able to deal equally with both the villains and the local ranchers or townspeople.

A typical example of Hart's good badman screen persona is shown in *The Aryan* (1916). Hart plays Steve Denton, a man who has been robbed and rejected by a dance-hall girl, and so becomes a bandit. He finds a wagon train of marooned settlers in the desert but refuses to help them. Heroine Mary Jane Garth (Bessie Love) comes to his hideout to beg for help. At first he refuses and tells her that his villainous gang of Mexicans and half-breed desperadoes is going to attack the wagon train. She persists, however, and finally persuades him to help her. He realizes that he has to accept some moral responsibility and attacks his own gang and rescues the settlers.

A similar movie was *Hell's Hinges* (1916). Hart plays Blaze Tracy, the leader of a gang of gunmen and killers in a town appropriately named Hell's Hinges. The townspeople want to build a church and they invite preacher Robert Henley (Jack Standing) from the East to administer it. Tracy plots with the proprietor of the saloon to run the new preacher out of town. Meanwhile, Tracy falls in love with Henley's appropriately named sister, Faith (Clara Williams). She converts him to Christianity and he undergoes a change of heart. So, instead of conspiring with the scum of the town, he traps all the prostitutes, gamblers, and dance-hall girls in the saloon and sets it on fire. Eventually the fire spreads and the entire town burns down. The preacher is killed trying to defend the church, and Tracy and Faith escape to continue their missionary efforts somewhere else.

Like Broncho Billy, Hart used his Western hero screen persona to promote Christianity, moral reform, and other Victorian values. Over the years, his films developed into the same formula with only minor revisions. His characters evolved into a stereotypical hero who was square-jawed and steely-eyed. His films were triumphant justice designed for families and church-goers. The plots were based on the dramatic conflicts of frontier life with Victorian purity added in. In Hart's films the heroine often appears physically and emotionally childlike.

After World War I America changed and movie audience tastes shifted as people drifted away from the Victorian principles of restraint and self-denial. Women's fashions and hairstyles became more daring, and women smoked, drank, and wore short skirts. Hart's popularity started to decline in the 1920s as urban theatergoers turned away from his type of movies and started to embrace the new moral climate. They wanted manly heroes with strength, virility, and masculine aggressiveness.[16]

Hart remained popular with rural and small-town audiences, particularly among young men and small boys, but this was not the audience the studios wanted. One article in *Views and Film Index* of January 1911 claimed that young boys made up most of the audience for cowboy-and-Indian pictures. An article by Stephen Bush in *Moving Picture World* in 1911 complained of "unwashed boys in the front seats."[17] Some films tried to reflect this trend to appeal to this specific audience. In *Terrible Ted* (1907) a young boy pulls his gun to rescue another boy from a policeman in New York, foils a stagecoach robbery, shoots a card cheat, saves a woman from a bear, and kills Indians who tie him to a tree before the audience realizes that he has been asleep and this is a dream.

This popularity among men and young boys created a problem. Exhibitors wanted to increase their profits by appealing to respectable middle-class adults and families and felt that the genre was driving that audience away. They started to avoid showing Westerns, as they felt that Westerns appealed to a rough crowd. Studios wondered how to continue to produce profitable Westerns but downplay the blood-and-thunder. The trend was to introduce more romanticism and more idealized Western characters. Rough characters became not so rough.

One of the goals of theater-owners was to attract more affluent viewers to the movies and moviemakers tried whatever they thought would boost movie attendance. One unusual attempt was when Nestor Motion Picture Company in 1912 went into a business arrangement with Frank V. Tousey, the dime-novel publisher. The two companies arranged to simulta-

Popular plot elements in early short movies were cowboys, light comedy, and a little romance. This was amply supplied in *The Real Thing in Cowboys*, a 1914 comedy short from Selig Polyscope. Tom Mix starred as Wallace Carey opposite Goldie Colwell as Elsie Mitchell (Library of Congress).

neously release a movie and a print version in Tousey's *Wild West Weekly* based on the same story. The printed version was available for purchase in the theater showing the movie. The idea was not successful with exhibitors or the trade in general and only lasted a few weeks.[18]

After 1920 Hart's movies began to earn less money. Though he was still popular, exhibitors felt that his themes were old-fashioned. His career was also dragged down by hints of scandal. In 1922, his estranged wife, actress Winifred Westover, charged him with abuse. Then another woman, Elizabeth MacCaulley, accused him of being the father of her illegitimate child. Both women later retracted their stories, but the widespread press coverage that accompanied both incidents was a blow to Hart's screen image as a moralist and he stopped making movies.[19]

The success of *The Covered Wagon* (1923) rekindled an interest in Westerns among audiences, and Hart's studio, Paramount, asked him to return to starring roles. Hart, however, would not compromise on his vision of the West and Westerns. He saw himself as an expert on the West and wanted complete control of his movies. He condemned Westerns made by other producers. He even criticized Owen Wister, the popular author of *The Virginian*, for inaccuracy in his writing, despite the fact that Wister had lived in the West during the cowboy period and had visited the locations he wrote about.[20] Paramount asked Hart to change his approach, but he refused and their contract ended.[21]

Audiences, for their part, saw Hart's vision of the West as outdated and were attracted to the new type of action movies that starred the up-and-coming Tom Mix. Hart did not do the flashy physical stunts that were Mix's trademark. Hart later tried to make a comeback, but audience tastes had changed and they were not interested in his vision of authenticity. His film career was over by the mid–1920s.

The "realism" for which contemporary critics praised Hart was his simple clothing, dilapidated town sets, dusty streets, and rough interiors. However, as modern film critic Jon Tuska has observed, "Hart's plots as plots are *not* realistic. They are keenly romantic, sentimental, melodramatic, occasionally ridiculous—but ridiculous in the spirit of Don Quixote." He goes on to say, "What ruined Hart in actually a very short time was his dogged insistence on overstated, fragrant, idealistic and sentimental plots."[22]

The Last of the Mohicans

Western novels provided suitable stories for movies, and filmmakers realized early on that popular books had a built-in audience for a film version. Cooper's novel *The Last of the Mohicans* was made into a movie under various titles in 1909, 1911, 1920, 1932, 1936, 1947, and 1992. In *The Last of the Mohicans* (1992), Natty Bumppo became Nathaniel Poe.

This romantic adventure was a natural for the screen. In general, the character of Hawkeye was left as a hero who had a great depth of knowledge about Indians, but in the screenwriting process the rest of the story underwent changes from the book. In the screen versions, the endings with Uncas, Cora, Chingachgook, and Magua were variously altered from the original to conform to what the particular filmmaker preferred. But Uncas and Cora still had to die because of the threat of an interracial liaison and Magua dies because he lusts after a white woman.

The novel was first brought to the screen as *Leather Stocking* (1909) by D.W. Griffith.

Anticipating the reaction to the changes that had been made in many adaptations of Western stories, promotion for the film included the statement, "While we have made no attempt to follow his story closely, we present a vivid appreciation of his work."[23] The story was remade as *The Last of the Mohicans* (1911), and again as what is considered to be a better version in 1920. The first sound adaptation of the book was made by Mascot as a twelve-part serial in 1932. To conform to the requirements of a multi-part serial, the plot was expanded to include an obligatory cliff-hanger that put the sisters in peril at the end of each episode. Actor Randolph Scott played Hawkeye in *The Last of the Mohicans* (1936). The story was remade again as *Last of the Redmen* (1947).

9

Tom Mix and the Flashy Showmen

The Old West is not a certain place in a certain time, it's a state of mind. It's whatever you want it to be—Tom Mix[1]

As dime novels and Wild West shows faded in the early 1900s, movie screenwriters took over from them as the primary storytellers of the mythic West. By the 1920s the star system was established in the film industry and the early years of the decade saw a rising popular acceptance of the cowboy figure in Western movies. Westerns evolved from the gritty depictions of Hart to a mythic land inhabited by cowboys who never worked with cattle. The first Western stars were actors who gained recognition by repeatedly appearing in a series of roles depicting a consistent character with whom they could be identified from movie to movie.

In the 1920s Western films expanded in length to six reels, or about sixty minutes. Movies became so popular that large ostentatious theaters were built to attract elite audiences. During the mid to late 1920s, however, exhibitors with these fancy first-run houses started to downplay Westerns because they were not popular with the audiences they wished to attract. For a film to play in a large first-run theater it had to attract middle-class women and families who wanted an appealing hero. William S. Hart's film persona was shaped in part by the need to appeal to this audience.[2]

The few Western movies that continued to play in the large theaters were the epics, which might have a running time of two hours or more. This type of Western was set around real historic events in the West, such as the coming of the railroad, the excitement of the Pony Express, pioneer wagon trains and settlers, and the Oklahoma Land Rush. One example that used the railroad was *The Iron Horse* (1924). These Western extravaganzas, however, were expensive to make, which limited their appeal for the studios. *The Covered Wagon* (1923) cost $782,000 to produce, which was a very large budget for the time (even though it later grossed $3.8 million). As a result, cheaper Westerns started to dominate the studios' output.

Movie studios continued to make low-budget "shoot-'em-up" Westerns primarily for male audiences for showing in smaller neighborhood movie houses and second-run theaters for abbreviated runs. Because the income from these small theaters was lower than the movie palaces, studios had to keep the costs down. Smaller budgets therefore led to a formula approach. This was well received by audiences, because small boys and other fans did not want their cowboy stars or the plots to change from a basic formula. Plots mattered less than who was in them. Hart was a victim of this shifting popularity, as he was unwilling to make low-budget Westerns.[3]

Tom Mix

The most recognizable cowboy movie figures in the early 1920s were the heroes defined and popularized by Broncho Billy Anderson, William S. Hart, and Tom Mix. Mix had the largest following, as he emphasized excitement, stunts, and bravado in his films. In the early 1920s Mix surpassed Hart as the best-known Hollywood cowboy. Mix turned the simple cowboy into a hero with fancy costumes and daring stunts. He introduced dazzling showmanship and a slick, polished format that was later followed by other movie cowboys, such as Ken Maynard and Hoot Gibson.

Mix claimed to have been born in a log cabin near El Paso, Texas, in 1880 to a Cherokee mother and a father who was a captain in the Seventh Cavalry. His studio biography said that he joined the Texas Rangers, served as a scout during the Spanish-American War in the Philippine campaign, fought alongside Teddy Roosevelt at San Juan Hill, and fought in the Boxer Rebellion in China and the Boer War in South Africa. In reality, Mix never left the United States during his military service and never fired a shot in combat. He was allegedly a wilderness guide for Teddy Roosevelt and supposedly served as a sheriff in Kansas, Colorado, Montana, and New Mexico.[4] Other stories were that he was nearly adopted by Buffalo Bill, was a lumberjack, and rode with Mexican revolutionary leader Pancho Villa.[5] To put it mildly, however, his public biography was romanticized and consisted of manufactured yarns about his beginnings.[6] His only verifiable stint as a lawman was that he served briefly as a deputy sheriff in Dewey, Oklahoma.[7] Much of his biography may have been created by Mix and his press agents at Fox. As film historian William Everson tactfully put it, "When Mix ultimately became a big star at Fox Studios, publicity created a biography for him far more colorful than any of his movie roles."[8] Though the truth seemed to be blurred, the movie-going public loved the fantasy world of Hollywood stars and did not really care either way. The Hollywood star system invented many a childhood to fit an actor's later screen image.

Mix worked at the Miller Brothers' 101 Ranch, where he developed many of the riding tricks that he later used in his movies. In 1909 he left the Millers to form his own troupe but was not successful. Mix was on the point of settling down to ranch life when Selig Polyscope Company decided to shoot a ranching documentary in Dewey, Oklahoma, called *Ranch Life in the Great Southwest* (1910), showing the round-up and shipping of cattle. Mix was hired to handle the livestock and help organize the cowboys. He asked for a part in the film, so they obliged and filmed him doing a bronc-busting sequence. After the film was complete, Selig asked if he would be interested in helping with livestock, stunts, and technical advice for a series of Westerns they were making. Mix went to California and worked for Selig Polyscope as a general stock manager. After this he made one- and two-reel Westerns as a regular in Selig productions, writing scripts, directing, and starring. Mix realized that movies were dominating entertainment. Whereas thousands of people might attend Wild West shows, movies could be seen by millions. Between 1911 and 1917, the years that marked Broncho Billy's rise and decline and Hart's rise to major stardom, Mix made almost a hundred films for Selig.

Tom Mix movies didn't offer much in the way of plot, characterization, or atmosphere, but they provided good stories, escapist entertainment, and lively action. Mix's movies were intended to display his riding and roping talents and show off the cleverness of his horse. Most of his movies consisted of stunts, fights, chases, and some comedy, set against beautiful

Film star Tom Mix made almost a hundred short (one reel) silent Westerns for Selig Polyscope. This is a promotional poster from *The Sheriff's Reward* (1914) with Mix playing the sheriff, opposite Goldie Colwell as Rose Borland. Here the sheriff ponders the warning that the cattle thieves are after him (Library of Congress).

backgrounds in the West. Many of his early pictures were filmed in Colorado. Two of his favorite filming locations were Canon City, Colorado, and Las Vegas, New Mexico. He established a film studio in Las Vegas and between 1914 and 1915 made twenty silent films there for Selig. Mix once commented that if he could escape from Hollywood he would like to live there forever.

Mix's screen performances came to the attention of William Fox and, as a result, Mix went to work for Fox's studio in 1917, where he made sixty or so films.[9] Fox was a moderately successful company at the time, but Mix's movies made the company flourish, as did Gene Autry movies later for Republic. Mix acted in comedy Westerns, straight dramas, and movies that showed off his riding stunts and showmanship. His pictures were so popular with the public they helped to pay for movies that Fox made for prestige reasons but which had low financial returns. Mix made the majority of his films on location and he particularly liked to film in America's national parks because he wanted audiences to experience the rugged natural beauty of the West.[10]

Tom Mix replaced William S. Hart's dusty authenticity and melodrama with flamboyant showmanship. Mix was the prototype of the hero with the white hat. His riding skills and daredevil stunts led him to be dubbed "America's Champion Cowboy." His movies were rugged and action-packed, with fights, chases, and escapist drama. He did not want realism, but showcased the outrageous riding stunts learned earlier in his career. Mix's films did not champion any weighty issues and nobody was expected to take his movies seriously.

Just like William S. Hart, Tom Mix became identified with the "real West." Even though Mix's reality of the West was no more correct than Hart's, Mix projected his own vision of authenticity on his movies. His West was theatrical, adventurous, glamorous, and filled with fast-moving action. He helped to create the clean-living, non-drinking hero, an image that lasted until the late 1940s and 1950s when violence started to creep back into Westerns.

Like Hart, Mix's movies projected strong moral values and avoided romance and excessive violence. His Westerns were lighthearted and fast-paced, and his on-screen persona projected a likeable hero with no vices. He certainly never smoked, drank, or swore. Mix established the formula for the sexless Western, what author Buck Rainey has called the "flirt-and-run" style, with no prolonged love clinches or romance.[11] He was a hard-riding hero, but he rarely used his guns and his movies contained little shooting. Mix did not kill or wound the villain, but subdued him with fists, roped him, or captured him through fancy stunt work, as opposed to Hart before him, who was a deadly, no-nonsense gun-slinging avenger. Mix preferred fistfights on the tops of trains, cars, and perilous cliffs, and he often simply lassoed the bad guys and tied them up. And he genuinely liked his horse. Mix performed most of own stunts, many of which involved airplanes, trains, automobiles, motorcycles, and cars.[12] As a previous Wild West performer, he believed he should do all his stunts himself; however, he did suffer broken bones and other injuries. When he grew older he used a stunt double, though the film crew was sworn to secrecy.[13]

While Hart wore grubby costumes, Mix was flamboyant. At first Mix dressed fairly realistically on-screen, saving his expensive fancy costumes for personal appearances.[14] Then he changed his image to become a glamorously dressed cowboy and started wearing fancy silk shirts, a hand-tooled gunbelt and holster, gloves, and boots with intricate designs. Mix was a showman and his lavish Western outfits reflected circus costuming. He wore a huge hat with an oversized brim that had a rolled edge and a ribbon trim. The crown was very high, with a large crease down the front. His colorful outfits bore no relationship to what real cowboys wore, except that he introduced leather gloves to movie cowboys because his hands were soft and the gloves provided protection during fights and other stunts. His vivid style brought the colorful covers of pulp magazines to life with flashy outfits. His flamboyant costuming helped to exaggerate the romance and adventure of the Old West. The bad men in his movies looked downright shabby in contrast to his exotic outfits.

Mix was definitely a Western hero and fans typecast him as a cowboy. In an attempt to appeal to female audiences in the first-run movie palaces, Fox tried to put him in swashbuckling period roles such as *Tom Mix in Arabia* (1922) and the costume drama *Dick Turpin* (1925). His audiences in the second-run theaters did not like him in these roles and rejected this change in image. As these movies were not a success, Fox did not try to change his image again.[15]

Mix films didn't portray the real West and Mix had no desire to be in melodramatic vehicles. He realized that the public wanted a good story rather than authenticity, so this was what he provided. He openly admitted that his screen character was not intended to parallel that of the authentic Westerns and he made no pretense of showing the West as it really was. His movies were primarily geared towards young boys, so the love mush was replaced by a nonstop parade of fistfights, chases, and riding stunts. As a businessman Mix knew that entertainment was what sold and so he provided nonstop action. He minimized bloodshed, emphasized morality over historical accuracy, amplified the role of villains, and minimized the participation of Indians and women. Indians were war-painted savages who opposed civilization. Women were pure, helpless and innocent, and the chivalrous Mix rescued them from the villain. Villains were usually cheats and bullies, people in positions of power who preyed on others weaker than themselves. Mix offered a romantic vision of the past and played a rugged individual who was moral and courageous, and brought villains to justice. He showed that truth and justice triumphed in his mythical West. He instilled morals that were clean and wholesome by promoting perseverance, humility, hard work, patriotism, courage, kindness to animals, personal health, cheerfulness, courtesy, and honor. The cowboy became a whitewashed stereotype who served as a model for youth.

The off-screen Mix was a flamboyant, glamorous Hollywood hero with an extravagant and lavish lifestyle. By 1925 he was earning $17,500 a week.[16] He wore dandified Western costumes, drove a luxurious car, and had a fancy home. Later B Western movie stars such as Tim McCoy, Ken Maynard, Jack Hoxie, Hoot Gibson, and William Farnum were patterned on the flamboyant Mix character. In spite of his clean screen image, though, in real life Mix smoked and drank liquor in Hollywood nightclubs, and married and divorced several times.[17] He had a yacht, five wives, plenty of money, and used it to live a gaudy, lavish lifestyle. He built a mansion in Beverly Hills, complete with an English butler, a seven-car garage, a swimming pool, and a large sign of his initials on the lawn that was lit up at night. He owned the Diamond S Ranch in Prescott, Arizona, and a collection of fancy cars with hand-tooled leather upholstery and silver trim.

At the height of his career in 1925, Mix reportedly toured with a baggage car that was devoted to only his wardrobe. The same year, he contracted with John B. Stetson to endorse his signature hat, which had a five-inch brim and a seven-inch crown. This endorsement popularized the ten-gallon hat. The bigger star Mix became, the more outrageous his outfits became. He popularized the pointed-yoke Western shirt with smile pockets and long multi-button cuffs. He appeared like this in *Teeth* (1924). In *Riders of the Purple Sage* (1925) he wore a black shirt with white-piped pointed yokes and smile pockets with embroidered arrowheads and long cuffs. For trousers he wore tight black riding breeches with a double seat outlined in white. He became so famous for his white suits and other fancy clothing that he was called the Beau Brummel of the West. Mix evolved the impractical and uneconomical "uniform" that dominated the Western hero through the Gene Autry and Roy Rogers years.

Mix was killed unexpectedly on October 12, 1940, when his car failed to make a curve at a detour sign for a bridge under repair eighteen miles south of Florence, Arizona. The car veered into a dry wash and his neck was broken by a metal suitcase that hit him when the car crashed. Flamboyant to the end, he was buried in a silver-plated coffin with his initials on it. After his death, his collection of custom-built automobiles and $250,000 worth of his collection of Western artifacts were put on display at the Tom Mix Museum in Dewey, Oklahoma.

An off-screen Tom Mix standing on the running board of a convertible shows off the typical attire of his screen persona, with his huge trademark hat along with fancy boots and spurs. The license plate from the District of Columbia dates this photograph at 1925 (Library of Congress).

Ken Maynard

Another Western film personality who played strong cowboy roles from the 1920s to the 1940s was Ken Maynard. His significance in forming the changing role of the Western movie hero was that he introduced the singing Western. He was also a dazzling trick rider who did most of his own stunts. Maynard's popularity peaked in the early 1930s as talking motion pictures were being introduced.

In keeping with the tradition of many of the other movie stars who tried to forge closer links to the West to impress their fans, studio publicity said that Ken Maynard was born in Mission, Texas, but he was actually born in Vevay, Indiana.[18] In the 1910s, Maynard worked for several Wild West shows, including Buffalo Bill's *Wild West* and *Kit Carson's Buffalo Ranch Wild West*. In these shows and in circus acts, Maynard acquired the skills for doing the stunts and trick riding that would later make him a spectacular action star in Western movies. Sometimes these experiences were used as a basis for plots for his movies, such as *The Wagon Show* (1928), which had a circus background to allow him to show off his riding skills. Similarly, in *Parade of the West* (1930), he played a daredevil circus performer.

Like Mix's films, Maynard's were also characterized by stunts and action. All of his films contained at least one good fistfight. *Branded Men* (1931) starts with a brawl and fisticuffs among some of "the boys." Maynard rides up and sees that the fight involves two of his buddies, so he wades in and immediately defeats three of the bad guys to help them. At the end Maynard and one of the henchmen fight it out with fists, rolling around on the edge of a precipice. Maynard slips over the cliff and hangs on by the tips of his fingers as the villain stomps on his hands. Maynard's horse, Tarzan, sees what is going on and comes to the rescue. Faced by the rearing horse, the villain is seen falling backwards over the cliff, presumably to his off-screen death. *Tombstone Canyon* (1932) ends with Maynard involved in another frantic fight on the edge of a high cliff, with two villains eventually going over the edge. In *Drum Taps* (1933), the title music is played at a fast tempo to set the pace for the movie. Within a few minutes the plot involves a thundering horse chase that ends when Maynard leaps onto the galloping villain and both fly off their horses down into a rocky gulch. Meanwhile, back at the ranch, so to speak, Maynard almost immediately gets into an extended fistfight where the participants roll around on the floor to the accompaniment of labored grunting and gasping on the soundtrack. Then come more horse chases.

Maynard liked to do spectacular horse mounts, either from the side where he jumped up and quickly slipped his foot into the stirrup, or from the back where he vaulted over the horse's rear end with two hands. Like other popular Western stars of the 1920s to the 1950s, Maynard had a favorite horse that shared movie billing with him. Maynard named his horse Tarzan at the suggestion of his friend Edgar Rice Burroughs.[19]

Maynard had musical talents and recorded several Western songs for Columbia Records. He was able to use his musical skills in his films, as he had negotiated a large amount of creative control. In *Sons of the Saddle* (1930), he fitted two songs into the plot, with three other cowboys providing accompaniment. In several subsequent movies he added more musical numbers. In *The Fiddlin' Buckaroo* (1933), even the bandits had a musical number. In *Heroes of the Range* (1936), the bad guys joined in an impromptu performance when Maynard, posing as the notorious outlaw "Lightnin' Smith," had to prove his identity by singing a song.

There have always been jokes about how the movie cowboy liked his horse better than women. This was not always a joke. For the Western *In Old Santa Fe* (1934) Maynard sang one of his own compositions, which included thoughts about marital problems and how he liked his dog better than he did women.[20]

In 1936 Maynard organized his own *Diamond K Ranch Wild West Circus and Indian Congress*. It was a large spectacle that employed 400 performers and supporting crew. Like many other Wild West shows that came late on the scene, Maynard's show did not make a profit and was forced to close after only a few performances.

Perspective on Movie Heroes of the 1920s

Cowboy movie heroes were very popular in the 1920s perhaps, as suggested by Raymond White in his essay *Ken Maynard: Daredevil on Horseback*, because "the Western film hero's innocence and simple codes of justice provided Americans with a link to their past."[21] Tom Mix's clean-living, non-drinking screen persona helped pave the way for the clean-cut heroes later portrayed by Gene Autry and Roy Rogers. This image persisted among the B Western stars until the early 1950s, when Wild Bill Elliott and others took the hero image back to a rougher, tougher type of westerner.

Fans of Western movies of the 1920s and 1930s wanted tough, authentic heroes who showed physical prowess and dexterity with fists, guns, and skill in riding a horse. Important also was the real life of the stars. Studios went to great lengths to convince theatergoers that their stars were just as rugged and clean-cut in real life as in their movies.

Five Western stars were dominant in the 1920s: Tom Mix, Ken Maynard, Buck Jones, Hoot Gibson, and Tim McCoy. All were white men of about the same age, all had served in the military, all were physically somewhat similar, and all had connections to the Millers' 101 Ranch. Their studios emphasized their Western backgrounds or, in some cases, invented or embellished them. This created the impression that they were not just movie stars but authentic figures from the West who had developed their skills on ranches and in Wild West shows. All five were excellent horsemen and indeed had experience in Wild West shows and rodeos. Tom Mix worked for the Miller Brothers' 101 Ranch in 1906. Ken Maynard had worked as a trick rider and for Buffalo Bill's *Wild West* and the Ringling Brothers' Barnum and Bailey Circus.[22] Hoot Gibson had performed in 1910 with the *Dick Stanley–Bud Atkinson Wild West Show* before he worked during the summers for movie studios Selig and Biograph, looking after horses and acting as a stunt double.[23]

Daredevil stuntwork established Ken Maynard as one of the top Western stars of the 1920s and he started the 1930s as one of the most popular stars of Western movies. His action sequences set the standard for later B Western stars. His use of songs revolutionized the B Western and ushered in the era of singing cowboys Gene Autry and Roy Rogers in the late 1930s and 1940s. While perhaps not as good a songster as some of the later singing cowboys, Maynard set the trend that became the standard for the future singing Westerns to follow.

Buck Jones started caring for horses before becoming a leading bronc rider. The name "Buck" may have come from his army days.[24] He became a film extra and stunt double in movies, performing stunts for William S. Hart and Tom Mix, among others.[25]

Hoot Gibson was born Edmund Richard Gibson. There are two versions of how he picked up the nickname "Hoot." One was that he received the name when he worked for Owl Drug Company as a boy.[26] Another version says that the name may have come from his habit of hunting owls as a youngster in Nebraska.[27] Whichever was the case, he became an expert horse breaker and cattle drover as a teenager before he performed with the Millers.

The public wanted authentic male heroes and these heroes had to perform movie feats that proved their strength, courage, and manliness. The public believed that these dashing stars performed their own stunts. This was not always the case, as some stars were not physically capable of dangerous stunts, particularly when they grew older. Though some of them did some of their own stunts, in most cases their studios would not let their valuable stars risk injuries doing a dangerous stunt. This would have halted costly production while the star recovered. It was less risky to the finances of a picture if a stuntman were to be injured than the expensive star. To maintain the star's image, however, stunt doubles were sworn to secrecy.

Real cowboys were attracted to Hollywood in the 1920s as jobs at cattle ranches became harder to get. Cowboys were perfect to become stuntmen in Hollywood Westerns. As they looked at it, stuntmen and extras in Westerns earned $10 a day, plus their lunch, just for falling off a horse. Many were glad to have the job even though it was hard, dangerous work.

The star's horse became an important character in Western movies and was always identified with the same star. Hart's favorite horse was Fritz. Tom Mix's horse was named Tony and he was treated as a costar. Tony could perform tricks and became the best-known animal in the movies at the time. This set the trend for many of the movie cowboys of the 1930s, 1940s, and 1950s. Other well-known horses were Champion, who performed with Gene Autry, Trigger with Roy Rogers, Buttermilk with Dale Evans, Koko with Rex Allen, and Topper with Hopalong Cassidy (William Boyd). These clever horses could untie ropes, go for help, help the hero up if he was knocked out, and serve as a diversion during mushy love scenes. In *Son of Paleface* (1952), when Junior (Bob Hope) and Roy Rogers are tied up by the villains, Trigger comes along and unties the knots to free them.

Stars of the 1920s appeared in a dozen or so low-budget Westerns every year. Their success depended on wide distribution in small-town and neighborhood theaters. Audiences in the smaller theaters were adequate, but without the income from the large movie palaces, production costs had to be minimized, so films were made quickly and cheaply. Plots were standardized to save money but also because that was what audiences wanted and expected. Audiences wanted the same basic structure, which consisted of horseback chases, extended fight scenes, sensational stunt work, rugged scenery, and a familiar star dressed in a fancy cowboy costume. Stars were supposed to use physical strength, ingenuity, and dexterity to overcome all obstacles. The studios had created larger-than-life heroes with exaggerated personas, so audiences expected impressive riding skills and fancy stunts.

The primary audience was young boys who did not want any change in their heroes. Kids dressed like their heroes and acted out cowboy fantasy stories from the movies they watched. Filmmakers tried to keep the heroes suitable for this audience, so the stars did not drink or smoke or swear in their films. They were always clean and neat. Young boys didn't like kissing or romantic scenes so these were kept to a minimum. The hero could be a pal to the heroine or help her or sing to her, but could not have tender romance scenes with her. As a result, leading ladies had only a limited relationship with the hero. Stronger relationships were created with the hero's horse, his younger brother, a saddle-pal, or an older sidekick.

A hero in a big white hat, a heroine mounted behind him on his horse, blazing guns, and one of the villains falling to the dust. What more could the audience watching a Western movie of 1926 ask for? This is Jack Hoxie (on horse) and Helen Holmes in *The Highwayman* (Library of Congress).

Horses or sidekicks were often included in romantic scenes to divert attention from the girl. To further appeal to young men and boys, many of the heroes were younger men who were free from the obligations of older adults. As a result, as Western stars aged and became heavier and didn't look like young heroes any more, their popularity often faded, and younger men took over from them.

Silent movies made movie stars into inscrutable gods but, when sound came in, many actors were transformed from gods back into mere mortals, as many of their voices could not make the transition to talking pictures. Around 1930 the box office successes of *In Old Arizona* (1928) and *The Virginian* (1929) reinvigorated the movie industry. The popularity of the novel *The Virginian* and its adaptation as a play had guaranteed a good audience for the movie. Towards the end of the decade, audience preferences changed again and the singing cowboy of the 1930s became the new popular hero of the silver screen.

Hollywood Indians

The counterpart of the fictitious Hollywood cowboy was the fictitious Hollywood Indian. The iconic Hollywood image of the Indian is a painted, bare-chested native with a feathered headdress riding bareback on a painted pony. This was the generalization of a few characteristics taken from only a few Native American tribes, mostly from the Indians of the Great Plains. These actors were not representative of a specific Native American Indian tribe, but were a Hollywood and dime novel creation. Filmmakers paid little attention to Indian clothing or cultural practices. Most movies showed them as inaccurate stereotypes, which produced false ideas in audiences about Indian culture and history. Indians were depicted in countless Westerns as savage killers ready to scalp the Whites at a moment's notice. Indians were generally shown as shrieking savages until *Broken Arrow* (1950). Films were rarely presented from the Indian point of view until *Dances with Wolves* (1990), when Native Americans were changed into a wronged and noble people.

Not all early actors who portrayed Indians gave convincing performances. One early journalist who was unconvinced said, "To be a stage Indian, swell out your chest, put a bulldog curve on your lips, grunt occasionally, and assume the same gestures of a ham actor in the role of Virginius."[28]

In Westerns of the 1930s and afterwards, Indians became faceless, nameless hordes giving out war whoops as they swooped down on wagon trains in uncountable numbers. Typical examples of this type of plotting occurred in *The Big Trail* (1930), *Union Pacific* (1939), and *Stagecoach* (1939). The movies portrayed violent contacts with Indians in which the heroic White man, such as a soldier, settler or cowboy, subdues the screaming savages and wipes them out by the score. The Indian is portrayed as one of the hazards that faced those who sought to tame the wilderness of the West. They are shown as a terrifying all-purpose enemy just waiting to attack a wagon train, a cavalry patrol, or an isolated pioneer settlement. They were portrayed as treacherous and bloodthirsty, threatening rape, mutilation, and death to the Whites. Bad Indians were Cheyenne, Sioux, Comanche, and Apache, the ones that the real army was fighting in the West. Good ones were considered to be the Pawnee and Arapaho. However, all were treated as having the same manner of dress, culture, and customs. All supposedly wanted to capture White women as wives, and all practiced scalping.

In general, in movies made before the 1950s, the Indians were played by white actors and various other ethnic backgrounds, including African Americans. Ironically, real Native Americans sometimes played the part of other nationalities. The result was a Hollywood caricature of Native American tribes. In some cases real Native Americans were used, but they were shown as the wrong tribes and often spoke the wrong language. For example, in *Cheyenne Autumn* (1964), Navajo actors were used to portray Cheyenne. Tony Hillerman's novel *Sacred Clowns* tells of a Navajo theater audience watching the film and laughing at both the use of Navajo tribesmen to play Cheyenne and the use of obscene or comic lines spoken in Navajo (supposedly Cheyenne) unknown to the filmmakers or to white audiences.[29]

10

Pulp Magazines and Mass-Market Paperbacks

A legend is more interesting than the actual facts—John Ford[1]

Dime novels were popular from about 1865 to 1910, with a peak in sales in the early 1880s. By the early 1900s, acceptance by the public of Western plays, melodramas, and dime novels was diminishing. Part of the reason was that many of these literary heroes had become unbelievable. One astute observer summed this up well: "Readers undoubtedly were dissatisfied with a continuous line of heroes who fought off twenty Indians and rescued the heroine, even with one arm badly wounded. They wanted a gallant and strong protagonist, but one that was, nonetheless, believable."[2] Though dime novels struggled on into the early twentieth century, they essentially faded away by 1920 as the rise in popularity of the nickelodeon and movies finished them off.

During the 1890s, lavishly illustrated magazines such as *Collier's* and *Saturday Evening Post* started to replace *Harper's Weekly* and *Frank Leslie's Illustrated Weekly* as popular reading material. These new magazines featured Western and adventure tales by writers such as Jack London and used the premier illustrators of the time such as Frederic Remington and Howard Pyle.[3]

But while motion pictures were on the rise in popularity, the other printed forms of Western entertainment had not been idle. At the same time that movie actors were evolving as individual stars, hack Western writers were churning out pulp novels which featured a White male hero challenged by a variety of situations and human opponents. Though the hero was usually a cowboy, he often became a generic frontier rider, perhaps a lawman or gunman, rather than a working cowboy. The heroines were typically young, innocent, and beautiful.

Western Novels

The Western novel was a part of the popular fiction of the late nineteenth century before *The Virginian* was published. Serious Western novels and romances from respectable publishing houses began to appear in the 1880s. These books were superior in literary and physical quality to the dime novels and enjoyed fair sales. They also provided inspiration for later writers. *Ramona* by Helen Hunt Jackson, for example, published in 1884, was an immensely popular novel about the plight and mistreatment of Native Americans. The book went through more than 135 printings.[4] It was first made into a film in 1910, then was remade under the same title in 1916, 1928, and 1936.

One of the first true novels set in the West was *The Colonel's Daughter,* published in 1881 by Captain Charles King, who is considered to be the inventor of the cavalry novel. King was a veteran officer of the Fifth Cavalry during the Indian Wars. Stationed at military posts in the West, he rode in campaigns against the Apache chiefs Cochise and Geronimo, and fought the Sioux before becoming a writer of military fiction after his retirement. King wrote sixty-nine novels between 1885 and 1909. His novels were based on his army experiences, but were nonetheless Victorian romances that featured and popularized the cavalry.

Cavalry novels, and the later cavalry movies, were characterized by honor, loyalty, and gallantry. King's plots and heroes were generally simplistic, typically involving a romance between a refined young lady and her aristocratic military boyfriend, and were set against a background of the regular army. During the course of the story, the two lovers are separated by obstacles such as status and jealousy, but sometimes by abduction and captivity that results in a daring rescue. Love and virtue, of course, triumph in the end as the two are reunited. Typical of King's books were *Foes in Ambush*, about Indian fighters battling with strikers. A similar novel was *An Army Wife*, which used the same general theme as a regiment of Indian fighters battling savage strikers.[5]

Some of the prose in the romantic novels of the time was a little heavy by our modern terms. The following is an example from *Ben Blair: The Story of a Plainsman* by Will Lillibridge: "Great splendid animals were the men who gathered there; hairy, powerful, strong-voiced from combat with prairie wind and frontier distance; devoid of a superfluous ounce of flesh, their trousers, uniformly baggy at the knees, bearing mute testimony to the many hours spent in the saddle; the bare unprotected skin of their hands and faces speaking likewise of constant contact with sun and storm."[6] A sentence written a few pages later is couched in the following language, which may have shocked proper Victorian readers: "'May Satan blister your scoundrel souls, all of you!' he cursed."[7]

Pulp Magazines

Coinciding with the decline of the dime novel was the rise of the pulp magazine. Pulp magazines were mass-produced reading material intended to provide cheap thrills for the common masses. Pulp magazines, like the dime novels, were an inexpensive form of literature named for the cheap, rough, untrimmed paper they were printed on. The stories were melodramatic and the covers were gaudy and lurid. The heyday of the pulps was also the heyday of illustrations for Western fiction. Covers contained dramatic titles in screaming print overlaying vivid images. This lurid cover art helped to evoke and maintain the myth of the Old West, as well as sell magazines.

The pulps initially sold for a nickel or a dime, rising later to a quarter. The genres published were many and varied. There were pulp magazines devoted to aviation stories, hard-boiled detectives, mystery, adventure, war, the Old West, romance, African adventures, horror, science fiction, and science fantasy.[8] The conquest of distant lands and their savage inhabitants were subjects of pulp adventure stories for many years—for example H. Rider

A forerunner of the lurid pulp magazines, the *Police Gazette* specialized in spicy gossip about popular actresses illustrated by cheesecake pictures, and stories about the violence of the Wild West. This type of picture from 1882, showing a shootout between detectives and desperadoes, was particularly thrilling for eastern readers and in their minds confirmed everything they had heard about the Western way of life, thus helping to perpetuate the legend (Library of Congress).

Haggard's *King Solomon's Mines*, published in 1885. The Westerns, science fiction and fantasy, and the hard-boiled detectives continued on into later movies and television.

Between 1920 and 1950 pulp magazines were the most popular form of fiction in the United States. At the height of their popularity in the mid–1930s, there were more than 200 titles on the market. The Western pulps helped to enhance and perpetuate the myth of the West and the cowboy-gunfighter image. Much of the pulp fiction that was published, however, was poor in quality and hastily written. Like the dime novels, the cheap paper the magazines were printed on was also poor in quality and the high acid content made it deteriorate, thus the pages rapidly discolored and crumbled with age.

For a long time the pulps were considered to be inferior literature and not worthy of academic study. W.H. Hutchinson, a professor of history at California State University, in his essay *Virgins, Villains and Varmints*, gave the view of an academic when he said, "The pulp paper magazines—looked down upon by any and every right-thinking literary person."[9] More modern thinking now accepts that dime novels and the pulps were the forerunners and foundation for much of popular Western fiction and that they contain valuable information that reflects the popular culture of their times. From a different perspective, no matter how much critics looked down on the literary values of pulp stories, they sold in large quantities. *Argosy*, for example, published six million words of new material a year.[10] Another interesting footnote to any discussion of popular Western reading is that Richard Etulain reported in 1999 that the scholarly journal *Western Historical Quarterly* published only 2,500 copies of each issue. By contrast, *Wild West* magazine, written for the popular market, sold more than 150,000 copies bimonthly.[11]

The era of the pulps started in 1896 when publisher Frank Munsey decided to switch *Argosy* magazine to a format that used a low-grade pulp paper like the dime novels. Munsey felt that the story was more important than what it was printed on. His concept of using cheaper paper and high-speed printing presses, coupled with inexpensive second-class postage, allowed pulp magazines to successfully compete with dime novels. Profitable general readership magazines at the time might sell millions of copies. Pulp magazines, on the other hand, could succeed and still make a profit by selling only a few hundred thousand copies at a cheap cover price. This strategy also allowed pulp magazines to successfully publish for specialized markets, such as for fans of Westerns, science fiction, or romance, and still make a reasonable profit.

One of the first of the Western pulps came from Street & Smith, the successful dime-novel publishers. In 1919 the firm changed their dime novel periodical *New Buffalo Bill Weekly* into a pulp magazine and called it *Western Story* and priced it at ten cents. Within a year the circulation had reached 300,000 per issue.[12] Sales further exploded in the 1920s when Street & Smith made the magazine into a weekly. To cash in on their success, they quickly added *Far West* and *Wild West Weekly*.

Success, of course, stimulated competition. Publisher Doubleday quickly brought out *West* and *Frontier Stories*. Among others that proliferated were *Western Story*; *Ace-High Western*; *Super Western*; *Texas Rangers*; *Crack Shot Western*; *Lariat*; *Thrilling Western*; *Popular Western*; *Masked Rider*; *Triple-X Western*; *All Western*; *Golden West*; *Cowboy Stories*; *Six-Gun*; *Double Action*; *Spicy Western*; *Range Riders*; *Dime Western*; *.44 Western*; *New Western*; *Star Western*; and *Western Adventures*. All were laced with vicarious thrills and mythical interpretations of the West. For the ladies, *Ranch Romances* pioneered the Western love story and told it from the heroine's point of view. In 1952, one newsstand in California reported displaying thirty-three Western pulps and six Western "love" magazines.[13] Like the dime novels, the pulps were developed around particular heroes and story types. The heroes of Western pulp tales were red-blooded adventurers who were dominant in their genre of action and excelled in fighting skills and male attractiveness.

To further boost circulation, publishers of pulps developed a new type of sales strategy. While traditional magazines were sold mostly by subscription, the pulps sold mostly on newsstands, making them ideal for an impulse purchase. To catch the eye of a potential purchaser and stimulate sales, the pulps developed catchy artwork on the cover, popularly featuring lurid illustrations of damsels in distress or ghoulish monsters.

The decline and fall of many of the pulp magazines started with the poor economic conditions of the Great Depression. Others merged with or were bought out by competing publishers. In the end, a paper shortage during World War II killed off many of these magazines. Though most of the pulps were already gone by the end of the 1950s, the popularity of radio, television, and motion pictures further decreased the popularity of the pulp magazines for entertainment and helped to speed the demise of the remainder.

Western Pulp Novels

The Western pulp novel continued the hero tradition of bravery, chivalry, romance, and excitement. Along with pulp magazines, the formula mass-market novel was responsible for keeping alive the mythic West that continued to spark the imagination of many readers. Many of the novels that made their way onto the sales rack were stuffed with lurid tales of daring cowboys, sinister villains, marauding Indians, and smoke-filled gunfights.

Some literary critics have separated the Western novel into two categories, the popular "formula" novel and the literary novel. The former was generally considered to be pulp trash that was written simply for entertainment and to make money for the author and publisher. The latter was a serious literary form considered to have been written "for artistic expression and fulfillment"[14] The first, however, is what has endured while the second is often neglected.

EDGAR RICE BURROUGHS

One of the most influential of the pulp writers was Edgar Rice Burroughs. Born in 1875 in Chicago to a father who owned an automobile manufacturing company, the younger Burroughs didn't do well in school but was intelligent enough to attend Michigan Military Academy in 1892. He wasn't a particularly good student, but he did stick with academics long enough to graduate. He applied to West Point but was turned down. Instead, he enlisted in the Seventh Cavalry (earlier commanded by Lt. Col. George Armstrong Custer). Burroughs was assigned to Fort Grant, Arizona, where he didn't see the action he had hoped for. He didn't particularly like the boring life of a soldier, which consisted mostly of building roads, so his father used his influence to have him released from service.[15] Burroughs worked as a railroad policeman, a door-to-door salesman, and a construction supervisor. Then he decided he wanted to write fantasy.

His first novel, published in 1911, was titled *Under the Moons of Mars*. The book was reissued the next year under its more common title of *A Princess of Mars*. This novel brought him writing success and spawned ten books in the Martian series. As part of this fantasy writing, Burroughs transferred Western plots of action and adventure into outer space. Though mostly set on Mars, but with some on Venus, his fantasy novels contained all the elements of a successful Western melodrama. The highlights were adventure, action, improbable plots, and a beautiful princess (or several princesses as the series progressed) to be fought for, wooed, and won.

Burroughs wrote novels in several genres, including Westerns, spy stories, fantasy, and Oriental adventures. Among other memorable characters, he created Tarzan of the Apes. His Western writing had an authentic background to it, as Burroughs had his Western military experience to call on and he had worked for a while on a cattle ranch in Idaho.

ZANE GREY

One of the most successful of all Western authors was Zane Grey, probably one of the most popular Western writers of all time and one of the first millionaire authors. Grey continued to churn out novels from his first in 1912 until his death in 1939. In all, he wrote over ninety books, most of them about the West, recounting the simple virtues of Western life. By 2012 Grey's books had sold over forty million copies and had undergone 112 film adaptations.

Zane Grey specialized in the larger-than-life hero, the innocent heroine, the chase, the duel, and the triumph of good over evil. He created melodramatic novels that were wonderful stories full of atmosphere. His books contained many convenient coincidences, but audiences loved them anyway and showered him with fame and fortune. Zane Grey's novels were better plotted than many of the time, but some critics have claimed that the characters were weakly portrayed. Author Jim Hitt, for example, says they are "wooden and unbelievable."[16] However, Grey helped to cast the stereotypical Western hero into the mold of silent, steely-eyed, and fast on the draw.

Grey was born in Ohio in 1872. In adulthood he studied dentistry and played baseball. In his thirties he traveled to the West as a tourist and used the knowledge he gained to create vividly written books that were a combination of the forest romances of James Fenimore Cooper, the blood-and-thunder dime novels, and the cowboy stories of Owen Wister. After visiting Utah in 1907, Grey used the state's scenic canyons and deserts as the background for his version of the hero myth in which heroic men fought nature and stereotypical villains. He developed a unique image for the hero as a cowboy-gunfighter agent of retribution who righted wrongs according to what Grey envisioned as the Code of the West. Grey was an easterner who lived in and knew the West, so many of his stories revolved around an easterner who went to live in the West and learn about it and finally accepted Western ways.

Grey's first novel (and probably his most popular), *Riders of the Purple Sage*, appeared in 1912. The book sold over a million copies in its hardcover edition and helped define a new type of Western novel for subsequent authors.[17] In the first few pages of the book Grey introduces Lassiter, a black-clad gunman who by his mere presence and reputation is at odds with a villain who threatens heroine Jane Withersteen and continues to do so until the end. Setting the trend for books and movies for years to follow, Lassiter is the iconic hero of Western films and novels. He is a gunman with a steely-eyed gaze, is clothed all in black, has a two-gun lightning-fast draw, and has high morals. Lassiter's role is that of the implacable avenger who hunts down the man who massacred his family and seduced and abandoned his sister.

Lassiter's image as a gunman is summed up succinctly when at one point he comments, "Gun-packin' in the West since the Civil War has growed into a kind of moral law. An' out here on this border it's the difference between a man an' somethin' not a man."[18] Describing a confrontation between Lassiter and Mormon Tull, Grey writes, "The rider dropped his sombrero and made rapid movement, singular in that it left him somewhat crouched, arms bent and stiff, with the big black gun-sheaths swung round to the fore."[19]

Grey's heroes are freedom-loving individuals who defend honest westerners dispossessed or oppressed by powerful men or businesses. The hero achieves this objective by being a gunfighter with two menacing guns, the proper gunfighting stance, and a lightning-fast draw. Grey's heroes are all similar: brave, uncomplaining, hardworking, laconic, reserved with strangers, hospitable, chivalrous, have a sense of humor—and they all dress the same. The formula was rigid and the action was colorful, with rugged cardboard heroes who are noble but primitive.

Reduced to its essentials, a typical Zane Grey story involves a White woman of upper-

Zane Grey was born in Ohio and started to write Western novels after he traveled in the West in the early 1900s. His first novel, *Riders of the Purple Sage*, appeared in 1912 and sold over a million copies in its hardcover edition. Grey helped to define a new type of Western novel for subsequent authors. This is Grey's study at his home in Lackawaxen, Pennsylvania, with part of his collection of Western artifacts in the background (Library of Congress).

class birth and money pitted against a wealthy and powerful villain who somehow threatens her money and inheritance. The conflict is resolved by a mysterious stranger who roams the West and happens by at just the right time. The resolution is some spectacular act of violence on the part of the hero. This transforms the woman, who then realizes that she loves the hero and wants him for a future husband. The following is how Fay Larkin's awakening is described in *The Rainbow Trail:* "Love had made her a woman and now the woman in her was speaking.... She had been hidden all her life from the world, from knowledge as he had it, yet when love betrayed her womanhood to her she acquired all its subtlety."[20]

Grey's plots often involved corporate greed or land-grabbing on the part of the villain, who is trying to crush "the little guy." The essential plot of *Knights of the Range,* set in New Mexico in 1874, is that Holly Ripple's father dies and leaves a great cattle empire to her. She has a choice of going back to the city where she grew up, or she can stay and fight for what is rightfully hers against killers, hired gunmen, and rustlers who are flooding the territory. As the leader of her "knights of the range" she picks outlaw Renn Frayne, who finally conquers the opposition and wins her love. This was an old plot structure that harked back to earlier dime novels and oppression by the ruling classes, but Grey came up with so many variations and combinations of this theme using original characters and different situations that the plotting seemed fresh. Pulp and paperback Western writers from Max Brand in the 1930s to Louis L'Amour in the post–World War II period copied the fundamental structure of Zane Grey novels.

Grey's version of the West consisted of hidden valleys, lost worlds, and isolated empires, often set among the rugged landscape of Utah. In *The Heritage of the Desert,* Martin Cole says to August Naab, "You're strong, stronger than any of us, far off in your desert oasis, hemmed in by walls, cut off by canyons, guarded by your Navajo friends."[21] The hidden valley in the desert is always a lush secret hideaway, in this book later described as follows: "August Naab's oasis was an oval valley, level as a floor, green with leaf and white with blossom, enclosed by a circle of colossal cliffs of vivid vermilion hue."[22]

Rape is often implied in Grey's books in the form of kidnap, seduction, and the forced marriage of the heroine. The cover of a 1961 paperback version of *The Rainbow Trail* knowingly describes the plot: "A determined tenderfoot risks his life to save a woman from a Mormon village of 'sealed' wives."

Like other novels of the time, including Wister's *The Virginian*, some of Grey's prose is a little circumspect, such as this quote from *The Heritage of the Desert*: "Then, at the sharp crack of the rifles, leaden messengers whizzed high in the air over horse and riders..."[23] The grand shoot-out at the finale is described in the following brief and mild terms: "Hare's hand leapt like a lightning stroke. Gleam of blue—spurt of red—crash!"[24] A similar short description describes the final shoot-out in *The Virginian*. In all fairness, though, much of Grey's prose has to be judged by the writing style of the time, which is not the same as today's fast-paced ways of describing action scenes. This example comes from Grey's *The Rainbow Trail*: "She slipped off the stone to her knees, swayed forward blindly with her hands reaching out, her head falling back to let the moon fall full upon the beautiful, snow-white, tragically convulsed face."[25]

Another of Zane Grey's extremely popular novels was *The Vanishing American*, which formed the basis for several film adaptations. The plot follows an Indian named Nophaie (the Warrior), who has the heritage of an Indian chieftain. As the novel opens, a group of well-meaning Whites traveling in the West kidnap Nophaie as a young boy, thinking they are doing a noble deed in "rescuing" him. One of the women in the group sends him to a school in the East for the next eighteen years, where "he had earned great fame as a football star." Grey describes when the heroine, Marian Warner, sees him for the first time in college as a star athlete, in typical romantic language: "Her eyes fell upon a tall bareheaded athlete, slenderly yet powerfully built, his supple form broadening wide at the shoulders."[26]

After Nophaie leaves the East, Marian, now in love with him, goes to the West to find him, planning to stay and be a teacher and do other charitable work on his reservation. When she arrives in the West, "Flagerstown, the first Western town Marian had ever been in, was not at all like what she had imagined it would be. Her impressions of the West had come from books and motion pictures, which mediums, she was to learn, did not always ring true to life."[27] She is in awe of "the marvel of color, the immensity of these uplands, and the weird, fantastic, and sublime nobility of sculptured shafts of stone."[28]

The following describes the moment she first sees Nophaie again: "An Indian stood silhouetted against the gold of sky. Slender and tall, motionless as a statue, he stood, a black figure in singular harmony with the wildness and nobility of that height."[29] Grey included very topical issues. World War I and the great influenza epidemic of 1918–1919 appear in the background of the book and affects all the characters' lives. As in other Grey novels, the heroine Marian does not at first realize that she loves the hero, "but she awakened to a terrifying consciousness that she had inflamed the savage in Nophaie." In response, she finds that "tenderness, gentleness, love had no part in this response to her woman's allurement. His mastery was that of the primal man denied; his brutality went to the verge of serious injury to her."[30]

Difficulties arose when *The Vanishing American* was first serialized in *Ladies' Home Journal* in 1922. At that time the elements of rape, stealing from the Indians, and interracial marriage were controversial. In Grey's original ending, Nophaie recovers from the rampant influenza epidemic, kills the villains, and marries the White girl, Marian. The problem was that an Indian married a White woman from the East, though perversely a White man marrying an Indian woman would have been acceptable at the time. Contemporary moral sentiment dictated that the end as Grey wrote it was not publishable in his lifetime.[31] Interracial marriage could not be allowed to last and be happy-ever-after. The editors of *Ladies' Home Journal* insisted on changing the outcome for serialization so that Nophaie dies at the end. By the time the book version was released by Harper's in 1925, Nophaie indeed suffers a relapse of influenza and dies. Two movie versions made from the book in 1925 and 1955 made further considerable changes to the plot. It was not unusual that Hollywood changes were made to plots to make a gloomy ending come to a more upbeat conclusion.

In movie interracial marriage, the world had to be set right by one of the characters dying or leaving.[32] This was usually the woman. In *The Squaw Man* (1914) Nat-U-Ritch (Princess Red Wing, birth name Lillian St. Cyr) commits suicide. In 1950, racial barriers meant that Tom Jeffords (James Stewart) and Indian maiden Sonseeahray (Debra Padget) in *Broken Arrow* (1950) could not settle down to blissful matrimony, so she is duly killed off before the end of the movie. An alternative solution for scriptwriters was for the man to die, such as Nophaie (Richard Dix) being shot by a fellow Navajo Indian in one early film version of *The Vanishing American* (1925).

Grey continued to write Western novels into the 1930s but updated his later ones, such as *Code of the West*, which was published in 1934, to include automobiles, telephones, and threshing machines. Just as in the anachronistic later Gene Autry and Roy Roger movies of the 1940s, Grey's plot also included horses, riders on horseback, and blazing six-guns. And, of course, like any Western worth its salt, the crucial resolution in the last few pages developed into a pounding fistfight.

Many of Grey's novels were subsequently made into motion pictures. Grey was so passionate about the West that he insisted the films be shot on the location where they were supposed to have taken place.

Some Other Novelists

Pulp magazines and paperback thrillers set the pattern for mass-market Westerns in a form of rip-roaring adventure story that made use of romance, excitement, and nostalgia for the Old West. They created an established formula that sold novels by the score. Commercial writers tried for realism and detail, but they often overdramatized and romanticized the West and its heroes. W.H. Hutchinson summed up the plot of this type of novel as a combination of "virgins, villains, and varmints."[33]

B.M. Bower (the pen name of Bertha Muzzy, a ranch wife in northern Montana) wrote over seventy novels, including the popular *Chip of the Flying U* in the early 1900s. She wrote about honest young people falling in love and overcoming obstacles to happiness against a background of the wide-open spaces of the West. *Lonesome Land,* first published in February of 1912, was so well received that it was reprinted three times in February, three times in March, twice in April, and again in August.

One of the major authors of Westerns during the first half of the 1900s was William MacLeod Raine, who wrote novels as well as short stories and articles. From 1908 to 1954 he averaged two books a year, publishing over eighty novels and numerous short stories. Raine was an authentic westerner who grew up on a cattle ranch near the Texas-Arkansas border and had known real lawmen and bandits.

Clarence E. Mulford wrote a series of connected short stories, published as a book in 1906, titled *Bar-20.* One of the characters was a tough, ornery, red-haired, hard-drinking, smoking, cursing cowboy who caroused with his buddies. This rough yet ethical cowhand was named Hopalong Cassidy. More stories and books about him followed and the character eventually appeared in the movie *Hop-A-Long Cassidy* (1935), starring William Boyd. During the sixty-five Hopalong Cassidy B Western films that followed between 1935 and 1948, the character was toned down and became milder. Boyd's screen character of Hopalong Cassidy was not like Mulford's original. He became a clean-living, square-dealing, congenial doer of good deeds. He also championed "the little guy," which, like the mythic Jesse James and Deadwood Dick before him, appealed to depression-era audiences. Hoppy never shot first and used his brain instead of brawn. Cassidy became a gentlemanly and idealistic hero who didn't drink, smoke, or curse. Mulford's original books were rousing action stories, but Boyd's movies became morality plays with simplistic detective-like plots. After Boyd became popular in the movie role of Cassidy, Mulford's novels were modified and partly rewritten before being reprinted to conform to Boyd's new image of Cassidy.[34] Thus the hero myth was altered and reflected into the original creation. Boyd's interpretation of Cassidy has lasted, and the original wild and vice-ridden cowboy has been forgotten.

Probably the most prolific pulp Western author was Frederick Faust, who wrote novels under nineteen different pseudonyms, including George Owen Baxter, Evan Evans, Peter Dawson, George Challis, David Manning, and, his most famous pen name, Max Brand.[35] He was one of the undisputed kings of the Western pulps. He wrote quickly, sometimes churning out 12,000 words on a weekend and writing an entire novel in three weeks.[36] Brand was more polished and less extravagant with words than many of the other contemporary Western authors. Starting as a writer in 1918, he completed over 300 books and hundreds of short stories that included mysteries, historical romances, and science fiction. Brand was known to author an entire issue of *Western Story* magazine with different stories written under different names. He once claimed the following was a guiding formula for pulp stories and B Westerns: "Action, action, action is the thing. So long as you keep your hero jumping through fiery hoops on every page you're all right."[37]

Another writer who believed in plenty of action was Wayne D. Overholser. The following is a typical excerpt from his 1939 story "Lawyer Two-Fist" in *Western Story*: "He ducked, came up under Lengel's right, and both his own fists went out in a paralyzing one-two to Lengel's jaw that rocked the big man to his heels.... Lengel's breath went out in a wheezing gurgle and he went down into the dust of the street."[38]

Frederick Dilley Glidden, who took the pen name Luke Short after the real-life gunman,

Movies are often remembered by the locations used. This background scenery, very familiar to fans of B Westerns, is the Alabama Hills backed by the Sierra Nevada Mountains, near Lone Pine, California. The Lone Ranger, Gene Autry, Hopalong Cassidy, and many other B Western stars galloped their way through these rocks and along the dusty roads as they chased villains across the screen. It has been estimated that more than 300 movies were made here between the 1920s and the 1950s (author's collection).

was a popular paperback author who began writing in 1936.[39] Glidden wrote Western fiction using colorful stories that had an authentic flavor of the Old West. His specialty was frontier justice and right triumphing over evil. His heroes were strangers on horseback who rescued heroines from villains against overwhelming odds. He created a popular formula that sold over thirty million books. Many of his novels were turned into films.[40]

One of the more recent popular writers was Louis L'Amour, who wrote many Western novels that have been turned into movies. He continued the tradition of lively, well-plotted adventure stories about the West, using courageous heroes who fight against villains and Indians. L'Amour's 100 novels and 250 short stories had sold 320 million copies by 2010. As well as adventure stories, L'Amour wrote several continuing stories about Hopalong Cassidy under the pen name of Tex Burns.

The Rise of the Mass-Market Paperbacks

In the 1930s, books were expensive, with many costing as much as $2.50 (about $34 in today's dollars). A further inconvenience for readers was that most books had to be purchased in bookstores in large cities. As paper shortages and rising costs during World War II pushed some of the pulps out of business, some of the others became smaller and thicker. Thus, as the pulp magazine format declined, a new reading format, the cheap paperback book, emerged.

A creative individual named Robert Fair de Graff realized he could change the way people bought books by making them cheaper and small enough to fit both the hand and the pocket. He obtained backing from publisher Simon & Schuster and launched a series of books under the business title of Pocket Books in May 1939.[41] The size was four inches by six inches and the cost was only thirty-five cents. Looking for profitable niche markets to be filled, De Graff put these small books where they hadn't been previously sold, such as grocery stores, drug stores, and vending machines. By selling the books in airports, train stations, and bus terminals, he provided travelers with cheap reading material to while away their trips. These cheap paperback novels started to become a dominant form of entertainment for the masses and within two years Pocket Books had sold seventeen million copies. The business model was such a financial success that it attracted other major publishers. Bantam, for example, sold twenty-five million books with Western titles between 1947 and 1951.[42] Early paperback publishers reprinted hardback stories, but then the popularity of the format forced them to expand into paperback originals to supply enough material.

Publishers had tried to introduce cheap mass-market paperbacks in this sort of format before World War II, but shortages of paper during the war limited growth. In the economic boom that came after the conflict was over, paperback books became popular and succeeded wildly. Many people who had not previously been considered part of the traditional book market started to read. In a practice that extended back to the dime novels, the biggest sellers in paperbacks were Westerns, mysteries, and thinly veiled lurid crime stories. Books by popular authors such as Zane Grey were republished in paperback form year after year with tantalizing front covers and thrilling descriptions on the back cover to hook the reader. A 1951 paperback version of *Forlorn River* says on the cover, "Forlorn River is a story of the old West—of the lawless days of cattle-stealing and the thrilling pursuit and capture of wild horses. It is full of the intensity and dash which made up life then and which Zane Grey brings vividly to life in print." The gunman on the front cover looks suspiciously like Alan Ladd in the motion picture *Shane* (1953), even though the book appeared before the movie.

In a further boost to popularity, American filmmakers adapted many of these thrilling novels into Western movies. Books had a built-in audience of readers who were more likely to go to a movie when they had read and enjoyed the book. On the negative side, filmmakers tended to tinker with book plots, adding and subtracting elements as they fancied. Plots were changed for the movie version either because the book was too long to make a suitable movie, or sometimes because the book did not translate well into a visual image, or the outcome was too depressing. Most moviegoers wanted excitement and a happy ending. Sometimes studios wanted only the popular or snappy title of a book for marketing reasons.

Western Nonfiction

Other literature about the West helped to maintain and amplify the image of the westerner as a rugged outdoor individual, and many nonfiction books were highly influential in supporting the myth of the West.

In 1883, when the buffalo were vanishing, future president Theodore Roosevelt traveled to the West to add a specimen to his collection of hunting trophies before the animals became extinct. He was so taken with the West that he purchased two ranches in North Dakota. He later wrote a series of reminiscences based on his experiences in the West as a rancher and a sportsman. These articles, illustrated by artist Frederic Remington and published in *Century* magazine, were collected into a popular book as *Ranch Life and the Hunting Trail* (1899). Roosevelt presented the cowboy as a heroic figure struggling with the wildness of the West, and not as the common laborer that he really was. It is significant that Wister, Roosevelt, and Remington were prime supporters of the Western myth and worked in concert to promote it. Roosevelt was so enthusiastic about the subject that his descriptions helped to create Western mythology and promoted travel to the West. Remington illustrated Roosevelt's writings in a manner that supported the myth. Wister and Roosevelt were friends and Wister dedicated *The Virginian* to him.[43] Wister and Remington wrote "The Evolution of the Cow-Puncher" for *Harper's New Monthly* magazine in 1895, in which they portrayed the cowboy as a modern-day knight. After the publication of *The Virginian*, a flood of Western illustrations appeared in books and magazines, all following in the tradition of Remington and Russell.

After the heyday of the real West was over, nostalgic and romanticized reminiscences of the myth appeared in novel form such as *The Virginian*. Accounts of authentic cowboy life also carried on the mythic tradition under the guise of realism. *A Cowboy; or, Fifteen Years on the Hurricane Deck of a Spanish Pony* by Charles Siringo, *Log of Cowboy* by Andy Adams, *We Pointed 'Em North* by "Teddy Blue" Abbott, *Fiddlefooted* by Mat Jones, and others, were mostly romanticized tales blending fact, fiction, and folklore and were based on typical events in the life of a cowboy rather than serious histories.

Other nonfiction writers turned to historical figures to promote their vision of the heroes of the West, again reflecting the writers of the dime novels. One of the more interesting examples of creating a folk-hero was the legend of Wyatt Earp. In 1927 Stuart Lake was writing for films and magazines when he heard that Earp was still alive and living in Los Angeles, and Lake decided to write his biography. In 1931, Lake published *Wyatt Earp: Frontier Marshal*, which featured Earp as a hero who single-handedly cleaned up the worst hell-holes on the frontier. Due to this exaggerated and mostly fictional account created by Lake, Wyatt Earp became one of the most famous lawmen of the days of the American Old West. Yet, as historian John Mack Faragher has pointed out, "Earp, unlike other frontier legends in their own time, was a minor figure until a popular writer named Stuart Lake concocted a legend for him."[44]

The book subsequently became the authority for nearly all the films that featured Earp. Acknowledging Lake's biography on-screen lent a kind of historical authenticity to these films, but the trouble was that the book contained imaginative fabrication mixed with just enough fact to lend it credibility. Although Lake claimed to have interviewed Earp and he used Earp's authoritative first-person voice throughout the narrative, Faragher states that "Lake later confessed that, 'as a matter of cold fact, Wyatt never "dictated" a word to him.'"[45]

Lake's chapter "At the O.K. Corral" was the basis for *Gunfight at the O.K. Corral* (1957) with Burt Lancaster playing Wyatt Earp, which solidified the title and the man in the public's mind. In point of fact, the famous gunfight didn't take place at the O.K. Corral, but just off Fremont Street in a vacant lot behind the corral. Deputy sheriff Billy Breakenridge, who was in Tombstone at the time, called it "The Incident Near the O.K. Corral." As author Jeff Guinn points out, it would not have the same ring if it was called "The Gunfight in the Empty Lot on Fremont Street."[46] The Earp legend was further promoted by newspaperman Walter Noble Burns in his book *Tombstone: An Iliad of the Southwest* in 1927 and by Billy Breakenridge in *Helldorado* in 1918. Both books were written with an eye more to drama than to fact.

11

Warbling Cowboys and the Silver Screen

The Western is an American folklore: A mythology, depending on fantasy rather than history—Brian Garfield[1]

Another boost to the heroic cowboy image came in the 1920s and 1930s. While the written word about the West, whether serious fiction, nonfiction, or the pulps was popular, the prime mythmaker of the Western hero was the motion picture industry. The movie hero was a cowboy who rode the open range and fought outlaws and other villains until social stability and moral order were restored. Within the framework of Western film, the hero had a natural awareness of right and wrong and did what a man had to do without consequences as he followed his personal code of honor. Most Westerns, and particularly the ones of the 1930s and 1940s, ended on a positive note, as the hero righted wrongs and overcame injustice. This image stretched back to the early good badmen of Broncho Billy and William S. Hart, who restored justice as they personally atoned for their wrongdoings.

The "A's" and "B's" of the 1930s Westerns

In spite of the success of *The Virginian* (1929) and *In Old Arizona* (1928), and even though Warner Baxter won the Academy Award for best actor as the Cisco Kid for *In Old Arizona* (1928), Hollywood believed that lavish outdoor Westerns were doomed with the introduction of sound movies. Some studio executives thought that Westerns could not succeed because of the technical difficulties of recording sound on location outside, away from an interior studio set. After 1929 the depressed economy, coupled with the high costs and complexities of producing sound films, made studios reluctant to finance major Westerns and caused the studios to steer away from the genre. Warner Brothers apparently agreed with that perception because they bought First National in 1929 and immediately phased out Westerns. In 1930, even Carl Laemmle, president of Universal, felt that sound Westerns were too much of a financial risk. He stopped making them, a decision that he reversed three years later, however, when the problems of recording sound on location had been solved.

Another factor that made producers leery of making sound Westerns was that the lavish epic *The Big Trail* (1930) did poorly at the box office. *The Big Trail* was released after the stock market crash of 1929 depressed the general economy, which rebounded onto Hollywood and the movie industry. William Fox declared bankruptcy and Fox Studios went into receivership.[2] Another unfortunate impact of the Great Depression was that 4,000 theaters closed in 1931 and 1932.[3] Hollywood was reluctant to invest large sums of money even when the Western *Cimarron* (1931) won the 1931 Academy Awards for Best Picture, Best Screenplay, and Best Art Direction, in addition to being nominated for Best Director, Best Actor, and Best Actress. Between 1931 and 1939 the major studios essentially abandoned Western movies.

All these factors helped to push the Western into a period of change in the 1930s that lasted until the entry of America into World War II in 1941. As moviemaking became more technical and more expensive, two kinds of Westerns emerged. The "A Westerns" were high-quality motion pictures about the West made with big stars and big budgets and were backed by the full weight of the studio publicity machines. The "B Westerns" were equivalent in the film world to the dime and pulp novels in the literary world. They were made on a tight budget and received limited marketing by the studios. They were expected to sell themselves by using the same established stars and keeping the same plots, which consisted primarily of action, drama, comedy, and a happy ending.

Between 1930 and 1941 a total of 1,336 Westerns were made. But of this large number, only sixty-six were A Westerns.[4] In 1930 only eight A Westerns were released and five in 1931. In 1934 no A Westerns were made.[5] Four were made in 1938, but after the success of *Stagecoach* (1939) the number went back up to fourteen in 1940. Some of the A Westerns of the 1940s continued the mythic and romantic heroic images, dominated by director John Ford's romantic visions of the Old West. Though Ford did not make many Westerns, his films, such as *Stagecoach* (1939), *My Darling Clementine* (1946), *She Wore a Yellow Ribbon* (1949), *Rio Grande* (1950), and *The Searchers* (1956), defined much of the popular image of the West from 1939 to 1956. His films portrayed the rescue of civilized frontier people from violent malevolent forces by a heroic man with superior skills in dealing with frontier life.

The Western as a genre remained popular in the 1930s, so the lack of A Westerns fueled the demand for B Westerns. First-run theaters started to show fewer Westerns, but the smaller houses continued to book them. This resulted in less profit for filmmakers, which in turn meant that studios had to cut production costs to the minimum and led to cheaply made, low-budget B Westerns. The name B Western has been interpreted as Budget Western (which indeed they were), but the name actually came from the practice of theaters running double features in order to make patrons feel they were getting their money's worth. The B Western ran on the second or lower half of the bill, which was the B position.

B Westerns continued to be cranked out at a furious pace during the 1930s and into the 1940s to satisfy audiences who sought to escape from the everyday worries of the poor economy. Hollywood in the 1930s was driven by the "Big Five" major studios: Paramount, Fox, MGM, Warner Brothers, and RKO. Next in line were the "Little Three," consisting of Columbia, Universal, and United Artists. At the bottom of the chain of filmmaking were what were called the "Poverty Row" studios, such as Victory Pictures Corporation, Puritan, Mascot, PRC, Monogram, World Wide Pictures, Supreme Pictures Corporation, and First National (before being absorbed by Warner Brothers), all of whom cranked out cheap B Westerns.[6]

The "B" Westerns

The B Western studios were geared towards the mass production and marketing of as many films as possible. Profitability depended on the studios' ability to read audience trends and then to produce many similar films. As a result, the limited budgets that were imposed on the producers of B Westerns in the 1930s caused the genre to become defined by several standardized plot devices. These included the comic sidekick, the villain in the black hat, and the sexy saloon girl whose unmentioned real profession remained questionable. The central conflict was between the hero and the villain. The central relationship was between the hero and his sidekick, rather than involvement with a female love interest. In the singing Westerns, the ranch hands who doubled as a backup band consisted of the "boys," who helped the hero whenever needed. Thus, the central group that these movie revolved around was essentially male. Usually even the hero's horse was male.

B Westerns relied on chases, gunfights, stampedes, and fistfights to keep the plot moving at a fast pace. Justice was fair and firm but inevitable. In the B Western the hero always won, but he won with good sportsmanship. These plot devices helped to define the genre of the B Western and the Western hero of the 1930s and audiences came to expect them. These factors complemented and reinforced each other. As audiences came to expect and enjoy certain plot conventions, moviemakers tended to keep them in their movies. Conversely, the more these standardized conventions occurred in the movies, the more the audiences expected them and grew to believe that they represented the real West.

The plots of B Westerns were mostly minor variations on a basic formula that was designed to be reliable rather than innovative, and they were based on recurring character types and performers. Villains were figures of authority motivated by greed—crooked bankers and politicians, and crooked ranchers swindling an heiress out of an inheritance or conspiring with local outlaw gangs. The heroes of these action pictures were always involved in fights. Columbia's B Westerns contained five or six fights per picture and just as many chases. Mascot Pictures specialized in rapid pacing and frantic action, such as the hero or a posse on horseback chasing outlaws escaping in an automobile. These routine action movies have been derisively called "oaters," "horse operas," "programmers," "formula Westerns," "shoot-'em-ups," and "blood-and-thunder epics." The emphasis on action did not always leave much time for a complex plot.

The majority of the source material for A Westerns came from contemporary serious novels, plays, short stories, and magazine articles. Most of the scripts for B Westerns were written directly for the screen by teams of writers at a studio, similar to the way scripts were later developed for television series. The B Westerns were, in particular, strongly influenced by the melodramatic plots of the dime novels. The valiant hero fought villains, outlaws, bank robbers, cattle rustlers, and stagecoach bandits. He might pretend to be an outlaw in order to get close to the villains before he pounced on them. The villain was motivated by some element of greed, such as robbery, theft, or control of land or water rights. Similar to the dime novels, one common plot twist was that the hero was an outlaw who had reformed and settled down to make a new life in a community that did not know of his past. Other common elements in these plots included former partners who came back to haunt the reformed hero and a wronged man hiding out from the law in a new life. In foreshadowing many of the 1950s Westerns, the hero might be seeking revenge for the killing of his family.

B Westerns were expected to show heroes and villains with plenty of action. Right and justice were always supposed to triumph in the end, as illustrated in this 1926 publicity still from *The Holdup of the Pony Express* showing the clean-cut hero holding a gun on the masked villain after capturing him (Library of Congress).

To combine plot lines, the murders might even have been done by his former partners in crime.

Acting ability in the B Westerns was not always the most polished. One of the old sayings in Hollywood was that actors in B Westerns had to master two expressions. One was with their hat on and the other was with their hat off.[7] This was put a little more crudely by Reb Russell, who made twelve Westerns in the 1930s: "...you only needed two expressions to be a western actor—constipation and relief."[8]

The real-life identity of the hero-actor in these movies often became merged with his screen persona and audiences identified a particular star with a particular screen image.

Popular Western star of the silent films George O'Brien, for instance, was known for creating athletic fights in his movies. Tom Mix's trademark was his on-screen daredevil stunts. Ken Maynard excelled in trick-riding skills. Tex Ritter, Gene Autry, and Roy Rogers sang and dressed in fancy show-business clothing like Tom Mix. Wild Bill Elliott and Johnny Mack Brown played tough guys. Stars did, however, use various gimmicks to try to differentiate themselves from the others. Wild Bill Elliott, for example, wore his twin .45 Colts in holsters with their butts facing forwards for a cross-draw, in the manner of the real Wild Bill Hickok, who wore his backwards tucked into a wide sash.[9] Both Lash LaRue and Whip Wilson used whips as their weapon of choice.

The mixing of screen persona and the actor's real life evolved into confusion for the audience between the actor and his screen role. Roles in films were seen as a type of biography or history of how this new type of hero lived. The confusion between fiction and real life was further promoted by the studios when cowboy stars such as Gene Autry and Roy Rogers used their real names in their movies. Buffalo Bill Cody achieved success by playing himself as "Buffalo Bill." B Western stars kept the same convention by keeping their same names in different films to provide continuity and project the image of their screen and real selves as being the same.

The actor's fictional hero persona was assumed to be the way he lived in real life. By the same token this led to actors who starred primarily in Westerns finding themselves narrowly type-cast into a certain image, which did not allow them to expand into other roles, as Fox found out when the studio tried to put Tom Mix into costume dramas. This association of an actor with a particular role then led to the illusion that the actor lived in this fictional Western world. For example, audiences assumed that William S. Hart, Gene Autry, and Roy Rogers lived on ranches in the Wild West, and that Tom Mix was a flashily dressed cowboy all the time. On the other side of the coin, this identification led to stars' projecting some of their image back into their real lives. Tom Mix and Gene Autry did indeed wear Western clothes, boots, and hats in their everyday lives.

The virtues of these movie cowboys were parodied in the later movie *Rustler's Rhapsody* (1985), which includes all the clichés and stereotypical characters from B Westerns of the 1940s. The plot includes villains dressed in black, the rancher's pure daughter, the hooker with a heart of gold, the town drunk, and a hero with a collection of tall, peaked white hats like Tom Mix.

The Series Westerns

As Western movies changed and were driven by the economics of cheap production methods, series Westerns emerged as a new sub-genre of the traditional Western. The series Western followed a set formula, had a set running time, and was geared for a particular audience who wanted to keep seeing the same star in the same plots. These Westerns were inexpensive to produce, mostly used outdoor settings on the studio's back lot or ranch to avoid the need for elaborate sets, contained as much action as possible, and were tremendously popular among audiences.

The primary pressure from the studio was that the producer had to bring in a saleable product on time and under budget. To help achieve this, the shooting schedule for these movies was very short. For economy, producers often repeated successful formulas and plots and used recycled footage from previous movies from the studio's library to keep costs low. The reuse of film from previous movies meant that actors might have to use clothing worn by early silent stars to match the footage. Sometimes this was not done and the mismatch was obvious to even casual audiences. Poverty Row studios made heavy use of existing permanent sets and towns on their back lot or movie ranch. These movies made such frequent use of the same sets and locations that experienced audiences could identify the movie ranch or exterior location that was being used. Sharp-eyed fans could recognize Movie Flats near Lone Pine, California, or Red Rocks Canyon State Recreation Area, north of Los Angeles, both of which were used heavily for B Western locations.

The need for speed and economies of production meant that several directors often worked on the same picture at the same time. One director might film the dialog scenes while another director was doing second unit work that consisted of the action scenes and fights, often using doubles for the actors at long range so that filming could be hurried along. The use of premier stuntmen such as Yakima Canutt and Cliff Lyons gave an added boost to the hero's actions. Actors worked so fast they often didn't know what they were supposed to be reacting to because the film was shot so much out of sequence. Scripts were often revised on the fly on location to incorporate new bits of action or to explain some situation that hadn't been properly worked out in pre-production or in the script.

Directors worked so fast that often parts of the plot were inadvertently left out. Due to budget constraints, there wasn't time for retakes or to add missing material because the cast and crew were already working on the next movie. Much of the final story might be left to the film editor, who had to piece together a patchwork of raw film into a coherent story. If the filmed story contained a serious jump, narration (as kind of a *deus ex machina*) was sometimes added to explain gaps in the story. At other times no attempt was made to figure it out at all.

Most of the series Westerns of the 1930s and 1940s did not represent either the historical or the modern West but used contemporary settings. The heroines were often dressed in contemporary fashions and had 1930s hairdos. These movies did not claim to represent the West with any authenticity, but dealt with the economic, social, and cultural issues of their audiences. Plots commonly involved issues raised by the New Deal or the Great Depression. Frequent plot elements were a failed bank or crooked banker, a dishonest foreman, or a kidnapped rancher. Heroes in B Westerns during World War II fought saboteurs and cattle barons with foreign accents and worked references to various evil foreign powers into the plots.

Many of the characters were stereotyped so that movies audiences could easily identify them. The villain was often a banker or real estate developer who seemed respectable to the honest townsfolk, but who carried on schemes to swindle the heroine behind this facade. Favorite plots involved a dishonest banker who cheated unsuspecting landowners out of their ranches or a crooked saloon owner who cheated customers in crooked card games. Many of the villain's henchmen were typecast by wearing scruffy boots, badly fitting dark clothes, and a black hat. They seemed shifty by their actions, as they popped in and out of the villain's respectable office in town via the hidden back door. The smooth villains typically dressed in contemporary business suits and drove fast modern cars, while the hero in cowboy clothes rode his favorite horse.

The Serial Westerns

Series Westerns presented the same star, usually under his own name, often with the same sidekick, in a string of unrelated movies with different plots. Serial Westerns, on the other hand, presented one long convoluted plot but broke it up into twelve to fifteen chapters, usually screened in local theaters as one chapter a week.

To entice the audience to return to see the next chapter of the serial, a cliff-hanger was written into the end of each weekly segment. The cliff-hanger placed the hero in a perilous situation and the audience had to watch the next chapter to see how he escaped. A typical cliff-hanger was to have the hero fighting the villain in a speeding driverless car or on top of a runaway stagecoach as the vehicle careened towards a cliff. Plot-writers of Western serials relied on speed to give a feeling of action. Therefore they used horse chases, automobiles, trucks, planes, fast boats, and speeding trains to create a feeling of tension and urgency. Another cliff-hanger was that the hero was left injured or unconscious after a fight and lying on a railroad track as a train sped towards him or on a road as a truck was about to rumble over him. Other perilous situations that the hero became trapped in might be a fall from a cliff, being caught in the direct pathway of a stampeding herd of cattle or horses, being trapped in a burning building, lying unconscious in a runaway wagon or automobile, being buried in a mine disaster, or about to be lynched by an angry mob. The next chapter of the serial would start with a recap of the impending peril and then carry on to its resolution.

These cliff-hangers were often forced and overplayed. For example, at the end of one chapter of *The Vigilantes Are Coming* (1936), star Bob Livingston was supposedly crushed by a giant piece of machinery. The start of the next chapter, however, showed that he had miraculously jumped out of the way before being squashed and the plot continued as if nothing had happened. Similarly, at the end of one of the chapters of *Winners of the West* (1940), Dick Foran is shown being run over by a train. At the beginning of the next chapter, however, he has reacted just in time and is off the track before the train hits him. Sometimes the resolution to the cliff-hanger was not explained. At the end of one chapter of *The Oregon Trail* (1939), star Johnny Mack Brown disappears under a herd of stampeding horses. Yet at the beginning of the next episode he carries on as if nothing had happened.

Singing Stars

Cowboy heroes started to sing after Ken Maynard introduced songs into several of his movies in the early 1930s. The music was worked in with the plotline. With the movie *In Old Santa Fe* (1934), Maynard created a new Hollywood genre that became known as the horse opera. The Poverty Row studios soon realized that there were several financial and commercial advantages to adding songs to films. One reason, as Republic's B Western director William Witney commented, was that singing numbers were cheaper to stage and film than fights and brawls that involved stunt work.[10] Another reason was to increase crossover promotion between films and recorded songs. Singers such as Gene Autry helped to promote sales of their songs on records by featuring them in their movies.

Depression-era audiences enjoyed the cheerful light touch of a singing musical Western. These movies were set in a carefree West that was filled with music and fun and where justice

Yodeling movie cowboys were not the only ones who popularized Western singing, or what was earlier called "hillbilly music," a type of music extremely popular during the Great Depression. This typical small band, consisting of two guitars and a fiddle, is entertaining at a mobile camp for migrant farm workers in Odell, Oregon, in 1941 (Library of Congress).

and good always triumphed over villainy. Accordingly a new type of plot evolved that was based on a decent story, had good music and comedy relief, retained action sequences with chases and fights, and sometimes introduced a little romance. Audiences also liked the notion that their cowboy hero was bashful around the heroine but became very confident when singing to her. All this was played out against an untamed land of sweeping desert scenery, snow-capped mountains, and the vastness of the western sky.

By the mid–1940s, musical accompaniment had become more elaborate and sometimes featured extravagant production numbers that included singers and dancers performing on lavish sets, even though the plot was supposed to be taking place in small nightclubs in remote, dusty western towns. Sometimes the hero sang while out riding the range. It must have been a puzzle to small kids who wondered where all the orchestral music accompanying the hero and his sidekick came from.

This new romantic hero kept his hat on, even during fight scenes and even when rolling around on the ground. In one movie, Gene Autry is shot off his horse. As his stunt double rolls down a hill into a brush-filled draw, he is seen holding his hat tightly on his head as he tumbles end-over-end down the slope, both to maintain his image and to hide his identity as a stunt double.

Two types of villain emerged. The smooth villain was still a banker, lawyer, or businessman who stole money from his clients and the safe, but now some of the villains operated Broadway nightclubs and lavish entertainment in small cow towns. The other heavy was a mean, grizzled, unshaven, rumpled, unwashed villain who did all the dirty (so to speak) work. The latter was typified by the characters later played by actors Royal Dano and Jack Elam.

The new musical Westerns were a departure from the traditional B Westerns. They were set not in the real American post–Civil War West, but in the contemporary West, as evidenced by the use of modern cars and trucks. The background characters were usually dressed in contemporary 1930s work clothes. As a result, studios like Republic Pictures invented their own historical Western fantasyland. Their plots were set in the modern West, with stars like Gene Autry as a radio or rodeo star (always under his own name), and involved high-powered cars, army tanks, airplanes, and radio stations. The hero was often linked to a radio show that promoted his music. The story lines addressed contemporary social problems such as politics or the problems of raising cattle. But plots still included stagecoaches, horse chases, cowboys wearing guns, and barroom fights. The plots of the 1930s mixed cowboy individualism and nostalgia with twentieth century realism but continued the theme of the traditional Western fantasy.

The singing cowboy was accompanied by a backup band that consisted of at least a guitar, fiddle, and bass. The back-up group was often made up of "the boys," who were the singer's band dressed in Hollywood's idea of Western clothing as they hung around the dude ranch where the star worked and sang as an entertainer. Acting excellence was not mandatory in the singing B Westerns, but the presentation of personality and the ability to sing was.

The movie cowboys of the 1930s duplicated Buffalo Bill Cody's flashy outfits and improved on them. The stars wore ornate clothing that was more suited to shooting exhibitions, circuses, and rodeo parades than to working cowboys. Singing cowboys wore stylish Western wardrobes with tight pants, gaudy shirts with yokes, high-button cuffs and smile pockets, ornate boots, and a tall white hat with a distinctive crease.[11] Rex Allen, the last of the singing cowboys, sometimes wore rhinestone-fringed gold-lamé outfits.

The 1930s sometimes made symbolic use of black hats and white hats to differentiate between the hero and the villain. The villain wore a black costume and a black hat. The hero wore white or light-colored clothing, a white hat, and rode a white or palomino horse. One exception was William Boyd as Hopalong Cassidy, who wore outfits that were black or navy blue (which filmed as black in black-and-white films). Another visual symbol of the bad guy was that he had a moustache, as facial hair was associated by audiences of the time with villainy.

Gene and Roy

The Gene Autry and later Roy Rogers movies were musicals, not Westerns, and actors such as Autry in fancy costumes were not cowpunchers but entertainers who blurred the lines between singer, performer, and movie star. The Westerns of Autry and Rogers combined traditional elements such as horse chases, cattle stampedes, gunfights, and saloon fights with modern elements such as nightclubs with chorus girls, Western singers, airplanes, trucks, fast cars, and television.

Autry, billed as the original Singing Cowboy, took Ken Maynard's basic idea and expanded the role of the singing hero until this formula dominated the B Westerns.[12] Autry's films combined music, light humor, action, chases, fights, stunts, and a little romance. Comedy relief was provided by the sidekick. Even though romance was toned down, the singing cowboy occasionally kissed the heroine. In *Oh, Susanna!* (1936), Gene Autry gave Mary Ann Lee (Frances Grant) a big smooch in the closing scene. He ends up in a similar clinch in the final scene of *The Old Corral* (1936).

The Westerns of the 1920s started out as sixty minutes of furious action. Gene Autry developed a new format for the Western that had as much music as gunplay. By 1936 the musical content of Autry pictures had overwhelmed the action of the traditional Western films. The Western hero was supposed to be tough, but Autry was mild-mannered with a soft voice. Autry movies were made to adhere to a "cowboy code." His movies had no bad language, no violence, and no excess gunplay—and certainly nothing that suggested that men and women slept in the same room. His movies were a form of escapism where people could get their minds off real life and the problems of the Depression. As Autry says in *Springtime in the Rockies* (1937), "It's hard to sing and be mean at the same time." He proves it in the movie when he diverts the lynching of a sheepman by angry cattle ranchers by having the villain sing a few verses of "When It's Springtime in the Rockies" and the "boys" all join in. Other bucolic scenes are the ranch hands singing around the chuckwagon at lunchtime.

Discounting such obvious aberrations as Autry's *The Phantom Empire* (1935), which involves a hidden civilization of advanced beings with ray guns and television located under Radio Ranch, and *Round-up Time in Texas* (1937), which was a Western set in Africa, most of Autry's cowboy films of the 1930s had standardized plots. In *Man from Music Mountain* (1938), a greedy and unscrupulous land promoter named Scanlon (Ivan Miller) sells worthless property in the ghost town of Gold River and its worked-out mine by telling investors that water and power will be coming soon from the new Boulder Dam. This type of plot played on the fears and worries of poor depression working folk of being taken advantage of by the rich classes. Autry and sidekick Smiley Burnette outwit the land promoters and have Scanlon buy back the property by pretending that they have made a new discovery of gold in the mine. All this, plus horse chases and shoot-outs, takes place to the accompaniment of seven songs, along with three musical novelty numbers played on cowbells, horse bells, and the Lone Ranger's theme (from the William Tell Overture) played on a xylophone. Not bad for a running time of fifty-three minutes and eighteen seconds.

In *The Old Barn Dance* (1938), Autry is a horse dealer who uses a radio show to promote his horses. Unknown to him, the show is sponsored by a crooked finance company which loans money to farmers for tractors and then forecloses on the debt if they cannot pay. This movies is full of Depression themes and "big bad business" taking advantage of the little guy. The resolution to the plot is for Autry to clear his good name and restore harmony to the community.

These films were made by Autry when he was under contract to Republic, before he enlisted in the Air Force (then the Army Air Corps) in 1942 during World War II. After the war was over he moved to Columbia Studios. *Rim of the Canyon* (1949) is an example of his later Columbia releases, which featured fewer songs, more serious complex plots, and a longer running time.

The appeal of Autry and Rogers movies for audiences was that the traditional fictional cowboy hero can individually and effectively deal with a variety of contemporary Western problems and villains. This may have been tinged with some nostalgia for days gone by when the times were presumed to have been better. As author Raymond White said, "In the uncertain times of the Depression-era 1930s and the war years of the 1940s, these films reassured Americans of their ability to face and survive crises. Perhaps one could not change his or her immediate economic or employment status or do much about the horrors of World War II, but in the darkness of the local theater, Roy Rogers could solve society' problems in about one hour."[13]

Like Tom Mix and others before them, Autry and Rogers cultivated the image of the clean-cut cowboy. They did not smoke or drink in public and avoided plots that went against their image. This put a great deal of pressure on a star to live up to his own persona and code. Being only human, mistakes in judgment occasionally occurred that disappointed fans who believed in the screen image. One time a drunken Gene Autry fell off his horse at the Fort Worth Coliseum Rodeo and smashed his guitar.[14] This departure from the clean-living hero of his movies startled and disappointed the young fans in attendance. On the other hand, these stars realized the impact that their hero images had on young children and genuinely tried to influence them to lead a clean-cut and positive life. Following are the rules from Roy Rogers' Riders Club as listed in Jim Arndt's *How to Be a Cowboy* (97):

1. Be neat and clean.
2. Be courteous and polite.
3. Always obey your parents.
4. Protect the weak and help them.
5. Be brave but never take chances.
6. Study hard and learn all you can.
7. Be kind to animals and take care of them.
8. Eat all your food and never waste any.
9. Love God and go to Sunday school regularly.
10. Always respect our flag and our country.

As successors to the earlier Westerns, the singing cowboys provided fantasy and escapist entertainment that reaffirmed the role of the mythic West. Though their movies contained modern elements, guns and horses were still the main attraction in an imaginary West where past and present were mixed together.

The Trusty Sidekick

Another successful element in the B Westerns of the 1930s and 1940s was the strong role of the sidekick, originating with comedian Smiley Burnette in the Autry movies. The sidekick was the hero's likeable companion who shared his adventures and helped him out in times of trouble. Although the concept of the comic sidekick has been a long-standing tradition in many entertainment forms, the Autry movies enlarged this role in B Westerns and made it a mainstay of the genre. Sidekicks were not as handsome as the hero and not as good with a gun or fists, but they provided comic relief by letting the audience laugh with them. In a traditional plot element that had its origin in early literature, a young hero was often paired with an old timer. The sidekick was a buddy, father, and brother all rolled up into one. Popular actors who played sidekicks in Westerns were Smiley Burnette, Pat Buttram, Walter Brennan, "Fuzzy" Knight, George "Gabby" Hayes, and Andy Devine.

The sidekick functioned as a sounding board so that the hero could discuss elements of the plot. He was also used to change the mood or pace in a film when required. Some sidekicks had comic physical limitations, such as an obvious stutter like Roscoe Ates, played his lines without teeth like Gabby Hayes, or were on the chubby side like Andy Devine and Smiley Burnette. None of this bothered the sidekick and these factors were played up to accentuate comic situations. The sidekick was not intended to be a stooge or a figure of fun. Though well-meaning, he was an often-bumbling friend who tried to be helpful. The sidekick hardly ever got a girl at the end and usually came out on the short end of the stick in most situations.

The sidekick often supplied the link between life and death for the hero if he was bushwhacked or captured. A common plot device was to place the star in danger, such as threatening him with a lynching or being locked up in jail, and then having him rescued with the help of the sidekick.

Outlaws as Heroes

Another common plot device for films of the 1930s was to use a hero who was, or had been in real life, an outlaw. As in the dime novels, a whole group of Western films revolved around outlaws like Billy the Kid and Jesse James. The first in this cycle was *Billy the Kid* (1930), which presented a whitewashed account of the Kid and his life. At the end, Billy (Johnny Mack Brown) and his girlfriend, Claire (Kay Johnson), escape across the border to Mexico as lawman Pat Garrett (Wallace Beery) shoots halfheartedly after them and deliberately misses. In the tradition of William S. Hart's good badman, Billy was portrayed as a man who was basically good but went bad due to circumstances beyond his control.

In *Billy the Kid Returns* (1938), Roy Rogers played dual characters, one of which supposedly looked just like the Kid. After the usual obstacles and twists, the plot is resolved to the accompaniment of seven songs. Producers Releasing Corporation (PRC) made a series of *Billy the Kid Outlawed* (1940), *Billy the Kid in Texas* (1940), *Billy the Kid's Smoking Guns* (1942), and *Blazing Frontier* (1943). Billy the Kid plots continued to be popular for decades with *The Left Handed Gun* (1958), *Dirty Little Billy* (1972), *The Great Northfield Minnesota Raid* (1972), *Pat Garrett and Billy the Kid* (1973), and *The Long Riders* (1980).

Jesse James (1939), with popular stars Tyrone Power and Henry Fonda, was a great success at the box office. The movie claimed to be historically accurate but misrepresented both the facts and the issues. The screenwriters of *Jesse James* (1939) justified Jesse's being forced into outlawry by a corrupt railroad man, Barshee (Brian Donlevy), who kills Jesse's mother. Jesse's subsequent attack on the railroad was justified as avenging the murder. In the movie, Jesse was martyred as a defender of wife, child, and home against the evil railroad. The success of *Jesse James* (1939) was followed quickly by *The Return of Frank James* (1940). Republic churned out *Days of Jesse James* (1939), *Jesse James at Bay* (1941), and *Jesse James Jr.* (1942).

Other studios had to come up with similar "heroes" and plots, and they jumped on the bandwagon with movies such as *When the Daltons Rode* (1940), *Bad Men of Missouri* (1941),

Belle Starr (1941), and another *Billy the Kid* (1941). The themes, characters, and plots for all of these movies were essentially derived from *Jesse James* (1939). The outlaws were put in a sympathetic light, and plots tried to make the audience believe that most of the West's badmen had been forced into a life of crime by a set of unfortunate circumstances beyond their control, such as encounters with crooked law enforcement officers. In *Days of Jesse James* (1939), Roy Rogers plays a detective who joins the James gang to catch Jesse, but finds out that he is an upstanding family man who has been framed by a crooked banker. Roy Rogers' portrayals of western outlaws like Billy the Kid were well done despite extensive character revisions by the writers to present him in a sympathetic light.

Jesse James continued to be a popular "hero" character with *Jesse James Rides Again* (1947), *Adventures of Frank and Jesse James* (1948), *The James Brothers of Missouri* (1950), and *Stranger at My Door* (1956). Among others were *The True Story of Jesse James* (1957) and *Alias Jesse James* (1959). These movies eventually degenerated into bizarre vehicles such as *Jesse James Meets Frankenstein's Daughter* (1966), in which the grandchildren of Baron Frankenstein want to experiment on Jesse and his wounded pal and turn the pal into a robot with a brain operation. Billy the Kid plots suffered the same fate in movies such as *Billy the Kid vs. Dracula* (1966), in which Dracula (John Carradine) shows up at a ranch where a reformed Billy (Chuck Courtney) is working and abducts ranch-owner Betty Bentley (Melinda Plowman). In the best vampire tradition, Billy tracks Dracula and the girl to a lair in a nearby mine and finishes the vampire off.

Other Cowboy Heroes

The high period of the singing cowboy occurred in the 1930s. Though singing Westerns continued to be produced during the 1940s, other Western screen heroes rebelled against this musical image. George O'Brien, Bob Baker, Donald Barry, Johnny Mack Brown, Sunset Carson, Monte Hale, Buster Crabbe, Wild Bill Elliott, Russell Hayden, Tom Holt, Tom Keene, Allan "Rocky" Lane, George Houston, Jack Randall, and Charles Starrett all starred in dramatic Westerns.

One innovative trend in the 1930s was the use of not one hero in a movie, but three. One of the heroes would be a romantic young lead to appeal to girls in the audience, another was a level-headed handsome hero for young boys and women, and the third was an older or fatter humorous character to provide comedy relief. Writer William Colt McDonald developed Republic's Three Mesquiteers series, which placed three White cowboys straight from Alexandre Dumas' *Three Musketeers* into a Western setting. This popular series, full of action-packed predicaments rescuing helpless women and children, ran from 1936 to 1943. The trend in trios continued with Buck Jones, Tim McCoy, and Raymond Hatton in Monogram's Rough Riders series. Another series was Ken Maynard, Hoot Gibson, and Bob Steele as the Trail Blazers. This type of plotting involved twelve different actors in nine different trios in fifty-one feature films.[15]

Wild Bill Elliott created a different kind of image for the hero in a series of Westerns for Monogram and Allied Artists. He could be ruthless, unsportsmanlike and selfish if it served the purposes of the plot. In *Bitter Creek* (1954), Clay Tyndall (Bill Elliott) needs information from the villain, so he proceeds to beat a response from him while keeping him covered with a gun. The villain protests: "You wouldn't get away with this if you'd put that gun down." In older Westerns the hero, such as Tom Mix, would have dropped his gun and gone at the villain in a fistfight just to be fair. Elliott, however, replies, "But I'm not going to put it down" and continues to pound on him until he gets the confession. Elliott played a man of integrity, but he often violated some of the earlier taboos of the singing cowboy. He would drink in a saloon if the plot called for it. If he played an outlaw, he played the real thing. In *Waco* (1952) and *Topeka* (1953), Elliott played an outlaw, not just a lawman posing as an outlaw. Unlike many of the heroes of the 1930s Westerns who sported improbable outfits, Elliott wore more traditional clothing of jeans and colored shirts.

A series of movies made by Lash LaRue contained violence and blood and were tinged with sadism. His hero image, with his trademark weapon of a whip, was more sinister than some of the other stars, as he dressed all in black.

Another popular nonsinging hero of the 1940s was Charles Starrett, who played the Durango Kid, an avenger righting wrongs. The Kid dressed entirely in black, including a black mask like the Lone Ranger wore, and rode a black stallion. A typical plot was that a town or a rancher was being threatened by an outlaw or a whole gang of outlaws when a tall, mysterious stranger rode into town. He was the Durango Kid, of course, but the local townspeople didn't know that. At the crucial moment, he would run behind a clump of bushes and emerge in the black masked outfit of the Durango Kid. (Often he was even able to apparently change the color of his horse at the same time.)

Meanwhile, back at the few Westerns produced by the big studios, two themes emerged. One was a social justice theme that explored the rights of the individual citizen versus the interests of the majority. Social injustice is imposed by the town boss, cattle baron, or local railroad and the hero has to correct the problem. Examples of this were the "town-tamer" Westerns like *Dodge City* (1939) and *My Darling Clementine* (1946). The other theme was the cavalry epic, such as *Santa Fe Trail* (1940) and *They Died with Their Boots On* (1941). This soldier theme explored war as something wanted by profiteers and fanatics but that the principled, civilized soldier did not want.

Singing Cowboys Ride Off the Screen

Westerns moved towards a new era after World War II as singing cowboy pictures lost their appeal for audiences. Public tastes had changed again and the global conflict brought a demand from audiences for a realism in both films and literature that did not include sequined cowboys. Though both the pulps and B Westerns continued after the war, they began fading in popularity.

The era of the singing Westerns came to an end in 1954 with *Phantom Stallion,* starring Rex Allen. Allen, born on a ranch in Mud Springs Canyon near Willcox, Arizona, was a latecomer to the singing movies, winning a contract with Republic in 1949. Between 1950 and 1954 he starred in nineteen singing Westerns and was one of the top ten box office draws of his day. Though his career as a movie star drew to a close in the 1950s, he went on to star in a television series, was a popular narrator for documentary films, and was a sought-after entertainer at rodeos and fairs.

Though the singing cowboy left the silver screen, cowboy music and the cowboy image continued to appeal to mass audiences. Singer Woody Guthrie, for instance, used frontier hero themes and cowboy ballads as he sang about Western outlaws such as Belle Starr, Billy the Kid, and Jesse James. Singing cowboy Tex Ritter, who starred in more than fifty B Westerns between 1936 and 1945, continued to appear at rodeos as a singer and entertainer. His singing career received a tremendous boost when he belted out the pounding Oscar-winning song that permeated *High Noon* (1952). Even popular crooner Bing Crosy recorded several cowboy-type songs in the 1930s.

Among the profound changes that occurred in American culture in the 1920s was the

Early recordings of country music were made on wax cylinders (shown with cylindrical storage box at upper right) and later on flat "records" made from shellac plastic (lower left) that revolved at 78 rpm. The record's sound information was contained in a series of grooves on the surface. Each ten-inch disc played for approximately 3½ minutes, thus songs were typically written to last for that length of time. This one happens to be "A Four Legged Friend" sung by Roy Rogers from the movie *Son of Paleface* (1952) (author's collection).

Early phonograph to play 78 rpm records used a hand-wound spring to power a mechanical motor, a steel needle to ride in the grooves to pick up the sound, and an acoustic horn to amplify and project it (author's collection).

ability to play recorded music at home and hear it over the radio waves. Radio, the phonograph, and Western movies were three new technologies that promoted cowboy songs and increased the popularity of Western music. Some singers were authentic cowboys, and some were showmen who dressed in cowboy outfits and sang cowboy songs. Either way, they popularized Western music and helped to further develop the romantic image of the cowboy.

This type of music was at the time called hillbilly and was aimed at rural audiences. Record companies quickly realized that there was a niche market for hillbilly music and cowboy songs, and quickly moved to record and promote this type of music. Phonographs, found in seven million American homes, were available for about $25. The first known recorded country music consisted of two fiddling tunes by Eck Robertson and Henry Gilliland, recorded and released in 1922 by Victor Talking Machine Company (later RCA Victor).[16] The first genuine cowboy to record a cowboy song was Carl T. Sprague, who recorded "When the Work's All Done This Fall" for Victor in 1925.[17] No slouch, this recording is estimated to have sold 900,000 copies.[18]

The sales of records were eventually hurt by the competition from radio, which was free compared to records that sold for about $1 each. By 1924, six hundred radio stations were broadcasting over the airwaves.[19] Radio programs were broadcast live and old-time hillbilly music was commonly used to fill the gaps between programs. Radio station WLS ("World's Largest Store"), owned and operated by Sears, Roebuck & Company, broadcast programs such as the WLS *Barn Dance*, which featured old-time rural music consisting of string bands with guitar, fiddle, bass, and banjo. Another leader in broadcasting hillbilly music was competing radio station WSM ("We Shield Millions") owned by National Life & Accident Insurance Company in Nashville. WSM went on the air in 1925 with 1,000 watts of power, broadcasting old-time country music and their own *Barn Dance* with lively fiddle music and banjo tunes and a regular cast of hillbilly acts.[20] This very popular program became the *Grand Ole Opry*, which continues today. In 1927 WSM increased its transmitter power to 5,000 watts so that it could reach homes in a much wider area of the country.[21]

Some Western bands were named or renamed to feature their radio sponsor. Bob Wills' band was called the Aladdin Laddies when he was sponsored by Aladdin Lamp Company. He later changed their name to the Light Crust Doughboys when he was sponsored by Light Crust Flour. The Light Crust Doughboys appeared backing Gene Autry in *Oh, Susanna!* (1936) as part of a crossover promotion between Western songs, cowboy bands, and Western movies.

A popular entertainer in the late 1920s and early 1930s was Jimmie Rodgers, who adopted Western-style clothing and recorded western-themed songs, including his characteristic yodel. Yodeling first came to America with troupes of touring Tyrolean musicians who used alpine yodeling in their acts in nineteenth century vaudeville.[22] This novel form of music was imitated and adopted by singers such as Jimmie Rodgers and, later, Gene Autry and Roy Rogers, who incorporated yodeling into many of their movie cowboy songs.

Jimmie Rodgers' style influenced Gene Autry, who tried to imitate Rodgers singing hillbilly music before he went into films. Autry's record producer, Art Satherly, steered him towards cowboy songs and billed him as "Oklahoma's Singing Cowboy."[23] After Autry went into movies, his records promoted his films and his films promoted his records. Sears, Roebuck (owner of station WLS) promoted Autry recordings through Gene Autry branded guitars, songbooks, and other merchandise the star endorsed. This trend was followed by the Western songs and merchandising of Roy Rogers.

These songs of the movie cowboys were not those of the real old-time cowboy, which were often derived from old folk tunes that arrived with immigrants from England or Ireland. The popular song "Streets of Laredo," for example, was a song that was modified and cleaned up by cowboys. It was from an old English sixteenth-century street song called "The Unfortunate Rake," about a young man dying from syphilis. The new cowboy music, on the other hand, came from the professional songwriters of New York and later from Hollywood, who promoted the romantic and idyllic version of the West that appeared in the movies. During the heyday of singing Westerns in the 1930s and 1940s Hollywood attracted scores of musicians and songwriters. The real cowboy songs, by contrast, originated as occupational songs of working cowboys. They were not the romantic ballads of the movie cowboy of the 1930s but reflected the harsh realities of life and dangerous work on the range.

Driven by the radio and recording industries, Western music styles shifted over the years from early folk music and hillbilly to country and western and then to country. Roy Rogers' musical group Sons of the Pioneers, who appeared in most of his movies, used a singing form more properly called Western than country, creating such classics songs as "Cool Water" and "Tumbling Tumbleweeds." They specialized in close harmony singing, backed by fiddle and guitars. Rogers was a founding member of the group under his real name of Leonard Slye and appeared in several movies as a member of the group before he attained starring roles. In Gene Autry's *The Old Corral* (1936), Rogers had several lines and was forced to do a yodel for Gene Autry as part of the plot. After Rogers was promoted to starring roles, Sons of the Pioneers remained his backup group in his movies, often supposedly working at the same ranch, thus again blurring the line between music and film. They were depicted as working cowboys and ranch hands who lent a hand when needed and were part of the pivotal action in the story. Their type of vocal harmony continues today with groups such as Riders in the Sky and Sons of the San Joaquin.

The singing cowboy movies helped to promote the musical cowboy trend. As the singing movie cowboy changed to flashy costumes—such as cowboy hats and boots, tight pants, fringed vests and colorful neckerchiefs—hillbilly performers started to change their traditional costumes of bib overalls and floppy hats to those of the movie cowboys. These costumes radiated showmanship on the stage and came at just the right time to accompany the sounds of the new emerging style of Western songs that included Western swing, bluegrass, honky-tonk, and the Western crooners. Popular performers such as Bob Wills, Ernest Tubb, Bill Monroe, and Roy Acuff brought new styles and voices to country music. These performers also crossed over to movies. Roy Acuff appeared in eight feature films between 1942 and 1949, including *Hi Neighbor* (1942), *My Darling Clementine* (1943) (not the John Ford version of 1946), *Night Train to Memphis* (1946), and *Smoky Mountain Melody* (1948).

The costume of the singing movie cowboy became the iconic image of country music during the 1930s. Country singer Hank Williams' back-up band was called the Drifting Cowboys, even though his music was not about the Old West. Many entertainers adopted this mode of dress, and the *National Barn Dance* (broadcast from Chicago) encouraged its performers to adopt Western clothing. One of the first to promote the style at Nashville's *Grand Ole Opry* was Pee Wee King and his Golden West Cowboys, who dressed in flashy Western costumes with boots and hats like the cowboy movie stars.[24]

Female singer Patsy Montana wore shirts with smile pockets and decorative flowers that imitated those of the movie stars. By that time country music was not music for hicks and hillbillies. Montana's 1935 hit record "I Wanna Be a Cowboy's Sweetheart" sold a million copies and was the biggest hit up to that time for a female hillbilly singer. As the trend continued, the movie tailors used by Gene Autry and Roy Rogers provided over-the-top rhinestone cowboy clothes for singing performers such as Hank Snow, Webb Pierce, and Little Jimmy Dickens.

12

Brooding Heroes

Maybe this isn't the way it was, but this is the way it should have been—The Life and Times of Judge Roy Bean[1]

Throughout most of the immediate post–World War II era, the Western was one of the most popular forms of film entertainment. Though Westerns were not one of the film industry's prestige genres, they were good moneymakers and continued to flourish into the 1950s.

As Rex Allen ushered in the end of the singing cowboy era, the mainstream screen Western hero changed from the happy-go-lucky, footloose action star of the 1930s and 1940s to a brooding, tormented, and angst-wracked gunman in the 1950s. The first half-century of Western films slowly replaced the early hero image of cowboys Broncho Billy and William S. Hart with that of the cow-less gunfighter. This new hero was often a melancholy drifting loner who had no home or settled life, lived by his gun, and always wore the same clothes. In reality, most cowboys were not gunfighters, even though they occasionally used guns. Those who lived by the gun in the Old West had to have superb skills with a revolver. They were not cowboys and could make more money by hiring out their expertise and becoming lawmen or range detectives.

In the 1940s and 1950s popular psychology and sociology swept Hollywood and the hero became troubled, complex, fallible, and even eccentric. In the 1950s, the image shifted from the wandering cowboy-gunfighter to one bent on personal revenge. Even the villain now had a psychological taint that drove his villainy. Movie screenplays of the 1950s tended to emphasize moody psychological dramas and pseudo-psychological analyses, such as *Man of the West* (1958) with psychotic Dock Tobin (Lee J. Cobb) and the weariness and desperation of Jimmy Ringo (Gregory Peck) in *The Gunfighter* (1950). Other examples of psychologically driven characters appear in *Saddle the Wind* (1958) and *Gunman's Walk* (1958). A further addition to this complexity was a heavier emphasis on sex and neuroses, which were considered to make up the new realism. Ironically, in spite of a demand by audiences for more realism in their movies, the post–World War II impact of the Cold War was to bring less realism into popular movies by focusing on the potential horrors of the nuclear age and science fiction monsters created by atomic radiation.

The new Western hero image included gunfighters who were professional killers, often for pay, such as the lead characters in *The Magnificent Seven* (1960). Screenplays reflected a change in moral values to propose that these professional gunfighters were merely doing their job, thus creating audience sympathy for their characters. Professional bounty hunters appear in *The Naked Spur* (1953), *The Bounty Hunter* (1954), and *The Tin Star* (1958). *Rio*

Bravo (1959), *El Dorado* (1967), and *Rio Lobo* (1970), all made by Howard Hawks, featured the professionalism of a man with a gun who fights alongside professional colleagues.

In the 1950s, the costume image of the flashy singing cowboy hero underwent a sharp reversal and the new breed of heroes became unglamorous in an attempt to portray so-called realistic cowboys. This trend was typified by Marshal Kane (Gary Cooper) in his nondescript clothing in *High Noon* (1952). Cooper created a distinctive interpretation of the Western hero as a masculine character, but one with a touch of sensitivity and uncertainty. The film echoed the popular theme of a man with human fears and doubts who goes about his dangerous job as a lawman or professional killer in spite of the community's reluctance to help him. (This role helped to define the lonely courage of the hero as a strong central figure who must confront and try to overcome evil (along with his own inner neuroses), even at the risk of his life. This movie in particular incorporated some further unplanned "realism." Cooper looked haggard and worn, as would any lawman in this situation, because he was experiencing chronic back problems, the results of a recent hernia operation, and a painful ulcer.)[2] Ex-gunfighters who have to take up their gun again when their town or woman is threatened showed up in *Fort Worth* (1951), *The Fastest Gun Alive* (1956), and *The Hanging Tree* (1959). Further debunking of the hero is shown in *Cowboy* (1958) and *3:10 to Yuma* (1957), which respectively show the unglamorous life of a cattle drive and that of a small farmer in the West.

In *The Bravados* (1958), Jim Douglass (Gregory Peck) is a grim-faced obsessive rancher looking for the four men he believes raped and murdered his wife. He takes the law into his own hands to track down and dispatch his wife's killers, only to find out when he catches up with the fourth man that he has killed the wrong group of men. Revenge was not always sweet. The plot was made legally and morally acceptable because the men he hunted down were supposedly guilty of other evil deeds and deserved to be punished.

Sidebar 12-1
Standardized Endings for Western Movies

1. The hero rides off alone by choice: *Shane* (1953), *The Searchers* (1956), *Pale Rider* (1985).
2. The hero leaves because he cannot stay: *High Noon* (1952), *The Magnificent Seven* (1960).
3. The hero stays and settles down with the girl: *Topeka* (1953), *The Sheepman* (1958), *Hallelujah Trail* (1965).
4. The hero stays after he has resolved his issues: *Winchester '73* (1950), *The Naked Spur* (1953).
5. The hero dies: *The Gunfighter* (1950), *The Shootist*, (1976).

Brooding Gunmen

As the 1940s came to a close, the concept of misunderstood outlaws such as Jesse James—painted as noble despite his sins—was on the wane. Instead, the theme of unrepentant evil and inevitable doom crept into plots in the fashion of film noir. The new psychological Westerns changed the traditional fast pace of the genre into long brooding moments of reflection and analysis. Good men went bad and vice versa. In *Warlock* (1959), gunfighter Johnny Gannon (Richard Widmark) changes sides to become the town's sheriff.

A popular theme with film audiences of the 1950s was the revenge Western. The hero has suffered a grievous injustice and is trying to correct or seek revenge on those who did him wrong. Between 1949 and 1961, ten of the top-grossing Westerns used vengeance plots.[3] In the 1950s James Stewart made a series of harsh revenge Westerns for director Anthony Mann. The films *Winchester '73* (1950), *Bend of the River* (1952), *The Naked Spur* (1953), and *The Far Country* (1955) transformed Stewart's screen persona from a gentle domestic figure of the 1930s and 1940s into a violent, driven protagonist out for revenge and justice. The general theme is that after a considerable series of setbacks, the main character finds reconciliation. Lin McAdam in *Winchester '73* (1950), Howie Kemp in *The Naked Spur* (1953), and Will Lockhart in *The Man from Laramie* (1955) (all played by Stewart) were normal men who had been driven by circumstances to exact vengeance. They are obsessed with avenging the past and only then can they return to carry on their lives. Other characteristics of these films is a love-hate relationship between a charming villain and the psychotic hero, who are often blood relatives, such as in *Winchester '73* (1950), which involves conflict between brothers. The plots used violent punishment as a test for the hero and the main character is often graphically mutilated. In *The Man from Laramie* (1955), McAdam (James Stewart) is dragged over the ground at the end of a rope and then shot in the hand at point-blank range.

In the Westerns made by Mann, the hero is a lonely individual driven to extreme physical and mental anguish by some personal or family tragedy. He is pushed outside his community, which is pictured as stability and sanity, and into a harsh and violent wilderness. He is lonely and full of raw emotion as he tries to eradicate his psychological and physical injuries. Justice is an eye for an eye. Mann's obsessed and neurotic vengeance heroes do not seem to be happy even after they resolve their issues.

Anthony Mann also made the violent *Man of the West* (1958), in which Link Jones (Gary Cooper) has renounced his evil ways but is forced by circumstances to rejoin his previous associates in a gang dominated by his uncle. Jones is robbed and stranded when his train stops for wood and water. He joins up with Billie Ellis (Julie London), a singer at the Longhorn Palace (thus an implied "bad girl"), and ends up at a cabin with the train robbers and crazy Dock Tobin (Lee J. Cobb). Link used to be a violent outlaw riding with Dock, but he is mentally tortured by his past and previous evil deeds. The violence is graphic as various participants are killed off throughout the movie. Coaley (Jack Lord) holds Link with a knife at his throat and tries to make Billie undress but is stopped by Dock. After a subsequent violent fistfight between Link and Coaley, Link tears off Coaley's clothes in retribution and Dock is forced to shoot the underwear-clad villain. Link rides into the town of Lasso to rob the bank, leaving Billie in a wagon with Dock. Link subsequently kills the rest of gang in a series of graphic gunfights. Link goes back to Billie to find that Dock has raped her, so Link has his final vengeance and shoots Dock. Jones goes through inner turmoil as he realizes that he is as bad as the rest of them. Nobody comes out happy at the end of this plot.

To round out the psychological aspects of the new type of hero, Oedipal father-son relationships were used in Westerns such as *The Tin Star* (1957), in which temporary sheriff Ben Owens (Anthony Perkins) seeks help from surrogate father image Morgan Hickman (Henry Fonda), an ex-sheriff and bounty hunter who rides after outlaws. A similar father-son love-hate relationship had been used earlier in *Red River* (1948) between Tom Dunson (John Wayne) and Matthew Garth (Montgomery Clift).

The magnificent scenery of Monument Valley dwarfs a visitor viewing the towering rocks from John Ford Point, so named because it was one of the iconic locations that the director used often in his movies. This location is remembered well by movie buffs for the night scene in *The Searchers* (1956) where Martin Pawley (Jeffrey Hunter) drops down off the edge to spy on Indian chief Scar's camp in the valley below and rescue Debbie (Natalie Wood) (author's collection).

Even director John Ford, who had presented romantic images of the West in the 1940s, turned to the revenge motif in his one Western of the 1960s, *The Searchers* (1956). This dark Western is probably John Ford's most bitter film and as Peter Cowie said, "Ethan [Edwards] must be the most unsympathetic 'hero' in all of Ford's work."[4] Edwards (John Wayne) taunts Martin Pawley (Jeffrey Hunter) about his Cherokee bloodline, and displays blatant racism throughout the film. Edwards rejects the moral and legal authority of the Rev. Capt. Samuel Clayton (Ward Bond). He has acquired illegal Mexican gold. He deliberately shoots out the eyes of a dead Comanche so that the man cannot see where he is going in the spirit world. He scalps Indian chief Scar (Henry Brandon), who murdered his family and kidnapped his niece Debbie (Natalie Wood). Ethan Edwards is a bitter, obsessed figure, not the nice character that would be used as an upstanding example of a clean-cut hero. He cannot be reconciled with society and, at the end, the closing door literally and figuratively shuts him off from reuniting with his family.

A similar man driven by inner torments is the hero of *Welcome to Hard Times* (1967), Blue (Henry Fonda), who is taunted for being a coward and not standing up to the villain. A veteran screenwriter once said (only semi-humorously) that the way to establish the character of the villain is when he rides into town. The first thing he should do when he gets off his horse is to kick a nearby dog to establish his rotten persona. In *Welcome to Hard Times* (1967), the "Man from Bodie" (Aldo Ray) does that with a vengeance.[5] He rides into town, drinks, shoots the bartender and a patron in the saloon, beats up a dance-hall girl, kills a man by hitting him on the head with a log, then shoots the local undertaker, dumps the body in his hearse, and runs the carriage out of town. In one sadistic scene, he even shoots his own horse. And, finally, to prove his toughness he burns down the entire town. His character was perhaps overdone, but the screenplay certainly established that here is a *real* villain.

Hollywood invented the professional gunfighter who was a formal gunman and killer. This combination of gunfighter and cowboy was a useful character for Hollywood plots as he was not restricted to a particular time or place in society. His character could be used for many situations, historical periods, and geographical settings, unlike a Wyatt Earp or a Jesse James, whose histories were limited to a particular time period and situation. Usually the plot is vague about what the gunfighter actually does for a living, but he is a particular character who resolves a wide range of conflicts in a variety of settings. The gunman's fame as a professional killer is based on his speed with a gun. He might be a bounty hunter (Colonel Mortimer [Lee Van Cleef] and Monco [Clint Eastwood] in *For a Few Dollars More* [1965]), a hired assassin (Tom Horn [Steve McQueen] in *Tom Horn* [1980]), a mercenary (the principals of *The Professionals* [1966] and *The Magnificent Seven* [1960]), or some type of lawman (Wyatt Earp in *Gunfight at the O.K. Corral* [1957] and *Tombstone* [1993]). Hollywood found a further advantage to gunfighters in that their stories had to reach a climax and end with an exciting fast-draw shoot-out.

Another theme was the hero as a professional gunfighter who was troubled by something in his past. His limitations and issues were ideal for these "psychological" Westerns. *The Gunfighter* (1950) is Jimmy Ringo (Gregory Peck), a lonely man hounded by his reputation as one of the West's fastest guns. He is constantly surrounded by violence and the challenge of someone faster on the draw. Ringo comes to town to see his wife and son but is challenged by young punk Hunt Bromley (Skip Homeier), and is eventually shot by him. This type of conflict was another popular Hollywood theme that became part of the movie gunfighter legend. This made gunfighting seem like a profession, where young upstarts were always trying to defeat the older reigning champion, as in boxing or golf.

The new type of 1950s hero was not always on the side of the law. Joe Erin (Burt Lancaster), for example, in *Vera Cruz* (1954) is amoral. He is part of a team of American gunfighters, ex-soldiers, and outlaws who are advising the Mexican government on suppressing a revolution. In reality they care nothing about Mexico or the freedom of the revolutionaries and are only looking out for their own gain. Erin takes pride in killing and in his skill with a gun, which gives him power over other people. He does not respect anything or anybody. He values only power and pleasure. He is capable of any degree of violence against man, woman, child, the strong, or the weak. His values are contrary to the long-standing cowboy code and the American concept of fair play by the hero. The conglomeration of characters in *Vera Cruz* (1954) provided a blueprint for later Western plots. Mercenaries acting as a mixed force of Americans and Mexicans appeared in *Treasure of Pancho Villa* (1955), *Bandido!* (1956), *Santiago* (1956), *Last of the Fast Guns* (1958), *Villa!* (1958), *The Magnificent Seven* (1960) and *The Wild Bunch* (1969). Though the lead characters of *Vera Cruz* (1954) are all looking out for themselves, the movie contains interesting symbolism from previous decades. Erin is the "bad" bad hero and is dressed all in black, including a black vest, gunbelt, and hat. Ben Trane (Gary Cooper) is the "good" bad hero and is dressed in light-colored clothing, including a tan hat.

As well as promoting a different portrayal of the hero, Western movies after the 1950s had a different feel to them. Older movies used dialog to develop characters and give them some depth. This can be seen in many comedy and drama movies of the 1950s and early 1960s that were adapted from stage plays. These movies seem very static and talky in today's terms. Then movie directors and editors started to edit movies into very brief scenes and to use rapid jump-cuts (two sequential shots that give the impression of jumping forwards in time), hopping from one piece of action to another without filling in the details, as also occurs in many novels of today that contain very short chapters.[6] This technique speeds up the pace of a novel or movie and allows more time for action scenes, which is what audiences want. But it also leaves less time for character development, which means that the characters become more superficial. As dialog is reduced, actors have to rely on other methods to show development of the character. Earlier Westerns were concerned with character development, whereas modern ones are focused on action. A good example is to contrast the two versions of *3:10 to Yuma*. The 1957 version is primarily about the interaction between farmer Dan Evans (Van Johnson) and outlaw Ben Wade (Glenn Ford) as they wait in a hotel room for the train to take Wade to Yuma. The 2007 version has more action and less interaction between the characters.

Randolph Scott

One of the stars of iconic Western hero roles of the 1950s was Randolph Scott. Scott starred in romantic roles for a long time. In these early years, Scott was too distinguished and handsome for most cowboy roles. He did, however, star in the early 1930s in several movies based on Zane Grey stories and was Hawkeye in *The Last of the Mohicans* (1936). He appeared in *Jesse James* (1939), where he played well-intentioned U.S. Marshal Will Wright, who sympathizes with the fictitious injustices done to the James boys but cannot condone defiance of the law. *Rage at Dawn* (1955) was another Scott film patterned on the James gang. The story, set after the Civil War, involved the four Reno brothers, who were real bank and train robbers in 1868.[7] Scott's role was based on a Pinkerton detective who infiltrated the gang to catch them.[8]

Scott also appeared as the spokesman for law and order in *When the Daltons Rode* (1940) and *The Desperadoes* (1943). He starred in *Belle Starr* (1941) and *Western Union* (1941), neither of which was historically accurate. Though he appeared in many Western films, Scott didn't come into his own as a Western star until he was older and had more lines on his weathered face. After World War II, he was the most prolific hero of the Westerns, starring in thirty-eight films from 1946 to 1960. Most were medium-budget, color A Westerns. He never had a major hit but relied on a stream of solid, action-filled, entertaining movies that featured outdoor action with a minimal reliance on studio shots.

Scott is best known for his Ranown movies, which were made by his production company (*Ran*dolph and Br*own*) with partner-producer Harry Joe Brown and directed by Budd

Boetticher. Together they made *Seven Men from Now* (1956), *Decision at Sundown* (1957), *The Tall T* (1957), *Buchanan Rides Alone* (1958), *Ride Lonesome* (1959), and *Comanche Station* (1960). By now Scott was weathered by age, which gave him an air of courage, dignity, and assurance. These movies were noted for their realism, though they were more violent and downbeat than most movies of the time. The plots often involved themes of betrayal and revenge and were not always concluded by the gentlemanly code of fair play but were more an eye for an eye. In *Coroner Creek* (1948) Chris Danning (Randolph Scott), in a brutal fistfight with Ernie Combs (Forrest Tucker), crushes Combs' hand with his foot as Combs had done to him. He also threatens to scald another bad man with a frying pan. Other examples of popular Scott Westerns were *Santa Fe* (1951), *Man in the Saddle* (1951), *Hangman's Knot* (1952), and *The Stranger Wore a Gun* (1953).

Western movie stars often faded away into a series of bad movies until they disappeared altogether. In fact, a recurrent plot element in Westerns of the 1960s and 1970s was the displacement of aging individuals as the West came to a close, because the stars were aging. Scott left on a high note with *Ride the High Country* (1962). His movie persona was a symbol of unwavering honesty and rugged individualism. A tribute to Scott's stature as a hero came unexpectedly in Mel Brooks' Western farce, *Blazing Saddles* (1974). Sheriff Bart (Cleavon Little) asks for twenty-four hours to come up with a plan to save the town. The townspeople resoundingly say, "No." Bart replies, "You'd do it for Randolph Scott." At that the townspeople take off their hats, reverently bow their heads, and sing the words "Randolph Scott" like a heavenly choir.

Shane

Another of the iconic movie and fictional heroes of the 1950s was Shane. The movie was developed from a short story titled "Rider to Nowhere" by Jack Schaefer, which appeared in *Argosy* magazine in 1946. In 1949 Schaefer expanded the plot into a novel called *Shane*. The film version of *Shane* (1953), starring Alan Ladd as Shane, contains many of the images associated with Western heroes, and its box-office success boosted the gunfighter into a prominent position as a movie hero. In a tradition going back to James Fenimore Cooper, Shane's buckskin clothing associates him with the wilderness and self-sufficient independence. There are images of virility and manhood as Shane and gunfighter Jack Wilson (Walter "Jack" Palance) give each other sinister looks and unspoken challenges while each drinks from a tin water cup when they first meet. In what was perhaps unconscious irony, Wilson is so sinister that the dog in the saloon gets up and runs away when the gunman first comes to town. Joey (Brandon de Wilde) shows his youthful obsession with guns as he spies on the

Opposite: Movie revolvers can be identified by their shape. Though real Westerners used a succession of handguns, from Colt's early cap-and-ball revolvers of the 1850s and 1860s (at top) to the double-action revolvers of the 1880s (bottom), the iconic movie cowboy hero of the 1950s and 1960s nearly always sports a Colt .45 single-action revolver with a short 4¾-inch barrel (called the Civilian Model by Colt) (center). This gun had a classic look and appeal and, because of the short barrel, was faster to draw for silver screen heroes than the original 1873 army Colt, which had a 7½-inch barrel. The use of this gun, nicknamed the Peacemaker, is often anachronistic, appearing frequently in movies about the Civil War and immediately afterward, whereas it wasn't manufactured and sold to the public until after 1874 (author's collection).

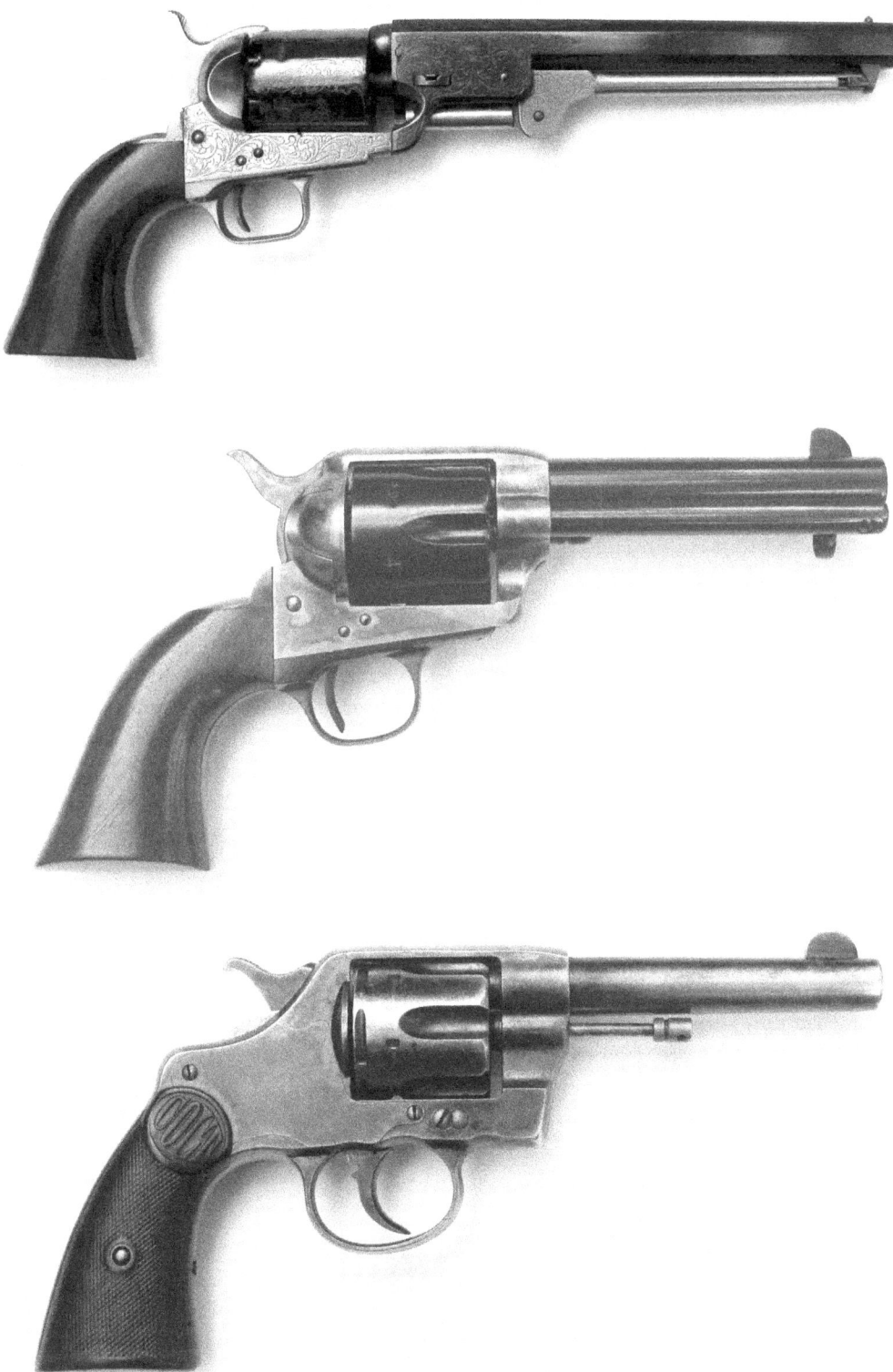

gunfighters from under the saloon door and secretly unwraps and admires Shane's hidden gun. The movie concludes with one of the classic Western movie endings. After the obligatory climactic gunfight, the hero Shane is the sole survivor and has to ride out of town, weary from all the killing. Even though he shoots gunfighter Jack Wilson and villainous rancher Rufus Ryker (Emile Meyer), he is unable to escape his violent past and has no place in the community. He is a gunfighter, not a farmer. He has to ride away. He knows that his fate is to go to more towns with similar problems that will be resolved only with his guns. Plots similar to *Shane* (1953) were used in *Man Without a Star* (1955), *At Gunpoint* (1955), *Johnny Concho* (1956), *Tall T* (1957), *Fury at Showdown* (1957), *Gun for a Coward* (1957), *Proud Rebel* (1958), and *Last of the Fast Guns* (1958).

Towards the end of the 1950s audiences started to tire of psychological Westerns and all their angst-ridden heroes. A new direction was charted with *The Magnificent Seven* (1960), which signaled a return to adventure and focused on a smaller group of heroes than the epic Westerns. In spite of this, Hollywood Westerns were breathing their last gasp and the trend was towards independent film productions and a darker kind of Western that came with the Sergio Leone Italian-made Westerns and the violence of *The Wild Bunch* (1969).

Television Heroes

By the end of the 1940s, Westerns were starting on a road to decline that carried into the 1970s. Among the reasons were that the top Western stars were aging and retiring from the movies, and studios saw a large rise in production costs, which put Hollywood in financial straits. The peak of the period of classic Westerns was 1958, with fifty-four feature films produced. By 1960 this number was down to twenty-eight Hollywood films. In 1963 it was eleven, and by 1965 it was twenty-two. By 1977 only seven were produced.[9] A major change in entertainment that affected Westerns in the 1950s and 1960s was television, which changed both the genre and the hero.

The Federal Communications Commission (FCC) authorized commercial television in 1941, but World War II put broadcasting on hold while all efforts to develop new electronics went into the war effort. After the war ended in 1945, television quickly replaced the movies as the primary medium of mass entertainment. People preferred to stay home rather than deal with the inconvenience of going out to a movie theater, particularly if a family had small children, many due to the postwar baby boom. Plus television was free. By 1946 there were approximately 7,000 television sets in America. In 1948 there were fewer than twenty stations broadcasting, but the medium was growing rapidly and regular programming was available. By the mid–1990s there were 1,500 stations. From 172,000 household televisions in 1948, the number of sets rose to 17 million in 1952 and to 125 million in the 1980s.[10]

Early television entertainment consisted primarily of variety shows such as those hosted by Ed Sullivan and comedians such as Milton Berle, Jackie Gleason, and Red Skelton. The background of these entertainers was vaudeville and they mostly re-created vaudeville-type acts on television. The Westerns that appeared on television in the late 1940s were edited versions of the popular cowboy movies of Hopalong Cassidy, Gene Autry, and Roy Rogers in half-hour formats.

By the late 1950s, television was embracing drama shows, including Westerns, many of which—such as *Gunsmoke*, *Wyatt Earp*, and *Have Gun, Will Travel*—had started on radio. Other Western series were specifically made for television, such as *The Adventures of Kit Carson*; *Wild Bill Hickok*; *Rin Tin Tin*; and *Annie Oakley*. Many of the early television Westerns were geared towards children, with heroes who had a high moral code as role models. The goal was good, clean, wholesome entertainment with no drinking or swearing and a sense of fair play. The hero, modeled after the B Western cowboys, was brave, smart, just, kind, and tough. The television Western hero was like a medieval knight or a modern Boy Scout. He helped widows, orphans, and the elderly through honesty, integrity, fairness, courage, hard work, tolerance, and patriotism. The good guy never shot first and the hero always shot the gun out of the bad guy's hand. These early TV Westerns were made with a juvenile audience in mind, so the plots were simple and to the point. The basic message was that good triumphed over evil, and crime did not pay. The bad guy always lost in the end. Gene Autry, in *Back in the Saddle Again* (184), outlines the "Cowboy Code":

1. The cowboy must never shoot first, hit a smaller man, or take unfair advantage.
2. He must never go back on his word, or a trust confided in him.
3. He must always tell the truth.
4. He must be gentle with children, the elderly, and animals.
5. He must not advocate or possess racially or religiously intolerant ideas.
6. He must help people in distress.
7. He must be a good worker.
8. He must keep himself clean in thought, speech, action, and personal habits.
9. He must respect women, parents, and his nation's laws.
10. A cowboy is a patriot.

Among the early television Westerns was the five-part Walt Disney series of shows of *Davy Crockett* (1954–1955), with Fess Parker as Crockett. The plot echoed the fictional adventures of the legendary frontiersman who died at the Alamo. At the time, Crockett's character in a coonskin hat became a national rage. The song *The Ballad of Davy Crockett*, with the refrain "King of the Wild Frontier," was a #1 hit song and sold four million records.[11] Triple Nickel Books published *The Adventures of Davy Crockett*. Like the previous dime novels about woodsmen heroes, the cover of the initial 1955 magazine showed a man in a coonskin cap carrying a rifle through the woods, with an Indian stalking him from behind. *Daniel Boone* (1964–1970), again with Fess Parker, was a similar fictional retelling of the adventures of the legendary frontiersman, pioneer, and explorer during the latter half of the eighteenth century.

Other real-life Western characters showed up as heroes in television series. *The Adventures of Kit Carson* (1951–1955), with Bill Williams as Carson, was a mix of a real Western character with a large dose of fiction. The television Carson roamed the Wild West chasing desperadoes with his sidekick, El Toro (Don Diamond), in the 1880s (even though the real Carson died in 1868). *Buffalo Bill, Jr.* (1955), with Dick Jones in the title role, was a story of the adventures of Buffalo Bill, Jr. and his young sister Calamity after their parents were killed. The character was supposedly the son of Buffalo Bill Cody. *Annie Oakley* (1953–1956) starred Gail Davis as the first Western female lead on television. The series was supposedly based on the real Annie Oakley, the sharpshooter from Buffalo Bill's *Wild West*. As usual, it was more fiction than fact as Davis in pigtails and a fringed buckskin suit jacket and skirt fought crime in fictional Diablo County, Arizona, in the 1860s. As with the earlier dime novels, these three series were good examples of the blending of real heroes from history and their fictional exploits. These television shows continued the practice of commercial tie-ins, where a series program spawned a host of products aimed at youngsters. This included Western costumes, comic books, lunch boxes, cameras, toy guns, and songs featuring a favorite television hero or heroine such as Gene Autry, Roy Rogers, Davy Crockett, Daniel Boone, or Annie Oakley.

Television, due to the restrictions of its nature, told only a limited story about a small group of people within a rigid framework. Television Westerns had to conform to a definite time slot, the insertion of commercial breaks, a low budget, and, for early Western series, the oversight of the sponsor, who could cancel a series if there were enough complaints by viewers (which of course equated to the number of customers for their products).

In a structure that harked back to the movie serials of the 1930s that ended each chapter with a cliff-hanger, television Westerns had some sort of plot climax before each advertising break in order to try to keep the audience watching in the hope that they would not change the channel during the commercials. Even the plots were structured by formula and included a certain amount of fighting or perhaps a violent death at periodic intervals to keep the audience interested. Even today's suspense novels are structured this way. Modern thrillers have short chapters with cliff-hangers at the end to ensure that readers keep turning the pages. Just as in television, they are written with a formula that includes the good guy, the bad guy, the heroine, and plot conflict.

Later television shows were written to appeal to a more mature audience (the so-called adult Westerns) and dealt with the real-life problems and struggles of adults. As plots turned towards these themes, their heroes changed to be more human, with human flaws. These heroes had doubts and made mistakes. Shows added more violence for the adults and didn't deal with problems in simplistic ways. Villains were subtly altered so as to not be completely evil, but motivated by various complex causes. As with theatrical films before them, violence and sex crept into these stories. What remained were shifty villains, beautiful girls, and shoot-outs.

The basic hero image also remained. Though Paladin (Richard Boone) in *Have Gun, Will Travel* was a gunman for hire, his character had a strict code of ethics and often dictated to his employer what he would and wouldn't do. He even sometimes turned against the people who hired him as he followed his own pathway of fairness and justice.

A sampling of the television series of the 1950s and 1960s shows how diverse the plots and heroes were, though often recycling previous characters and plots from older movies and novels. The stories of Zane Grey remained popular. *Dick Powell's Zane Grey Theatre* (1956–1962) was a popular anthology series adapted from the novels of Zane Grey with the film star and co-owner of the production company, Dick Powell, as host. In *The Big Valley* (1960s) Barbara Stanwyck played Victoria Barkley in the soap-opera saga of a strong-willed owner of a 30,000-acre cattle ranch. *The Virginian* (1962–1970), played by James Dury, was a loose adaptation of Owen Wister's novel with Trampas (Doug McClure) changed from the villain into a rowdy and irresponsible ranch hand at the Shiloh Ranch in Wyoming in the 1880s. A series named *Custer* (1967), with Wayne Maunder, was set at Fort Hays in Kansas in 1867 and fictionalized a personal war between Custer and Crazy Horse and the Cheyenne tribe (even though Crazy Horse was a Sioux war chief).

Starting in 1955, the television series *Gunsmoke* created Marshal Matt Dillon (James

Arness) as a composite of Western lawmen. *Gunsmoke* began as a radio program in 1952, with William Conrad as the voice of Dillon. The television *Gunsmoke* starred heroic-looking six-foot-six James Arness. Rather than presenting nonstop action and chases, *Gunsmoke* focused on interpersonal dramas and relationships and was intended for adults. Dillon was portrayed as having the human failings of anyone trying to do his job. He drank occasionally and used force when necessary.

By 1960 critics were complaining about the amount of violence on television and its effects on young children. As one example of the concerns, many youngsters in the 1950s were injured by blows to the head from toy cap guns as they emulated their heroes in knocking out the bad guy.[12] Further controversy arose when the surgeon general announced that there was a relationship between violence on television and in real life.[13]

The response was to make television Westerns with less violence, such as *Bonanza* (1959–1973), which emphasized family values and was about a father and his three grown sons (no mother to get in the way of plots) running a ranch near Virginia City, Nevada, in the days of the Old West.[14] It also perpetuated the myth that the "good old days" in the West were glamorous and comfortable. In *Sugarfoot*, the main character of the same name (Will Hutchins) was a pacifist cowboy law student who tried to avoid violence.

There were more than twenty-five Westerns on television each week in the fall of 1957. The number of Western series peaked at thirty-two between 1958 and 1961. Between 1957 and 1960, nine to twelve Western shows were in the top twenty-five. In 1958 twelve of the top twenty-five television series were Westerns, including seven of the top ten shows.[15] From 1957 to 1961 the top-ranked show was always a Western. The average audience share for Western series between 1957 to 1961 was about 35 percent. No other genre of action show had such a high share of prime time for so many years. But by 1965 the networks and audiences had lost interest and the number of television Westerns was back to eight each week.[16]

Other factors were at work in the decline of television Westerns. By the 1970s demographics became more important than numbers. *The Virginian*, for example, went off the air not because it was unpopular but because the primary audience was rural and working class, and not the middle-aged affluent urban audience advertisers wanted.

As with earlier movie stars, there was a blurring between television actors and their characters in order to promote their television personas. Rodeos were popular during the 1950s and 1960s in the heyday of Western television series, and many television actors appeared as headliners in rodeo programs to create a draw based on their popularity. Actors such as Lorne Greene and Dan Blocker from *Bonanza* made frequent appearances at rodeos. They often served as marshals at local rodeo parades and led the Grand Entry to the arena. This type of showmanship was not always appreciated by the real working rodeo cowboys, who felt that they were risking injury competing in dangerous events while the television stars were making far more money for merely singing and entertaining. Even the stars of *Gunsmoke*, James Arness (Matt Dillon), Amanda Blake (Miss Kitty), and Milburn Stone (Doc) created a rodeo act in which they sang, danced, and acted out humorous skits.

Gail Davis played the part of Annie Oakley from her television show in rodeos starting in 1955. She spent half her time making her television series and the other half in personal appearances. She was an accomplished horsewoman and did her own riding and shooting. She was a good shot and did displays of trick shooting. In the 1930s tradition, she wore glamorous costumes in the arena that were trimmed with sequins and fringes. Film and television star Rex Allen was a popular rodeo entertainer. He had a special feeling towards rodeo and its contestants as he had competed in local rodeo events when he was growing up on the family ranch in Arizona. After his film career declined when singing B Westerns were phased out in the 1950s, he appeared as a rodeo entertainer and headliner into the mid–1970s.

Ironically, television began by running edited movies of Gene Autry, Roy Rogers, and Hopalong Cassidy for children. As new programs developed, they started to disappear from broadcast television. But then in the 1980s, the rise of cable television revived the Western with reruns of old Autry and Rogers movies and television shows such as *Bonanza* and *Gunsmoke*. Though the production of traditional Western films declined in the late 1960s and 1970s, many of these old Western movies are still alive and well today on cable and satellite television. Many are still shown at retrospectives and revival festivals of old Western movies.

The Vanishing West

As the traditional stars of Westerns aged and grew into older hero roles, movies turned to the theme of the passing of the West. *Ride the High Country* (1962), *Monte Walsh* (1970), and *The Ballad of Cable Hogue* (1970) depicted traditional westerners trying to cope with the passing and changing of the West. In the 1960s and 1970s this led to movies that were portraits of individuals threatened by the new social order as the Old West disappeared and the traditional cowboy vanished. In *Will Penny* (1968) and *Wild Rovers* (1971) the heroes suddenly realize that they have nothing to show for their years as cowboys. *The Rare Breed* (1966) and *The Cowboys* (1972) show the fading importance of the cowboy. *The Gunfighter* (1950) is the story of a celebrated but weary gunman who wants one last chance to settle down, but he discovers he is unable to find a place in a changing world. *The Shootist* (1976) is similar, when J.B. Books (John Wayne) goes to Carson City in 1901 and finds trolley cars and streetlights.

Wooly chaps made from goatskin or sheepskin with the hair still attached were worn by real cowboys to help keep their legs warm in the bitterly cold winters of the Northern Plains. Later, big wooly chaps became a movie and television comedy symbol for a clueless dude from the East who knew nothing about the West (author's collection).

12. Brooding Heroes

In *Monte Walsh* (1970), the hero of the same name is a longtime cowboy who is part of a dying breed around the turn of the nineteenth century as the West he knows fades away. Capitalists have taken over the ranches, and barbed wire and the railroad are changing his way of life. His friends fall on the same hard times and have to find their way under altered circumstances. In the end Walsh rides off with only his horse for company, but he still has his westerner's code of honor.

In a more modern sense Jack Burns (Kirk Douglas) is the same in *Lonely Are the Brave* (1962) as he represents the free spirit of a cowboy of the Old West in conflict with the modern way of life. He is disgusted by vapor trails and the sound of jet aircraft flying overhead as he camps out, and he has difficulty avoiding cars and trucks as he crosses a major highway on horseback. At the end of the story he and his horse are hit by a semi truck in a final encounter as he crosses the highway and tries to escape from the law and civilization to Mexico. The group of modern loners in *The Misfits* (1961), who catch wild horses for a living, are the same.

In *The Ballad of Cable Hogue* (1970), Hogue (Jason Robards) has trouble adjusting to the vanishing West that he understands and is finally run over by a new-fangled motor car, the symbol of the progressive West. In *Will Penny* (1968), Penny (Charlton Heston) is a lonely, illiterate cowhand who drifts through life and has no particular place to go. *Ride the High Country* (1962) shows that Steve Judd (Joel McCrea) is out of place when he comes to town. A policeman tells him, "Get out of the way old man" as Judd is almost run over by a camel race down the main street. His old saddle pal, Gil Westrum (Randolph Scott), is working as a carnival barker wearing a bushy false beard and wig, looking like Buffalo Bill, which is the best he can do. There is no place for either of them in this new West, but they want to have one last success and retire.

13

And a Suitable Heroine

There has to be a woman, but not much of one. A good horse is much more important—
Max Brand[1]

The typical Western plot is set on a frontier caught between the anarchy of lawlessness on the open range and the impending approach of settlement and civilization, so plots typically used the male vision of national and gender identity. Although women have always appeared in Western films, the genre has traditionally been dominated by male heroes. Built-in movie audience biases resulted in Westerns being aimed primarily at males, melodramas and romances at women, and science fiction at teenagers. In the 1930s and 1940s audiences were made up of small boys who didn't particularly want women in the plot, only the male hero and lots of action, so love interest and romance were negligible.

The Western is the supreme male Hollywood genre, where the hero seeks the comforting company of fellow men and the outdoors. Shoot-outs, brawls, horse chases, and other cowboy antics allow the audience to view masculinity in action. In spite of this male machismo, with very few exceptions the Western plot has to have a heroine. Women personify refinement, virtue, culture, and all the best elements of civilization. The heroine, whether she is the refined daughter of a rancher or an easterner, represents the moral fiber of the Western community. The message is that the hero cannot fulfill himself without a woman at his side to provide comfort and companionship. But he secretly fears civilization and women and the settled life that they symbolize. The hero is by definition a drifting cowboy or gunfighter, which makes him what he is, and a woman's civilizing influence can be only destructive. At the end of the movie he has to either ride off again into the sunset or settle down with the girl. The latter situation ends *Gunfight at the O.K. Corral* (1957) when Wyatt Earp (Burt Lancaster) drops his lawman's badge and expresses the hope that Laura Denbow (Rhonda Fleming) will be waiting for him in California. This symbolizes his change from gunfighter to settled husband.

Women's roles in Western films tended to reflect a male perspective that emphasized the male hero and male expectations of female behavior, such as a woman depending on a man for happiness and security. This was because men were primarily the ones who wrote and directed Westerns. Women's roles often reflected male-perceived feminine traits, such as passivity, dependence on males, gentleness, and sensitivity. The women in these plots were placid, smiling, and obedient. They were depicted as helpless, subservient creatures, useful as mothers, wives, and schoolmarms, but as little else. Some heroines were merely decorative and were present to provide an association with the domestic life of the traditional role of women in the West, consisting of civilization, the schoolhouse, the church, and the family.

They often had no mother but a father who always seemed to need help. Common was the rancher's daughter without a visible mother, a feisty heroine who rides horses and fights back. Women's roles were often marginalized. For example, when Billy (Jack Buetel) and Doc (Walter Houston) gamble in *The Outlaw* (1943), they both want to win the horse, not the voluptuous Rio (Jane Russell).

The heroine may suffer at the hands of the villain, even when she plays only a peripheral role. Director Sergio Leone's violent Western world was a male one, for example, with a general absence of leading women's roles, though secondary women are included, often as rape victims. Leone was quite frank when he said, "In my films, the women tend not to play a very important role because my characters had no time to fall in love or court someone. They were far too busy trying to survive." He added, "So the roles for women in Western films usually tend to be kind of ridiculous. The Rhonda Flemings in *Gunfight at the OK Corral*. What's she there for? To make Burt Lancaster seem even more of a hero. If you had taken her out altogether, the film would have worked better and moved faster."[2] *Once Upon a Time in the West* (1968), directed by Leone, was unusual because a woman, Jill McBain (Claudia Cardinale), was at the center of the story. In discussing women in Western films, director Budd Boetticher once remarked that "what counts is what the heroine provokes, or rather what she represents. She is the one, or rather the love or fear she inspires in the hero, or else the concern he feels for her, who makes him act the way he does. In herself the woman has not the slightest importance."[3]

Similar to the attitudes of the film industry, characters in Western novels often reflected these prevailing ideas about women. One of the cowboys in Zane Grey's novel *The Heritage of the Desert*, ruminating about women, says, "It's funny about a woman, now, ain't it? ... One minnit she'll snatch you bald-headed; the next, she'll melt in your mouth like sugar."[4] In the movie *The Outlaw* (1943), Doc Holliday (Walter Houston), talking about women, says, "Ah, they're all alike.... There isn't anything they wouldn't do for ya [spit] ... or to ya [spit]."

Actresses in motion pictures have observed (correctly) that our society allows men to age into older movie roles as a result of both our culture and the film industry. Male Western actors such as Henry Fonda, James Stewart, John Wayne, Joel McCrea, and Randolph Scott shifted into Western hero roles and endured even after their youthful appearances were gone and their looks became rugged and weather-beaten. Male stars dealt with their age as they grew older and continued their acting careers. The working life of female stars, on the other hand, was generally short. As soon as they lost their youthful looks, they found it difficult to find starring roles. Survival and success in the motion picture industry has always demanded that stars increase in popularity and rank among top box-office attractions.

Stereotyping Women in Westerns

Just as Indians were misrepresented in Westerns, so were women. The Victorian view of women, reflected in most early novels and films about the West, was that they were frail and had a duty to marry, have children, and devote their lives to the care of their husband, children, and home. Even the real women of the nineteenth century were essentially invisible. A common complaint was that the only times their names were in the newspaper was for their marriages and their deaths.[5]

In early films the heroine was a helpless maiden. Zane Grey novels created heroines who were more active, but in a crisis they were still helpless. In the Gene Autry era the heroine was characterized by jackets and skirts with fringes and fancy boots. In the 1950s and the years of the brooding heroes, the good woman was the one who hoped that her man would give up his gun. She wore jeans and rode a horse, emphasizing her femininity by her masculine actions. She entered the man's world but needed a dedicated man to help her through.

In the traditional Western there are several stereotypes of women. Western movies show women as the girlfriend, mother, schoolteacher, prostitute, or saloon girl. One invisible role is the stereotype of the nonspeaking supporting part of the pioneer wife. The pioneer wife is given little shading or complexity and often receives demeaning treatment in the movies. In reality, these women played a large part in taming the West. They cooked, sewed, tended the livestock, had babies at home, and were the family doctor in times of need. They provided stability in the unstable world of the frontier. They are often treated in a marginal role in films or as a passive helpless figure. In reality, pioneer women were diverse, they were supporters of Prohibition, farmers, wives, suffragettes, and doctors. The tough conditions of the pioneer West took a high toll on women. Although movies fade out with a kiss, the real years ahead would be tough, and pioneer women aged quickly beyond their years as their beauty and youth faded into the reality of ranch work.

Another movie stereotype is the "good" woman, who is perceived as representing the Christian moral principles that are essential to a civilized order, as opposed to males, who represent violence. She is the unsullied pioneer heroine who is in short supply and has to be protected and respected. She might be the virtuous wife, the rancher's virginal daughter, or the local schoolteacher. A third type is the naughty girl. She wears tights and spangles and works in the local saloon, dancing, singing, and drinking whiskey. The saloon girls wore short skirts and stockings, low-cut dresses that revealed their cleavage, showed off their legs, and danced the can-can. They are plentiful, available, and community property. They have names like Frenchy (Marlene Dietrich in *Destry Rides Again* [1939]) or Feathers (Angie Dickinson in *Rio Bravo* [1959]). Though this may seem like an oversimplification of women into two types, that was the Victorian reality.[6] Stereotypical roles of the woman as gentle and dependent nurturer and civilizer or as a vamp reflected this polarized Victorian view of women. In *My Darling Clementine* (1946) the eastern heroine is Clementine Carter and the saloon girl is Chihuahua.

Just as stereotypical heroes wear white hats and villains wear black hats, the good heroines are often blonde, as is Amy Kane (Grace Kelly) in *High Noon* (1952). They represent love, purity, and lawfulness. The naughty women tend to be dark-haired. Again to use *High Noon* (1952) as an example, Helen Ramirez (Katy Jurado) with her flowing black hair represents passion and recklessness as "the other woman" in Marshal Will Kane's (played by Gary Cooper) past. The heroine Mescal in Zane Grey's novel *The Heritage of the Desert* says, "My mother was a Navajo, my father a Spaniard," implying that she herself is a hot-blooded cross-breed.[7] The feisty heroines are often red-haired, symbolizing spirit without vice. This would be Laura Denbow (Rhonda Fleming) in *Gunfight at the O.K. Corral* (1957).

The traditional cowboy hero had great respect for women, offering such bashful sentiments as "Shucks, Ma'am" while dragging his boot toe in the dirt. But this changed with the likes of *High Plains Drifter* (1973), where the stranger (Clint Eastwood) drags a woman he meets on the street into a barn and rapes her. In the Westerns of the 1930s the image of

Real women of the West filled many roles. Lucille Mulhall was an expert trick rider and the daughter of Colonel Zack Mulhall, who started *Mulhall's Congress of Rough Riders and Ropers* in 1899. Called the "Queen of the Range" and "America's First Cowgirl," she was a champion roper who specialized in lassoing bulls and tying them up. Here she shows off her equestrian skills in 1909 by standing on the saddle of a horse that is sitting down (Library of Congress).

romance was that "the hero would kiss his faithful horse and ride off alone into the sunset."[8] Even the stoic hero William S. Hart kissed the girl.

Women in the Wild West shows were more robust and participated in male activities. They wore revolvers, did trick riding and roping, and participated in horse races. Women in early rodeos performed bulldogging, and in real life participated in roundups and other activities to raise cattle. Perversely, in acts such as "Attack on the Deadwood Stage" and the attack on the settlers cabin, the women performers played the part of helpless victims who required rescuing by men. In reality, many women in the real West who were isolated on ranches had to be proficient with firearms. They might be left alone at home with the children while their husbands were out on the range or at a roundup. They had to be prepared to defend themselves from wild animals, Indians, or any other undesirables who might happen by.

The Changing Heroine

Just as the hero of Western books and movies evolved and changed, so did the heroine. In the 1880s, novelist Mary Hallock Foote wrote about women and families in the newly settled West. As one example, she wrote *The Led Horse Claim* about life in a mining camp in the Northern Rocky Mountains. In a departure from masculine action, most of the story is told from the perspective of the heroine. Foote also featured romance, such as that in *The Last Assembly Ball*, about an easterner who comes to the West to forget a love affair and falls in love with a servant girl. Foote illustrated her own books. Her paintings, however, were not as action-filled as those of other artists, such as Remington, and did not show the grand sweep of the Rockies as did Bierstadt and Moran. Rather they showed the domestic side of life in the West, focusing on women, children, and animals. Because her vision did not conform to the generally held image of the Wild West, her books and paintings have been forgotten.

Author Zane Grey was not above some racy material and lurid writing about his heroines. Several of his plots were based on abduction and included several narrow escapes for the heroine from the fate worse than death. In Grey's novel *Riders of the Purple Sage*, a mysterious masked rider is seen at the head of a band of cattle rustlers. Venters shoots the rider off his horse then runs over to find that the rider is only wounded in the chest. As he pulls off the mystery rider's sombrero he sees bright curly chestnut hair and a youthful pale face. Venters is overcome with remorse, thinking that he has shot a boy. He rips open the bloody shirt to inspect the bullet wound. "First he saw a gaping hole, dark red against a whiteness of skin, from which swelled a slender red stream. Then the graceful beautiful swell of a woman's breast!"[9] Venters realizes that he has shot a woman by mistake, nurses her back to health in secret, then, to appease reader sensibilities, marries her at the end of the book.

Marriage was not always the outcome of Grey's happy romances. Part of the plot in *Riders of the Purple Sage* involves Deception Pass, the narrow gateway into Surprise Valley, a huge, well-watered valley covered with cottonwood trees and surrounded by impenetrable cliffs where rustlers stash their stolen herds. At the end of the book, the hero tumbles a giant rock into the pass and seals off the valley, isolating him and Jane Withersteen, where they are trapped to live happily together without the benefit of marriage.

The cowboy hero of films has always been tough, resolute, and masculine. The heroines in Western movies have been portrayed differently at different times, depending on the plot and the era during which a film was made. In the first portrayals and throughout most of the 1920s the woman was a strong pioneer. Later she became the stereotype of a frail, helpless woman who was forever turning to her hero for protection.

Broncho Billy used women as featured players in some of his early Selig Polyscope films. *The Girl from Montana* (1907) featured Pansy Perry as a young woman who makes a determined effort to rescue her sweetheart after he is captured by a gang of toughs. The heroines of Broncho Billy and William S. Hart films were mostly portrayed as virtuous women who had a profound effect, changing the hero and redeeming him from his life as an outlaw. Hart introduced the tradition of the beautiful but helpless heroine whose cattle or ranch or other property was being threatened by the villain. Any brothers or father were often eliminated early and there was no mother. In the early days of the Western movies the heroine often required rescuing, so the hero spent much of his time getting her out of predicaments. In spite of all the fighting and killing, the heroine's love was the only reward that the hero got by the end of the picture.

By the 1920s the movie hero was portrayed as a virile, red-blooded, go-getting, rough-and-ready he-man. The movie heroine, by contrast, was portrayed as being sweet and fond of children and animals. She often wore white to symbolize her purity, at least when her purity was threatened. Her ability and intelligence were often irrelevant and unmentioned.

During the 1930s and 1940s some sex appeal was added. In *Dodge City* (1939) Ruby Gilman (Ann Sheridan) and six singing girls in abbreviated costumes dance on the stage. In *Abilene Town* (1946), in the saloon theater, the lead singer wears an abbreviated costume with dancing chorus girls in similar costumes backing her up. The heroine emerged again as self-reliant, athletic, and often sexier, with a robust build and tight pants that emphasized the female figure. In *The Desperadoes* (1943), the heroine, Allison McLeod (Evelyn Keyes), wears tight-fitting leather pants when she works in the stable or rides hard. Abby Nixon (Virginia Mayo) in *Devil's Canyon* (1953) wears tight jeans that show off her figure to advantage. Movie critic Jon Tuska once recalled that leading lady "Peggy Stewart, under contract at Republic Pictures, once confided in me that she resented making Westerns because her backside was to the camera more than her face."[10]

The hero wore Western outfits, but women in Westerns of the 1930s typically wore the clothing and hairstyles that were stylish and in fashion at the time the movie was made.[11] Leading ladies in Westerns of the 1930s and 1940s were portrayed as contemporary and smart women, not the damsels in distress of the 1910s and 1920s. They were educated, independent, and fashionable women, not virgins on a Victorian pedestal. This changed image may in part be due to screenwriters such as Betty Burbridge, Luci Ward, and Connie Lee, who worked on Autry movies and tended to feature women in the plotlines and show their independence.[12] This altered characterization resulted in appeal of these movies for female audiences.

One actress who exemplified this new role in Westerns was Dale Evans. Evans was named Lucille Wood Smith when she was born in 1912, but her name was later changed by her parents to Frances Octavia Smith while she was still a child. She started her career as a singer using stage names of Frances Fox and Marian Lee, then settling on Dale Evans before becoming the wife of Western movie and singing star Roy Rogers. When Evans was paired with Rogers by Republic Pictures, women were mostly background scenery in Westerns. Evans, by contrast, rode fast, roped, and shot six-guns. Her trademark outfit was a split riding skirt with fringes, a bolero top, and fancy boots. In *My Pal Trigger* (1946) she is suitably feminine in frilly clothing as Gabby Kendrick's (Gabby Hayes) daughter, Susan, but she is competent and strong enough to wield a gun when she mistakenly blames Rogers for shooting her horse Golden Sovereign. Another strong leading lady was Gail Davis, who was the first woman to star in a Western television series, *Annie Oakley*.

After women became an integral part of the workforce during World War II, their screen depiction changed from shy, demure, and acquiescent to tough women who cracked the whip, though Western films of the 1940s and 1950s were still essentially masculine. Men were men and women were either chaste or bad. Women were portrayed in director John Ford's Westerns as either fragile and protected or as sturdy pioneer women who had learned to cope with life on the frontier. Heroines often wore pants and shirts when doing chores or riding but changed into dresses to get their man.

Mexican women, such as Rio (Jane Russell) in *The Outlaw* (1943), Pearl (Jennifer Jones) in *Duel in the Sun* (1946), and Helen Ramirez (Katy Jurado) in *High Noon* (1952), were portrayed as hot-blooded and passionate They generally had to die or be abandoned by the hero at the end of the film in order to get rid of the "bad woman." In *Destry Rides Again* (1939) the tarty Frenchy (Marlene Dietrich) was not good enough to marry Destry (James Stewart) and had to die at the end.

Melodramatic theatrical plots in early movies overlapped and closely paralleled stories from dime novels and the stage and were often adapted from them for the screen. In this 1907 theatrical poster advertising *An Arizona Cowboy*, a pretty girl and her handsome hero show that they are accomplished riders, a skill that was automatically expected of Westerners by audiences. Before the advent of movies, traveling stage plays were a primary form of entertainment (Library of Congress).

In some later Westerns it becomes hard to tell the good girls from the bad. Just as the male hero was affected by his internal psychological struggles, these issues began to affect women's roles. In *Hang 'Em High* (1968), for example, Rachel Warren (Inger Stevens) continually rejects Marshal Jed Cooper (Clint Eastwood), not because she is a virginal heroine but because she underwent a gang rape, which made her frigid.

By the time of *Unforgiven* (1992), women and sexuality were as explicit as the violence in the plot. When Ned (Morgan Freeman) and widower Will Munny (Clint Eastwood) are discussing women, Munny says he doesn't miss it that much, but the two exchange some graphic comments. Munny points out that the love and civilizing influence of a good woman has reformed him and Ned from killers into farmers.

Strong Female Roles

The classic Western was indifferent to women, and few females played the lead star in Western films. There were, however, some females who played tough roles. One of the few no-nonsense early female movie stars was Texas Guinan, who had worked previously as a chorus girl in vaudeville. She acted in shoot-'em-ups such as *Get Away Kate* (1917), *The Gun Woman* (1918), *The Love Brokers* (1919), and *The Girl Sheriff* (1921). She was billed as the female equivalent of William S. Hart and played her parts as a tough, gritty, pants-wearing cowgirl who fought as hard as any man with a whip and a revolver. She was probably ahead of her time. Male stars were considered to be role models, but a woman was not, and Guinan was considered by critics to have a corrupting influence on young boys. After making several movies, she left the film industry to become a nightclub hostess.[13]

Rita Hayworth played the masked leader of a band of Mexican vigilantes in the B Western *Renegade Ranger* (1938) at a time when it was rare to have an active female star. *Johnny Guitar* (1954) showed strong-willed, hard-bitten saloon owner Vienna Jones (Joan Crawford) in conflict with neurotic rancher Emma Small (Mercedes McCambridge). The two strong-willed women are involved in a hotbed of passions. Unlike male-dominated movies of the time, this movie does not have much action because a large amount of the plot takes place in Vienna's saloon. In *Belle Starr* (1941), Gene Tierney plays an aristocratic southern girl forced by circumstances and carpetbagger Yankees to turn gunfighter. In *Montana Belle* (1952) Belle Starr (Jane Russell) is a tough woman quite the equal of her male cohorts, but she ends up being killed by the Daltons.

Later women had more success in leading roles. In *Cat Ballou* (1965) Catherine Ballou (Jane Fonda) matures from an innocent demure schoolteacher on her way out West into a self-confident train robber and gang leader. *Rooster Cogburn* (1975) shows Eula Goodnight (Katharine Hepburn) as a feisty spinster. *The Ballad of Josie* (1967) shows Josie Minick (Doris Day) as she transforms into an aggressive and successful sheep farmer. Among some of the other strong-willed notables were Marlene Dietrich in *Destry Rides Again* (1939), Raquel Welch in *Hannie Caulder* (1971), Claudia Cardinale in *Once Upon a Time in the West* (1968), Sharon Stone in *The Quick and the Dead* (1995), and Madeleine Stowe, Mary Stuart Masterson, Andie MacDowell, and Drew Barrymore in *Bad Girls* (1994).

Another strong actress was Barbara Stanwyck, who made ten Westerns in the 1940s and 1950s, often playing a tough-talking, hard-working woman. In *Cattle Queen of Montana*

(1954), Stanwyck played Sierra Nevada Jones, a woman trying to hold on to her father's ranch with the help of gunman and secret government agent Farrell (Ronald Reagan). In *The Violent Men* (1955), Stanwyck played Martha, the scheming, cheating wife of rancher Lew Wilkison (Edward G. Robinson). She was a woman outlaw in *The Maverick Queen* (1956). In *Forty Guns* (1957), she played Jessica Drummond, the dangerous whip-wielding boss who controlled Cochise County with the aid of forty armed gunmen who killed and destroyed at her request. Stanwyck's best-known role came in the 1960s when she played Virginia Barkley, the iron-fisted matriarch of television's *The Big Valley*.

Sex and Censorship of the Mythic West

As author Frank Miller succinctly put it, "The impulse to censor, to control what other people are allowed to see, hear, and think, is as old as humanity itself."[14] The concern of the would-be censors of Westerns, like other genres, was violence, sex, bad language, excessive drinking, and poor morals. As early as 1916, the National Association of the Motion Picture Industry (NAMPI) was created by the major film studios to preserve screen morals. Among other subjects, material considered to be unsuitable for the screen were nudity, prostitution, drunkenness, and illicit love affairs. Any studio that violated these taboos was to be expelled from the group. In practice, however, the rule was largely ignored and it was business as usual.[15] In the late 1910s and early 1920s, changing audience tastes and acceptance of previously taboo morals in real life allowed more frank treatments of these subjects in movies.

After World War I, skirts became shorter, bobbed hair was the fashion, and new dance trends such as the Charleston were widespread among the youth of the day. Cigarette smoking for women became acceptable. In this looser moral climate, films became more lurid. Filmmaker Cecil B. DeMille, for example, made comedy-romances with racy divorce themes such as *Why Change Your Wife?* (1920). He also started to add bathroom scenes to his movies, including undressing, bathing scenes, and even partial nudity. Though such behavior was considered to be acceptable in the context of a bathroom, it was really added to provide erotic titillation.[16] Encouraged by acceptance, De Mille moved on to the bedroom and included lingering scenes of undressing and dressing.

Early Westerns did not have to have blatant eroticism. The type of clean-cut image shown in this 1909 photograph was popular among young eastern men who dreamed of a cowgirl from the West who was pretty, who could handle a gun as well as a man, and who could excel at poker. However, the fringed buckskin pants outlining this girl's legs, the gun, and the poker chips gave this photograph a naughty connotation in late Victorian times (Library of Congress).

By 1921, however, looming censorship worried the film industry. In response, they created the Motion Picture Producers and Distributors of America (MMPDA—later renamed the Motion Picture Association of America) to try to avoid censorship and create goodwill towards Hollywood. The office was headed by Will Hays, a former postmaster general under President Warren Harding. Hays formulated a series of rules for the studios to limit sex, violence, and other subjects deemed unsuitable for the movies. This became known as the "Hays Code," which was in theory adopted in 1924 by the studios.[17] Little, however, changed onscreen.

At the same time, real-life scandals involving sex, alcohol, narcotics, and riotous living among movie stars began to show up in the national press. One prominent scandal featured the death of a minor actress named Virginia Rappe after a disorderly party in San Francisco in 1921. Popular comedian Roscoe "Fatty" Arbuckle was arrested for her rape and murder though there was no proof to connect him to any crime. A jury that later acquitted Arbuckle stated that a great injustice had been done to him. However, even though he was cleared of any wrongdoing in her death, the stigma was there and he never worked in Hollywood again.[18] Another scandal involved the death of director William Desmond Taylor, who was found shot to death on the floor of his Hollywood bungalow in 1922. Links appeared to leading lady Mary Miles Minter and popular comedienne Mabel Normand. Minter had written an indiscreet love letter to Taylor which subsequently ruined her career.[19] Normand, who was the last to see him alive, was cleared of any connection with Taylor's death. Another problem among actors was drugs. Actor Wallace Reid died at age thirty of a drug overdose.[20] Scandals such as these helped to reinforce the need for a code of behavior among stars both off and on the screen.

During the 1920s, Hollywood fed the censorship fire with movies that showed wild orgies on the screen. Movies such as *The Mad Whirl* (1925) showed scenes of drinking and gambling. Films such as these tended to be an hour of sin followed by a few minutes of repentance by the characters at the end. By ostensibly policing themselves in this way, Hollywood hoped to avert a national censorship board. Another issue was to avoid local censorship that might have different standards of judgment of what should and should not be seen, hence either making different cuts to the same film or banning it completely. State boards charged a fee for screening movies for cuts and often charged for each print distributed within a state.[21]

Continued flouting of the code led in 1927 to a specific list of thirty-six subjects in films that consisted of "Don'ts and Be Carefuls."[22] Studios were supposed to submit screenplays to the MPPDA before shooting started, but this was generally ignored, and nudity and near-nudity kept popping up on the screen. DeMille's *The Sign of the Cross* (1932), for example, included a fully naked Christian chained to a Roman statue, though she is festooned with garlands of flowers to cover the appropriate places. Similar draping of nudity was used in *Dante's Inferno* (1924).

As movie attendance declined during the early years of the Great Depression, Hollywood turned to more sex and violence to try to draw in bigger audiences. Although the sex was not overt, even ordinary films featured partial nudity and lingerie, as was the case in *Red Hair* (1928) and *Breach of Promise* (1932). Films of the so-called flaming youth type became popular. *Dance, Fools, Dance* (1931), for example, showed a lingerie party on a yacht with young male and female participants lounging around in their underwear.

In the 1930s, complaints about sexuality and violence on the screen led Hollywood to start making cleaner, more wholesome (e.g., sexless) pictures. A production code office was created to monitor scripts and completed films. The code outlined how studios should treat sex, crime, profanity, and costuming (e.g., no nudity). Economic pressures on the studios to attract bigger audiences, however, still led to gangster violence, risqué dialog, and sexual candor.

In response to blatant avoidance of the code, in 1934 Hays set up the Production Code Administration (PCA) headed by Joseph I. Breen. Member studios agreed not to release films without the MMPDA seal of approval. The PCA scrutinized film scripts and costume drawings to eliminate poor morals and nudity on-screen. For example, the Hays Office code said that crime must not only not pay, but must also be punished. After the censorship code became stronger, the B Westerns emphasized fighting and singing cowboys with action, fist-fights, and riding stunts, and romance was kept to a minimum.

The Hays Office created the Studio Relations Committee to monitor code compliance, but by 1933 critics regarded these efforts as ineffective. Three examples of pre-code non–Western movies show why. In *Baby Face* (1933) Lily Powers (Barbara Stanwyck) is a woman prostituted by her father in his run-down speakeasy. She leaves and goes to New York, where she sleeps her way up the corporate ladder, ruining various men in the process.[23] In *Red-Headed Woman* (1932), "Lil" (Jean Harlow) uses her sexuality to get what she wants during the Great Depression. She carries on several affairs and also sleeps her way to the top. The sex is not graphic, but the dialog contained so much innuendo that it was banned in England. *Waterloo Bridge* (1931) is about out-of-work chorus girl Myra Deauville (Mae Clarke) making a living as a streetwalker picking up men on Waterloo Bridge in London. She is a woman who "plays for pay" as it was delicately put. The film includes a voyeuristic scene of chorus girls taking off their clothes in their backstage dressing room and standing around in their underwear.

Another film that was responsible for the adoption of stricter regulations was *Tarzan and His Mate* (1934). In it a man undresses to the buff and takes a bath for no reason that advances the plot. At another point, Tarzan (Johnny Weissmuller) fondles Jane's (Maureen O'Sullivan) stockinged leg and the men ogle her silhouette as she dresses in a backlit tent. The clincher was a swimming scene with Jane totally naked underwater, with full frontal and rear nudity.[24]

Sexuality was used in a similar voyeuristic sense in *To the Last Man* (1933). This was one of the film versions of the Zane Grey novel based on the real Graham-Tewksbury feud known as the Pleasant Valley War in the Tonto Basin of Arizona. Almost all the participants in the two families killed each other. During the feud between the Colbys and the Haydens (the renamed movie feuding families), there is a nude bathing scene when Ellen Colby (Esther Ralston) is swimming in a pond. Jim Daggs (Jack La Rue) watches her and taunts her to come out and get her clothes. Lynn Hayden (Randolph Scott) comes upon the scene and knocks Daggs in the water instead. This was a popular type of Hollywood voyeuristic erotic scene.

Other, more subtle, sexual themes appeared in the Westerns. Heroines were mostly beautiful to provide added titillation for the male audiences. Some, however, though feminine, went around dressed as men. A popular theme was to have the heroine dressed up as boy, as in *Riders of the Purple Sage*, where Venters shoots the mysterious masked rider and opens her shirt to check the wound. In Zane Gray's earlier book *The Border Legion*, Jack Kells abducts Joan Randle and forces her to cross-dress as a bandit in a black outfit and mask. She dwells on her appearance and how her male costume "strangely magnified every curve and swell in her body." A tomboy heroine was off-beat at the time and appealing to many men. An early Calamity Jane in *The Heroine of Whoop-Up* was a hard-riding, card-playing, swearing whiskey-drinker. In *Western Girls* (1912), two sisters disguise themselves as cowboys to capture a gang of bad guys.

Another erotic theme that showed up in Westerns was the hero spanking the heroine, which provided sexual titillation in the taming of a tomboy and focused on her bottom. Spanking heroines appeared in *Gold Mine in the Sky* (1938) with Gene Autry, *Outlaws of the Desert* (1941) with William Boyd, *The Guns of Fort Petticoat* (1958) in which Audie Murphy spanks Kathryn Grant. In *True Grit* (1969), La Boeuf (Glen Campbell) spanks Mattie Ross (Kim Darby) until Rooster Cogburn (John Wayne) tells him to stop because he's enjoying it too much. *McClintock!* (1963) had two spanking scenes. Katherine McLintock (Maureen O'Hara) is spanked by G.W. McLintock (John Wayne) with a small coal shovel. In a previous part of the movie McLintock's daughter Becky (Stefanie Powers) is spanked in a similar fashion by her fiancé, Devlin Warren (Patrick Wayne).

Sex Returns

Moviegoing became very popular during World War II, partly as a temporary escape from reality. To try to attract audiences, sex emerged from Hollywood again as an ingredient in Westerns. Two films were notable for introducing blatant sexuality into the Westerns in the 1940s. One was *The Outlaw* (1943), which promoted sex in the form (pun intended) of Jane Russell and the relationships between the three main characters. The other film was *Duel in the Sun* (1946), directed by King Vidor and produced by David Selznick. Selznick disliked Westerns, but said, "Seeing how profitable Westerns always were, I decided that if I could create one that had more spectacle than had even been seen in a western and combine it with a violent love story, than [sic] the two elements would give me a great success."[25]

The Outlaw (1943) was the first movie to openly defy the code. The plot was an invented three-way love triangle between Billy the Kid (Jack Buetel), Doc Holliday (Walter Huston), and a fictional girl named Rio MacDonald (Jane Russell). The film did not receive a seal of approval from the PCA because of controversy over the emphasis on Rio's bosom. Production was completed in 1941. Producer and director Howard Hughes refused to make cuts and released the film without a seal of approval to any exhibitors who were willing to take it. It received limited release in 1943 but did not go into general release until 1946, after Hughes reluctantly cut about thirty seconds of footage that accentuated Russell's bosom. Other blatant scenes include one where Billy is wounded and unconscious, so Rio jumps into bed with him to warm him up. To gain approval from the censors, Rio is suddenly and inexplicably married to Billy the next day to explain why they spent all night in the same bedroom together.

The story of *Duel in the Sun* (1946), rather unkindly called "Lust in the Dust" by some critics, follows the affair between lecherous Lewt McCanles (Gregory Peck) and tempestuous half-breed Pearl Chavez (Jennifer Jones). To set the tone of what is to follow, the opening narration states that this is a story of "wild young lovers who found heaven and hell in the shadow of the rocks." The plot opens with Pearl, the half-breed daughter of a white father and an Indian mother, performing a sensual dance in a saloon. The mother, doing the same, goes off with a customer, and the father follows and shoots them both. As a result, Pearl goes to live with her cousin on a ranch. What follows is a plot full of leering, lust, and innuendo. To set the tone for their later liaison, Lewt leers at Pearl's departing rear while the camera pans down her legs as she walks away with Lewt watching appreciatively. During a swimming scene in the local waterhole, Lewt watches and Pearl won't get out, as presumably she doesn't have any swimsuit.

Lewt and Pearl's first union in the bedroom is accompanied by a symbolic thunderstorm. Pearl flares her nostrils, bares her teeth, and writhes around in Lewt's arms as an indication of her passion. This kind of acting was advanced for the time. To add further spice to the plot, Lewt's mother, Laura Belle McCanles (Lillian Gish), had a previous affair with Pearl's father, but dies right after confessing her sin. At the climax of the story, Pearl and Lewt end their passionate affair in a grim and bloody mountain-top encounter in which they fatally wound each other in a gunfight. Pearl claws her way up Squaw's Head Rock, crawling through the dirt for one final lusty kiss before they die in each others arms. In Hollywood fashion this ending was to gain redemption for their sins for both of them. Selznick turned out to be right. Sex in *Duel in the Sun* made it a sweeping box-office success and it was the second highest moneymaker of 1947.[26]

One of the changes for the film industry in the 1950s and 1960s was including sexual themes as a way to win back audiences from television. Moviemakers added spice wherever they could, even though most situations were less obvious than that of Lewt and Pearl. In *Jubal* (1956), ranch hand Jubal Troop (Glenn Ford) lusts after the boss's (Shep Horgan played by Ernest Borgnine) sexually frustrated wife, Mae (Valerie French). Their thwarted passions lead to conflicts that could get him killed.

Shane (1953) showed an implied illicit attraction between Shane (Alan Ladd) and Marian Starrett (Jean Arthur), but their relationship ends unfulfilled. This relationship is depicted more obviously (and physically) in the similar attraction between the Preacher (Clint Eastwood) and Sarah Wheeler (Carrie Snodgrass) in *Pale Rider* (1985), which echoes the plot of *Shane* (1953). Andy Wahol's *Lonesome Cowboys* (1968) involved five lonesome homosexual cowboys and a transvestite sheriff (as expected it received an X rating). *Paint Your Wagon* (1969) featured two men married to one woman.

Harking back to the earlier bathroom scenes in the films of De Mille, it was not unusual for Westerns to contain an obligatory scene of a girl in a bathtub. One example is when Harmonica (Charles Bronson) bursts into the room of Jill McBain (Claudia Cardinale) as she is taking a bath, in *Once Upon a Time in the West* (1968). He uses her window as a vantage point for a gunfight brewing in the street below while she glares at him out of a mound of soap bubbles.

Usually bathing involved a woman in the tub, such as Jill McBain in her bubbles or Hildy (Stella Stevens) in *The Ballad of Cable Hogue* (1970) in the outdoor bathtub. However, unlike other genres, men are occasionally seen bathing in Westerns to allow voyeuristic admiration of the male body by female audiences. In *MacKenna's Gold* (1969), the bandit chief Colorado (Omar Sharif) sits naked (though thankfully cross-legged) by the side of the pool where Hesh-Ke (Julie Newmar) is swimming nude. In *The Good, the Bad and the Ugly* (1966), bad Tuco (Eli Wallach) takes a bath (and casually brushes his teeth with his finger and the bathwater) when an even badder villain breaks in and Tuco shoots him with a gun hidden in the water under all the suds.[27] Tuco continues his bath, then, hearing a sound in the hallway, gets out of the tub on full camera (naked except for a few thin suds) to investigate the noise.

In the Western comedy *The Hallelujah Trail* (1965), the ladies of the temperance group take a bath while the soldiers are literally falling out of the nearby trees to watch them. In a reverse twist earlier in the movie, Colonel Thaddeus Gearhart (Burt Lancaster) is taking a peaceful bath after being out on dusty patrol when temperance worker Cora Massingale (Lee Remick) charges into the room to confront him. With total aplomb he says, "You'll forgive me if I don't get up."

Bathing was not even necessary to show off the male physique. In *Duel in the Sun* (1946), Lewt (Gregory Peck) lounges around suggestively (actually poses might be a better word) on corral rails and rocks. Jeff Chandler in *The Battle at Apache Pass* (also known as *Cochise*) (1952) and Rock Hudson in *Taza, Son of Cochise* (1954) appear as bare-chested Indians with muscular arms. Shane (Alan Ladd) strips off his shirt when he and Joe Starrett (Van Heflin) are struggling to solve the challenge of chopping out the stump in the backyard. In *Day of the Evil Gun* (1968), Apache Indians strip Owen Forbes (Arthur Kennedy) to the waist before staking him out on the ground, a scene done mostly to show off his manly chest. Similar masculine themes appear in Western novels. The men are all handsome, broad-shouldered dreams. The physiques and rippling muscles of Wister's Virginian and Zane Grey's Lassiter and Venters are all described in glowing, almost erotic, terms. Molly finds the Virginian after he is left for dead following an Indian attack, so she undresses him and nurses him back to health.

Western clothing gradually became eroticized, particularly the high-heeled boots and tight pants worn by Western movie heroes of the 1930s through 1950s. The use of tight leather cowboy chaps by some Western stars tended to emphasize the groin area. As author Lee Mitchell has half-humorously pointed out, Westerns are the only genre that allows men to wear tight leather pants without homoerotic connotations.[28] One of the more unusual Western clothing themes was the British-made *The Singer Not the Song* (1961) with Anacleto Comachi (Dirk Bogarde) as a leather-clad homosexual sadist in Mexico. Leather pants were not only for the female audience to enjoy. In *The Plainsman* (1936), Calamity Jane (Jean Arthur) wore tight black leather pants.

The Threat of Rape

One persistent theme in Westerns dealt with rape. The stereotypical Hollywood Indian was often portrayed as lusting after any and all white women.[29] The plot in *Sergeant Rutledge* (1960) involves the court martial of a black cavalry sergeant accused of raping a White girl and murdering her father. The heroine in *Hannie Caulder* (1971) goes on a blood-thirsty revenge quest against three men who raped her and killed her husband. At the beginning of *Two Mules for Sister Sara* (1970) Hogan (Clint Eastwood) interrupts three bandits who are getting ready to rape Sara (Shirley MacLaine). In *The Outlaw Josey Wales* (1976) Laura Lee (Sondra Locke) is stripped from top to (literally) bottom by bandits during an attempted rape. In *Pale Rider* (1985) Josh LaHood (Christopher Penn) tries to rape Megan Wheeler (Sydney Penny), but the Preacher (Clint Eastwood) shows up just in time to rescue her and shoots Josh in the hand.

Closely connected to the rape theme was "save the last bullet" to escape the "fate that was worse than death," the euphemistic expression for the rape of a White woman by Indians. This was a widely established convention from earlier Western books and plays. The concept, however, was based on reality, for example, "Besieged by Sioux and Crows on the Plains in 1867, an army wife wrote in her diary that the women had 'decided that if the Ft [fort] could not be held then we preferred to be shot by our own officers rather than to be taken captive.'"[30]

One of the earliest examples of this theme in the movies is a scene in *The Invaders* (1912), where the commandant is ready to shoot his daughter when rescue arrives. A similar scene was shown in *The Battle at Elderbush Gulch* (1913). The cavalry troops arrive just in time to prevent a rancher from using the last bullet on Melissa Harlow (Lillian Gish). A similar scene occurs in *Stagecoach* (1939), where the gambler Hatfield (John Carradine) is just pulling the trigger on Mrs. Malloy (Louise Platt) when the sound of distant bugles brings the cavalry to the rescue. In *Winchester '73* (1950), Lola Manners (Shelley Winters) looks at the loaded gun in her hand and knowingly says, "I understand about the last one," meaning the last bullet was to be saved for herself.

The secondary message in these plots showed prejudice against a woman who had been raped. In the book *Apache Uprising*, which was made into the movie *Duel at Diablo* (1966), Ellen Graf is rescued from Indian captivity. She is told, "'You were even a wife to one of them.' 'Not because I wanted to be.' 'Then why were you? Any decent woman would kill herself before...'"[31] In *Two Rode Together* (1961), Marshal Guthrie McCabe (James Stewart) is hired by the United States Cavalry to bring back white captives from the Comanche. Elena de la Madriaga (Linda Cristal) has been the captive of Stone Calf (Woody Strode) for five years. During a dance at the fort, the white women are shocked that Elena did not kill herself rather than submitting to an Indian. In *The Searchers* (1956), Ethan Edwards (John Wayne) is focused on killing his niece Debbie (Natalie Wood) because of what he perceives as the physical and mental humiliation she has endured as a captive of the Indian chief Scar when she grew to womanhood. To his eventual surprise, she is resigned to her new life as Scar's wife and says of the Indians who captured her, "These are my people." In the vision of filmmakers of the 1950s, the pure hero had to end up with a virginal heroine. Only the villain, a man of questionable virtue and morals himself, could have a liaison with a prostitute or a disgraced woman.

Dressed and Undressed

One of the trends in the treatment of women in Western films was an emphasis on their bodies, eventually to include total nudity. *Man of the West* (1958) contained a scene full of sexual overtones when Billie Ellis (Julie London) is forced to undress in front of the gang while the villainous Coaley (Jack Lord) holds a knife on Link Jones (Gary Cooper). The situation is resolved before she removes more than the top of her dress, revealing her bodice and petticoat, but that was nevertheless racy for the 1950s.

In the late 1950s, foreign "art" films started to challenge the handling of nudity in the movies. Cheap sexploitation films featuring nudity and sex provided increased box-office competition for the major studios.[32] One of the breakthroughs for nudity in the United States was the humorous *The Immoral Mr. Teas* (1959), made by cheesecake photographer Russ Meyer. In the movie, Mr. Teas (Bill Teas), a door-to-door salesman for dental appliances, has the ability to look at women and see them without their clothes on. Unlike the traditional porno movies, there was no touching and no sex. Teas only ogled the women. The concept was a first in voyeurism for respectable theaters. By today's standards, it was a very mild nudie film with no sexual contact or male nudity, but for the time it was very daring. The film earned $1 million profit and, for the first time, a nudie film appeared in legitimate movie theaters. Because of its theme, however, the film tended to be shown at drive-in movies or second-run theaters, rather than the first-run movie palaces.

By the mid–1960s, morals were changing in America. Unmarried couples were living together, young people were experimenting with drugs such as marijuana and LSD, and teenage pregnancy was rising. Nudity started working its way into the arts and motion pictures. On the stage, the play *Who's Afraid of Virginia Woolf?* and the later motion picture had sexual themes and very strong language for the time, all while being nominated for thirteen Academy Awards. Theater productions, such as *Hair* in 1967 used hippy nude male and female actors who cavorted among the audience. There was more sexual candor in books and advertising. And the movie code eventually collapsed.

With the relaxation of attitudes towards sex in the 1960s, film producers turned towards more sensationalistic plots to attract patrons, and nudity and sexual themes started to creep back onto the screen. Films presented such subjects as the May-December romance of *Lolita* (1961) and a customer baring her breasts in *The Pawnbroker* (1965). Brief female rear nudity appeared in *Cry Tough* (1959), *Splendor in the Grass* (1961), *Cleopatra* (1963), and *Of Human Bondage* (1964). These scenes were cut for American audiences but were shown in European release.

By the mid–1960s the moral prohibitions of the code had gradually eroded away. In 1966 Jack Valenti took over the MPAA (Motion Picture Association of America) and turned out to be far more liberal than the previous president. By 1966 a new code was issued that did not necessarily prohibit some previously banned activities but said rather that they should be handled with restraint. Nudity, for example, was now cautioned by "indecent or undue exposure of the human body shall not be presented," and swearing by "undue profanity shall not be presented."[33] An example of this new liberality occurred in *The Way West* (1967), where "Mercy McBee (Sally Field) is so horny that at one point her lusty father points out that if she doesn't get a husband pretty soon, they'll have to mate her to an ox, which is all well and good, considering oxen, like mules, don't mate. Her constant flirtations end when she is raped, not seduced."[34]

In 1968 Valenti finally scrapped the production code in favor of a system modeled after film ratings in Britain and other countries. The American system was organized under the name of the Code and Ratings Administration (CARA). CARA gave its ratings based on the final film, rather than supervising scripts and production as had the MPPDA. Ratings were "G" for general audiences, "M" for mature audiences, "R" restricted (under 16 admitted only with an adult); and "X" for nobody under 16 admitted. Later PG, (parental guidance), PG-13, and NC-17 (no children under 17 admitted) were added. The X rating was changed to NC-17 to avoid the stigma of X-rated porn films being attached to legitimate Hollywood productions. An X or NC-17 rating was feared by Hollywood, because this rating might cost a film 50 percent to 75 percent of its bookings, compared to an R rating. Many theaters refused to book X or NC-17 films, many newspapers would not take ads for them, and many video stores would not stock them. The non–Western gangster movie *Scarface* (1983) was very violent, with a sophisticated special-effects bloodbath with a machine gun at the end. It originally earned an "X" rating before the decision was appealed and amended.

Sometimes the application of these ratings seemed arbitrary, as slasher films with gruesome violence might rate an "R" or even a "PG-13" rating, whereas sex and nudity might receive an "NC-17" rating or undergo severe cuts in the final film to achieve a lower rating. This editing might alter the director's vision. In a perverse twist of unintended consequences, adults would often not attend a PG or PG-13 film as being too childish. Some films then added gratuitous nudity or profanity in order to raise the rating of a film to attract adult audiences who would only view an R film and would stay away from a PG-13 version.

Total nudity returned to Westerns films such as *MacKenna's Gold* (1969) with Hesh-Ke (Julie Newmar) swimming naked in a water hole and *The Ballad of Cable Hogue* (1970), where Hildy (Stella Stevens) emerges from a bathtub and runs across the desert with nothing on. *Heaven's Gate* (1980) contains several scenes of full frontal nudity (both genital and breast) and rear nudity of Ella Watson (Isabelle Huppert), who runs a brothel.

By the 1970s, even bawdy houses had emerged into acceptability in Westerns such as *The Cheyenne Social Club* (1970), *McCabe and Mrs. Miller* (1971), and *Paint Your Wagon* (1969). The hero was now allowed to occasionally indulge himself. Previously in Westerns, dance-hall and saloon women were not labeled directly as prostitutes, but either their vocation was obvious or, as in Victorian times, they were called by euphemistic names, such as dance-hall girl, waiter girl, or saloon woman.

14

Violence Returns

Chili con carnage—Sir Christopher Frayling[1]

Several factors were involved in the decline of the Hollywood Western. First, in 1948 the settlement of a long-running antitrust suit against the major studios forced them to sell off their profitable theater chains, which resulted in dramatically lowered profits and a drastic cut in production budgets; hence fewer movies were being made. At the same time—as the 1950s progressed—studio costs in Hollywood rose to the point where Westerns were not profitable, which led to a further decline in production. A third factor was that by 1960 many of the Western movie stars from the classic period of the 1940s and 1950s were aging or had retired from the screen. The older appearance of those stars who continued in films had to be reflected in the plots, which did not always attract young audiences. And the popularity of free television Westerns, such as *Gunsmoke* and *Maverick*, created fierce competition for theatrical releases and further cut into movie audiences. To compete with the popularity of the small screen and attract sophisticated audiences, feature Western films had to present more daring themes and visual images than what could be broadcast under the watchful eye of the FCC to homes with families or with children present. As the 1960s progressed, lowered movie censorship barriers allowed Western filmmakers to exploit more graphic themes, including rape, nudity, hanging, whipping, sex, and sadism. The new heroes were cynical and cold-blooded.

The decline of Hollywood production in the late 1960s created a shortage of Western movies for the overseas market. This created a business opportunity as Westerns were still profitable in Europe, particularly in Germany and Italy. To meet this demand, several European countries decided to make their own Westerns. As one example, the Western comedy *The Sheriff of Fractured Jaw* (1959), with English actor Kenneth More and American actress Jayne Mansfield, was a British production made in Spain.

As the 1970s progressed, audience tastes shifted to the occult, horror, science fiction, thrillers, kung-fu movies, and outer space themes, such as the *Star Wars* and *Alien* cycle of films. Interest in Western films declined and, by the 1970s and 1980s, Hollywood Westerns were rare. In an attempt to attract audiences back, the romantic view of the Old West gave way to a different vision that was the supposed harsh and unflattering "truth." The movie West was transformed into a bleak and violent world that was dirty, dangerous, and full of undesirable characters.

Heroes became scruffy rascals and free-living colorful spirits like Dingus Billy Magee (Frank Sinatra) in *Dirty Dingus Magee* (1970), Cable Hogue (Jason Robards) in *The Ballad of Cable Hogue* (1970), and the quartet of gambling rogues in *4 for Texas* (1963). As in the dime novels, outlaws and bandits were glorified again in *Butch Cassidy and the Sundance Kid* (1969), *Waterhole #3* (1967), and *The Duchess and the Dirtwater Fox* (1976). Though these films were comedies on the surface, they presented the notion that everyone in the West was violent, greedy, and devious. The hero image was modified to become equally violent and devious.

Other new themes included compromise and betrayal with more serious consequences. An example was the shoot-out between Alamosa Bill (Jack Elam) and Billy the Kid (Kris Kristofferson) in *Pat Garrett and Billy the Kid* (1973). Both participants were supposed to count to ten before shooting at each other. Alamosa cheated and only counted to eight before firing, but Billy beat him by being even more devious and only counting to three. This was considered to be acceptable and even humorous.

Violence and Changing Morality

Censorship of Western plots has been directed at various themes and not just sex. Two concerns among critics that dated back to the beginnings of dime novels and motion pictures were corrupted morals and violence. When Edward Wheeler created Deadwood Dick, he was the first dime novel writer to create a Western hero who was outside the law and even defied it. In Dick's case, Dick disrupted the social order by robbing stagecoaches. Western bad-men like this, however, became very popular with working-class audiences who felt themselves exploited by the capitalist class, as represented by railroads, banks, and other powerful corporate figures. While this theme was used heavily in dime novels, critics felt that movies should not use the same type of plotting, as they were watched by children and the working class.[2] Whether such films were or were not historically accurate, the actions portrayed in them were often not moral. Early movies about Jesse James, for example, were banned by censors, and exhibitors in several large cities refused to show them.[3]

The portrayal of excessive violence in Westerns has always received criticism. As one example, in *The Man from Hell* (1934), Clint Mason (Reb Russell) is "hung" as part of the plot. Yakima Canutt, the premiere stunt man and second-unit director, constructed a system of piano wires for support that made the hanging seem real. In fact, it was so realistic that censors thought the scene was too vivid and had it removed from the release version.[4] By the 1960s, however, this attitude had softened and the beginning of *Hang 'Em High* (1968) opens with the detailed lynching of Jed Cooper (Clint Eastwood), who is left dangling by the lynch mob, with his feet twitching, until he is, luckily, cut down just in time. This introductory scene of an innocent man being victimized provides the rationale for why he becomes a vengeful marshal who follows his own code of justice.

A Reinvigorated Pattern of Violence

Violence in the movies has a long history and has been highlighted since the first Westerns. *The Battle at Elderbush Gulch* (1913) contains one particularly violent and distasteful scene where an Indian swings a child over his head as he crushes its skull on a rock. *The Spoilers* (1923) has a protracted bloody fight between McNamara (Noah Beery) and Glenister

Since the early days of dime novels and Western movies, cowboy violence has persisted in popular entertainment. In this photograph, actors stage a main street walk-down and face-to-face gunfight for the delight and entertainment of tourists (author's collection).

(Milton Sills) that is so drawn-out the two have to stop and rest between bashing each other. A similar exhausting fight scene takes place in *The Big Country* (1958) between James McKay (Gregory Peck) and Steve Leech (Charlton Heston) as they try to resolve their conflicts out behind the barn.

Western novels can be even more violent than their film counterparts. In the original novel of *The Shootist*, Marshal J.B. Books was a more violent character than in the film of the same name. For example, in the book there is one detailed scene where Books shoots a man in the rear end, shattering the man's spine.[5] Other descriptions in the book are much more intense than the film. The graphic description of a gruesome head shot is one example: "On the tile floor under what remained of Jay Cobb's face lay an eyeball and the brain matter which housed the accumulated knowledge of his twenty years...."[6] At the end of the novel Books is shot in the back by the bartender and then asks Gillom to shoot him. Gillom complies. Toning this down in the movie, Gillom (Ron Howard) shoots the bartender and then throws away the gun, leaving Books dying on the floor.

A turning point in depicting violence in Western movies came with *Shane* (1953). Previously, and particularly in B Westerns, the loser in a gunfight simply threw his arms up in the air and swooned dramatically to the ground, usually with no blood on his shirt. Typical was *The Sheepman* (1958), where Jason Sweet (Glenn Ford) is shot in the shoulder but has no hole in his jacket and no blood leaking out. But in *Shane*, when Stonewall Jackson (Elisha Cook Jr.) is shot down by gunman Jack Wilson (Walter "Jack" Palance), Cook was rigged with wires so that he was jerked violently backwards by the apparent impact of the bullet. This graphic effect created a new type of "realism" in shootings which thrilled and titillated audiences so much that it became a standard in Western gunfights.

The classic Westerns of the 1940s and 1950s promoted the traditional American view that violence was the fault of evil men. In 1960s, as filmmakers presented a more intense portrayal of violence, new attitudes emerged, perhaps in part reflecting a jaded view towards violence. Film writer Ted Sennett, for example, has pointed out that *The Missouri Breaks* (1976) was considered by many to be an extremely violent, unpleasant Western "full of wretched excesses."

Sergio Leone and the Spaghetti Westerns

In 1948, one-fourth of all movies were Westerns. In spite of the addition of sex and violence, by 1964 the number of Westerns had dropped to about 7 percent.[7] Then the late 1960s and the 1970s saw an abrupt change in the direction of the depiction of the Western hero as films and plot themes became dominated by the efforts of Italian film director Sergio Leone and American director Sam Peckinpah.

In the 1950s and early 1960s, as the Hollywood Western continued to promote the myth of heroic cowboy-gunmen fighting Indians and each other on a wild frontier, the Italian film industry was dominated by the "sword-and-sandal epics" such as the series of *Hercules* gladiator films starring Steve Reeves. In the mid–1960s, however, the Italian film industry, like Hollywood, went into a slump.

A new vision of the West emerged with director Sergio Leone's "Dollars Trilogy," which consisted of *A Fistful of Dollars* (1964), *For a Few Dollars More* (1965), and *The Good, the*

Bad and the Ugly (1966). These films made an icon of a poncho-clad gunfighter whose anonymity was played up for marketing purposes to add mystique to the character. He became known in publicity as "The Man with No Name," even though in the first movie he was called "Joe" in a couple of places, in the second he was "Monco," and in the third "Blondie."

These three movies presented a more cynical version of the Western hero. He is a tough, laconic fortune hunter with a lack of morals and driven by survival and material success. The first of the trio was *A Fistful of Dollars* (1964), which reenergized the Western film industry and led to a host of copies. The characters are greedy and power hungry. Human decency and morality have no place in their violent world. Like other directors before him, Leone tried to re-create what he perceived was the real West and filmed the story in the desert country around Almeria in Spain, which he felt showed the harshness and toughness of the West. A stranger (Clint Eastwood) rides into an isolated town ruled by factions warring in a conflict involving profit and power. Leone and Eastwood present this "hero" as an amoral, hard-bitten, sell-your-soul-to-the-highest-bidder gunfighter.[8] Eastwood, previously known for his portrayal of the clean-cut, grinning Rowdy Yates in the television series *Rawhide*, was transformed into a squinty-eyed, terse-lipped, stubble-chinned, cigarillo-smoking antihero. His version of the hero does not care about the rights or wrongs of the situation but plays both sides against each other.[9] The stranger is punched, kicked, has tequila poured on his open cuts, and a cigar ground out on his hand. At one point he is severely beaten, complete with vivid renderings of a split nose, a swollen eye, and a battered face, but he eventually recovers to defeat the strongest villain. In a world of immorality with sadistic villains, the anonymous hero's superior craftiness and skill with a gun let him come out on top. The level of violence in the film resulted in cuts by censors and some versions of the film still do not show Leone's full vision.[10]

Yet, it must be admitted, the stranger is not totally without virtues. He exhibits a sense of old-time morality when he rescues Marisol (Marianne Koch) from the gang of baddies and restores her to her husband and child with a wad of stolen money to help them make a new start. When she asks why, he replies, "I once knew someone like you. There was no-one there to help."

American critics used the name "spaghetti Western" as a derisive label to describe this and similar Westerns made in Italy and Spain between 1963 and 1977 with Italian directors and international casts.[11] Two dozen or so of these Spanish-Italian oaters had been made before Leone filmed his Dollars Trilogy. Some of these films were distributed in the United States, but American audiences didn't find them particularly appealing. Many of the plots were rehashes of old American Westerns starring declining secondary actors who had previously played supporting roles in Hollywood A Westerns.

Several hundred of these movies were to follow Leone's lead. Leone did not create the spaghetti Western but brought it into prominence, thus creating a new genre for Hollywood. Critics and reviewers complained that the three Dollars movies were poor Italian imitations of American Westerns, but audiences loved them. Forty spaghetti Westerns were produced in 1966, seventy-four in 1967, seventy-seven in 1968, thirty-one in 1969, thirty-five in 1970, forty-seven in 1971, and forty-eight in 1972.[12] In all, more than 500 were made. The popularity of the Dollars movies even spawned direct imitators, such as *For a Few Dollars Less* (also named *The Good, the Ugly, the Cheeky*) (1966), and *The Handsome, the Ugly, the Cretinous* (1967).

The spaghetti films were different from the traditional Hollywood Western. They featured a newer, younger type of Western hero, instead of the aging Western stars of Hollywood at the time. This new hero was distinctively dressed in dusty, dirty, sloppy clothing, with a battered hat-brim pulled low. The bad men are really bad, such as Angel Eyes (Lee Van Cleef) in *The Good, the Bad and the Ugly* (1966), who guns down a peasant and his wife and child at the beginning of the movie (similar to the concept of the bad man kicking the dog). Even these villains presented a new type of morality. Before the peasant is shot, he offers Angel Eyes money to kill whoever hired him. Angel Eyes takes the money, returns to his original employer, and kills him also. This may show poetic justice, but it also makes the character deceitful, double-dealing, devious, and a cheat. Tuco (Eli Wallach), another of the unpleasant protagonists in *The Good, the Bad and the Ugly* (1966) has a background of murder, swindling, armed robbery, rape, arson, perjury, bigamy, and deserting his wife.

The Dollars films incorporated a large amount of violence for the time, such as the brutal beating of No-Name (Clint Eastwood) in *A Fistful of Dollars* (1964) and the wholesale machine-gunning of Mexican soldiers as the Rojo gang steals their shipment of guns. Another violent segment is the slaughter of the Baxter family by the Rojos when they dynamite the Baxter house, set it on fire, and then methodically gun down everyone as they run out, including Baxter and his son. This is done to the accompaniment of the maniacal laughter from the killers in the Rojo gang. They even shoot Baxter's wife in cold blood, which establishes them as really, really bad.

For a Few Dollars More (1965) contained a graphic rape and suicide of the sister of Colonel Mortimer (Lee Van Cleef) by Indio (Gian Maria Volontè). In one scene, Indio shoots one of his henchmen twice, then three times more at point-blank range. This was not the behavior of a hero, or even of a traditional villain.

In *The Good, the Bad and the Ugly* (1966), Tuco is beaten until his face is a bloody pulp and his teeth are falling out. Blondie's face becomes a mass of disgusting disintegrating blisters as he is forced by Tuco to walk across the desert in the blinding heat of the desert sun. Tuco kills the sadistic sergeant who beat him in the POW camp by hammering his head on a rock. Scores of men are blown up and die for some remote cause as expendable Mexicans and Civil War soldiers take over the previous role of expendable Indians. The overall theme of the films was brutality and gore. The earlier Hays code did not allow a single frame of film to show both a shooting and the bullet hitting the victim. They were supposed to be separate film shots (so to speak). However, supposedly Leone didn't know that and filmed it anyway.[13] Even with all this blood-drenched violence, Leone claimed that his Westerns were "fairy tales for adults."[14]

Another change from the traditional Western was that Leone's filming style kept audiences off balance. He included bizarre-looking secondary characters and focused on lingering close-ups of eyes and the faces of ugly desperadoes. The hero's part was played in a minimalist style. Eastwood felt that his part in *A Fistful of Dollars* (1964) would be more effective by not saying much, therefore much of the scripted dialog was cut. Eastwood later said, "I don't just do something. I stand there."[15] Some critics have claimed that this may have been due to Eastwood's inability to speak Italian; however, these movies were shot without sound and the dialog dubbed in later, so this may be inaccurate. The films were shot without audio so that different sound tracks could be incorporated for different international markets during postproduction.[16]

Leone's films were also different, as they introduced a new type of musical sound track particularly for a Western. Typical Hollywood Western music at the time consisted of powerful melodies and lush orchestral scores by composers such as Elmer Bernstein for *The Magnificent Seven* (1960), or the driving beat of the ballad sound tracks of Dmitri Tiomkin in *High Noon* (1952), sung by Tex Ritter, and *Gunfight at the O.K. Corral* (1957), sung by Frankie Laine. By contrast, for the Dollars movies, composer Ennio Morricone blended conventional orchestral music with electronic sounds, whistles, human voices, musical chimes, metallic clanging noises, strident solo instruments, gunshots, odd noises (such as the creaking of the windmill in *Once Upon a Time in the West* (1968)), and melodies carried by the ethereal soprano voice of Edda Dell'Orso.[17] In a reversal of the usual method of adding music, which was traditionally done in postproduction, much of the music for Leone's films was composed before filming and Leone played it on the set to help create the mood he desired. The violence of the Dollars trilogy and the hero as brutal and amoral continued into Leone's next Western project, *Once Upon a Time in the West* (1968). Critical opinion of this movie has changed over time. At first the film did not receive much praise from critics, but it is now considered to be one of Leone's best works.

At the beginning, a group of gunman hired by the evil railroad baron Morton (Gabriele Ferzetti) massacres the entire McBain family, consisting of Brett (Frank Wolff) and his two sons and daughter, at their farm at Sweetwater as they are preparing a celebration picnic for the arrival of stepmother Jill (Claudia Cardinale). The gunmen wear saddle slickers in order to project a more sinister image. The leader of the shooters is seen first from the rear, then the camera moves around his head and the audience suddenly sees that it is Henry Fonda. *Henry Fonda is the bad guy!* This was a shocker for the audience. Henry Fonda had built up a career over a thirty-year span as a traditional Western hero playing the good guy. In this movie he acts a reversal of his traditional role of the good guy and plays the despicable villain Frank, who shoots the entire family. In the best tradition of movie villains, Frank smiles with pleasure as he shoots.

In preparing for the part, Fonda thought he should look like a villain. He grew a moustache and went to an optometrist and purchased brown contact lenses to disguise his baby-blue eyes.[18] Leone would have none of this and told him to go back to looking like Henry Fonda. The point of the cynical joke by Leone was the shock value of a traditional hero playing an evil villain. There is an obligatory walk-down at the end as Frank, all in black (except for a dark-brown shirt), circles Harmonica (Charles Bronson), dressed in light tan. In this way, Leone included the old Western imagery of evil in black versus a good hero dressed in white.

The New Violence and Brutality

As the spaghetti Westerns soared in popularity among audiences of the mid–1960s, production companies rushed to film and release this new type of Western while the craze was still strong. So many movies were produced with heroes that were unshaven, gritty, dark, and mean that filmmakers tried to create some distinction among them. The results were almost comic. As Christopher Frayling has pointed out, "There were one-armed gunmen, handless gunmen, gunslinger priests, blind gunmen, mute gunmen, epileptic gunmen, a ghost gunman, and on one celebrated occasion, gay gunmen."[19]

Most of the location shooting for the spaghetti Westerns took place at outdoor movie towns in Spain and on Western movie town sets around Rome. Interiors were filmed on rented Italian studio sets and sound stages. Though mostly Italian or Spanish-Italian coproductions, some were also made by the West Germans, a nation that loves Westerns. One German example was the very popular *The Treasure of Silver Lake* (1962).

Spaghetti Westerns were typically filmed in Spain. Casts were usually an American star or a European one with an Anglicized name or a pseudonym to appeal to English-speaking audiences. This was also done so that the audience would think the movie was a real American Western. Actor's names were altered to appeal to different audiences. For example, a German name might be used for German audiences. The bandit leader in *Navajo Joe* (1966), Mervyn Duncan, was Alfredo Brell, also known as Aldo Sambrell.[20] Similarly, blue-eyed blonde Italian actor Mario Girotti became Terence Hill in *My Name Is Nobody* (1973). Carlo Pedersoli was credited in movies as Bud Spencer.[21]

The spaghetti Westerns had no particular social message and presented a hero with no clear sense of moral right as the heroes of the earlier generations of Westerns had. Their new motivation was financial. This redefined the Western hero, who dispensed his own violent

Is this the desert country of Almeria in Spain from a spaghetti Western? Monument Valley in Arizona from a John Ford Western? Or the mythic West? The vision of a harsh landscape of sandstone buttes and arid desert country has become associated with the primary location of the West of movies and Western novels. This particular scene could be any of these places but is actually the real West of Utah's canyon country, the setting of many of Zane Grey's novels (author's collection).

form of justice in gratuitous carnage and incredible plots. Other Westerns of the late 1960s added this intense violence and a lack of heroic motivation of the protagonist. The new "heroes" were grim outlaws surrounded by death and sadistic behavior. Typical of the harsh and violent world of the Hollywood Westerns of the 1960s was *Welcome to Hard Times* (1967). Blue (Henry Fonda) is the hero, but he is also a coward, as he and the townspeople allow "The Badman from Bodie" (Aldo Ray) to terrorize their town. Blue tries to survive and stay out of the conflict but is finally pushed to his limit and shoots the bad man in an almost accidental, haphazard way rather than the traditional heroic face-to-face showdown and shoot-out.

The violence in these Westerns became more realistic, elaborate, and sensational. Makeup artists and special-effects wizards found ways to depict violence and its effects more graphically and with seeming realism. Audiences started to expect this level of violence in other films, as in the violent shoot-out at the end of the non–Western *Bonnie and Clyde* (1967). Carnage appeared in *Soldier Blue* (1970), a movie based on the real Sand Creek Massacre that took place in Colorado in 1864, an appalling episode from history in which a regiment of volunteer cavalry slaughtered between 130 and 175 Cheyenne and Arapaho and mutilated the bodies. In the movie version of the battle, the director used amputees with false limbs to set a new standard for spouting blood and hacked-off body parts. That was a bit of a stomach-turner for many viewers.[22]

Valdez Is Coming (1971) is full of sadistic violence, such as where Valdez (Burt Lancaster) is beaten and his arms lashed to two huge poles tied together in the form of a symbolic cross as he tries to drag himself and the wooden cross back home. In *Lawman* (1971), when villainous rancher Vince Bronson (Lee J. Cobb) sees his sons dead in the street, he blows his own brains out on camera in a shockingly vivid scene. *The Hellbenders* (1967) contained graphic scenes of the hanging of three Mexican bandits, which by this time was considered to be so routine that it received only an "A" (Adult) rating from censors in England. In the beating scene in *Day of Anger* (also known as *Gunlaw*) (1967), one of the characters is kicked and punched so that he has blood pouring from his mouth. This was so graphic that it was cut by censors.

The ways to kill off characters became more and more macabre. In one scene in *A Professional Gun* (1968), after he interrogates a wounded bandit, one of the characters stuffs a grenade in the other's mouth, pulls the pin and runs out of the way. In the later *No Country for Old Men* (2007), villain Anton Chigurh (Javier Bardem) carries a compressed-air tank hooked up to a portable pneumatic cattle-killing device from a slaughterhouse to assassinate his victims.

Django Kill (1967) is possibly one of the most gruesome and perhaps the most violent of the spaghetti Westerns. The gratuitous violence includes a scalping, a man's chest being ripped open, a mass lynching, an implied male rape, a man killed by a torrent of molten gold, and an entire gang and their horses blown up with dynamite. Other delightful scenes include a half-dead man clawing his way up out of a grave, a man vomiting outside a saloon, and a woman biting a man's hand.

This became a little much for even some of the actors. When Burt Reynolds made *Navajo Joe* (1966) in Spain, he reportedly became tired of performing stunts with no let-up in the action, so he asked the director to include a love scene to quiet the pace. Director Sergio Corbucci refused and replied, "We have improved the American western by removing all the boring stuff. We have taken out the love scenes and all the talk, talk, talk."[23] It was a gruesome movie to begin with, complete with scalpings, whippings, and killings by knife, garotte, and tomahawk. The story is a grim and violent one about a group of hunters who kill Indians for the bounty on their scalps. The film contains vivid and graphic depictions of scalping and, at one point, a tomahawk is thrown into the villain's forehead. Minor incidents are a bloody beating with fists and a rifle butt, and a skull smashed with a rock.

These new themes of extraordinary brutality, violence, and cruelty in the spaghetti Westerns was hailed by some critics as a fresh, realistic approach and a removal of stereotypes. This was self-defeating because these characters became stereotypes when they were copied again and again, just as the traditional cowboy hero became a stereotype after his newness wore off.

Other antihero themes crept into Westerns. *Butch Cassidy and the Sundance Kid* (1969) ended with the death of the two bandit-heroes, which was a new twist. *True Grit* (1969) showed John Wayne in an unusual role for him, where he was vengeful instead of fair, liked to drink, and was motivated by money instead of the desire for justice. In a peculiar piece of masochistic imagery, when the son of wagon train organizer Irving Tadlock (Kirk Douglas) is killed in a buffalo stampede in *The Way West* (1967), Tadlock orders his own flogging by his Negro servant.[24]

Gunfight at Red Sands (1964) is a spaghetti Western but, more like a parody of the old B Westerns, it contains fistfights, gunfights, wild wagon rides, horse chases, and a characteristic saloon can-can dance scene that has nothing to do with the plot. At the end, the hero and the villain walk towards each other for a traditional face-off and shoot it out in the main street. The hero, of course, wins and rides out of town to the accompaniment of a ballad sung in the fashion of Frankie Laine in 1950s Hollywood Westerns.

The Wild Bunch

Meanwhile, in the United States, director Sam Peckinpah was also moving towards more violent movies. The gallant virtuous hero on horseback did not fit in this new world of violent Westerns. Eight of Peckinpah's fourteen films end with the death of a major character.[25] *Ride the High Country* (1962) contains savage characters who abuse women and brutalize each other, while the two heroes try to maintain their own moral codes. Morals were slipping for everyone, however. Gil Westrum (Randolph Scott) is a rascally hero who plans to steal the gold they are transporting from his more idealistic partner Steve Judd (Joel McCrea).

Peckinpah extended excessive violence into *The Wild Bunch* (1969), which glorified and promoted the amoral and violent hero. Rather than the traditional clutch-your-chest-and-fall when someone was shot in the older Westerns, this movie used special effects to make the depiction of bullets striking a body as realistic as possible. Slow motion filming was used to make killing seem esthetic.

The opening contains several cruel images of children watching two scorpions being overwhelmed by an army of ants. Then the children douse the entire anthill in kerosene and burn it. Also at the beginning is a massacre where the outlaw gang uses a group of hymn-singing temperance marchers to shield them as they make their escape after a failed robbery of the town bank in San Miguel. As the surrounding posse of townspeople continues to blaze away in the ensuing mayhem, a woman is trampled, a marching musician is killed, and bystanders are maimed and shot down in the streets while the gang make their getaway. This sequence, where the posse continues to shoot at the gang and their hostages, killing innocent women and children, breaks with the earlier film taboo of killing women. This happens again later in the film with the shooting of Teresa (Sonia Amelio) as she is sitting on General Mapache's (Emilio Fernández) lap.

In a radical change in the hero image, Pike Bishop (William Holden) professes the virtues of loyalty, comradeship, and professionalism. However, he also has a dark side. He abandons Crazy Lee (Bo Hopkins) to be shot by the posse that storms the bank during the initial raid so that the others can escape. He shoots the blinded Buck (Rayford Barnes) because he is slowing down their escape. He lets Freddie Sykes (Edmond O'Brien) fend for himself when the posse chasing them catches up, as he feels that Sykes will create a diversion while the rest of them escape. Bishop later changes sides for money and allies himself with the villainous Mapache to steal guns from the Americans.

The other characters are just as bad and brutal. Dutch Engstrom (Ernest Borgnine) abandons Angel (Jaime Sánchez) to his fate, which turned out to be very unpleasant when he is tied up and dragged behind a speeding car. Angel shoots his previous girlfriend Teresa and spatters everyone with her blood when he believes she has become Mapache's whore. Rebels shoot without hesitation at a fellow soldier who shoots prematurely at Bishop and the wagon of guns they are stealing. The gang all drink and swear and consort with whores.

The ending is resolved by the typical gunfighter scenario of the hero forcing direct and personal combat with the chief of the evildoers. Following the stylized scenario of the Western, the long final walk by Bishop is like that of the traditional gunfighter, leading the audience to suspect how the plot will end. But to the audience's surprise, the final bloodbath is cold and brutal, with the machine-gunning of almost everybody. This was filmed in great detail by special effects crews using exploding blood squibs. Reportedly 90,000 rounds of blank ammunition were used.[26] The ending of *The Wild Bunch* (1969), as well as *Butch Cassidy and the Sundance Kid* (1969), perpetuated the myth of the superiority of the Anglo gunman. In both movies it takes an entire regiment of troops to finally gun them down.

The last scenes of graphic violence in *The Wild Bunch* (1969)—where blood spurts rather than drips, and slaughter and blood-letting were shown in slow motion—led to the first R rating for a Western.[27] Even so, the producers had to cut a few minutes of violence to gain an R rating instead of an X. Nevertheless, audiences found the violence a bit too much. Thirty or so people walked out of a sneak preview in Kansas City, some of them physically sick.[28] Some critics were similarly outraged. After early screenings were not well received by the public, the studio cut a further thirty-five minutes. Warner Brothers announced a twenty-fifth anniversary rerelease of *The Wild Bunch* to restore the minutes that had been cut, but when the film ratings board gave the new version an NC-17 rating, Warners withdrew the idea.[29]

The Wild Bunch (1969) was the first violent and bloody American Western with violent stunts shot in extreme slow motion. As the main character, Bishop meets an unusual, protracted end for a hero. First he is shot in the back by a woman, so he promptly turns and blasts her with a shotgun. After more slaughter of Mexican troops, he is shot again in the back and killed by a young boy in a military uniform with a rifle. Gone were the days of the romantic stand-up duel.

Another groundbreaking subtle change in film style that made *The Wild Bunch* different was that the editing contained more cuts than any other Hollywood film. It contained 3,642 individual cuts (in the original unedited version) as compared to 600 or so for the typical Western.[30] Editing in this manner affects viewer emotions, with the increased pace raising the tension of the movie. An interesting humorous tribute to the creator of *The Wild Bunch* occurs in *My Name Is Nobody* (1973) when Nessuno (Terence Hill) walks past a grave, then stops and looks at the name on the wooden cross and says, "Sam Peckinpah. That's a beautiful name in Navajo."

Upside-down Heroes

The new trends in movie-making developed a peculiar breed of Western heroes. *The Professionals* (1966), for example, presented a reversal of plot themes. What starts out as a rescue mission for a kidnapped young woman turns out to be a kidnap mission. Twists and turns in the plot show that the apparent villain, Raza (Jack Palance), is not the evil kidnapper he is originally made out to be, but the woman's lover. Raza cold-bloodedly kills the Colorados (storm troopers of the local governing body), but this turns out to be in revenge for the death of his wife. The plot shows the use of immoral actions on both sides to justify their means, and the morality turns out backwards. These professionals, for example, show a willingness to kill their horses to avoid detection, which is different from the traditional hero, who bonded with his horse.

Good taste and morality both disappear in *A Fistful of Dynamite* (1971), which was inexplicably retitled *Duck, You Sucker* in the United States. The movie starts with Juan Miranda (Rod Steiger) urinating on an anthill as the camera shows the ants being washed away. Then he walks away from the camera, scratching his behind in a rather vulgar manner. This is a drastic change in the protagonist, as behavior like this would not have been acceptable in earlier movies or in polite company. The bad taste continues after Juan and his men rob the stagecoach and he forces passenger Adelita (Maria Monti) to look at his genitals before he rapes her. The bandits strip the male passengers of their belongings and force them to hand over all their clothes, providing a full-screen view of a bare male bottom and a rather graphic shot of a naked male tumbling end over end as the wagon the men are in crashes and they are all thrown out onto the ground. Except for a lack of spurting blood, there is violence similar to *The Wild Bunch* (1969) during mass killings as professional Irish mercenary Sean (James Coburn) and Juan blow up a bridge then wipe out an entire patrol of soldiers with two machine-guns while trying to rob a bank in revolutionary Mexico. A revenge scene shows soldiers shooting and killing innocent local civilians trapped in a trough.

By the 1980s, excessive violence was the norm, as exemplified by *The Long Riders* (1980). During the sequence featuring the Northfield bank robbery by the James and Younger gang (and indeed throughout the movie), the plot highlighted fighting and shooting, showing bleeding wounds and head shots and blood squibs exploding violently out through clothing. Some of this was filmed in stylized slow motion like *The Wild Bunch* (1969).

Dead Man (1995) contained even more violence. Charlie Dickinson (Gabriel Byrne) kills his fiancée by mistake when he finds her in bed with William Blake (Johnny Depp). Though wounded in the exchange of fire, Blake is forced to kill Dickinson in self-defense. Blake is befriended by an Indian (Gary Farmer) who nurses him back to health. In a revenge-type plot, after Charlie Dickinson's father, John (Robert

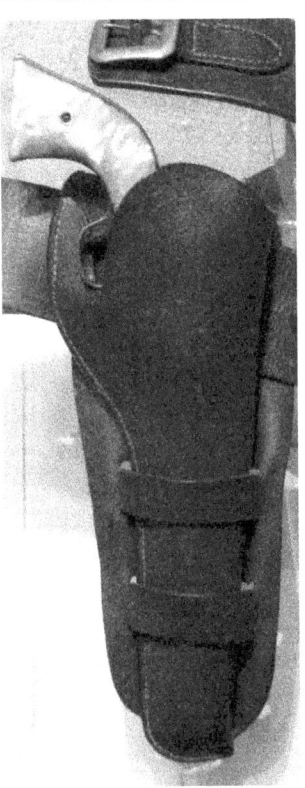

Right: The sides of holsters used in the real Old West were high and the gun sat deep in the sheath to protect it from the weather, to prevent it from accidentally falling out onto the ground, and to protect the trigger from snagging in bushes. The holster typically covered the trigger mechanism to prevent inadvertent discharge, which would shoot the wearer in the leg. This type of holster was worn high on the waist so it would not interfere with daily activities, and typically a cartridge belt was not part of the rig. *Below:* In 1950s Hollywood fast-draw expert Arvo Ojala redesigned the basic holster so that it would clear the leather sheath faster and allow a quicker draw by movie heroes. Ojala stiffened the leather pouch by adding a thin plate of metal to keep it away from the cylinder of the revolver. He also cut the top of the holster lower so that most of the gun was exposed and the hammer could be cocked during the draw. His design became the iconic symbol of the movie gunman. The lowered attachment loop on the belt for this type of holster allowed it to be worn low on the thigh and nearer to the hand for a faster draw. Because much of the revolver was exposed, a loop had to be added over the hammer to prevent the gun from falling out of the holster. A leather thong tied the bottom of the holster to the leg to prevent the holster from riding up with the gun as it was drawn. Cartridge loops were added to the belt so that a fast-shooting movie hero would have spare ammunition (both photographs, author's collection).

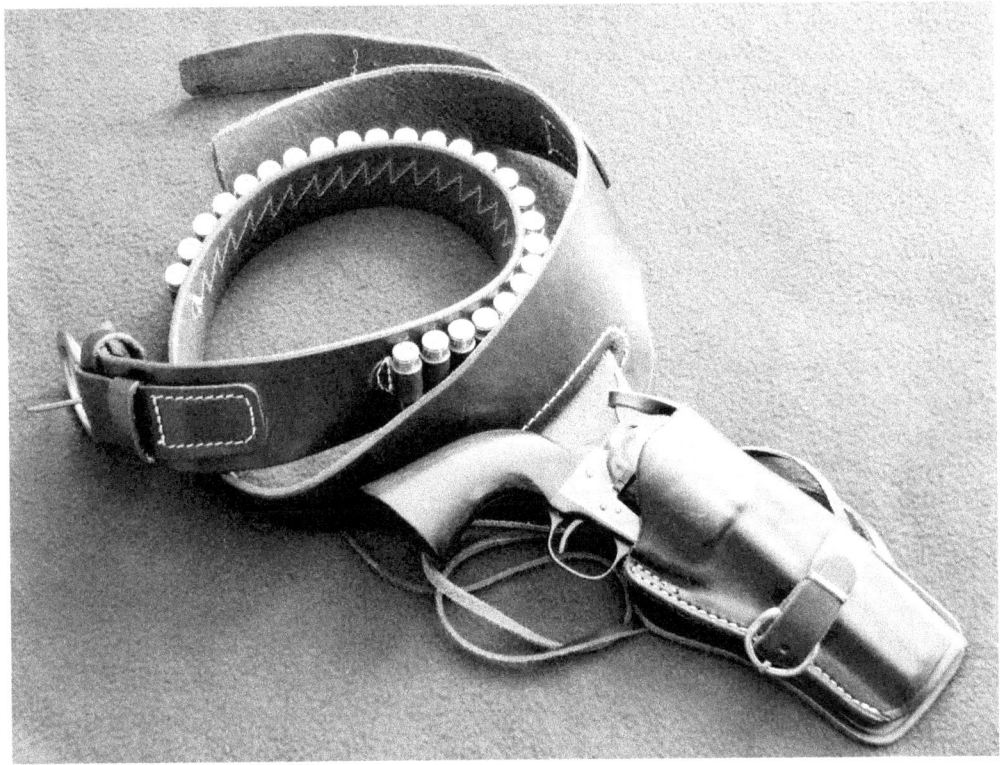

Mitchum), hires three killers to hunt Blake down, the movie degenerates into a maelstrom of violence. The language is vulgar and the shootings are graphic. The screen is filled with bizarre touches, including graphic representations of fellatio and sexual intercourse. One of the killers is a cannibal, another sleeps with a teddy bear, and John Dickinson addresses a stuffed grizzly bear when erratically talking to the men that he hires as killers. Blake has an encounter with three odd fur-trappers, one of whom is wearing a gingham dress. Cole Wilson (Lance Henricksen) stands on the face of a dead lawman that Blake has killed until the head splits open and blood squirts out. Wilson shoots one of his fellow bounty hunters and eats him. Blake stabs a combination storekeeper and preacher in the hand with a pen, then shoots him at point-blank range.

Other American Westerns contained the same type of violence and changed morality as the spaghetti Westerns did. *Bad Girls* (1994), which is unusual for a Western as the four protagonists are women, ends in a blood-spattered shoot-out. In *Tombstone* (1993), Curly Bill Brocius (Powers Boothe) and the cowboy gang shoot the groom in cold blood at a wedding. That particular sequence ends with Johnny Ringo (Michael Biehn) deliberately killing a priest.

The Last of the Mohicans (1992) contains five sequences of intense and graphic violence. One is the first Indian attack when Maj. Duncan Heyward (Steven Waddington), Cora Munro (Madeleine Stowe), Alice Munro (Jodhi May), and their escort are traveling to Fort William Henry. This contains intense images of the use of battle axes, muskets, tomahawks, and pistols in knifings, shootings, and scalpings. Spurting blood and bodies are everywhere. The second is the attack on Fort Henry, where soldiers are blown up by exploding mortar shells. Third is the slaughter of the troops leaving Fort Henry after the surrender to the French. This sequence lasts for four minutes of gory violence, including a scene of Magua (Wes Studi) cutting out the heart of Colonel Munro (Maurice Roëves) and brandishing it in the air. In the fourth, Major Heyward is burned alive at the Huron camp before Hawk-Eye (Daniel Day-Lewis) shoots him to put him out of his misery. Finally there is the fight between Chingachgook (Russel Means) and Magua as Chingacook chops Magua to pieces with his war sword.[31]

Clint Eastwood

The star and director who has probably had more influence on the shaping of modern Western movies and their heroes is Clint Eastwood. Eastwood's characters, though amoral, are men of mystery and mythic power. Eastwood plays the parts of lone-wolf antiheroes that are totally different from those of John Wayne. Wayne played a strong, independent and self-sufficient westerner in the way that most Americans would like to picture themselves. Eastwood's "heroes" are scruffy, amoral men who are virtually indistinguishable from the villains.

The plots of these new Westerns of Eastwood are also not those of Wayne's era. Traditional mythology has been changed. In *Pale Rider* (1985) the bad guys establish evil intent and define themselves by killing Megan Wheeler's (Sydney Penny) dog during the initial attack on the miner's camp. In *Two Mules for Sister Sara* (1970), the nun (Shirley MacLaine) that Hogan (Clint Eastwood) rescues from nudity and rape at the beginning of the movie turns out to be a whore in nun's clothing. In *High Plains Drifter* (1973), The Stranger (Clint Eastwood) appears out of a mirage like the apparition that he really is. In setting the initial scene (like the bad guy kicking the dog), he swigs whiskey, guns down three baddies, and rapes an aggressive woman in a barn. The plot contains a violent whipping murder scene and ends with a revenge motif with one of the bad guys being whipped to death.

In *Unforgiven* (1992), Will Munny's (Clint Eastwood) background is that of a violent gunman who has been reformed by his wife. He credits whiskey for most of his violent career. But he is now a widower, which frees him to take on a job of revenge. Now he is older, so he has trouble mounting his horse and is out of practice when he tries to shoot. But the violence in this film is still brutal and squalid. The plot opens with an attack on the whore Delilah (Anna Thompson) by cowboy Quick Mike (David Mucci), where her face is slashed with a knife. During the ensuing revenge gunfight, the violence is vicious and not the traditional type of shoot-out. It is hard to define who is good and who is bad. Both sides are gray. The cowboy has cut up the whore, but Munny and Ned (Morgan Freeman) and the Schofield Kid (Jaimz Woolvett) shoot him down in cold blood. They have no personal reason to kill except for money.

The Schofield Kid was raised on stories of the West. He believes the dime novels and wants to be part of the myth of the gunfighter. After shooting Quick Mike, however, the Kid realizes the difficulty of killing another human. He hasn't done this before and discovers that killing is not as glamorous as it seems. He vows never to kill again and runs away. The violence ratchets up as Ned is tortured and murdered and Munny is beaten. Further violence continues when Sheriff Little Bill Daggett (Gene Hackman) kicks and beats English Bob (Richard Harris) and runs him out of town.

During the final conflict, Munny shoots the unarmed Skinny (Anthony James) in cold blood. He shoots Fatty (Jefferson Mappin) in the back. He shoots Little Bill at point-blank range as Little Bill lies wounded on the floor. Yet Munny is not punished in the sense of the traditional Westerns for all this. According to the final crawl at the end of the movie, he goes to San Francisco with his children and prospers as a businessman.

Clint Eastwood once said that his fans liked to see movies with lots of action where the good guy wins in the end.[32] Though extremely violent, *Unforgiven* (1992) goes out of its way to deglamorize violence. The gunfights and killings reflect the incompetence, fear, and suffering of real gunfighters. Even the main characters (Munny, Ned, and the Schofield Kid) become disturbed by all the killing and violence.

The few remaining Westerns that have come out of Hollywood since then have been even more violent. Among them was *Django Unchained* (2012). Black slave Django (Jamie Foxx) teams up with bounty hunter/ex-dentist Dr. King Schultz (Christoph Waltz), who offers Django his freedom if he will become his partner to hunt down wanted criminals. This movie fits into the category of what has been called "exploding heads." In the beginning Schultz shoots one of two slave traders in the head, which explodes in a spray of blood and other unmentionable matter. He also shoots a horse in the head with the same results. As Schultz and Django leave, the remainder of the captured group of slaves finish off the other trader with shotguns and he is shredded in a violent fountain of exploding body parts. Schultz's theory of survival is that dead or alive means dead by shooting without warning, under the guise of being an officer of the court with a warrant. Schultz shoots the local sheriff (who turns out to be a wanted criminal) without warning. The violence includes the branding of a slave woman on the face and one slave beating another to death with a hammer. In a show of antihero nonchalance, Waltz shoots Calvin Candie (Leonardo DiCaprio) without warning with his derringer, turns, shrugs, and says that he couldn't resist it. He, in turn, is literally blown apart by the blast from a sawed-off shotgun. This leads to a bloodbath at Candie's mansion, with exploding fountains of blood spouting and spraying from bodies as Django cleans up the baddies. In a touch of irony the movie uses one of Ennio Morricone's themes from an earlier spaghetti Western.

15

The Image Persists

[T]he Western exists primarily as a curiosity, a once popular, once fashionable, once immensely profitable form of entertainment that wore out, exhausted its possibilities, and has, except for isolated reappearances, more or less vanished—Peter Rollins and John O'Connor[1]

From 1948 until 1965, Western films were at the peak of their popularity. In 1945 only eight Westerns of longer than eighty minutes running time (a typical B Western length) were made. In 1946 there were twelve, fourteen in 1947, thirty-one in 1948, but more than eighty in 1949. Production increased every year until 1955.[2] Fifty-four feature films were released in 1958.[3] Production remained high until the end of the 1960s, when the genre declined. Western movies reached an average release of twenty-four per year from 1969 to 1972.[4] Nineteen were released in 1971, but by 1973 this figure had declined to thirteen. In 1974 there were only seven. By the late 1980s, Westerns had fallen on hard times and even fewer were made.

The Decline of the Western Movie

Heaven's Gate (1980) has arguably been called one of the greatest box-office disasters of all times.[5] It was such a financial and critical failure that it almost sank United Artists studios and scared producers away from making Westerns. Critics feel that this effectively killed the genre of the Western. United Artists was saved only by their next James Bond film, which fortunately for them made $192 million worldwide.

Heaven's Gate (1980) was based on the real Johnson County War in Wyoming that pitted farmers and small ranchers against cattle barons in 1889. The film featured many of the same characters as the real incident, but their roles in the real war were altered to suit dramatic and cinematic needs. The director's cut ran 216 minutes, with the final release print running 149 minutes. Like other movies of the time, the film contained vulgar language and plenty of violence. Examples are the brutal gunning down of settlers by the regulators (self-appointed cattle detectives), the graphic rape of Ella Watson (Isabelle Huppert) by regulators who have just killed four other women in the brothel she runs, James Averill (Kris Kristofferson) killing a lookout by cutting his throat, Nate Champion (Christopher Walken) literally shot to pieces, and a close-up of a wagon running over a man's legs. The movie was so gory, including real cockfighting and the use of horse entrails, that the Humane Society started to monitor movies for animal violence and cruelty. Reportedly four horses died during the filming of the final battle scenes.[6]

All for a good cause. This local group is reenacting a street gunfight to raise money for charity. Kids (one with his fingers in his ears) and adults line the street to enjoy the spectacle of gunfire and smoke as the good guys shoot it out with the bad guys. In this instance it is difficult to tell one from the other, as both sides are wearing black hats (author's collection).

After this, as the Western genre faded, *Pale Rider* (1985) didn't do as well as hoped at the box office and neither did *Silverado* (1985), which was promoted as being a return to the good old days of the classic Westerns. *Young Guns* (1988) didn't generate much interest, but spawned a spin-off television series, *Young Riders* (1989–1992), and a sequel movie, *Young Guns II* (1990).

By the 1990s only a few Western movies were released. The story of the shoot-out at the O.K. Corral in Tombstone, Arizona, was retold as *Tombstone* (1993) and *Wyatt Earp* (1993). Remakes of the popular 1960s television shows *Maverick* (1994) and *The Wild Wild West* (1999) didn't do well at the box office. *Geronimo: An American Legend* (1993) didn't seem to excite audiences. Women starring in Westerns in *The Ballad of Little Jo* (1993), *Bad Girls* (1994), and *The Quick and the Dead* (1995) drew mixed audiences and reviews.

A complete change in theme and hero was *Dances with Wolves* (1990), which showed the West from a romanticized Indian viewpoint, with the Whites as corrupt and the Indian way of life in harmony with nature as being superior. The film set off a renewed brief craze for Westerns, as it won seven Academy Awards, including the Academy Award for Best Picture in 1990. The Best Picture award was taken again two years later by another Western,

Unforgiven (1992). The early 2000s were not much better. *Hidalgo* (2004), about a horse race in the middle East, was not a traditional type of Western. *Open Range* (2003), *The Missing* (2003), *The Alamo* (2004), and *Home on the Range* (2004) received mixed acceptance. So did *Brokeback Mountain* (2005), which focused on the love between two 1960s cowboys as they tended sheep in Wyoming.

The Western television series also essentially disappeared between 1972 and 1975.[7] After that, old Western films appeared primarily on cable television, along with occasional new productions, such as the History Channel's popular nonfiction *Wild West Tech*. The series *Deadwood* (2004–2006) on HBO television focused on Seth Bullock, a real early sheriff of Deadwood, and Al Swearengen, the real proprietor of the real Gem Saloon in the historic mining town of Deadwood, South Dakota, in 1876. The television series was gritty and violent. Calamity Jane (Robin Weigert) was played as a bad-tempered, foul-mouthed drunkard, but Weigert's portrayal must have been popular, as she won an Emmy nomination.

Tributes to Western Movies

Several movies that have perpetuated the Western image and heroes, albeit in nontraditional fashion, deserve some mention.

Mars Attacks (1996) featured the music of Western singing star Slim Whitman. When invading Martians hear his music played by a dotty old lady in a nursing home, their heads explode and in this manner earth is able to overcome them.[8] *Cowboys & Aliens* (2011) was an uneasy mix of Western and science-fiction genres that fans of 1920s Westerns and singing cowboys did not like. Many of the elements go back to William S. Hart, but the traditional villains were replaced by aliens. To sum up the plot, Jake Lonergan (Daniel Craig), the tough leader of a gang of desperados and gold robbers rides into the desert town of Absolution in 1873 with a futuristic bracelet-like device clamped onto his arm that turns out to be a powerful weapon. He teams up with his old gang, the local land baron, Colonel Woodrow Dolarhyde (Harrison Ford), and the last of the Chiricahua Apache warriors to battle aliens who have come to take over Earth and mine all the gold. Like Hart's Western films, there is the obligatory shoot-out with the chief alien at the end, in which the good badman is redeemed as he helps the locals defeat the aliens then rides off alone.

Quigley Down Under (1990) is an interesting homage to the Old West as a "Western" set in Australia. Mathew Quigley (Tom Selleck) is an American cowboy who thinks he has been hired to hunt dingoes (wild Australian dogs), but has really been hired by a land baron to exterminate aborigines. Villain Elliott Marston (Alan Rickman) is fascinated by the Old West. He says, "I am a student of your American West. I've read a great deal about it." He is impressed that Quigley had been in Dodge City and comments that Wild Bill Hickok must have been there. At the climactic end, Marston insists on an Old West shoot-out with Colt revolvers and obviously relishes the upcoming fast-draw contest. Before the final gunfight, Marston says to Quigley, "Some men are born in the wrong century. I think I was born on the wrong continent." Quigley replies, "This ain't Dodge City. And you ain't Bill Hickok." He then proceeds to outdraw his three opponents and gun them all down.

Thelma and Louise (1991) contains many of the same elements as the traditional formula

Western. Two heroes (in this case two heroines) are hunted by lawmen for the wrong reasons after an accidental shooting that leads to a crime spree. It involves an extended chase in cars, which replace the traditional horses, across vast Western landscapes by state troopers and federal agents, who replace the traditional marshals and sheriffs. The ending is reminiscent of *Butch Cassidy and the Sundance Kid* (1969), except instead of the two male heroes running out into a hail of Bolivian bullets, the two women deliberately drive off a cliff in Utah's canyon country.

Western themes and imagery have still maintained headway in other modern entertainment. The romance-adventure story *Romancing the Stone* (1984) used well-known images from the Westerns at the beginning as a subplot. As the film starts, writer Joan Wilder (Kathleen Turner) is finishing a Western novel about a girl of the Old West and her fictional lover, Jesse. The heroine, Angelina (Kymberly Herrin), is confronted by the ultimate lascivious villain, Grogan (Ted White), who has killed her father, raped and murdered her sister, burned her ranch, shot her dog (there is the dog again), and stolen her Bible. After she dispatches him by throwing a hidden knife strapped to her shapely thigh, she leaps onto her horse and rides furiously across the prairie to the strains of theme music from *How the West Was Won* (1962). She is chased by three brothers who ride dramatically along the skyline. The studly Western hero is a tall, rangy cowboy who rides to her rescue in the nick of time and downs all three villains with only three shots. This short vignette shows an ultimate Western fantasy set in a familiar red rock filming location of the B Westerns.

Perhaps an indication of how powerful the Western gunfighter hero image remains embedded in popular culture was shown in the science fiction *Westworld* (1973). Delos is a robotic amusement park for a fantasy vacation with three choices: Medieval World, Roman World, and Westworld, which is a re-creation of the Old West of the 1880s. As one vacationer who has just returned from Westworld says, when he and his friends played "cowboys and Indians" as kids they pointed their fingers at each other in the classical gun configuration and went "bang, bang." Now, as an adult, he can live out his fantasies by shooting cowboy robots that are programmed to look, talk, act, and bleed like real gunfighters in situations where guests cannot get hurt. The main robot is a gunfighter of the Old West who looks like Chris from the motion picture *The Magnificent Seven* (1960). In a clever twist, the part was played by Yul Brynner, who was the original Chris. Of course, the programming instructions in the robots go violently wrong and the gunfighter robot shoots and kills hero John Blane (James Brolin). Stereotyped Western scenes include a saloon peopled with characters looking like they just stepped out of Central Casting, all of whom get into a typical rowdy saloon fistfight.

Much of the humor in the Western satire *Cat Ballou* (1965) is derived from the plotline that Kid Shelleen (Lee Marvin in an Oscar-winning role) is a washed-up old drunk. He literally cannot hit the side of a barn when he shoots, but eastern hack writers have made him into a hero of dime novels. Shelleen, who supposedly worked for Buffalo Bill in the old days, only comes into his own as a crack shot after drinking a pint of whiskey. The villain, Tim Strawn (also played by Marvin), is dressed all in black and wears a silver cap over his nose, the nose having been bitten off in a previous fight. Hole-in-the-Wall, where the real Butch Cassidy hid out in the Old West near Kaycee, Wyoming, is peopled by an ancient Cassidy and a gang of washed-up has-beens. Even the saloon "wench" dressed in silks and satin is gray-haired and old.

A New Type of Western

Since the mid–1960s there has not been a single consistent formula for Westerns and Western heroes, though the existing trend includes increased violence, more violent heroes, excessive blood-letting, more acrobatic method of dying, and more-explicit sex. These features, however, only reflect a universal trend in American entertainment and culture.

In *No Country for Old Men* (2007), violence follows when a group of drug dealers are slaughtered in the desert after a drug deal goes wrong. Llewelyn Moss (Josh Brolin) finds and takes $2 million of their cash and is pursued by psychopathic hit man Anton Chigurh (Javier Bardem), who stops at nothing to get it back and murders almost everyone he comes in contact with.

Just as violent is *The Last Stand* (2013), which uses modern Las Vegas (though actually filmed in Albuquerque) and a small town in Arizona (in reality also in New Mexico) for its background. Although set in modern times, this is a traditional type of Western plot with a rugged Western hero standing up for good and justice pitted against a villainous drug lord who has escaped from federal custody and is trying to escape across the border to Mexico. Small-town sheriff Ray Owens (Arnold Schwarzenegger), with only a few deputies, stands ready to protect his town when the bad guys show up, in a plot reminiscent of *High Noon* (1952) and *3:10 to Yuma* (1957).

High speed horse chases in *The Last Stand* have been changed into high speed automobile chases and six-guns have been changed into modern machine guns and automatic weapons. The machine-gunning of the bad guys in the main street shoot-out rivals the final bloodbath in *The Wild Bunch* (1969). Bullets from automatic weapons, machine pistols, and high-powered rifles tear into cars, buildings, and the bad guys, stitching everything in sight with bullet holes. "Exploding heads" with blood spraying everywhere is a favorite. One bad guy is shot in the bandolier he is wearing with a cartridge from a flare pistol. This ignites all the ammunition in the belt and he literally explodes, with limbs and other body parts raining down out of the sky. Maintaining the Western theme, the leader of the gang attacking the town uses a huge single-action revolver that is a cartridge conversion of an early Old West black-powder pistol. In a tradition harking back to the movies of the 1930s and 1940s, it is never reloaded and never seems to run out of ammunition.

In the final confrontation between good and evil, the sheriff stands tall in the middle of the steel bridge the villains have erected over the Rio Grande in order to escape to Mexico. He stands motionless, blocking the way of the escaping drug lord and looking like the traditional Western gunfighter hero moved to a modern setting. The two proceed to beat each other to a bloody pulp with their fists, then stab each other with a knife before the hero finally prevails and handcuffs the drug lord. All this bloodshed, which received an R rating, is toned down by having the principals somehow all survive the mayhem to fight another day.

The Western Image Lives On

Even though Western movies have all but disappeared, the image of the hero of the Old West continues to permeate our culture.

THE WRITTEN WORD

Western novels by Zane Grey, Max Brand, and Louis L'Amour are still being reprinted and sold. Paperback original Westerns still form a popular genre that is widely published today and whose plots, characters, and settings in the never-never land of the Old West are a direct descendant from dime novels. A tribute to America's written Western heritage appears in the movie *The Third Man* (1949), set in post–World War II Vienna. Holly Martins (Joseph Cotten) is an American writer of pulp Western novels who has penned several thrilling titles such as *Oklahoma Kid, Death at Double-X Ranch* and *The Lone Rider of Santa Fe*.

The Old West and Western gunfighters continue to hold a fascination for readers, and controversy about "how it really was" still exists today. *Doc,* for example, is a new historical novel based on the life and times of Doc Holliday that features his early relationship with Wyatt Earp. The book tries to portray Holliday as he was during his time in Dodge City. Other books, such as Allen Barra's thoughtful *Inventing Wyatt Earp: His Life and Many Legends*, continue to analyze the O.K. Corral shoot-out.

An interesting contribution to the cowboy-hero myth is *How to Be a Cowboy*.[9] This book explains how to be a modern cowboy, including a detailed explanation of clothing, hats, boots and spurs, and how to select them. Instructions cover such diverse elements as cowboy lingo, cowboy poetry, hat etiquette, and the cowboy code. This is not the West of the real cowboy, however, but an updated, romanticized version of the mythic cowboy hero, including the latest fashions that might be found in Santa Fe, New Mexico. Though the modern cowboy philosophy in the book is based on the myth, it shows how strong the image of people wanting to be a cowboy is.

ADVERTISING

Advertising has always relied heavily on Western themes. A few representative historical examples are *Kirk's White Cloud Floating Soap*, which featured a scantily clad generic Indian warrior, *Black Hawk Brand Oranges*, with a stern-faced warrior on the label from the Arlington Heights Citrus Company of Riverside, California, and *Indian Queen Perfume* from the Bean and Brother factory in Philadelphia. Advertising for the Northwest Brewery featured a topless Indian maiden riding a buffalo across the prairie. Other Indian motifs were found on Sure Shot Chewing Tobacco, Dyer's Indian Cough Drops, and Totem Tobacco. As well as firearms, Buffalo Bill Cody endorsed a number of other products, and a wide variety of products carried the Cody name, including Cody cigars, Buffalo Bill Saddle Soap, commemorative spoons, medals, and *Wild West* program materials, clothing, calendars, a board game, and songbooks.

This same type of product endorsement continued with television. When cowboy movies and shows were popular, kids were targets of merchandising. Tom Mix endorsed toys, breakfast cereal (Ralston sponsored his radio program for children, called *Tom Mix and His Ralston Purina Straight Shooters*), hats, shirts, toy guns, boots, and charm bracelets. Gene Autry's name appeared on guitars, songbooks, wristwatches, toys, kids clothing, books, lunchboxes, and dolls. He performed on radio and television shows and made personal appearances to help sustain merchandising after his movie career had peaked. Roy Rogers

Iconic images of the West have always been used in advertising, and they live on today. Sign for a local brewery on a building in Cody, Wyoming, the town founded by Buffalo Bill Cody in 1895 (author's collection).

and Dale Evans endorsed more than 450 products, including children's clothing, breakfast cereal, lunch boxes, and flashlights. In the 1940s Rogers was second only to Disney in numbers of licensed products.[10] A special section of Sears, Roebuck was devoted to Roy Rogers products. Another shrewd businessman was actor William Boyd. Boyd purchased rights to his Hopalong Cassidy movies from the 1930s and 1940s, and reedited them for television in the 1950s. The flood of merchandising that accompanied the television series, including clothing and watches, made him a wealthy man.[11]

The deadly gambler himself is remembered by the Doc Holliday Tavern in Glenwood Springs, Colorado, where the real Doc Holliday died from tuberculosis in the Hotel Glenwood in 1887. He was buried in the local cemetery (author's collection).

In the 1950s licensed merchandise and premiums were tied to radio, television, and the movies. Pictures of Western stars appeared on such diverse items as ice cream, postcards, and comic books. As cowboys vanished from the screen, products endorsed by particular stars disappeared. In the 1960s, however, generic cowboys and Western heroes were still being used to promote products such as cars, tobacco, whiskey, beer, and the ubiquitous blue jeans, all of which helped to keep the Western image alive. Names for cars, such as Maverick, Pinto, Mustang, and Bronco, evoke images of wild western animals. Designer Ralph Lauren used the cowboy image and chaps, dusters, hats, and boots as a fashion statement when the cowboy presence returned under the influence of television programs such as *Dallas* (1978–1991) and others. Think also of the macho imagery associated with the Denver Broncos and the Dallas Cowboys.

One of the most recognizable advertising icons of the 1960s and 1970s was the Marlboro Man, created in 1954 by advertising man Leo Burnett. The slogan "Come to Malboro Country," with a virile cowboy-horseman riding in a lush Western landscape, was the epitome of masculinity and made the ad campaign a huge success. The image of the Marlboro cowboy on horseback wearing denim jeans and his hat pulled down was an advertising triumph that catapulted to fame a minor brand of cigarettes from Victorian England that was originally marketed to women in the United States.

The Western image received a boost with the urban cowboy craze of the early 1980s, named after the film *Urban Cowboy* (1980). Bud (John Travolta) is an oil worker who frequents the huge cowboy nightclub Gilley's (owned by real-life singer Mickey Gilley) in Houston.[12] One movie poster aptly promoted the movie with the theme of "hard hat days and honky-tonk nights." The film resulted in the opening of a rash of cowboy-style nightclubs with mechanical bulls for patrons to ride. The film was so popular that for several years even ordinary city slickers wore Western garb and went about their daily business wearing cowboy hats with feathers, flowered shirts, and fancy neckerchiefs. Western clothing and boots are still popular and commonly worn in states such as Texas, Montana, New Mexico, Wyoming, Colorado, and others.

Singers and Their Songs

Real cowboys on the trail mostly sang unaccompanied. If they used an instrument they used a fiddle, or perhaps a banjo. A fiddle could be packed and carried on the trail or on a chuckwagon easier than a guitar. Many cowboys used a harmonica for accompaniment, which was even smaller. The guitar in the style of the singing cowboys was impractical, as a cowboy on a horse couldn't play it and ride at the same time.

The Sons of the Pioneers, formed in the 1930s by Roy Rogers, is the oldest of the close-harmony Western singing groups, but their music is still available on CD today. The second-oldest similar Western group is the Flying W Wranglers of Colorado Springs, Colorado, formed in 1953. This group is still in existence today (with different membership) and sings Western songs while eager diners sit outside at the Flying W Ranch on wooden benches and eat a re-created cowboy meal of beef, beans, and rolls, with coffee served in tin cups. The ranch typically fed a thousand guests every night in the summertime before the buildings burned down in the disastrous Colorado Waldo Canyon fire of 2012. Other similar popular Western chuckwagon ranch venues exist in Durango, Colorado; Jackson Hole and Cody, Wyoming; Ruidoso, New Mexico; and Phoenix, Arizona. Modern Western singers, such as Don Edwards and the group Riders in the Sky, follow the pathway of these groups.

Modern cowboy and country western music that had its roots in the hillbilly music from the mountains of the South and from real cowboys continues to be popular. In 1959, singer Marty Robbins, who had variously recorded country, pop, the so-called lush Nashville sound, and rockabilly, released an album of cowboy music titled *Gunfighter Ballads and Trail Songs*.[13] It contained the hit "El Paso," which was both a pop and country #1 hit on the charts.[14] The cover showed Robbins decked out as a gunfighter dressed all in black.

As with other popular culture, Western music did not stand still. At a time when Nashville was primarily producing the smooth Nashville sound, singers Tompall Glaser, Waylon Jennings, Kris Kristofferson, and Willie Nelson produced a different type of music. In 1973 a disc jockey in North Carolina called their sound "outlaw music," a name that had a good marketing ring to it. The concept was picked up by RCA executive Jerry Bradley. He gathered some recordings, promoted the image of scruffy jeans, cowboy hats, and boots, and released an album called *Wanted! The Outlaws*. The cover was designed to look like an Old West wanted poster. The album went platinum and sold over a million records. Jennings, Kristofferson, Nelson, and Johnny Cash teamed up for *The Highwaymen* in 1985, which became a similar hit. The outlaw style became popular, and Waylon and Willie were all over the radio in the late 1970s promoting an image similar to the movie cowboys that was wild, freedom-loving, and self-reliant. The independent cowboy spirit they tried to project is summed up by the first two lines of "Mammas, Don't Let Your Babies Grow Up to Be Cowboys." The song by Willie and Waylon became a #1 hit.

In a further crossover marketing move, just like the singing cowboys of forty years before, country singers crossed entertainment forms and tried their hands at Western movies. Kenny Rogers' 1978 song "The Gambler" told a Western story and became a #1 country and #16 pop hit. The song provided the basis for five made-for-television Western movies between 1980 and 1994. In *Barbarosa* (1982), Willie Nelson played an old Texas Ranger who had turned into a wily bandit and lived by his wits.

Western and cowboy music still remains in fashion with newer singers such as George Strait, Dwight Yoakam, Alan Jackson, Toby Keith, Marty Stuart, John Anderson, Clint Black, and Garth Brooks, with big hats, jeans, and western wear. The early 1990s brought a new popularity in cowboy line dancing and "boot scooting." Significant is that in 1973 there were 700 country music stations in the United States. By 1994 there were 1,600.[15]

Dwight Yoakum, who burst onto the country music scene in 1986, has also appeared in movies. Yoakum wrote, directed, and produced *South of Heaven, West of Hell* (2000). Like other modern Westerns, the film included nudity and raw language (including the now-ubiquitous f-word) and a violent shoot-out at the end. Visual elements were folks dynamiting each other, shotgun blasts, machine-gun, and a man stabbed in the genitals with the broken glass chimney of a kerosene lamp.

Tourism

Some towns have found a new lease on life by using their Western image and heritage to attract tourists who want to experience the flavor of the Old West. Tombstone, Arizona, maintains historic Allen Street as a dirt road and offers daily reenactments of the gunfight at the O.K. Corral. Dodge City, Kansas, built a re-creation of Boot Hill graveyard and historic Front Street, where cowboys and cattlemen used to relax after the cattle drives from Texas to sell their herds. Deadwood, South Dakota, focuses on the killing of Wild Bill Hickok by drifter Jack McCall. Cody, Wyoming, founded by Buffalo Bill himself, offers nightly mock gunfights as a charity tourist promotion by a group of reenactors called the Cody Gunfighters, in front of Bill's Irma Hotel. The nearby Buffalo Bill Historical Center hosts thousands of visitors each year seeking to learn more about the Old West. Similarly, the Autry National Center in Los Angles and the National Cowboy and Western Heritage Museum in Oklahoma City continue to draw crowds.

Other local events with an Old West flavor are popular. The Range Riders in Colorado Springs, Colorado, dress up in Western gear and ride around nearby Pikes Peak to promote the town's annual rodeo, camping out like the old cowboys. In another event, cowboys drive cattle through one of main streets of this town of 400,000 people.

Cowboy poetry presented by the likes of Baxter Black and Bruce "Waddie" Mitchell is presented nationally at events such as the annual National Cowboy Poetry Gathering in Elko, Nevada.

Rodeo

The enduring image of the Old West and the Western hero as a cowboy on a bucking bronco has persisted in the sport of rodeo, where cowboys compete for prize money riding wild horses and steers, roping, and bulldogging cattle. The great cattle drives of the 1870s from Texas to Kansas are part of the romance of the era of the Old West and rodeo maintains this heroic image. Rodeo and Western frontier celebrations called Covered Wagon Days, Frontier Days, Pioneer Days, or Helldorado Days are held in towns such as Prescott, Fort Worth, Denver, and Cheyenne. Rodeo is not just a Western sport, but is held in almost every state and Canada and is covered as a sport by major television networks. In Wyoming and North Dakota rodeo is considered to be the official state sport.[16] Wyoming's license plate continues to have a bucking bronco on it. The National Finals Rodeo, where the year's champions are recognized, are held every year in Las Vegas in December.

Rodeo is tough and dangerous. The excitement and danger of the events cannot be choreographed. The original cowboys tamed wild horses, and roped and branded cattle for a living. Modern rodeo cowboys ride bucking horses wrestle steers, and ride Brahma bulls for a living. The word *rodeo* comes originally from the Spanish word *rodear*, which means "to surround" or "encircle." The word was originally used in the Southwest to describe rounding up cattle for branding. The term later became applied to exhibitions of horse riding, roping technique, bronc busting, and skills with cattle that were developed from working with cows. Rodeo eventually became a series of formalized competitive events sanctioned by the Professional Rodeo Cowboys Association (PRCA). Five standardized events are bulldogging, calf roping, bronc riding, bareback horse riding, and bull riding. A description of various rodeo events can be found at the end of this section.

The origins of rodeo are cloudy. As early as 1844 Major Jack Hayes of the Texas Rangers organized a contest of riding and shooting skills between Comanche warriors and Texas Rangers in San Antonio.[17] Early similar competitive events were held in Santa Fe, New Mexico, in 1847 while it was occupied by the American army during the Mexican War.[18] The first real rodeo appears to have been staged at Deer Trail, Colorado, on July 4, 1869, as a contest to see who was the best between rival cowboys from the Mill Iron, Camp Stool, and Hashknife ranches. The cowboys competed in various skills practiced on the trail, particularly bronc busting. There were no prizes, no trophies, and no rules. The top cowboy is thought to have been Emilnie Gardenshire from the Mill Iron ranch, as the other cowboys gave him the title of "Champion Bronco Buster of the Plains" for successfully riding a wild horse named Montana Blizzard.[19]

The Miller brothers of 101 Ranch fame claimed that they staged the first commercial rodeo when Colonel Miller staged a "roundup" in Winfield, Kansas, in 1882.[20] Other rodeos soon joined in. Cheyenne Frontier Days in Wyoming was first held in 1897, the Pendleton Round-Up in Oregon in 1910, and the first Prescott Frontier Days in Arizona on July 4, 1888.[21] Cheyenne Frontier Days, now called "The Daddy of 'em All," claims to be the oldest continuous rodeo, but the Prescott event started earlier. Cheyenne has the most contestants and biggest arena. Incidentally, movie star Tom Mix won the steer roping event at Prescott in 1915.

In bulldogging (steer wrestling), the contender jumps from a horse onto a running steer and wrestles it to the ground by twisting its horns. Bulldogging was developed by 101 Ranch cowboy Bill Pickett, who noted that bulldogs could subdue steers by biting them on the nose and hanging on. He did the same, jumping onto the bull from a running horse and biting its nose or lip to wrestle it into submission.[22] Pickett was a mixed-blood black man with some Cherokee and some white heritage. Because blacks were barred from most rodeo events he was billed as the "Dusky Demon."[23] During the 1890s, Pickett performed at fairs, rodeos, and shows across the West before he came to the attention of the Millers. He appeared with an all-black cast in the movie *The Bull-Dogger* (1923), made by Norman Film Manufacturing Company. The film played only in black theaters and did not do well. Pickett died at the 101 Ranch in 1932 after being kicked in the head by a horse he was trying to break.

By the 1950s rodeo had become a major professional competitive sport that promoted the cowboy image. Contestants were still called cowboys, but they did not bring beef to market. They rode a bull for eight seconds, roped a calf, or jumped from the back of a horse onto a steer and wrestled it to the ground. They traveled the rodeo circuit of thousands of miles, paid for their own entrance fees and equipment, suffered physical abuse of their bodies, and received no compensation if they were injured and could not compete.

The lines became blurred between rodeo and the Wild West shows as rodeos gradually included elements of the earlier shows, including Indians, drill exhibitions by soldiers, and street dances. Rodeo was further commercialized by bringing in singing movie star heroes such as Rex Allen, Roy Rogers, and Gene Autry, and roping tricks by performers such as Montie Montana (born Owen Mickel). In 1971, Montie Montana, Jr. tried to re-create Buffalo Bill's *Wild West* with 125 cowboys, cowgirls and Indians, and included the attack on the Deadwood stage, bronc riding, and trick roping. Unfortunately the show did not do well and eventually closed.

In the 1990s the *Wild West* was re-created with more success at Euro-Disney with a dinner show called "Buffalo Bill's Wild West," which featured Indians, cowboys, and horses.[24] A barbecue dinner and show for an audience of over a thousand at each performance re-created the tradition of the original *Wild West*. The modern show used up-to-date Disney technology, such as blank cartridges and clever illusions to highlight "Annie Oakley's" superior marksmanship.[25]

Popular Rodeo events are listed below:

Bareback Bronc Riding
The contestant has to ride a bucking horse for eight seconds while holding with one

hand only onto a single strap (the "rigging") cinched around the horse. The other hand has to stay in the air. The contestant is disqualified if he touches the horse, himself, or the equipment with his free hand.

Bull Riding

The contestant has to ride a bucking Brahma bull (which may weigh 2,000 pounds or more) for eight seconds, while holding onto only a strap cinched around the bull's midsection. Riding style is also important in the judge's decision. As in bareback bronc riding, the contestant is disqualified if he touches the animal, himself, or the equipment with his free hand.

Ladies Barrel Racing

In this fast-and-furious event for cowgirls, the contestant has to ride in a cloverleaf pattern at high speed around three barrels spaced widely apart without knocking any of them over. This event is timed to a hundredth of a second and the fastest time wins.

Saddle Bronc Riding

This is rodeo's classic event. Its origin was in breaking wild horses for use on a ranch. The contestant has to ride a bucking horse for eight seconds, holding on with only one hand, while continuously raking the horse's shoulders with his spurs. The other hand has to stay in the air.

Steer Roping

The contestant has to chase and rope a steer from a running horse, dismount, wrestle the steer to the ground, and tie three of its legs together. This skill was part of the original cowboy's work on the range and at the round-up.

Steer Wrestling (sometimes called Bulldogging)

The contestant on a galloping horse chases a running steer, slides off the horse onto the steer, and wrestles it to the ground using the steer's horns for leverage. The clock stops when the steer is on its side with all four legs pointing the same direction

Team Roping

Two cowboys participate in this event. One cowboy (the "header") ropes a steer around the head and neck, the other (the "heeler") ropes the back feet. Speed is essential to win the event.

Tie-Down Roping (previously named Calf Roping)

This event is similar to steer roping, but is performed with a calf. The event originated on ranches in the West when cowboys had to rope sick or injured cattle and calves to give them medical treatment. The calf is given a head start, then the cowboy rides out at full speed to rope, throw, and tie the calf's legs with a pigging string (a soft rope about six feet long). Experts can perform this feat in a little under seven seconds.

Breakaway Roping

In the ladies' version of calf roping, a woman rider ropes the calf over the head as fast as she can, but she does not throw and tie it. The event is timed instead for speed. Winning times can be in the two- to three-second range, with tenths of a second making the difference between winner and loser.

Kid's Events

Rodeo events are not just for adults, kids can join in too. The very little ones can participate in dummy roping and timed stick-horse races similar to barrel racing. Boys and girls from five to thirteen can participate in more rough-and-tumble events, such as "mutton busting" (riding sheep holding on with one hand and acting like steer riders), trying to ride young calves, or catching piglets. The ten- to thirteen-year-olds can participate in some steer riding.

Dude Ranches

Tourists are still drawn to the West by exciting expectations of grand landscapes, vast open spaces and skies, untamed wildlife, and adventure. A Western institution that continues to promote this Old West image is the dude ranch. A dude ranch lets city folks live out their own fantasies as a cowboy and temporarily become part of the hero image. "Dude" was originally a name for ranch vacationers with no disrespect attached, but it later became derisively associated with clueless easterners who knew nothing of Western ways, as portrayed by Bob Hope in *Son of Paleface* (1952). Junior's fiancé (Jane Russell) tells him to "go out West." When Junior (Bob Hope) wants to show that he has become a Westerner, he wears a tall outsized white hat like Tom Mix and white wooly chaps, the traditional movie outfit representing an eastern dude.[26] A female dude was known as a "dudess" or "dudine."

Guests at early dude ranches paid high prices to stay in rustic cabins, eat homemade food, and ride in cowboy clothing alongside real wranglers. These ranches, now euphemistically called guest ranches, are still popular and offer any variation from luxury accommodations with spas to working with stock and helping with cattle drives. This type of cowboy vacation life was parodied in the movie *City Slickers* (1991).

The first dude ranch appears to have been started by the Eaton brothers from Pittsburgh, who established several ranches near the town of Medora, in the Dakota Territory.[27] So many of their friends started to visit that expenses became prohibitive. As a result, in 1882, they started charging for room and board. Other Western ranches soon followed this move and took in vacationers who wanted to ride, fish, and hunt, or to escape urban life for a while. An expanded national railroad network allowed easy travel to the West and by the 1920s dude ranches were thriving.

Wealthy easterners sent relatives who were addicted to drink to the Eaton brothers' dude ranch as an alternative to a sanitarium. The hope was that a good dose of the outdoors and healthy living would dry them out. The ranch dutifully kept liquor away from their guests; however, some of the more addicted sneaked frequent forays into the nearby town of Medora, which at the time had over a dozen saloons. The results were predictable. Local cowboys said that "you couldn't put your hand in the crotch of any tree within a hundred yards of the Eatons' ranchhouse without coming upon a bottle concealed by a dude being cured of 'the drink.'"[28]

Three states eventually emerged as leaders in the dude ranch business. Wyoming had the attraction of Grand Teton National Park, Montana had Yellowstone National Park, and Colorado had Rocky Mountain National Park. These states were followed by New Mexico and Arizona, which were particularly attractive in the winter. Some of the trips into the mountains and nearby scenic areas were extensive. One outfitter who led a trip into Yellow-

A typical dude ranch cowboy of the 1940s. Cigarette smoking was in style, the holstered revolver was probably for show, and the batwing chaps and big hat are right out of the movies. Note an adult resemblance to the young would-be cowboy pictured in chapter 1 (author's collection).

stone with 173 guests from the San Francisco Sierra Club needed 200 mules and horses and had to take along 40 support workers.

Dude ranch cowboys had to be able to handle both regular ranching chores and a variety of visiting dudes. The cowboys were expected to know everything about the outdoors and had to be a combination of cook, accomplished horseman, singer, storyteller, and expert on cowboy folklore. They continued to wear traditional wrangler clothing and maintain cowboy customs, as that was what guests wanted to see. They also had to be personable, as guests expected them to strum a guitar and sing around the campfire at night. Life imitated art and real cowboys adopted the image of movie cowboys as that was what guests expected. Some of them even started to talk like the cowboys in the movies.

As early as 1905 the Miller brothers boarded guests at their 101 Ranch in Oklahoma. They attracted visitors from big cities who wanted to learn how to ride, rope, and live like a cowboy. Relaxation consisted of fishing and hunting. The Millers' first dudes lived in tents, but this type of vacation proved to be so popular that the Millers build a series of guest cabins with a communal dining room and a clubhouse. The complex, called Riverside Camp, drew guests from around the world.[29] The camp became another profit center for the Millers, but at the same time it fitted with their desire to keep the image of the Old West alive. To enhance the Western experience, guests purchased hats, boots, chaps, and shirts (in the Millers' store, of course). It was not necessarily an easy vacation. Guests could participate in as much cowboy work as they wanted, depending on their interests. Dudes helped with cattle roundups, broke horses, fixed fences, and dehorned cattle under the guidance of the Miller cowboys. They all ate at the chuckwagon. One of the cowboys who told tall tales and wild stories around the campfire was future movie star Tom Mix.

Cowboy Action Shooting

The ultimate reenactment of the heroes from cowboy movies is Cowboy Action Shooting, a sport in which competitors dress in clothing that would have been used on the Western frontier as they participate in shooting competitions with period revolvers, rifles, and shotguns using live ammunition. The participants dress as their favorite hero from the Old West or a favorite Hollywood character from Western movies as they adopt the name and mannerisms of real or fictional gunmen from the Old West.

Competition on the shooting range is a three-gun event with each contestant using single-action revolvers, lever-action rifles, and period shotguns. Some participants use original versions of these firearms, but with the rarity and value of antique weapons most competitors use modern replicas. The main event involves shooting at steel targets with live ammunition on a Western town street furnished with movie-like props. Varied scenarios are used to provide added authenticity. The fastest time to complete the event determines the winner. Favorite weapons for these modern gunfighters are the .45 caliber Colt single-action Peacemaker with the 4¾-inch barrel, the favorite (of course) of the movie cowboy and gunfighters of the late 1870s and 1880s. In a further quest for authenticity, some participants use cap-and-ball revolvers, such as a replica of the Colt Model 1860 army revolver, seen in some movies and a favorite of real gunfighters in the Old West.

Postscript

[T]he old folklore has maintained its appeal to audiences everywhere; and it seems there will always be a popular fascination with Westerns... —Brian Garfield[1]

The Old West of reality started to disappear around 1900. Historians argue whether the end of this expansion and colonization should be marked at 1890 with the end of the Indian Wars between the U.S. Army and the Sioux Indians at the battle of Wounded Knee, South Dakota, or when the superintendent of the U.S. Census Bureau stated that there was no clear line of advancing settlement in the West and historians concluded that the American frontier was gone by 1890, or when Arizona, the last of the territories in the West, gained statehood in 1912. Whichever one is the appropriate benchmark, the golden age of the mythic West undoubtedly drew to a close around the turn of the twentieth century.

In the early 1900s, as the West became more "civilized," the inhabitants of the frontier began to tire of the triple threat of excessive drinking, gambling, and loose women. These vices were gradually outlawed and the West settled into a more staid existence. As these bad influences were run out of town, gunfights also gradually declined and then disappeared. The West was settled, civilizing influences were on the ascent, and law and order had arrived.

As time passed and the Old West vanished into history, its reality was replaced by the memory of a myth that was created by the media. As the real cowboy started to fade from the Old West in the 1880s, the mythic cowboy was invented by Western entertainers, writers, and artists to provide a symbol of American freedom, independence, and courage. Dime novels, stage melodramas, pulp magazines, comic books, Wild West shows, radio, movies, and television contributed to an idealized representation of this small segment of American history. Popular fiction and Hollywood films created a vision of the West of gunfighters, saloon brawls, cattle stampedes, fights between settlers and marauding Indians, and the lone cowboy riding off into the sunset. Movies perpetuated the mythic image of the nineteenth-century frontier heritage by showing rugged cowboy heroes living in the wide-open spaces as they helped to tame the West. In the end, America's Western expansion would be remembered in terms of Buffalo Bill's *Wild West*. His cowboy was seen as America's folk hero, characterized by courage, independence, cheerfulness, and acceptance of hardship and danger. Images captured on film extended and perfected the myth of cowboy heroes dashing across the prairie to save the heroine from a fate worse than death. The image was sustained by nostalgia for the lost wilderness and the vanished frontier.

A question that naturally arises is why cowboys became mythic heroes. After all, the real cowboy's everyday life was dull, consisting mostly of tending cows and fixing fences. Yet a popular element in art today is that of a high-flying cowboy rider trying to tame a bucking

One of the enduring iconic images of the Western hero is that of a cowboy riding high on top of a bucking bronco, a spectacle that was a thrilling vision of manhood in action for nineteenth-century readers of eastern newspapers and dime novels. This cowboy is competing in a rodeo in the mid–1950s in New Mexico. Real cowboys in the Old West tamed wild horses like this to use for herding cattle and other ranch work. This concept still carries on in paintings and sculpture as an iconic image of the days of the Wild West (photograph by Tyler Dingee; author's collection).

bronco. One reason may be that the mythic cowboy of the media represented freedom from society, which was probably a wish of many urban working-class people of the late nineteenth century that continued into the mid-twentieth century. After *The Virginian* was published in 1902, even real cowboys started to incorporate what was in the book into their lives to fortify their own image of rough-and-tough individuals.[2] As one old-time cowboy remarked, "Well, maybe we didn't talk that way before Mr. Wister wrote his book, but we sure all talked that way after the book was published."[3] Rancher Carey McWilliams remembered that cowboys on his father's Colorado ranch read Beadles pulp novels and tried to imitate the cowboy heroes described in them.[4] Many working cowhands even adopted the clothing styles and look of the screen stars.

The mythic American West became a physical and spiritual place that represented the last frontier of freedom and individualism. This is shown by the continuing popularity of dude ranches that offer an escape into this legendary world, though dude ranches now include spas, massages, rafting, mountain biking, hot tubs, and other modern amenities along with traditional ranch activities.

Buffalo Bill created a vision of the West and the Westerner who led a simple and free life and solved problems easily and readily with his guns. The tendency has been to think of this mythic Western hero as one constant character. However, as we have seen, the representation of the Western hero has changed over the years. The image of the hero has changed so much that it is appropriate to reflect on some of the main trends. The novels of James Fenimore Cooper invented the buckskin-clad woodsman who was at home in the forests of the East. He changed into the dashing improbable hero of the dime novels. This hero diverged into the later hero of the pulps and the hero of serious novels. This literary breed has survived today in the paperbacks of Louis L'Amour and Larry McMurtry. Though McMurtry in *Lonesome Dove* and his other novels has tried to presented a less romantic West, the reading public is still fascinated by cowboy gunplay and violence.

The Western movie hero emerged as a definable character with the good badman of Broncho Billy and William S. Hart in the 1910s. This hero was strong, silent, and bashful. In the 1920s the image changed into the stunt-filled flashy cowboy showmen of Tom Mix and the other stars of the silent screen. By adding a few songs and toning down the seriousness of plots, the hero turned into the singing cowboy of Gene Autry and Roy Rogers of the 1930s. Serials and action oaters continued in the 1940s but turned the hero into the moody, psychologically driven angst-wracked gunman of the 1950s. When audiences tired of these plots, the hero reemerged in the 1960s and 1970s as an unshaven, violent, amoral gunfighter. The production of Westerns declined through the 1980s and as a genre they were essentially gone by the end of the 1990s.

A few other Westerns that are essentially modern tales set in the West have since appeared, such as *No Country for Old Men* (2007) and *The Last Stand* (2013), but these could probably be better characterized as violent action films that just happen to be set in the West. Graphic violence and eroticism continue as themes in many similar action films today. *Hansel & Gretel: Witch Hunters* (2013), for example, is a non–Western adult retelling of the Grimm's children's fairy tale, but it contains many of the same elements that appear in Westerns. The movie includes graphic scenes of violence, including a man literally blowing his head off with a shotgun, witches exploding in fountains of blood, a giant stepping on the sheriff's head and squashing it like a pumpkin, and blood splattering over the participants during many hand-to-hand fights. These are the same elements that have appeared respectively in the Western films *Lawman* (1971), *The Wild Bunch* (1969), *Dead Man* (1995), and *The Last Stand* (2013). Erotic titillation is included when the good witch takes off all her clothes and steps down into a pool in the forest to swim. This is shown on the screen in a full-length, full-rear lingering view as she walks away from the camera (think Isabelle Huppert in *Heaven's Gate* (1980)). Further titillation is included as implied sex in the pool between her and Hansel. Gretel even manages a few gratuitous naughty words now and then when things are not going well. All this received an R rating. These similarities to Westerns should not be construed as bad, however. *Hansel & Gretel* is an entertaining motion picture for those who like action films, but the point is that this new framework for these types of movies, as opposed to being part of the plot of a Western, is a reflection of the changing demands and expectations of audiences of today.

In their day, Gene Autry, Roy Rogers, and Dale Evans, and later John Wayne and Clint Eastwood, created such strong screen hero personas that just a mention of their names even today immediately recalls a specific embodiment of their Western image. Gene Autry and

Roy Rogers evoked images of flashy cowboys on horseback toting a gun and a guitar as they ride through the West singing a romantic ballad. Dale Evans portrayed an independent woman and showed that the Western heroine of the 1940s was more than a passive, dependent female who swooned at the first sight of danger. John Wayne, in his big hat, boots, and characteristic bib-front Western shirt with two rows of buttons, personifies Western heroism. Clint Eastwood conjures up images of a scruffy, unshaven antihero wearing a poncho and chewing on a cheroot.

The question remains: who or what is a cowboy today? Real cowboys arrived with the Spanish settlers in the Southwest. These were young men on horseback who tended cattle and later drove them to market at the railheads in towns such as Abilene and Dodge City in Kansas in the 1870s. Some purists claim that the only real cowboys today are those who still work with cattle, using their riding and roping skills as did cowboys over a hundred years ago.

Today there are relatively few real working cowboys who herd cattle for a living. Nobody really knows how many, but probably only a few thousand are left. And many of them no longer ride to tend their cattle. Horses have been replaced by pickups, ATVs (all-terrain vehicles), motorcycles, and even helicopters for the roundup. Real cowboys have been faced with challenges throughout the 1900s and early 2000s as the West changed. Economic pressures, mechanization, and creeping urbanization in the West have changed cattle ranching and the cowboy's way of life. They are having to cope with a new West.

More than that, the cowboy image carries on as a look and lifestyle. Real cowboys still work in Wyoming, Colorado, Montana, and other states in the West. Would-be cowboys walk the streets of Tombstone on the weekends in Old West fashions. Men and women in cowboy boots and Western hats are found in downtown Santa Fe wearing fashion statements that would have bankrupted the old-time cowboy. There is also the urban cowboy, the drugstore cowboy, the rodeo cowboy, the movie cowboy, and the singing cowboy.

We are left with a cowboy hero who is a legend, a mirage that is continually out of reach, never quite there, and never quite definable. He is mythic hero who still lives on to play a large part in our collective image of the Old West. To paraphrase Brian Garfield, quoted at the beginning of this postscript, it seems there will always be a popular fascination with the West.

Chapter Notes

Preface

1. Mitchell, *Westerns*, 259.
2. Bernstein, *Wild Ride*, 10.
3. Tuska, *The American West in Film*, 7.
4. Griffith and Mayer, *The Movies*, 397.
5. Wright, *Six Guns and Society*, 13.
6. Edward J. Whetmore, *Mediamerica: Form, Content and Consequences* (Belmont, CA: Wadsworth, 1995), 10–12, 170–171.
7. When Christopher Columbus arrived in the Americas he called the people he encountered "Indians" because he thought he had arrived in the East Indies. These people were later called "American Indians" to differentiate between India and the West Indies. In the twentieth century the name "Native American" became more popular, as the name "Indian" was perceived by some to connote a negative stereotype. As author David King put it, "most of the people in question still call themselves *Indians*—or by their specific tribe name. Today [2008] both *American Indian* and *Native American* are considered acceptable" (*First People*, 7).

Chapter 1

1. Slotkin, *The Fatal Environment*, 1.
2. The term "Manifest Destiny" was coined in 1845 by John L. O'Sullivan, editor of the *New York Morning News*.
3. Out of an estimated 250,000 to 400,000 people who traveled the Oregon and California trails, about 20,000 emigrants died during the trip, mostly from disease and accidents, whereas only an estimated 400 died from Indian attacks (Simmon, *The Invention of the Western Film*, 324).
4. Goetzmann and Goetzmann, *The West of the Imagination*, 290.
5. Sullivan, *Jeans*, 48.
6. Ibid., 49.
7. Goetzmann and Goetzmann, *The West of the Imagination*, 239.
8. Cowie, *John Ford and the American West*, 208.
9. Tuska, *The American West in Film*, 147.
10. Ibid., 193.
11. Simmon, *The Invention of the Western Film*, 108.
12. Josephy, Alvin, Jr., "They Died with Their Boots On," in Carnes, *Past Imperfect*, 148.
13. Helena Huntington Smith, "Sam Bass and the Myth Machine," *The American West* 7, no. 1 (January 1970), 32.
14. For more details and the background on this gruesome fight, see Agnew, *Smoking Gun*, 50–51, 60–61.
15. Ironically *Gunga Din* (1939), though set in India, was filmed in the Alabama Hills near Lone Pine, California, which was the location for scores of B-Westerns.

Chapter 2

1. Folsom, *The Western*, 1. Turner was a young Wisconsin historian who delivered a paper in 1893 at the World's Columbian Exposition in Chicago titled "The Significance of the Frontier in American History," in which he concluded that the American frontier was closed by 1890. He was not totally correct, as Western settlements continued to expand after 1890, but his thesis became part of the myth of the frontier.
2. It is interesting to note that there are no other regional designations for novels and movies. There are no "Easterns" or "Southerns" to correspond to the "Western."
3. Slotkin, *Gunfighter Nation*, 199.
4. King, *First People*, 121.
5. The 1675–1676 war in which Wampanoags and Narragansetts were slaughtered and enslaved was nicknamed King Philip's War. In June 1675, a loss of land and encroaching settlers led Indian leader Metacom to attack colonial villages in the Connecticut River Valley. Colonists gave him the derisive nickname of King Philip to mock his leadership of the tribe. Metacom attacked fifty-two villages and slaughtered many of the colonists. The colonists retaliated by killing several hundred Indians. On August 12, 1676, the colonial militia attacked and Metacom was shot. His head and hands were cut off and displayed for public viewing.
6. Hine and Faragher, *The American West*, 66.
7. Guinn, *The Last Gunfight*, 11.
8. Cooper, *The Last of the Mohicans*, iii.
9. Ibid., 110.
10. Ibid., 10–11.
11. Ibid., 105.
12. Ibid., 112.
13. Ibid., 182–183.
14. Ibid., 362.
15. This similar concept is seen in the *Death Wish*

and *Dirty Harry* series of modern movies, as well as in countless Westerns.
16. Slotkin, *The Fatal Environment*, 66.
17. Ibid., 67.
18. Guinn, *The Last Gunfight*, 11.
19. Taos means "people of the red willows" in the Tewa Indian language.
20. Simmons, *Kit Carson and His Three Wives*, xi.
21. Sides, *Blood and Thunder*, 251.
22. Ibid., 284.
23. Ibid., 392.
24. Ibid., 285.
25. Ibid., 251.
26. Ibid., 257–259.
27. A brevet rank was a temporary commission to a higher rank, without the formal authority consistent with the rank. Brevet ranks were commonly awarded during the Civil War for outstanding bravery or other distinguished service. Brevet officers were allowed to use their highest brevet rank, hence George Armstrong Custer was addressed as General Custer, even though he was only a lieutenant-colonel in the regular army.
28. Goetzmann and Goetzmann, *The West of the Imagination*, 222.
29. This image continued to remain popular. In the spring of 1942 the War Department printed 2,000 copies of the Budweiser lithograph and distributed it to army posts around the country.
30. Goetzmann and Goetzmann, *The West of the Imagination*, 225–226.
31. Slotkin, *The Fatal Environment*, 14.

Chapter 3

1. Tuska, *The American West in Film*, 193.
2. Wilson and Wilson, *Mass Media/Mass Culture*, 25.
3. Ibid., 106.
4. Ibid., 159.
5. Don Russell, "The Cowboy: From Black Hat to White," in Harris and Rainey, *The Cowboy*, 11.
6. Wilson and Wilson, *Mass Media/Mass Culture*, 134. The term was originally derived from a comic strip called "The Yellow Kid."
7. O'Neil, *The End and the Myth*, 32.
8. Cox, *The Dime Novel Companion*, xiii.
9. Wilson and Wilson, *Mass Media/Mass Culture*, 106.
10. Pearson, *Dime Novels*, 47.
11. The Victorian double standard placed a very high value on prenuptial virginity for women. A woman who strayed before marriage was considered to be a fallen woman who would never find a suitable husband. Men, however, were expected to gain some experience before marriage under the guise of "boys will be boys."
12. Murdoch, *The American West*, 35.
13. Ibid.
14. Etulain, *Telling Western Stories*, 17.
15. British currency of the time consisted of the pound, which was composed of twenty shillings, and each shilling was divided into twelve pennies.
16. Wister, *The Virginian*, 29.
17. Pearson, *Dime Novels*, 37.
18. Ibid 108–109.
19. Ibid., 68.
20. Buntline, *The Hero of a Hundred Fights*, xv.
21. Pearson, *Dime Novels*, 7.
22. This book started the formula for the main title with a secondary title. The double title was separated with a semicolon, an "or," and a comma. This became the fixed rule in book publishing and play titles for the next forty years or so.
23. Actor Richard Clarke was asked to portray Deadwood Dick in 1927 at Deadwood's Days of '76 parade. Clarke continued to play Deadwood Dick until his death in 1930.
24. "Pard" was short for "pardner," or "partner."
25. O'Neil, *The End and the Myth*, 34.
26. Slotkin, *Gunfighter Nation*, 144.
27. Murdoch, *The American West*, 52.
28. Pearson, *Dime Novels*, 107.
29. Wilson and Martin, *Buffalo Bill's Wild West*, 75.
30. Edwards, John N. *Noted Guerillas; or, The Warfare of the Border* (St. Louis: Bryan Brand, 1877).
31. The more things change, the more they stay the same and the media still slants coverage of events to suit their own purposes. In July 2013, *Rolling Stone* magazine featured the alleged Boston bomber, Dzhokhar Tsarnaev, on the front cover of their August issue in a glamorized portrait that many critics felt idealized and glorified the young man, in contrast to the more realistic police photographs that showed him covered in blood during his capture after he fled from authorities.
32. Slotkin, *Gunfighter Nation*, 133.
33. Tuska, *The American West in Film*, 136.
34. Slotkin, *Gunfighter Nation*, 137.
35. Frank Triplett, *The Life, Times and Treacherous Death of Jesse James* (St. Louis: J.H. Chambers, 1882).
36. Agnew, *The Old West in Fact and Film*, 111.
37. Sarf, *God Bless You, Buffalo Bill*, 100.
38. Slotkin, *Gunfighter Nation*, 147.
39. Ibid., 149.
40. Tuska, *The American West in Film*, 139.
41. William Keleher, *The Fabulous Frontier* (Santa Fe: Rydal, 1945), 125.
42. John Baumann, "On a Western Ranche," *Fortnightly Review* 47 (1887), 516.
43. Sarf, *God Bless You, Buffalo Bill*, 30.

Chapter 4

1. Parks, *The Western Hero in Film and Television*, 1.
2. O'Neil, *The End and the Myth*, 87.
3. Buntline, *The Hero of a Hundred Fights*, xx.
4. O'Neil, *The End and the Myth*, 54.
5. Buntline, *The Hero of a Hundred Fights*, xi.
6. Parks, *The Western Hero in Film and Television*, 65.
7. Wallis, *The Real Wild West*, 45–46; Agnew, *Entertainment in the Old West*, 125.
8. The accepted account of Buffalo Bill's service

with the Pony Express comes from his autobiography, published in 1879. Historian Louis Warren has questioned whether or not Cody actually rode for the Pony Express and concluded that this story may have been part of Cody's reinvention of his show business persona after he had become famous as a showman (Warren, *Buffalo Bill's America*, 18–21).

9. The animals commonly called "buffalo" are more correctly named American bison (*Bison bison*).

10. One of the lesser known was Charles (or maybe Jonathan or James or even Frank) White, nicknamed "Buffalo Chips Charlie." White attached himself to Buffalo Bill Cody when they were scouts at Fort McPherson. "Buffalo chips" was the polite name for the dried buffalo droppings that were found all over the Plains. Supposedly the nickname came about when White was introduced to General Phil Sheridan as "Buffalo Bill." As a part of this apocryphal tale, Sheridan supposedly looked at White and said, "Buffalo dung [or something more direct], more likely," and the name stuck.

11. Rosa, *They Called Him Wild Bill*, 243.

12. Mrs. Alderdice, unfortunately, was found dead from a blow with a tomahawk.
Mrs. Alderdice's husband, Thomas, had served as a scout at the earlier Battle of Beecher's Island in 1868. The child was killed shortly after capture.

13. Russell, *The Lives and Legends of Buffalo Bill*, 138.

14. O'Neil, *The End and the Myth*, 53.

15. Buntline, *The Hero of a Hundred Fights*, 424.

16. The story of the M'Kandlas gang with Hickok, called "Hitchcock," appeared first in a story by George Ward Nichols in the February 1867 issue of *Harper's New Monthly Magazine*. For more details see Rosa, *They Called Him Wild Bill*, 34–52. So where did Buntline really get his material?

17. Buntline, *The Hero of a Hundred Fights*, 5.

18. Ibid., 55.

19. Ibid., 160.

20. Russell, *The Lives and Legends of Buffalo Bill*, 193.

21. Buntline, *The Hero of a Hundred Fights*, xii.

22. Ibid., 163.

23. O'Neil, *The End and the Myth*, 55.

24. Kasson, *Buffalo Bill's* Wild West, 25.

25. Cody, *The Life of Hon. William F. Cody*, 481.

26. Sarf, *God Bless You, Buffalo Bill*, 35.

27. Rosa, *They Called Him Wild Bill*, 257.

28. A "combination" company presented only one play and moved from town to town, staying a few days in each location until the audience was played out. This is opposed to a "stock company," which presented several different plays on a rotating basis in one location.

29. After the battle, the name of the dead Indian Yellow Hair was mistakenly translated by an army interpreter as "Yellow Hand," thus creating a confusion of names. Both Yellow Hair and Yellow Hand will be found in various books describing the same incident.

30. Mountain man Jim Bridger was so famous for his tall tales that nobody at first believed his descriptions of the geysers and other wonders of the area that is now Yellowstone National Park.

31. Warren, *Buffalo Bill's America*, 18–20.

32. Ibid., 27.

33. Ibid., 154.

34. Ibid., 86–87.

35. Kasson, *Buffalo Bill's* Wild West, 28.

36. Ibid., 31.

37. Ibid., 36–37.

38. Warren, *Buffalo Bill's America*, 81.

Chapter 5

1. Reddin, *Wild West Shows*, xiii.

2. Wallis, *The Real Wild West*, 20–21.

3. Rosa, *They Called Him Wild Bill*, 162.

4. Wallis, *The Real Wild West*, 21–22.

5. Arthur H. Saxon, *P.T. Barnum: The Legend and the Man* (New York: Columbia University Press, 1989), 100–101.

6. Rosa, *They Called Him Wild Bill*, 164–167.

7. Wilson and Martin, *Buffalo Bill's* Wild West, 41.

8. Kasson, *Buffalo Bill's* Wild West, 44. Cody's wife, Louisa Frederici Cody ("Lulu"), in her biography, *Memories of Buffalo Bill* (New York: D. Appleton, 1919), consistently called him "Salisbury."

9. Ibid., 44.

10. Ibid., 54.

11. Wilson and Martin, *Buffalo Bill's* Wild West, 220.

12. Ibid., 68.

13. Ibid., 219.

14. Warren, *Buffalo Bill's America*, 244.

15. Ibid., 240.

16. McMurtry, *The Colonel and Little Missie*, 196.

17. Wilson and Martin, *Buffalo Bill's* Wild West, 142.

18. McMurtry, *The Colonel and Little Missie*, 196. See also Shirl Kaspar, *Annie Oakley* (Norman: University of Oklahoma Press, 1992).

19. McMurtry, *The Colonel and Little Missie*, 8.

20. Wilson and Martin, *Buffalo Bill's* Wild West, 62.

21. Warren, *Buffalo Bill's America*, 249.

22. Wallis, *The Real Wild West*, 309.

23. Ibid., 313.

24. Ibid., 316.

25. Wilson and Martin, *Buffalo Bill's* Wild West, 86.

26. Musically inclined readers may be interested in a re-creation of the music for the show as played by the Americus Brass Band on a compact disc titled *Wild West Music of Buffalo Bill's Cowboy Band*. The CD includes a short recording in which Buffalo Bill himself introduces the Congress of Rough Riders of the World, probably the version recorded in 1898 by the Berliner Gramophone Company.

27. Reddin, *Wild West Shows*, 77.

28. Ibid., 60.

29. Warren, *Buffalo Bill's America*, 228.

30. Ibid., 273.

31. Slotkin, *Gunfighter Nation*, 77.

32. Reddin, *Wild West Shows*, 144.

33. Ibid., 145.

34. Wallis, *The Real Wild West*, 268.

35. Ibid., 269.
36. Walker, *Westerns*, 118.
37. Garfield, *Western Film*, 12.
38. Walker, *Westerns*, 123.
39. O'Neil, *The End and the Myth*, 204.
40. Reddin, *Wild West Shows*, 76.

Chapter 6

1. O'Neil, *The End and the Myth*, 49.
2. Ibid., 49.
3. Frank James was Jesse's older brother. Cole Younger was the sole survivor of the Younger brothers who rode with the James gang. Cole later wrote about his exploits in a garish book titled *Northfield Bank Robbery (Real Fact)*.
4. O'Neil, *The End and the Myth*, 50.
5. Reddin, *Wild West Shows*, 165.
6. Wallis, *The Real Wild West*, 358.
7. The company principals were Charles O. Bauman, a former streetcar conductor; Adam Kessel, who was once a bookmaker; and Fred J. Balshofer, a former photographer who went into movie production.
8. Fred J. Balshofer and Arthur C. Miller. *One Reel a Week* (Berkeley: University of California Press, 1967), 76.
9. This was formerly a ranch named Topanga Malibu Sequit, after three old Indian villages in the area (Wallis, *The Real Wild West*, 371).
10. Wallis, *The Real Wild West*, 374.
11. Reddin, *Wild West Shows*, 179.
12. Wallis, *The Real Wild West*, 235–236.
13. Ibid., 237.
14. Ibid., 236.
15. Ibid., 245.

Chapter 7

1. George-Warren, *Cowboy*, 9.
2. Nachbar, *Focus on the Western*, 10.
3. Richard Etulain, "Cultural Origins of the Western," in Nachbar, *Focus on the Western*, 20.
4. *Frank Leslie's Illustrated Weekly*, January 14, 1882.
5. *Harper's Weekly*, October 16, 1886.
6. Agnew, *Smoking Gun*, 254; Don Russell, "The Cowboy: From Black Hat to White," in Harris and Rainey, *The Cowboy*, 7. In *The Virginian*, Wister spells the name as "cow-boy" on page 499. Publicity photos for Buck Taylor spelled it as "cow boy."
7. Philip D. Jordan, "The Pistol Packin' Cowboy," in Harris and Rainey, *The Cowboy*, 62.
8. Ibid., 63.
9. Buck Rainey, "The 'Reel' Cowboy," in Harris and Rainey, *The Cowboy*, 23.
10. Ramon F. Adams, *The Old Time Cowhand* (New York: Macmillan, 1961), 5.
11. Philip D. Jordan, "The Pistol Packin' Cowboy," in Harris and Rainey, *The Cowboy*, 57.
12. Wister, *The Virginian*, 4.
13. Frantz and Choate, *The American Cowboy*, 6.

14. Wister, *The Virginian*, 480–481.
15. Ibid., 465.
16. Ibid., 474.
17. Ibid., 476.
18. Ibid., 29.
19. Ibid., 96.
20. For examples, see the limericks and songs in "The Cowboy and Sex" by Clifford Westermeier, in Harris and Rainey, *The Cowboy*, 85–105.
21. Ibid., 91. However, even the name of Son-of-a-Gun Hill on Pikes Peak in Colorado was considered to be so naughty that it was replaced by Sun-of-a-Gun Hill.
22. Wister, *The Virginian*, 160.
23. Davis, *Playing Cowboys*, 6.
24. Lenihan, *Showdown*, 13.
25. Calder, *There Must Be a Lone Ranger*, 105.
26. Agnew, *The Old West in Fact and Film*, 168.
27. McDonald, *Shooting Stars*, 110.
28. Don Siegel, *A Siegel Film* (London: Faber and Faber, 1993), 32.
29. The bib-front or "fireman's" shirt had a large flap of material over the chest that was attached to the rest of the shirt by a row of buttons down each side. The original design of the shirt, made from heavy wool with its extra layer of cloth, was adopted by firemen in the Old West to protect the upper body. Later movie stars used more fashionable material, such as silk.

Chapter 8

1. Nachbar, *Focus on the Western*, 2.
2. Fenin and Everson, *The Western*, 11.
3. Wills, *John Wayne's America*, 311–312.
4. Shipman, *The Story of Cinema*, 36.
5. One reel of film ran for approximately ten minutes, thus two reels would last for about twenty minutes. The time for a reel of film was derived from the approximate length of a vaudeville act when early movies were shown as "acts" in vaudeville theaters.
6. Fenin and Everson, *The Western*, 11.
7. O'Neil, *The End and the Myth*, 205.
8. Smith, *Shooting Cowboys and Indians*, 137.
9. Slotkin, *Gunfighter Nation*, 236.
10. Black Maria is credited as America's first movie studio. It was a small, dark, cramped, overheated shed built by Edison in 1893 in West Orange, New Jersey. The name supposedly came from the studio's resemblance to a police wagon.
11. Smith, *Shooting Cowboys and Indians*, 61.
12. Slotkin, *Gunfighter Nation*, 236.
13. Moneymaking Westerns often were used to finance more-artistic types of films, many of which failed at the box office. Ince used this scheme and so did Fox Studios.
14. We apparently like tall heroes. Many popular Western stars have been over six feet tall: Buffalo Bill (6ft. 2in.), Buck Taylor (6ft. 4in.), Willian S. Hart (6ft. 2in.), Gary Cooper (6ft. 3in.), Randolph Scott (6ft. 3in.), John Wayne (6ft. 4in.), James Arness (6ft. 6in.), and Clint Eastwood (6ft. 4in.). Shane (Alan Ladd) was an exception at 5ft. 6in.

15. McDonald, *Shooting Stars*, 7.
16. Smith, *Shooting Cowboys and Indians*, 170.
17. *Moving Picture World*, October 21, 1911, p. 190.
18. Smith, *Shooting Cowboys and Indians*, 108.
19. Ibid., 179.
20. Slotkin, *Gunfighter Nation*, 244.
21. Griffith and Mayer, *The Movies*, 165.
22. Jon Tuska, "The American Western Cinema: 1903–Present," in Nachbar, *Focus on the Western*, 33.
23. Simmon, *The Invention of the Western Film*, 89.

Chapter 9

1. Quoted in the epigraph of Mitchell, *Westerns*.
2. Matinee idols Rudolph Valentino and John Barrymore were similarly promoted in costume dramas to appeal to female audiences.
3. Smith, *Shooting Cowboys and Indians*, 189.
4. O'Neil, *The End and the Myth*, 215.
5. Goetzmann and Goetzmann, *The West of the Imagination*, 303.
6. Fenin and Everson, *The Western*, 113.
7. Wallis, *The Real Wild West*, 602.
8. Everson, *A Pictorial History of the Western Film*, 64.
9. Fenin and Everson, *The Western*, 113.
10. Ibid., 116.
11. Buck Rainey, "The 'Reel' Cowboy," in Harris and Rainey, *The Cowboy*, 41.
12. Goetzmann and Goetzmann, *The West of the Imagination*, 304.
13. Reddin, *Wild West Shows*, 204.
14. Everson, *A Pictorial History of the Western Film*, 81.
15. Fenin and Everson, *The Western*, 117.
16. O'Neil, *The End and the Myth*, 217.
17. Griffith and Mayer, *The Movies*, 168.
18. Wallis, *The Real Wild West*, 601.
19. Ibid., 443.
20. Raymond White, "Ken Maynard: Daredevil on Horseback," in McDonald, *Shooting Stars*, 30.
21. Ibid., 28.
22. Smith, *Shooting Cowboys and Indians*, 206.
23. Ibid., 205.
24. Wallis, *The Real Wild West*, 444.
25. Ibid., 445.
26. Buck Rainey, *Saddle Aces of the Cinema* (New York: A.S. Barnes, 1980), 218.
27. Wallis, *The Real Wild West*, 602.
28. *Nickelodeon*, March 25, 1911, p. 336.
29. Tony Hillerman, *Sacred Clowns* (New York: HarperPaperbacks, 1993), 140–143.

Chapter 10

1. Cowie, *John Ford and the American West*, 190.
2. Nachbar, *Focus on the Western*, 21.
3. Goetzmann and Goetzmann, *The West of the Imagination*, 313.
4. Hitt, *The American West from Fiction (1823–1976) into Film (1909–1986)*, 84.
5. Slotkin, *Gunfighter Nation*, 93.
6. Will Lillibridge, *Ben Blair: The Story of a Plainsman* (New York: A.L. Burt, 1905), 1.
7. Ibid., 8.
8. One of the more lurid of the pulps was *Tales from the Crypt*, a comic book which specialized in sadistic horror.
9. Folsom, *The Western*, 36.
10. Pilkington, *Critical Essays on the Western Novel*, 27.
11. Etulain, *Telling Western Stories*, 151–152.
12. Rainey, "The 'Reel' Cowboy," in Harris and Rainey, *The Cowboy*, 17.
13. Pilkington, *Critical Essays on the Western Novel*, 28.
14. Ibid., xii.
15. Slotkin, *Gunfighter Nation*, 196.
16. Hitt, *The American West from Fiction (1823–1976) into Film (1909–1986)*, 137.
17. Pilkington, *Critical Essays on the Western Novel*, 26.
18. Zane Grey, *Riders of the Purple Sage* (London: Hamish Hamilton, 1952), 107.
19. Ibid., 10.
20. Zane Grey, *The Rainbow Trail* (New York: Cardinal, 1961), 183.
21. Zane Grey, *The Heritage of the Desert* (London: Pan Books, 1953), 5.
22. Ibid., 35.
23. Ibid., 154.
24. Ibid., 182.
25. Grey, *The Rainbow Trail*, 166.
26. Zane Grey, *The Vanishing American* (Roslyn: Walter J. Black, 1953), 15.
27. Ibid., 18–19.
28. Ibid., 56.
29. Ibid., 77.
30. Ibid., 278–279.
31. Simmon, *The Invention of the Western Film*, 331.
32. Hollywood was faced with a similar problem in non–Western movies. One example is *Showboat* (1951), where the marriage between Gaylord Ravenal (Howard Keel) and Julie LaVerne (Ava Gardner) was doomed from the beginning because interracial marriages were forbidden in the South.
33. Pilkington, *Critical Essays on the Western Novel*, 25.
34. Parks, *The Western Hero in Film and Television*, 69.
35. Pronzini, *Wild Westerns*, 1.
36. Hitt, *The American West from Fiction (1823–1976) into Film (1909–1986)*, 189.
37. Rainey, "The 'Reel' Cowboy," in Harris and Rainey, *The Cowboy*, 18.
38. Pronzini, *Wild Westerns*, 125.
39. Luke Short was a gambler, saloonkeeper, and dangerous gunman who was involved in several deadly gunfights in the 1880s and 1890s.

40. Hitt, *The American Westf from Fiction (1823–1976) into Film (1909–1986)*, 206.
41. Clive Thompson, "The Paper Chase" *Smithsonian* 44, no. 2 (May 2013),14.
42. Frantz and Choate, *The American Cowboy*, 5.
43. Wister also wrote *Roosevelt: The Story of a Friendship, 1880–1919* (New York: Macmillan, 1930).
44. John M. Faragher, "The Tale of Wyatt Earp: Seven Films," in Carnes, *Past Imperfect*, 154.
45. Ibid.
46. Guinn, *The Last Gunfight*, 318.

Chapter 11

1. Garfield, *Western Film*, 9.
2. The huge project had been a gamble to save the studio but instead pushed it over the edge. After Fox was taken over in 1930 by AT&T and Chase National Bank, earnings fell from $10 million in 1930 to a loss of $4 million in 1931. The studio lost nearly $11M in 1931 and 1932, which pushed it to the brink of collapse (Tino Balio, *Grand Design: Hollywood as a Modern Business Enterprise, 1930–1939* (New York: Charles Scribner's Sons, 1993), 15–17).
3. Wills, *John Wayne's America*, 55.
4. Cameron and Pye, *The Book of Westerns*, 25.
5. Slotkin, *Gunfighter Nation*, 255–256.
6. World Wide Pictures was popular among young boys for having a rather strange company logo in the titles: a smiling blonde woman holding two large world globes in front of her chest.
7. Simmon, *The Invention of the Western Film*, 174.
8. Lahue, *Riders of the Range*, 202.
9. William "Wild Bill" Elliott received his nickname for playing Wild Bill Hickok in the fifteen-chapter Columbia serial *The Great Adventures of Wild Bill Hickok* in 1939.
10. McDonald, *Shooting Stars*, 90.
11. The outlandish shirts, pants, and boots worn by the Western movie stars, which featured piped collars, shaped cuffs with multiple snaps and buttons, and stitched arrowheads, were primarily made by three tailors to the movie stars, Rodeo Ben (Bernard Lichenstein), Nathan Turk, and Nudie of Hollywood (Nutya Kotlyrenko). Among their customers were Hoot Gibson, Gene Autry, Roy Rogers, Dale Evans, Rex Allen, Audie Murphy, John Wayne, Glenn Ford, and Guy Madison.
12. One actor who didn't make it as a singing cowboy was John Wayne, as "Singin' Sandy" Saunders in *Riders of Destiny* (1933), who walked into the final shoot-out softly singing a ballad. Wayne didn't care much about being a singing cowboy, so this was his first and last attempt at being one.
13. Raymond White, "Roy Rogers and Dale Evans," in Etulain and Riley, *The Hollywood West*, 27.
14. Rainey, "The 'Reel' Cowboy," in Harris and Rainey, *The Cowboy*, 50.
15. George-Warren, *Cowboy*, 105.
16. Kingsbury, *The Grand Ole Opry History of Country Music*, 15.
17. Kingsbury and Nash, *Will the Circle Be Unbroken*, 100.
18. Ibid., 107.
19. Kingsbury, *The Grand Ole Opry History of Country Music*, 21.
20. Ibid., 22–26.
21. For comparison, today's clear-channel AM radio stations operate with 50,000 watts of broadcast power in order to be heard all over the country.
22. Stanfield, *Horse Opera*, 63.
23. Kingsbury, *The Grand Ole Opry History of Country Music*, 45.
24. Ibid., 49.

Chapter 12

1. From the prologue to the motion picture *The Life and Times of Judge Roy Bean* (1972).
2. Mitchell, *Westerns*, 180.
3. Wright, *Six Guns and Society*, 59.
4. Cowie, *John Ford and the American West*, 88.
5. The "Bad Man from Bodie" was a generic name for the roughest and toughest character around, who was willing to fight anyone and everyone. The name probably was a combination of the term "bad man," which was used as a popular name for a gunfighter, and the town of Bodie, California, which had the not undeserved reputation as the roughest, toughest, wickedest mining camp in the West.
6. For example, a novelist or screenplay writer doesn't describe how the hero travels from one place to another. The action stops when he leaves the first place and resumes when he arrives at the second.
7. In real life the Reno gang, led by brothers John, Frank, Simeon, and William, were similar to the James and the Dalton boys and were one of the first of the famous bandit train-robbing gangs.
8. The real Allan Pinkerton preferred to call his detectives "operatives," and they really did hunt outlaws in this manner. After an aborted train robbery and eventual capture, the real Renos were lynched in 1868.
9. Cameron and Pye, *The Book of Westerns*, 10.
10. Wilson and Wilson, *Mass Media/Mass Culture*, 264–265, 275.
11. Autry, *Back in the Saddle Again*, 102.
12. Wilson and Wilson, *Mass Media/Mass Culture*, 399.
13. George-Warren, *Cowboy*, 196.
14. In 1959 *Bonanza* premiered on NBC as the first color television show, in the hopes that it would boost sales of color television sets for its parent company RCA.
15. McDonald, *Shooting Stars*, 218.
16. Jackson, *Classic TV Westerns*, 19.

Chapter 13

1. A Western novelist, Brand is quoted in Ron Goulart, *Cheap Thrills* (New York: Arlington House, 1972), 134.

2. Frayling, *Once Upon a Time in Italy*, 76.
3. Tuska, *The American West in Film*, 224.
4. Zane Grey, *The Heritage of the Desert* (London: Pan Books, 1953), 175.
5. Simmons, *Kit Carson and His Three Wives*, x.
6. For a more detailed discussion on Victorian views of women, see Agnew, *Brides of the Multitude*, chapter 1.
7. Grey, *The Heritage of the Desert*, 10.
8. Everson, *A Pictorial History of the Western Film*, 3.
9. Zane Grey, *Riders of the Purple Sage* (London: Hamish Hamilton, 1952), 37.
10. Tuska, *The American West in Film*, 228.
11. This has not been unusual in other movie genres in an attempt to appeal to female audiences. For example the romantic comedy *That Touch of Mink* (1962) has a sequence that features a fashion show for the heroine, Cathy Timberlake (Doris Day), to choose her wardrobe.
12. Autry, *Back in the Saddle Again*, 66.
13. Smith, *Shooting Cowboys and Indians*, 209.
14. Miller, *Censored Hollywood*, 261.
15. Ibid., 27.
16. Griffith and Mayer, *The Movies*, 125.
17. Miller, *Censored Hollywood*, 36.
18. James R. Peterson, *The Century of Sex: Playboy's History of the Sexual Revolution* (New York, Grove Press, 1999), 98–99.
19. Ibid., 99–100.
20. Griffith and Mayer, *The Movies*, 182.
21. Miller, *Censored Hollywood*, 42.
22. Ibid., 39.
23. This movie is interesting for film buffs as it contains John Wayne in a very small part playing Jimmy McCoy, Jr.
24. O'Sullivan's nude swimming sequence was doubled by Olympic swimmer Josephine McKim. A swimsuit version was included for final release to appease the Hays Office, but the nude scene has been restored in modern versions.
25. Hitt, *The American West from Fiction (1823–1976) into Film (1909–1986)*, 255.
26. Mitchell, *Westerns*, 203.
27. To be technical, this movie was set during the Civil War, before the introduction of sealed heavy-caliber cartridges in 1873. The powder in his cap-and-ball gun would have become wet and could not ignite. No matter, it makes a satisfying dramatic scene.
28. Mitchell, *Westerns*, 165.
29. In reality, however, a woman could travel the Wild West in safety and most men behaved with utmost respect towards a lady. This courtesy, for example, allowed middle-aged Englishwoman Isabella Bird to explore 800 miles of the Rocky Mountains on horseback by herself in 1873.
30. Simmon, *The Invention of the Western Film*, 74.
31. Marvin H. Albert, *Apache Uprising* (New York: Fawcett, 1957), 32.
32. The term "sexploitation" came to mean low-budget independent films dealing with taboo subjects such as sex and drugs.
33. Miller, *Censored Hollywood*, 204–205.
34. Hitt, *The American West from Fiction (1823–1976) into Film (1909–1986)*, 65.

Chapter 14

1. Frayling, *Once Upon a Time in Italy*, 186. Frayling was an expert on Sergio Leone.
2. A similar concern among critics of early film was the fear that gangster movies would teach people how to commit a crime and would glorify criminals. Even if the movie law caught up with the gangster and left him dead at the end, moralists felt that films about crime would make the lifestyle attractive.
3. Smith, *Shooting Cowboys and Indians*, 138–139.
4. Lahue, *Riders of the Range*, 203.
5. Glendon Swarthout, *The Shootist* (New York: Doubleday, 1975), 84.
6. Ibid., 176–177.
7. Griffith and Mayer, *The Movies*, 471.
8. Etulain and Riley, *The Hollywood West*, xiii.
9. It has been suggested that this attitude reflected the new cynicism among audiences at the time of the failing Vietnam war and the Watergate scandal, which brought down President Nixon.
10. Similar cuts were made in the television versions of many movies, such as the violent Schwarznegger films showing bullets fired into heads.
11. Frayling, *Once Upon a Time in Italy*, 177.
12. Ibid., 177.
13. George-Warren, *Cowboy*, 201.
14. Hughes, *Once Upon a Time in the Italian West*, 254.
15. Mitchell, *Westerns*, 232.
16. On a business trip to Germany in the 1990s, I had the somewhat surreal experience of watching a well-known American Western film with a sound track that had been dubbed into French but was presented with German subtitles.
17. Hughes, *Once Upon a Time in the Italian West*, 52.
18. Interview with Henry Fonda (1975) in special features on the *Once Upon a Time in the West* (1968), special collector's edition DVD.
19. Frayling, *Once Upon a Time in Italy*, 177.
20. Hughes, *Once Upon a Time in the Italian West*, 90.
21. Frayling, *Once Upon a Time in Italy*, 181
22. The Sand Creek massacre involved mutilation of Indian corpses, including obscenities committed on women, similar to the taking of ears from dead soldiers as souvenirs of victory in the Vietnam War.
23. Hughes, *Once Upon a Time in the Italian West*, 86.
24. Hitt, *The American West from Fiction (1823–1976) into Film (1909–1986)*, 65.
25. Simons and Merrill, *Peckinpah's Tragic Westerns*, 4.
26. Hughes, *Once Upon a Time in the Italian West*, 215.
27. Mitchell, *Westerns*, 250.

28. Ibid., 315.
29. Miller, *Censored Hollywood*, 254.
30. Mitchell, *Westerns*, 247.
31. Though violent, this was similar to other movie genres of the time, such as *Rob Roy* (1995), in which Rob Roy (Liam Neeson) cleaves open Cunningham's (Tim Roth) chest in the final climactic sword fight after the earlier graphic rape of Rob Roy's wife, and *Braveheart* (1995), where William Wallace (Mel Gibson) is hanged, castrated, disemboweled, and beheaded.
32. McDonald, *Shooting Stars*, 193.

Chapter 15

1. Rollins and O'Connor, *Hollywood's West*, x.
2. Slotkin, *Gunfighter Nation*, 333.
3. Lenihan, *Showdown*, 6.
4. Slotkin, *Gunfighter Nation*, 627.
5. McVeigh, *The American Western*, 193.
6. Trivia section of Internet Movie Database for *Heaven's Gate* and "Special Features" on the DVD release.
7. Slotkin, *Gunfighter Nation*, 627.
8. The movie was based on a series of fifty-five science-fiction trading cards that were included with Topps bubble gum in the 1960s (Topps Company, *Mars Attacks*, New York: Abrams Comic Arts, 2012). In the original story, soldiers go by rocket ship to Mars and defeat the Martians on their home ground; the planet explodes as the soldiers return to Earth. It did not include the tongue-in-cheek singing Slim Whitman Western concept. Slim Whitman's singing style has suffered some of the same sarcasm that was directed at Liberace, though his fine baritone makes a pleasant change from nasal twangs describing drinking problems and the loss of women. It is also relevant to note that fans have bought over 100 million copies of his recordings.
9. Jim Arndt, *How to Be a Cowboy* (Layton, UT: Gibbs Smith, 2009).
10. George-Warren, *Cowboy*, 133.
11. Ibid., 134.
12. The real Gilley's nightclub in Houston has since burned down and been rebuilt.
13. The Nashville sound was smooth-sounding pop music that included violins and orchestras using experienced session musicians to accompany the singer. The "sound" was enhanced by using vocal harmony groups, such as the Anita Kerr Singers or the Jordanaires as backing.
14. Kingsbury and Nash, *Will the Circle Be Unbroken*, 226.
15. Wilson and Wilson, *Mass Media/Mass Culture*, 253.
16. Bernstein, *Wild Ride*, 15.
17. Wallis, *The Real Wild West*, 136.
18. O'Neil, *The End and the Myth*, 99.
19. Bernstein, *Wild Ride*, 24.
20. Wallis, *The Real Wild West*, 137; Slatta, *Cowboy*, 172–173.
21. Wallis, *The Real Wild West*, 136.
22. Ibid., 253.
23. Ibid., 254.
24. Kasson, *Buffalo Bill's* Wild West, 8.
25. Wilson and Martin, *Buffalo Bill's* Wild West, 256.
26. This became the dude image, even though real cowboys commonly wore wooly chaps made from angora or sheep's wool, called "woolies," particularly to stay warm in the brutally cold winters of the Northern Plains.
27. Lawrence R. Borne, "The Cowboy and the Dude," in Harris and Rainey, *The Cowboy*, 108.
28. Ibid., 109–110.
29. Wallis, *The Real Wild West*, 279.

Postscript

1. Garfield, *Western Film*, 9.
2. Sarf, *God Bless You, Buffalo Bill*, 77.
3. Murdoch, *The American West*, 81.
4. Carey McWilliams, "Myths of the West," *North American Review* 232 (November 1931), 428.

Bibliography

Adams, Andy. *The Log of a Cowboy.* Boston: Houghton Mifflin, 1903.

Agnew, Jeremy. *Brides of the Multitude: Prostitution in the Old West.* Lake City: Western Reflections, 2008.

_____. *Entertainment in the Old West: Theater, Music, Circuses, Medicine Shows, Prizefighting and Other Popular Amusements.* Jefferson, NC: McFarland, 2011.

_____. *The Old West in Fact and Film: History Versus Hollywood.* Jefferson, NC: McFarland, 2012.

_____. *Smoking Gun: The True Story About Gunfighting in the Old West.* Lake City, CO: Western Reflections, 2010.

Alter, Judy. *Wild West Shows: Rough Riders and Sure Shots.* New York: Franklin Watts, 1997.

Arndt, Jim. *How to Be a Cowboy.* Layton, UT: Gibbs Smith, 2009.

Autry, Gene. *Back in the Saddle Again.* Garden City: Doubleday, 1978.

Barbour, Alan G. *Saturday Afternoon at the Movies.* New York: Bonanza Books, 1986.

Barra, Allen. *Inventing Wyatt Earp: His Life and Many Legends.* New York: Carrol & Graf, 1998.

Bernstein, Joel H. *Wild Ride: The History and Lore of Rodeo.* Salt Lake City: Gibbs Smith, 2007.

Brant, Marley. *Jesse James: The Man and the Myth.* New York: Berkeley, 1998.

Breihan, Carl W. *The Complete and Authentic Life of Jesse James.* New York: Frederick Fell, 1953.

Buntline, Ned. *The Hero of a Hundred Fights: Collected Stories from the Dime Novel King.* Edited by Clay Reynolds. New York: Union Square, 2011.

Calder, Jenni. *There Must Be a Lone Ranger: The American West in Film and in Reality.* New York: Taplinger, 1974.

Cameron, Ian, and Douglas Pye, eds. *The Book of Westerns.* New York: Continuum, 1996.

Carmichael, Deborah A., ed. *The Landscape of Hollywood Westerns.* Salt Lake City: University of Utah Press, 2006.

Carnes, Mark C., ed. *Past Imperfect: History According to the Movies.* New York, Henry Holt, 1995.

Cody, William F. *The Life of Hon. William F. Cody, Known as Buffalo Bill.* Lincoln; University of Nebraska Press, 2011.

Cooper, James F. *The Last of the Mohicans.* New York: A.L. Burt, 1920.

Cowie, Peter. *John Ford and the American West.* New York: Harry N. Abrams, 2004.

_____. *Seventy Years of Cinema.* Cranbury: A.S. Barnes, 1969.

Cox, J. Randolph. *The Dime Novel Companion: A Source Book.* Westport: Greenwood, 2000.

D'Arc, James V. *When Hollywood Came to Town: A History of Moviemaking in Utah.* Layton: Gibbs Smith, 2010.

Davis, Robert M. *Playing Cowboys: Low Culture and High Art in the Western.* Norman: University of Oklahoma Press, 1992.

Etulain, Richard W. *Telling Western Stories: From Buffalo Bill to Larry McMurtry.* Albuquerque: University of New Mexico Press, 1999.

Etulain, Richard W., and Michael T. Marsden. *The Popular Western: Essays Towards a Definition.* Bowling Green: Bowling Green University Popular Press, 1974.

Etulain, Richard W., and Glenda Riley, eds. *The Hollywood West: Lives of Film Legends Who Shaped It.* Golden: Fulcrum, 2001.

Everson, William K. *A Pictorial History of the Western Film.* New York: Citadel Press, 1969.

Fenin, George N., and William K. Everson. *The Western: From Silents to the Seventies.* New York: Grossman, 1973.

Folsom, James K., ed. *The Western: A Collection of Critical Essays.* Englewood Cliffs: Prentice-Hall, 1979.

Frantz, Joe B., and Julian E. Choate, Jr. *The American Cowboy: The Myth and the Reality.* Norman: University of Oklahoma Press, 2001.

Frayling, Christopher. *Once Upon a Time in Italy: The Westerns of Sergio Leone.* New York: Harry N. Abrams, 2005.

French, Philip. *Westerns: Aspects of a Movie Genre.* New York: Viking Press, 1973.

Garfield, Brian. *Western Film.* New York: Rawson, 1982.

George-Warren, Holly. *Cowboy: How Hollywood Invented the Wild West.* Pleasantville: Reader's Digest Association, 2002.

_____. *Public Cowboy No. 1: The Life and Times of Gene Autry*. New York: Oxford University Press, 2007.

Goetzmann, William H., and William N. Goetzmann. *The West of the Imagination*. New York: W.W. Norton, 1986.

Griffin, Scott T. *The Centennial Celebration Tarzan*. London: Titan Books, 2012.

Griffith, Richard, and Arthur Mayer. *The Movies*. New York: Simon & Schuster, 1970.

Guinn, Jeff. *The Last Gunfight: The Real Story of the Shootout at the O.K. Corral and How it Changed the American West*. New York: Simon & Schuster, 2011.

Hamilton, John R. *Thunder in the Dust: Classic Images of Western Movies*. New York: Stewart, Tabori & Chang, 1987.

Hanners, John. *It Was Play or Starve: Acting in the Nineteenth Century American Popular Theatre*. Bowling Green: Bowling Green State University Popular Press, 1993.

Harris, Charles W., and Buck Rainey, eds. *The Cowboy: Six-Shooters, Songs, and Sex*. Norman: University of Oklahoma Press, 1976.

Hine, Robert V., and John M. Faragher. *The American West: A New Interpretive History*. New Haven: Yale University Press, 2000.

Hitt, Jim. *The American West from Fiction (1823–1976) into Film (1909–1986)*. Jefferson, NC: McFarland, 1990.

Hughes, Howard. *Once Upon a Time in the Italian West*. London: I.B. Taurus, 2004.

Jackson, Ronald. *Classic TV Westerns*. New York: Carol, 1994.

Kasson, Joy S. *Buffalo Bill's Wild West*. New York: Hill and Wang, 2000.

King, David C. *First People*. New York: DK, 2008.

Kingsbury, Paul. *The Grand Ole Opry History of Country Music*. New York: Villard Books, 1995.

Kingsbury, Paul, and Alanna Nash. *Will the Circle Be Unbroken: Country Music in America*. London: Dorling Kindersly, 2006.

Kitses, Jim. *Horizons West: Directing the Western from John Ford to Clint Eastwood*. London: BFI, 2004.

Kitses, Jim, and Gregg Rickman. *The Western Reader*. New York: Limelight Editions, 1998.

Lahue, Kalton C. *Riders of the Range: The Sagebrush Heroes of the Sound Screen*. Cranbury: A.S. Barnes, 1973.

Lake, Stuart N. *Wyatt Earp: Frontier Marshal*. Boston: Houghton Mifflin, 1994.

Lenihan, John H. *Showdown: Confronting Modern America in the Western Film*. Urbana: University of Illinois Press, 1985.

Lloyd, Ann, ed. *They Went That-A-Way*. London: Orbis, 1982.

Manns, William, and Elizabeth C. Flood. *Cowboys and the Trappings of the Old West*. Santa Fe: Zon International, 1997.

McDonald, Archie P., ed. *Shooting Stars: Heroes and Heroines of Western Film*. Bloomington: Indiana University Press, 1987.

McMurtry, Larry. *The Colonel and Little Missie*. New York: Simon & Schuster, 2005.

McVeigh, Stephen. *The American Western*. Edinburgh: Edinburgh University Press, 2007.

Miller, Frank. *Censored Hollywood: Sex, Sin and Violence on Screen*. Atlanta: Turner, 1994.

Mitchell, Lee C. *Westerns: Making the Man in Fiction and Film*. Chicago: University of Chicago Press, 1996.

Munn, Michael. *John Wayne: The Man Behind the Myth*. New York: New American Library, 2003.

Murdoch, David H. *The American West: The Invention of a Myth*. Reno: University of Nevada Press, 2001.

Nachbar, Jack, ed. *Focus on the Western*. Englewood Cliffs: Prentice-Hall, 1974.

O'Neil, Paul. *The End and the Myth*. Alexandria: Time-Life Books, 1979.

Parks, Rita. *The Western Hero in Film and Television: Mass Media Mythology*. Ann Arbor: UMI Research Press, 1982.

Pearson, Edmund. *Dime Novels; or, Following an Old Trail in Popular Literature*. Boston: Little, Brown, 1929.

Pilkington, William T. *Critical Essays on the Western Novel*. Boston: G.K. Hall, 1980.

Pronzini, Bill. *Wild Westerns: Stories from the Grand Old Pulps*. Boston: G.K. Hall, 1988.

Rabinowitz, Harold. *Black Hats and White Hats: Heroes and Villains of the West*. New York: Friedman/Fairfax, 1996.

Reddin, Paul. *Wild West Shows*. Urbana: University of Illinois Press, 1999.

Robinson, David. *From Peep Show to Palace: The Birth of American Film*. New York: Columbia University Press, 1995.

Rollins, Peter C., and John E. O'Connor, eds. *Hollywood's West: The American Frontier in Film, Television, and History*. Lexington: University Press of Kentucky, 2005.

Rollins, Philip A. *The Cowboy*. New York: Charles Scribner's Sons, 1936.

Rosa, Joseph G. *They Called Him Wild Bill: The Life and Adventures of James Butler Hickok*. Norman: University of Oklahoma Press, 1974.

_____. *Wild Bill Hickok: The Man and His Myth*. Lawrence: University Press of Kansas, 1996.

Russell, Don. *The Lives and Legends of Buffalo Bill*. Norman: University of Oklahoma Press, 1960.

Russell, Mary D. *Doc*. New York: Random House, 2011.

Ryan, Jim. *The Rodeo and Hollywood: Rodeo Cowboys on Screen and Western Actors in the Arena*. Jefferson, NC: McFarland, 2006.

Sarf, Wayne M. *God Bless You, Buffalo Bill: A Lay-*

man's *Guide to History and the Western Film.* East Brunswick, NJ: Associated University Presses and Cornwall Books, 1983.

Sennett, Ted. *Great Hollywood Westerns.* New York: Harry N. Abrams, 1990.

Settle, William A., Jr. *Jesse James Was His Name.* Columbia: University of Missouri Press, 1966.

Shipman, David. *The Story of Cinema.* New York: St. Martin's, 1982.

Sides, Hampton. *Blood and Thunder: An Epic of the American West.* New York: Doubleday, 2006.

Simmon, Scott. *The Invention of the Western Film: A Cultural History of the Genre's First Half-Century.* Cambridge: Cambridge University Press, 2003.

Simmons, Marc. *Kit Carson and His Three Wives.* Albuquerque: University of New Mexico Press, 2003.

Simons, John L., and Robert Merrill. *Peckinpah's Tragic Westerns: A Critical Study.* Jefferson, NC: McFarland, 2011.

Sklar, Robert. *Film: An International History of the Medium.* New York: Harry N. Abrams, 1993.

Slatta, Richard W. *Cowboy: The Illustrated History.* New York: Sterling, 2006.

Slotkin, Richard. *The Fatal Environment: The Myth of the Frontier in the Age of Industrialization, 1800–1890.* New York: Atheneum, 1985.

_____. *Gunfighter Nation: The Myth of the Frontier in Twentieth-Century America.* New York: Atheneum, 1992.

Smith, Andrew B. *Shooting Cowboys and Indians: Silent Western Films, American Culture, and the Birth of Hollywood.* Boulder: University Press of Colorado, 2003.

Speed, F. Maurice. *The Western Film Annual.* London: MacDonald, 1954.

Stanfield, Peter. *Hollywood, Westerns and the 1930s.* Exeter: University of Exeter Press, 2001.

_____. *Horse Opera: The Strange History of the 1930s Singing Cowboy.* Urbana: University of Illinois Press, 2002.

Stiles, T.J. *Jesse James.* New York: Alfred A. Knopf, 2002.

Sullivan, James. *Jeans: A Cultural History of an American Icon.* New York: Gotham, 2006.

Sullivan, Larry E., and Lydia C. Schurman, eds. *Pioneers, Passionate Ladies, and Private Eyes: Dime Novels, Series Books, and Paperbacks.* New York: Haworth, 1996.

Tefertiller, Casey. *Wyatt Earp.* New York: John Wiley & Sons, 1997.

Toll, Robert C. *On With the Show: The First Century of Show Business in America.* New York: Oxford University Press, 1976.

Tripplett, Frank. *The Life, Times and Treacherous Death of Jesse James.* Chicago: J.H. Chambers, 1882.

Tuska, Jon. *The American West in Film: Critical Approaches to the Western.* Westport: Greenwood, 1985.

Utley, Robert M. *Billy the Kid.* Lincoln: University of Nebraska Press, 1989.

Varner, Paul, ed. *Western: Paperback Novels and Movies from Hollywood.* Newcastle, England: Cambridge Scholars, 2007.

Verhoeff, Nanna. *The West in Early Cinema: After the Beginning.* Amsterdam: Amsterdam University Press, 2006.

Walker, Janet, ed. *Westerns: Films Through History.* New York: Routledge, 2001.

Wallis, Michael. *The Real Wild West: The 101 Ranch and the Creation of the American West.* New York: St. Martin's, 1999.

Warren, Louis S. *Buffalo Bill's America: William Cody and the* Wild West Show. New York: Alfred A. Knopf, 2005.

Weber, David J. *The Taos Trappers: The Fur Trade in the Far Southwest, 1540–1846.* Norman: University of Oklahoma Press, 1971.

Weston, Jack. *The Real American Cowboy.* New York: Schocken Books, 1985.

Wetmore, Helen C. *Buffalo Bill: Last of the Great Scouts.* Stamford: Longmeadow Press, 1994.

White, Raymond E. *King of the Cowboys, Queen of the West.* Madison: University of Wisconsin Press, 2005.

Wills, Garry. *John Wayne's America: The Politics of Celebrity.* New York: Simon & Schuster, 1997.

Wilson, James R., and Stan L. Wilson. *Mass Media/Mass Culture.* New York: McGraw-Hill, 1998.

Wilson, Robert L., and Greg Martin. *Buffalo Bill's Wild West: An American Legend.* New York: Random House, 1998.

Wister, Owen. *The Virginian.* New York: Macmillan, 1902.

Wright, Will. *Six Guns and Society: A Structural Study of the Western.* Berkeley: University of California Press, 1975.

Index

Page numbers in ***bold italics*** indicate pages with illustrations.

A Westerns 135–136, 187
Adams, James C. "Grizzly" 57
advertising 204–207; *see also* merchandising
allegory in Westerns 2, 17–18, 225
Allen, Rex 117, 142, 147, 152, 164, 210, 224
Anderson, Gilbert *see* Broncho Billy
Arbuckle, Roscoe "Fatty" 175
Astor Place Riot 45
Autry, Gene 11, 112, 114, 116, 117, 128, 130, 138, 140–144, 150–151, 160–164, 168, 171, 177, 204, 209, 210, 217, 224

B Westerns 91, 94, 100, 113, 116, 129, ***130***, 135–147, 161, 164, 176, 186, 199, 202, 219
Bad Man from Bodie 156, 191, 224
Barnum, P.T. 55, 57
Battle of the Little Bighorn 26–27, 51, 52, 65, 68–69
Beadle & Adams 31–32, ***33***, 34–39, 48, 216
Bierstadt, Albert 9, 170
Billy the Kid 14, 37, 42, 145–146, 148, 167, 177, 184
Bison 101 78
Black Maria 102, 222
Bogardus, Adam 58, 63, 65
Bonanza (television) 163, 164, 224
Boone, Daniel 8, 17, 19, 21, 22, 24, ***25***, 27, 30, 161, 162
Boyd, William 80, 117, 129, 142, 177, 205
Broken Arrow (1950) 2, 15, 100, 119, 128
Broncho Billy 100–102, 110
budgets, film 2, 199
buffalo (bison) 44, 45, 54, ***54***, 57, 58, 60, 68, 76, 132, 192, 204, 221
Buffalo Bill *see* Cody, William F.
Buffalo Bill and the Indians (1976) 43, 72
Buffalo Bill's *Wild West* 7, 10, 44, 53–55, 56–74, 83, 84, 96, 102, 103, 115, 116, 161, 210, 215
bulldogging 73, 77, 169, 209–211
Buntline, Ned *see* Judson, Edward Zane
Burke, John 44, 53, 56, 62, 63
Burroughs, Edgar Rice 115, 124
Butch Cassidy and The Sundance Kid (1969) 14, 184, 192, 193, 202

Calamity Jane 36, 37, 79, 177, 179, 201
Canutt, Yakima 139, 184
captivity narratives 18
Carson, Kit 14, 21–22, 23–26, ***23***, ***25***, 27, 30, 115, 161
Carver, Doc 57–58, 62, 63, 74
Cassidy, Butch *see* *Butch Cassidy and The Sundance Kid* (1969)
Cassidy, Hopalong 117, 129–131, 142, 160, 164, 205
Cat Ballou (1965) 30, 31, 173, 202
Catlin, George 9, 170
cavalry novels 121
censorship in movies 95, 174–177, 183–187, 191
chaps (clothing) 11, 61, 72, 94, 164, 179, 207, 212, 213, 226
Cheyenne Autumn (1964) 119
children as fans 6, 7, 62, 101, 144, 161, 163, 164, 181, 183, 184, 204, 205
Clarke, Richard 220
cliffhangers 24, 29, 108, 140, 162
clothing 43, 86, 104, 114, 139, 142, 147, 151, 157, 158, 171, 179, 188, 204, 207, 213, 214, 216, 224
Cody, William F. "Buffalo Bill" 14, 21, ***25***, 39, 44–73, ***59***, ***64***, ***70***, 74, 78–79, 80, 84, 93, 98, 103, 138, 142, 161, 204, ***205***, 221; origin of the name "Buffalo Bill" 45, 46, 54, 72, 221; *see also* Buffalo Bill's *Wild West*
Colt .45 revolver 12, 63, 85, 94, 138, ***159***, 201, 214, 225; holsters ***195***
combination, theatrical 221
cone effect 3
Constructed Mediated Reality (CMR) 3
Cooper, Gary 92, 153, 154, 157, 168, 180, 222
Cooper, James Fenimore 8, 12, 19–21, 22, 30, 36, 72, 89, 91, 107–108, 125, 158, 217
cowboy action shooting 214
cowboy bands *see* music in Wild West shows
cowboy code 88, 92–93, 143, 144, 161
cowboy wannabes 6, 7, ***11***, ***213***
cowboys, authentic 10, 30, 39, 60, 66, 82, 84–86, ***85***, 88, 90, 113, 117, 164, ***164***, 207, 213–216, ***216***, 218, 226
Crockett, Davy 7, 17, 21, 22, 24, 25, 27, 30, 52, 53, 161, 162
Custer, Elizabeth "Libbie" 26, 29
Custer, George Armstrong 7, 26–27, 39, 50, 51–52, 55, 58, 61, 65, 67, 68–69, 103, 124, 220
Custer's Last Rally 68–69; painting 26

Davis, Gail 161, 163, 171
Deadwood Dick 15, 30, 34, 36–40, 104, 129, 184, 220

Index

Deadwood stage 44, 58, 67, 68, 169, 210
Diamond Dick *see* Tanner, Richard
dime novels 1, 2, 4, 7, 9, 12, 14, 19, 21–27, 28–43, **29**, **33**, 44–57, 66–69, 72, 83–85, 92, 96–98, 100, 101, 104–105, 109, 120–123, 136, 184, 202
Django Unchained (2012) 197–198
dog as symbolism 119, 156, 158, 188, 196, 197, 202
Dracula 72, 146
Drama of Civilization 67–68
dude ranches 76, 80, 83, 142, 212–214, 216
Duel in the Sun (1946) 171, 177–179

Eastwood, Clint 3, 92, 156, 168, 173, 178, 179, 180, 184, 187, 188, 196–197
Edison Company 96, 99, 102, 222
Edison Trust *see* Motion Picture Patents Company
Edwards, John Newman 40–41
Elliott, William "Wild Bill" 116, 138, 146–147, 224
Evans, Dale 117, 171, 205, 217–218, 224

Flying W Wranglers 207
folklore *see* myth-making
Fonda, Henry 10, 145, 154, 155, 167, 189, 191
Fonda, Jane 31, 173
Ford, Bob 41
Ford, Glenn 157, 176, 186, 224
Ford, John 10, 12, 28, 120, 135, 151, 155, 171, 190
Fox Studios 110, 112, 113, 135, 138, 222, 224

Garryowen 67
Gibson, Hoot 80, 110, 113, 116, 146, 224
Girl of the Golden West 50
The Great Train Robbery (1903) 38, 81, 96–97, 100, 101, 102
Grey, Zane 13, 100, 124–128, **126**, 131–132, 157, 162, 167, 168, 170, 176, 179, 204
Gunfight at the O.K. Corral (1957) 15, 133, 156, 166, 168, 189
gunfight, concluding *see* showdown, final
The Gunfighter (1950) 152, 153, 156, 164

Gunsmoke (television) 161, 162–163, 164, 183

Hansel & Gretel, Witch Hunters (2013) 217
Hart, William S. 3, 11, 36, 91, 103–107, 109–112, 116, 117, 134, 138, 145, 152, 169, 170, 173, 201, 217, 222
Hawkeye *see* Leatherstocking
Heaven's Gate (1980) 182, 199, 217
heroes, tall 222
Hickok, James Butler "Wild Bill" 14, 22, 34, 42–43, 46–47, 49–50, 53, 57–58, 66, 88, 138, 161, 201, 208, 221
hillbilly music 149–151, 207
Holliday, John H. "Doc" 14, 167, 177, 204, **206**
Hopalong Cassidy 117, 129, 130, 131, 142, 160, 164, 205
horses of movie stars 91, 117
Hoxie, Jack 113, **118**
Huppert, Isabelle 182, 199, 217

Ince, Thomas 102–103, 222
Inceville 78, 102
Indian movie era *see* Native American movies
Indian scouts 45–46
Indians, Hollywood stereotypes 3–4, 14, 18, 100, 119, 179, 200
Ingraham, Prentiss 39, 48, 51

James, Jesse 14, 34, 37, 40–42, 48, 104, 129, 145–146, 148, 153, 156, 157, 184, 194, 222
Jennings, Al 102
Jones, Buck 80, 116, 146
Judson, Edward Zane 7, 44–49, 72

King, Charles 52, 54, 71, 121
King Philip's War 17

Lancaster, Burt 72, 133, 156, 166, 167, 179, 191
language, bad 35, 88, 96, 121, 143, 174, 177, 181, 196, 199, 208, 222; dime novel 35, 88
LaRue, Lash 147
The Last of the Mohicans (movies) 107–108, 157, 196
The Last of the Mohicans (novel) 18–19, **20**, 21, 107–108
The Last Stand (2013) 14, 16, 203, 217
Leatherstocking 18–21, **20**, 30, 36, 91

Leone, Sergio 3, 160, 167, 186–189
Lillie, Gordon W. 70–71, **75**, 76, 78
literacy rates 28, 36
Lone Pine, CA **130**, 139, 219

The Magnificent Seven (1960) 13–14, 92, 152, 153, 156, 160, 189, 202
Maleska 35–36
Man from Bodie 156, 191, 224
Man of the West (1958) 152, 154, 180
marketing *see* merchandising
Mars Attacks (1996) 201, 226
Marvin, Lee 202
Maynard, Ken 80, 110, 113, 115–116, 138, 140, 143, 146
McCoy, Tim 74, 80, 113, 116, 146
merchandising 5, 52, 65, 95, 150, 162, 205, 206
Miller Brothers' 101 Ranch Wild West Show 7, 71, 76–79, 80, 102–103, 110, 116, 210, 214
Minter, Mary Miles 175
Mix, Tom 3, 18, **29**, 79–80, 94, **106**, 107, 109–119, **111**, **114**, 138, 144, 147, 204, 210, 212, 214, 217
Montana, Montie, Jr. 210
Montana, Patsy 151
Monument Valley 8, **155**, **190**
Moran, Thomas 9, 170
Morlacchi, Giuseppina 48, 49, 50
Morricone, Ennio 189, 198
Motion Picture Patents Company 98
"movie flats" *see* Lone Pine, CA
movie ratings 178, 181–182, 193, 203, 217
Mulhall, Louise 80, **169**
Mulhall, Col. Zack 76, 80, 169
music in Wild West shows 58, 67, 77, 221
My Name Is Nobody (1973) 194
myth-making 2, 5–14, **11**, **38**, 43, 60, 72, 92, 122, 129, 132, 204, 215, 220

Native Americans, as actors 3–4, 48, 66–67, 78, 119; movies 15, 99–100, 120–121, 119, 128, 219
Ned Buntline *see* Judson, Edward Zane
New York Motion Picture Company 78
nickelodeons 96, 98, 120
No Country for Old Men (2007) 14, 191, 203, 217
Normand, Mabel 175

Index

nudity in Westerns 174–179, 180–183, 196, 208

Oakley, Annie 34, 62, 63–66, 73, 96, 161–162, 163, 171, 210
O.K. Corral 7, 14, 15, 84, 93, 133, 200, 204, 208
Omohundro, James Burwell "Texas Jack" *25*, 34, 39, 48, 49, 50, 57, 58
The Outlaw (1943) 167, 171, 177
The Outlaw Josey Wales (1976) 179

Pale Rider (1985) 153, 178, 180, 196, 200
paperback novels 131–132, 204, 217
Pawnee Bill *see* Lillie, Gordon W.
Peck, Gregory 152, 153, 156, 177, 179, 186
Peckinpah, Sam 2, 186, 192, 194
penny dreadful 34
persona, definition 4
plots, standardized 15–16, 32–34, 83, 97–102, 117, 132, 135, 139, 153–154
Police Gazette 28–30, 90, 98, *122*
Poverty Row studios 135, 139, 140
printing press 28, 123
Production Code 175–177, 181, 188
The Professionals (1966) 14, 156, 194
pulp literature 3, 15, 21–27, 28–43, *29*, 120–133, 135, 147, 204, 216, 223; *see also* dime novels

radio 5, 83, 123, 142, 143, 149–150, 161, 163, 204, 206, 224
Ranch Life in the Great Southwest (1910) 103, 110
rape themes 35, 119, 127–128, 153–154, 167–168, 173, 179–180, 183, 188, 191, 194, 196, 197, 199, 202
Rappe, Virginia 175
ratings *see* movie ratings
recordings of songs 115, 140, 148–150, *148*, *149*, 161, 208
Reid, Wallace 175
Remington, Frederic 9–10, 120, 132, 170
Reno Gang 157, 224
Republic Studios 39, 112, 140, 142, 143, 145, 146, 147, 171
revenge Westerns 15, 37, 46, 152–155, 158, 179, 194–197
Ritter, Tex 138, 148, 189

rodeo *13*, 57–58, 72, 76, 79, 80, 81, 83, 95, 116, 142, 144, 147, 148, 163–164, 169, 209–212, *216*, 218
Rogers, Roy 11, 39, 93, 114, 116, 117, 128, 138, 142–144, 145–146, 148, 150–151, 160, 162, 164, 171, 204–205, 207, 210, 217, 218, 224
Roosevelt, Theodore 54, 69, 110, 132
rough-rider 69, 74, 146, 221
Rowlandson, Mary 17–18
Russell, Charles 9, 132
Russell, Jane 167, 171, 173, 177, 212
Rustler's Rhapsody (1985) 138

saloon girls 168, 171
Salsbury, Nate 44, 60, 61, 62, 65, 66, 67, 69, 221
Schreyvogel, Charles 10
Schwarzenegger, Arnold 203
Scott, Randolph 108, 157–158, 165, 167, 176, 192, 222
The Scouts of the Plains 56
The Scouts of the Prairie 48–49, 56
The Searchers (1956) 15, 94, 135, 153, *155*, 180
Selig-Polyscope Studios 97, 102–103, *106*, 110, *111*, 112, 116, 170
Selznick, David 177, 178
serial Westerns 140, 162, 217
series Westerns 138–139
Seth Jones 36
sex in Westerns 3, 19, 92, 112, 152, 162, 173, 174–184, 196, 203, 217
Shane (1953) 2, 13, 132, 153, 158, 160
The Shootist (1976) 93, 153, 164, 186, 225
showdown, final 16, 87–89, 91–93, 125, 127, 186, 191, 193–194
sidekicks 144–145
singing cowboys 1, 83, 115–117, 119, 140–144, 146–151, 152, 153, 158, 163, 164, 176, 201, 207–208, 213, 217, 224, 226; groups 136, *141*, 142, 150–151, 207
Sitting Bull 37, *64*
Smith, California Frank 66
Smith, Lillian 65–66
songs, cowboy 88, 115, 116, 140, 143, 145, 148–149, *148*, 150, 151, 161, 162, 204, 207–208, 217, 222
Sons of the Pioneers 150–151, 207

spaghetti Westerns 3, 21, 186–192, 196, 198
spanking in movies 177
stage melodramas 44–52, *51*, 60, 67, *99*, 172
"The Star Spangled Banner" 67
statistics 95, 160, 163; *see also* Western movie production statistics
steam literature 28
stock company 221
Street & Smith 34, 37, 38, 41, 48, 123
stunts 60, 80, 81–82, 102–103, 112, 113, 115, 116, 117, 139, 140, 184
Summit Springs battle 10, 46–47, *47*, 71

Tall Bull 46–47, *47*
Tammen, Henry 71
Tanner, Richard *29*, 38–39
Taylor, William "Buck" 34, 39, 62, 66, 69, 83, 86, 222
Taylor, William Desmond 175
television 1, 5, 7, 12, 14, 22, 49, 83, 91, 95, 160–164, 178, 183, 200–201, 204–207;
Texas Jack, *see* Omohundro, James Burwell
Tilghman, Bill 102
tourism 20, 57, *185*, *200*, 208–209, 212–214
Tousey, Frank 34, 41, 48, 105–107
train robbery *see The Great Train Robbery* (1903)
trick riders 66
trick shooters 62–66
True Grit (1969) 94, 177, 192
Tuska, Jon 2, 12, 107, 171
Tutt, Davis (Dave) 47, 88
"The Two Bills Show" 70
Two Mules for Sister Sara (1970) 14, 179, 196

Unforgiven (1992) 43, 92, 173, 197, 201
United Artists Studios 135, 199

The Vanishing American (1925) 15, 100, 128
The Vanishing American (novel) 100, 127–128
villains 4, 14, 16, 18, 37, 51, *51*, 88, 100, 104, 139, 152, 155–156, 162, 188
violence 2, 15, 21, 30, 35, 72, 77, 92, 100, 112, 147, 154, 156, 162–163, 183–198, 203, 217

The Virginian (movies) 118–119, 134
The Virginian (novel) 18, 35, 86–90, **89**, 107, 118, 120, 127, 132, 179, 216, 222
The Virginian (television) 162, 163

Wayne, John 7, 30, 93–94, 154, 155, 164, 167, 177, 180, 192, 196, 217, 218, 224, 225
Wenona, Princess 66
Western movie production statistics 95, 112, 135, 160, 187, 199
Western movies as allegory 2, 225
Westerns' appeal to small boys 105, 109, 166
Wheeler, Edward 34, 36–38, 184
whips 138, 147, 197
White, Charles "Buffalo Chips Charlie" 221
Whitman, Slim 201, 226
The Wild Bunch (1969) 2, 14, 156, 160, 192–194, 203, 217
Wild West see Buffalo Bill's *Wild West*
Wilson, Whip 138
Winchester rifle 12, 63, 66
Wister, Owen 86–90, **87**, 107, 125, 127, 132, 162, 179, 216, 222
women, attitudes towards 19, 35, 79, 105, 149, 166–182, 193, 225
Wyeth, N.C. 10

Yellow Hair (Yellow Hand) 51–52, 54, 61, 71, 221
yellow journalism 30
yodeling 73, 141, 150

Zanuck, Darryl 12

www.ingramcontent.com/pod-product-compliance
Ingram Content Group UK Ltd.
Pitfield, Milton Keynes, MK11 3LW, UK
UKHW050533150426
5217IPUK00026B/1917

9 780786 478392